Library of
Davidson College

Society As the Patient

SOCIETY AS THE PATIENT

Essays on Culture and Personality

BY

Lawrence K. Frank

KENNIKAT PRESS/PORT WASHINGTON, N. Y.

SOCIETY AS THE PATIENT
Copyright 1948 by The Trustees of Rutgers College in New Jersey
Reissued in 1969 by Kennikat Press by arrangement with the
Rutgers University Press
Library of Congress Catalog Card No: 72-86568
SBN 8046-0559-9

Manufactured by Taylor Publishing Company   Dallas, Texas

ESSAY AND GENERAL LITERATURE INDEX REPRINT SERIES

Preface

THIS book is concerned with new and more fruitful ways of thinking about man and his society which we have been developing within recent years, indicative of the new climate of opinion now emerging in science, philosophy, art, and especially literature.

One expression of this reorientation in our thinking we are calling the *psychocultural approach,* because it utilizes the concepts and findings, the insights and understandings, as well as the methods, of psychiatry, psychoanalysis, and psychology, together with those coming from cultural anthropology and sociology.

This synthesis has many advantages over the older ideas and assumptions. It helps us to see that social order arises from the beliefs, activities, and feelings of the individuals making up the group life, and that those individuals are the product of our traditional culture.

In terms of culture and personality, we may view the widespread social disorders and conflicts and also the prevalent unhappiness and personality difficulties of individuals as different expressions or symptoms of our disintegrating cultural traditions.

This seemingly circular conception replaces the long accepted, but unresolvable dilemma of the individual versus society—and, like modern physics, locates the dynamics of social life in individuals, living in a social and cultural field which they themselves maintain.

Perhaps the major gain from this new approach is that it provides a constructive substitute for the increasingly bitter polemics and apologetics and also the growing defeatism and "failure of nerve" of today. If we can see ourselves as carrying on the endless endeavor to develop a human way of life, we will not shrink from accepting the great privilege and immense responsibility of renewing our culture and reorientating our social order, as the task we and our children must undertake.

For this task, we have the resources of these new concepts and insights and the guidance of our enduring aspirations toward a democratic social order, dedicated to human dignity and respect for the individual personality.

For many years I have been concerned with the development of this psychocultural approach. These essays, written for different journals and on special occasions, present successive efforts to deal with the varied problems of this emerging synthesis of culture and personality. They are offered not as pronouncements but as invitations to new ways of thinking.

While earlier exploratory statements have been elaborated and further clarified in later formulations, I hope they will be of value to students now entering this field and also to the general reader who is seeking illumination upon the contemporary scene.

The appearance of this volume is due primarily to the interest and persistent efforts of my friend, Houston Peterson, who helped to select and arrange these essays and enlisted the interest of the Press in their publication. To him, and to Lyman Bryson, who has written the Introduction, I offer my grateful acknowledgment and affectionate regard.

Lawrence K. Frank

Cloverly
Holderness, New Hampshire
September, 1947

Acknowledgments

ASIDE from some minor corrections, these essays appear as originally published, except that "The Emancipation of Economics" has been cut and the original manuscripts of several papers have been used in place of the printed papers (which had been edited before publication). Footnotes and references given in the original papers have largely been omitted as unnecessary or inappropriate in this volume. The name of the journal and the date of publication are given at the end of each essay.

Acknowledgment and thanks are due to the editors and publishers of the following journals for permission to reprint these papers: *American Journal of Sociology; The Journal of Political Economy* and *The International Journal of Ethics* of the University of Chicago Press; *Plan Age* of the National Planning Association; *The Political Science Quarterly; The American Economic Review; The Saturday Review of Literature; The Annals of The American Academy of Political and Social Science; The American Journal of Orthopsychiatry; Psychiatry; Journal of the Biology and the Pathology of Interpersonal Relations; School and Society; Journal of the National Education Association; Education; The Magazine of Art; The Scientific Monthly; The Journal of Aesthetics and Art Criticism; Free World* (now *United Nations World*); and *Mental Hygiene. The Journal of Social Philosophy, Case and Comment,* and *The Social Frontier* have discontinued publication, so no permission could be obtained.

Contents

	PAGE
Introduction	xi
SOCIETY AS THE PATIENT	1
SOCIAL PROBLEMS	10
THE COST OF COMPETITION	21
THE PRINCIPLE OF DISORDER AND INCONGRUITY	37
THE EMANCIPATION OF ECONOMICS	47
THE SIGNIFICANCE OF INDUSTRIAL INTEGRATION	61
SOCIAL PLANNING AND INDIVIDUAL IDEALS	77
APOLOGY FOR IRRESPONSIBILITY	84
SOCIAL LEGISLATION AND THE POLICE POWER	97
SOCIAL CHANGE AND THE FAMILY	102
THE MANAGEMENT OF TENSIONS	115
THE CONCEPT OF INVIOLABILITY IN CULTURE	143
SOCIAL ORDER AND PSYCHIATRY	151
FREUD'S INFLUENCE ON WESTERN THINKING AND CULTURE	162
CULTURAL COERCION AND INDIVIDUAL DISTORTION	166
FREEDOM FOR THE PERSONALITY	193
TWO TASKS OF EDUCATION	207
GENERAL EDUCATION	213
MENTAL SECURITY	226
THE REORIENTATION OF EDUCATION TO THE PROMOTION OF MENTAL HYGIENE	239
MENTAL HEALTH IN SCHOOLS	253
ART AND LIVING	266
SCIENCE AND CULTURE	275
WHAT IS SOCIAL ORDER?	286
THE HISTORIAN AS THERAPIST	298
DILEMMA OF LEADERSHIP	308

	PAGE
TIME PERSPECTIVES	339
MAN'S MULTIDIMENSIONAL ENVIRONMENT	359
THE ARTS IN RECONSTRUCTION	380
WORLD ORDER AND CULTURAL DIVERSITY	389

Introduction

FOR a number of years we have had a good deal of talk in educational and scientific circles about the need to study the relation between culture and personality. We have watched the psychologists and anthropologists wrestling with new ways of getting precise descriptions of the person and the society in which he lives; and we have known that we would want practical applications of those theoretical analyses as soon as we could get them. It is Lawrence Frank's special importance, I think, that he has been both a pioneer thinker and worker in this field, and the book that is now being published establishes the fact that his thinking has gone along with his practical work.

Mr. Frank has spent part of a lifetime (and has, happily, a good part of it still to spend) on projects, public and private, that were all directed toward bettering the culture in which he lives. A careless observer might think that this has been only another of those useful and admirable but uncreative lives of service. Lawrence Frank would be the first to insist that simple goodness and good will are valuable qualities and that men and women who merely serve good causes are needed in the world. But his own service has been nevertheless of a different sort, informed by a more searching philosophy, productive of bold generalizations and far more significant for the future.

The essence of his philosophy and practice is given best, I think, in this sentence from the first essay, p. 8, "This idea that man can remake his culture . . . repudiates the concept of purely individual responsibility and of personal salvation, regardless of the ruin of others, for the larger concept of social responsibility that directs attention to the creation of a culture to serve human needs and values...."

This is very clearly said. It will doubtless be misinterpreted and misrepresented, chiefly because the "discovery of the plasticity of culture" is a tremendous step toward human freedom, and the officials of institutions do not generally like the freedom-giving ideas. Such discoveries shake too many temporal powers.

It would be lacking in respect for Lawrence Frank's own splendid detachment to pretend that I agree with everything he has said in these papers. No one who feels deeply the importance of the chief principles set forth in this book can fail to treat all Mr. Frank's material with the most rigorous caution. He is not interested, I am sure, to have anything that he has written stand at all unless it can stand up against that kind of reading. This is a serious business, remaking the social patterns in which we live. He demands that we re-examine our most sacred loyalties. He insists that we gain for ourselves, in spite of discomfort, the freedom to think out afresh all the traditions and institutional attachments that hamper our growth.

We realize how much a pioneer he has been when we see that the essential point of view was already expressed in papers published twenty-five years ago, and also when we see that the essential principles have been applied to art, to education, to the practice of medicine, to economics, and to government; in fact, to all the important business of life. These are aspects of the life of society, and society is the patient.

In reading these essays, one is struck by the fact that they show a remarkable consistency as well as growth. Since each is an independent composition, there is some

INTRODUCTION   xiii

repetition, but it has seemed best to reprint them as they stand. The content often betrays the date, and the problems used to illustrate the principles are sometimes shadows out of the past. In spite of this, the book can be read straight through with steadily cumulative effect.

One almost inevitable misinterpretation needs, I think, to be warned against in advance. The older forms of democratic idealizing in America have set the welfare of the person, of the individual, as the aim of social organization and centered the processes of betterment largely in the individual himself, acting in freedom and realizing himself "in spite of" society. This idea that freedom is the revolt of the individual, struggling against social pressures, runs all through our literature and our philosophic writing.

The new point of view, implicit in all of Mr. Frank's writing and often spelled out, does not change the aim of social organization; the individual is still the locus of wellbeing. The individual is not sacrificed to the state or to society, as in primitive groups, or in the well-known modern states that are dictatorial and thereby anachronistic. Nor is there any change in the idea that the individual will realize himself by being free of social pressures. The change comes in the new realization that social pressures exist in the mind of the individual; that the individual has built the taboos and restraints into his own conscience and will resist their extirpation; that obsolete traditions and institutions must be attacked as mental habits and changed in the minds of the members of the group; and finally that other new institutions can be devised to do, not evil to the free person, but constructive good.

This is almost certain to be mistaken in some quarters for what it precisely is not, i.e., an exaltation of the group above the members, of the state above the citizens. Lawrence Frank is arguing for freedom, and anyone who has argued so well, so consistently, and so subtly for twenty-five years must have had, in all those years, an immense faith in what men would do with freedom if they ever got it. That moral courage, that trust in humanity, is as much a part of his philosophy as is his science. Together they indicate a kind of leadership that we may, to our own great benefit, learn to follow more often in the future.

LYMAN BRYSON

November 24, 1947

Society As the Patient

ONE

Society as the Patient

THERE is a growing realization among thoughtful persons that our culture is sick, mentally disordered, and in need of treatment. This belief finds expression in many different forms and from a variety of professions. We have had, for example, *The Sickness of an Acquisitive Society*, by Tawney, and *Modern Education*, by Rank, wherein society, not merely the individual, is portrayed as the patient.

Anyone who reflects upon the present situation in which our Western European culture finds itself cannot fail to see that we have passed from the condition in which deviations from a social norm could be regarded as *ab*normal. Today we have so many deviations and maladjustments that the term "normal" has lost almost all significance. Indeed, we see efforts being made to erect many of the previously considered abnormalities into cultural patterns for general social adoption.

The disintegration of our traditional culture, with the decay of those ideas, conceptions, and beliefs upon which our social and individual lives were organized, brings us face to face with the problem of treating society, since individual therapy or punishment no longer has any value beyond mere alleviation of our symptoms. No one can complain that we in America lack self-appointed physicians who are ready, nay eager, to doctor our own society; and abroad we can see various treatments in progress which we are being invited to emulate.

The conception of a sick society in need of treatment has many advantages for diagnosis of our individual and social difficulties and for constructive therapy, although we may find it necessary to prescribe a long period of preparation before the patient will be

1

ready for the remedies indicated. Perhaps the most immediate gain from adopting this conception is the simplification it brings. Instead of thinking in terms of a multiplicity of so-called social problems, each demanding special attention and a different remedy, we can view all of them as different symptoms of the same disease. That would be a real gain even if we cannot entirely agree upon the exact nature of the disease. If, for example, we could regard crime, mental disorders, family disorganization, juvenile delinquency, prostitution and sex offenses, and much that now passes as the result of pathological processes (e.g., gastric ulcer) as evidence, not of individual wickedness, incompetence, perversity, or pathology, but as human reactions to cultural disintegration, a forward step would be taken. At present we cherish a belief in a normal, intact society against which we see these criminals, these psychopaths, these warring husbands and wives, these recalcitrant adolescents, these shameless prostitutes and vicious sex offenders, as so many rebels who threaten society and so must be punished, disciplined, or otherwise individually treated. This assumption of individual depravity or perversity gives us a comfortable feeling that all is well socially, but that certain individuals are outrageously violating the laws and customs that all decent people uphold.

It is, indeed, interesting to see how this conception of a social norm, with individuals as violators and frustrators of normality, runs through so much of our thinking. In political life we cherish a fond belief in the essential soundness and efficacy of representative government. The cumulative evidence of social injustice, of corruption in office, of legislative "deals" and intrigues—the whole slimy trail of graft and misfeasance is treated as the vicious practices of dishonest politicians. We save our belief in democracy and in our representative political organization by imputing all their faults and shortcomings to individual malefactors. The remedy for political chicane is then viewed as investigation and prosecution: "Turn the rascals out."

In our economic affairs we follow a similar practice. Rugged individualism, free enterprise, the money and credit economy, the price system with its supposed free play of economic forces and the law of supply and demand—all these are considered as naturally sound, effective economic practices based upon the very nature of society; if perverse and selfish individuals did not interfere with these natural forces, frustrate competition, and break these laws, we should have no economic troubles. When our industry and banking and commerce are crippled or paralyzed, we begin to look for the guilty persons who have interfered with normality. Some blame the stifling of competition, others the excess of competition, while others aim their accusations against this or that individual or organized group of individuals whose conduct is deemed to be uneconomic and therefore responsible for our troubles. The confusion over the nature and the perpetrators of these economic misdeeds provides occasion for vivacious, sometimes vituperative, argument, but we generally agree that the trouble comes from individual misdeeds that must be curbed by more laws, more regulation, and more severe punishment.

Likewise, in family life, difficulties are similarly treated in terms of individual wickedness and guilt, to be corrected by severe moral instruction and legal adjudication on a semicriminal basis, as in divorce. Similarly, the admitted inadequacy of the courts, both civil and criminal, is blamed upon individuals, corrupt judges, unprincipled shysters, and unethical practitioners, whose disloyalty to their high duty has stained the bright garments of Justice and prevented honest administration of the laws.

In every department and aspect of our social life we find the same pattern of thought about our society: that our social ills come from individual misconduct that must be corrected and punished so that these supposed underlying social forces and social laws can operate without hindrance, thereby solving our social problems. Nor is this point of view confined merely to the man in the street and the unscrupulous manipulator who has learned to utilize these social myths for his own purposes. Our social scientists, with few exceptions, are strong believers in these supposed social forces and laws and underlying natural processes that, if left unhindered, would operate smoothly. Much of our social research is a persistent search for these underlying social, political, and economic systems, the discovery of which will, it is expected, bring social progress, just as physical science revealed the underlying physical-chemical processes that gave us our modern industry and technology. Indeed, these conceptions of normality and inherent order in society have dominated both lay and professional thinking for many generations.

If, then, we abandon this social mythology, as a growing number of individuals are urging, for another view of the situation, what have we as an alternative? The term "society as the patient" is a good analogy for discussion, but we need something more than a clever phrase as a basis for reconsidering our social theory and revising our social objectives. The conception of culture and personality, emphasizing the patterned behavior of man toward his group and toward other individuals, offers some promise of help, for it indicates at once that our society is only one of numerous ways of patterning and organizing human life and that what individuals do, for good or evil, is in response to the cultural demands and opportunities offered them.

This cultural conception reveals human conduct, not as whimsical or volitionally controlled, but as the way the individual takes over the ideas, beliefs, and practices of the traditional group life and, under their guidance, carries out his life-processes. In a secluded group where, over a long period of time, men have worked out a unified culture with appropriate sanctions and beliefs, the individual ordinarily finds the pattern of his life prepared for him and, within the permissions and restrictions it offers, he can achieve his life goals and fulfil his social responsibility. His culture dictates what he will be aware of, how he will respond to it and explain it, and what he can and must do with his organic needs and functions. In homogeneous cultures individuals of aberrant temperaments are less likely to find it difficult to conform to the patterns laid down by their culture; when forced to do so, they can adapt themselves with a minimum of strain because their culture does not offer conflicting choices. In some cultures it is the practice even to give specific exemptions to an individual whose temperament makes it difficult for him to conform to the patterns that are recognized as socially normal; such exemption saves the individual deviant from anxiety or guilt.

When we regard Western European culture, which has emerged from an almost incredible background of conflict and confusion and mixture of peoples, and see that for centuries it has not been unified either in ideas and beliefs or in socially approved practices, we can begin to understand the etiology of the sickness of our society. Our culture has no unanimity of individual or social aims, no generally accepted sanctions, and no common patterns of ideas or conduct. All our basic ideas, conceptions, and beliefs have been in process of revision for the last three hundred years or more,

SOCIETY AS THE PATIENT

beginning with the displacement of the older notions of the universe and man's place therein and going on now to the supersedure of the traditional animistic, voluntaristic conceptions of human nature and conduct and man's relation to his society. The American scene, moreover, has been successively invaded by representatives of widely different nationalities, who have accelerated the decay of the early American tradition that our changing industry has made inevitable. The picture is sufficiently familiar and has been adequately described so that no prolonged description is needed here.

If we bear in mind this disintegration of culture, then our so-called social problems and the seeming perversity of individuals become intelligible. They are to be viewed as arising from the frantic efforts of individuals, lacking any sure direction and sanctions or guiding conception of life, to find some way of protecting themselves or of merely existing on any terms they can manage in a society being remade by scientific research and technology. Having no strong loyalties and no consistent values or realizable ideals to cherish, the individual's conduct is naturally conflicting, confused, neurotic, and antisocial, if that term has any meaning in the absence of an established community purpose and ideal. The more skilful contrive to profit from the social confusion and their own lack of scruples, while others evade or break laws, become mentally disordered or diseased, or otherwise violate the older codes of conduct, damaging themselves and those whose lives they touch. No one is happy, it is apparent; the successful are driven as relentlessly as the failures by their sense of guilt, their compulsions, and their frustrations.

We see, then, that continued faith in the myths regarding an underlying social system comes from a need to cling to something that offers some sense and meaning in the social confusion and keeps alive the hope that things may be better. Cynicism is, of course, the refuge of the majority of successful men, especially professional men, who shrug their shoulders, acknowledge the decay of their professional scruples, but go on "getting theirs." There is, apparently, no profession or occupation that has not succumbed to the current practice of racketeering, which means that the traditional ethics and sense of responsibility are breaking down, leaving each one to pursue his own personal ends. It is neither fair nor useful to upbraid the individual who could not singly maintain the old standards, even if they were workable, or withstand the competitive pressure to adopt the unscrupulous practices of the others. Campaigns for social reforms are unavailing since there are no new patterns or sanctions to which we can give allegiance, and we cannot return to the old since they offer no meaningful answers to our present perplexities. The only common faith we share at present is this social mythology which we cling to with increasing difficulty as the absurdity of such beliefs and the futility of our efforts to restore normality become more evident.

Where, then, does the cultural view help beyond providing another apt theory of social confusion which is useful as a point of vantage from which the intellectual can contemplate the vulgar scene? It transfers the focus of attention from the seemingly recalcitrant or perverse individual to the cultural patterns and sanctions. This revision of our thinking will modify the doctrine of individual responsibility and guilt that is not only an active factor in the growing criminality and insanity, but also a complete block to any understanding of the problem or any attempt at modification. If we accept the conception of society as the patient, absolve the individual from guilt, and regard these various social problems as symptoms of progressive cultural change, we can at least relieve some of our anxiety since we then have a definite and possibly manageable problem.

Here we must pause to take note of the chorus of objections this point of view always elicits. From many sides, but especially from religious and ethical groups and lawyers, vehement protest is made against any tampering with the concept of human volition, human autonomy, and individual responsibility. These ideas and beliefs have been of extraordinary value in the history of culture, since they made possible the devolution of social responsibility upon the individual and helped to create that belief in conscience which has so largely dominated conduct. To those who cherish this tradition and the moral gains it has brought, the undermining of the concept of individual responsibility appears as the greatest impiety and the beginning of social collapse. Is man to be viewed as a passive instrument of culture, deprived not only of volition and responsibility but also of self-determination? Is free will to be abandoned? But it must be recognized that the individual's conscience, his conception of right and wrong, his feeling of moral responsibility, are but the reflections of his culture. What we are learning to call the superego, that stern and implacable censor of our conduct and unrelenting director of our lives (the conscience of our moral tradition), is the culture that has been incorporated into the very personality of the individual. When the culture no longer provides for a superego that is integrated and wholesome, but by its many conflicts and ambiguities makes the superego socially ineffective, if not self-destructive, we must recognize the necessity of revising our ethical and moral ideas. Here we get a clue to the present situation wherein the lack of any clear, unambiguous patterns of conduct is producing distorted personalities who are not only wrecking themselves but ruining all others.

It is curious how fondly we cherish this belief in free will, volition, and individual responsibility, along with the social myths of implacable social forces that move with cosmic power. The two beliefs are, in truth, complementary, representing the two conceptions under which cultural conformity and individual variability have been expressed and given sanctions of extra-human cogency. It is one thing to impute the inadequacy and breakdowns of our industrial money economy to impersonal social forces; it is quite a different matter to regard our economic perplexities as a product of the cultural traditions that might be changed. Again, it is obvious that the idea of human volition, of the power of choice and the responsibility for consequences, provides one framework of individual and group life, while the concept of individual variability within a cultural setting, that may be and often is individually disastrous, shifts the whole orientation of our thinking and forces us to consider how culture can be revised to avoid or mitigate these individual disturbances.

Instead of clinging to the traditional conceptions of individual autonomy and moral responsibility that were dependent upon a coherent culture for their effective operation, we must begin to think in terms of individuals caught in social confusion wherein individual conduct and ethics are no longer socially tolerable. The individual, instead of seeking his own personal salvation and security, must recognize his almost complete dependence upon the group life and see his only hope in and through cultural reorganization. The tradition of individual striving that was ushered in by the Renaissance has been the very process of this cultural disintegration, for the individual, in striving to be an individual, has broken down the inherited culture of common, shared beliefs and activities. Now that this necessary cultural disintegration has been accomplished, almost to the point of unbearable confusion, we must face the task of constructing a new culture, with new goals, new beliefs, new patterns and sanctions, but predicated upon the enduring human values that must be continually restated and given renewed expression.

It is to be noted that in this need for redirecting individual lives toward a feeling of responsibility for the culture, helping the individual to realize that his personal fulfilment will come through and in the social life, we are in a very real sense completing a cycle. In the early period of Western European culture, especially Anglo-Saxon culture, the group was responsible for the individual and he, in turn, shared the common responsibilities, even legal guilt for the misconduct of other members of the group. Then, slowly and haltingly, came the emergence of the legal doctrine of individual responsibility and guilt for violating the social requirements and prohibitions and the replacement of status by contract. Today, we are moving toward a reinstatement of the ancient doctrine of group responsibility and a recognized status for the individual, with increasing individual subordination and allegiance to the group. The truly perplexing problem this trend presents is to prevent the stifling of individual ideas and experimentation by enforced conformity to the group patterns; but the current practices of repression and enforced conformity may be regarded as reactions of neurotic, if not psychotic, individuals against the present cultural disorder that produced their own distortions.

We are, indeed, asked to give up these time-honored beliefs in human volition and responsibility, but only to replace them with a larger and humanly more valuable belief in cultural self-determination, social volition, and group responsibility. This idea that man can remake his culture is, in that form at least, relatively novel, although it has many antecedents in the utopias that have been proposed in the past. It repudiates the concept of purely individual responsibility and of personal salvation, regardless of the ruin of others, for the larger concept of social responsibility that directs attention to the creation of a culture to serve human needs and values—a culture with a "vital sensibility."

Just as the emergence of the doctrine of individual responsibility brought an enormous gain to the individual and to society, so the doctrine of cultural responsibility will bring another great step forward in human life. It will give us both the courage and the faith to undertake the remaking of our culture, and it will provide the criteria for the new patterns and sanctions for the human needs of individuals who vary in capacities and skills but are basically alike in their physiological, psychological, and social requirements, and especially in their need of a common faith.

The process of remaking our culture is under way. The new social orders abroad have initiated the program, each with different goals and values, but agreeing in their repudiation of many of the older social theories and myths that forbade social change and in their relinquishment of the idea of human volition and an individualistic freedom with little or no social responsibility. Their specific aims and the frequently ruthless execution of these programs affront our sensibilities, but we must acknowledge that they are experimenting with cultural reorganization—the task which we must also undertake, peacefully and more humanely, we hope, and with real respect for individual differences.

In the history of ideas and social development it is not improbable that this discovery of the plasticity of culture may rank as one of the greatest of man's achievements since, from the beginning of history, he has been at the mercy of supposed necessities—the divine right of kings, the power of the church, and all the other forms of sovereignty and their justification by social and religious theorists, with the continual sacrifice of the individual life to the most aggressive or unscrupulous.

Today we must face the task of reconstructing our culture and creating our own design for living, in which the age-old cruelties, frustrations, and deprivations may, we must hope, be mitigated, if not eliminated. For that task we have need of more understanding of personality and culture and, above all, of faith in the value of human life which the new culture must serve. Until the culture makes the conservation of human values the dominant theme, the individual cannot, or will not, find his fulfilment.

(FROM: *The American Journal of Sociology,* 42 [1936]: 335–44.)

TWO

Social Problems

THE STUDY of social problems has reached such an advanced stage today that, in venturing to set forth the following discussion, I feel that I must apologize for my temerity. These remarks, which are offered, not as conclusions, but merely to indicate a line of inquiry, may perhaps suggest to more competent hands an enterprise of some moment.

1

WHEN WE speak of our social problems we refer usually to those subjects of earnest concern which are known severally as the housing problem, the infant-mortality problem, the child-welfare problem, the labor problem, the problem of crime and delinquency, and so on. And when we inquire into the occasion for housing as a problem, or any of the other numerous social problems, we find that each of these problems is associated with a situation involving a fairly large number of persons who are in distress. Further inquiry into the character of their difficulties shows that, as in the housing problem, people are embarrassed, to say the least, by an insufficient supply of houses in which to live. Or we find that the number of babies dying prematurely is too large to be viewed with complacency. Or, again, we see a large social class which we call labor unable to obtain a satisfactory basis of employment from another large class, called employers. Then, too, we find large numbers of adults and children breaking the laws of property and person so that, as individuals and as members of society, we see our rights and liberties menaced.

Being aroused by these evidences of social difficulties, we are concerned with discovering a solution of these problems which will reduce or eliminate the housing shortage, infant mortality, industrial friction, and lawbreaking. A social problem, then, appears to be any difficulty or misbehavior of a fairly large number of persons which we wish to remove or correct, and the solution of a social problem is evidently the discovery of a method for this removal or correction.

To all this, it is safe to say, will be given assent, as the familiar statement of a familiar theme. It is repeated here merely to assure agreement upon the topic to be discussed. And one of the first questions raised by the subject of social problems asks what the conditions are which generate these difficulties. For no one, it may be assumed, would be inclined to look for a housing problem among, let us say, the Eskimos, who construct their igloos personally from an inexhaustible supply of building materials; nor a labor problem among those African pygmies who have a hunting culture. This is merely to suggest that a social problem is related to the particular social conditions from which it arises, which is more or less a commonplace. Examining social problems and their generating conditions more closely, it appears that each social problem is specifically related to particular social conditions or social factors, namely, one or more social institutions. That is to say, a housing problem is related to the institution of private property, undoubtedly, for it may be presumed that people would not continue to suffer the housing shortage if they did not face, in the institution of private property and absentee ownership, *inter alia*, something which forced them to contemplate their uncomfortable position as a difficult problem. For were the land upon which to build and the materials and tools needed in building available to those in need of shelter, it is not unwarranted to expect that the housing shortage would be alleviated, in rather primitive fashion, to be sure, if done individually. If, however, the state were to take these requisites from their owners and construct homes in proper fashion, the housing shortage would be eliminated in appropriate form.

It may be further pointed out that each of the social problems is concerned with, or arises from, a social institution, which, like private property, acts as a deterrent or obstacle to the direct solution of the problem, or, like marriage, permits and encourages the bearing of offspring in such surroundings and by such mothers as, jointly or severally, to lead to high infant mortality. It is sufficient here merely to mention the connection between private property and crime, between private property, the "price system," and the high cost of living, the wages aspect of the labor problem, and so on.

Now the purport of these remarks upon the apparently obvious fact that social problems arise in a society with institutions, and that these problems and institutions are intimately related, is merely to call attention to what seems to be the unique character of social problems. In any other variety of practical or scientific problems, the task set by the problem is to find a method or technique for doing something, whether it be to launch a boat or bombard helium atoms with X rays. In doing this something, we endeavor to find the sequence of operations which will lead to the accomplishment of the task involved and to remove or abolish the factors or elements in the given situation which block our efforts in that direction.

But when we inquire into one of these social problems and the efforts made to solve it, we meet with this interesting situation. Let us take the housing problem for an illustration. There develops a shortage of houses of such a magnitude that many people are distressed. Manifestly, the usual and accustomed operations of house construction have been reduced or interrupted. Now, in the discussion which ensues, we meet these proposals: that the income tax on the interest from real estate mortgages be reduced; that the property tax on newly constructed houses be remitted for a period of years; that insurance companies and savings banks be required to invest a fixed portion of their assets in real estate mortgages; that labor unions in the building trades be supervised by the state; that the producers of building materials be regulated by a state commission; that people be persuaded to move to other cities or towns; that landlords be prohibited from increasing rents above a fixed percentage of existing rents, and so on. It would require many pages to enumerate the various and sundry proposals recently made for solving the housing problem.

It would be taken as a sign of eccentricity or feeble-mindedness, perhaps, to question the relevance of these proposals to the housing problem, so let us invoke that familiar figure of the man from Mars who views mundane affairs with an innocent eye. To this visitor, we may imagine the student of social problems, or the man in the street, patiently explaining that we had a serious housing problem.

SOCIAL PROBLEMS 13

And our visitor would reply with numerous questions, we may assume, about the state of the building art: Had we met with some new difficulty in constructing houses which our architects and builders could not overcome? The answer would have to be no, for there was no lack of skill there, nor in the ability of our building trades employes to erect houses. And the producers of building materials were possessed of tools and techniques for manufacturing building materials.

It is evident that our visitor would be somewhat perplexed to understand what was the nature of this housing problem, for surely there was no lack of ability and skill to build houses. What, then, was this housing problem and how were we trying to solve it? Again he would be told, with an exaggerated patience, that there was a shortage of houses for the population and that the legislators and economists, sociologists, social workers, and many other professional and lay persons, were engaged in finding a way to overcome this shortage, as partially described above. The bewildered gentleman would knit his brows, cough apologetically, and say:

Please be patient with one who is anxious to understand and to sympathize with your difficulties, for I cannot see how, if you are concerned with a housing shortage, you talk about income taxes, mortgages, and all these other seemingly unrelated subjects. If you need houses, why, in the name of intelligence, don't you build them or address yourself to finding ways of building them instead of talking about money, capital, and so on? Your architects and builders know how to construct dwellings, your building-material factories know how to produce materials, and the land awaits. Then, wherefore and why?

We should have to delegate an economist, a lawyer, a political scientist, a sociologist, and a historian to explain about the system of private property, the price system, popular government, congestion of population, transportation, and so on. And when they had severally and jointly expounded the complexities of the situation, pointing out that we cannot just build houses, but must rely upon individual initiative and private enterprise to enter the field of building construction, that we must use the "price system" to obtain the needed land which is someone's private property, to buy the necessary materials and to hire the skilled labor, that we must borrow capital on mortgages to finance these expenditures, paying a bonus to induce someone to lend that capital and also pay interest on the loan, together with amortization quotas, and then we must contrive to rent these dwellings in accordance with a multiplicity of rules and regulations about leases and so on—after all these sundry explanations, showing that to get houses built we must not infringe anyone's rights of private property or freedom to make a profit, and that what we want is to find a way of getting houses without interfering with anyone's customary activities, our visitor would suddenly exclaim: "Yes, I begin to see; have you any other such difficult problems, for this is exceedingly interesting."

Then we should go on to explain about the problem of infant mortality, how any persons of adult age may beget children with the sanction and approval of the state, provided they undergo a ceremony called marriage. When they do beget children, despite their physical infirmities and the lack of an adequate income or any technique for taking care of their infants, large numbers of their babies die in the first year of life, but no one can say or do anything to prevent this mortality because it is against the law and the constitution to interfere with an individual adult woman, especially in the care of her child. We have a difficult problem, therefore, of reducing these appalling losses of life, without restricting the liberty of individual mothers to beget more children than they should have, and to kill off their offspring through ignorance or the poverty which every person is by law entitled to enjoy, without let or hindrance (unless mitigated by charity). Of course, the application of modern medicine and hygiene can cut infant mortality to a very low rate, but about all we can do is to distribute enlightening pamphlets and establish infant-welfare stations, where, if they wish to do so, mothers can bring their infants for inspection and advice.

After telling about infant mortality, we would go into the intricacies of the problem of crime and delinquency, of alcoholism and drug addiction, the labor problem, the traffic problem (which would surely make our visitor puzzled to see how valiantly we are striving to find ways of increasing the number of vehicles and pedestrians on our streets), and all the sundry other social problems. If this visitor possessed the usual Martian keenness and penetration, he would probably interrupt our recital to say:

SOCIAL PROBLEMS

If it is not indelicate of me to remark, every social problem you describe seems to have the same characteristics as every other social problem, namely, the crux of the problem is to find some way of avoiding the undesirable consequences of your established laws, institutions, and social practices, without changing those established laws, etc. In other words, you appear to be seeking a way to cultivate the flower without the fruit, which is somewhat difficult, to say the least. And from what your historians tell me, every generation has its own peculiar social problems, or as I would prefer to say, its difficulties in keeping "business as usual" (one of your most expressive phrases) despite the exigencies of social life. I am reminded also of an account of the Melanesians written by one of your anthropologists, the late Dr. Rivers, who tells about a group in which canoe-building used to flourish as a fine art that died out several generations ago. As nearly as he could discover, there developed such an intricate set of rituals, ceremonies, taboo-raising practices, and the like, around the making of canoes, that it became a dangerous trade, so to speak; for, to omit any step in the propitiation of deities, the collaboration of the priests, the appropriate, ceremonial application of tools, and so on, exposed the wilful or neglectful one to the wrath of the whole community. So the building of canoes, which were really needed for their island economy, became gradually more infrequent and then died out entirely. It would appear that there is somewhat of a kinship between the life of these primitive peoples and of your highly civilized nations, although your institutions are much more rational, as your social theories clearly indicate. I am sorry I can offer no help in solving your problem and I assure you I have been greatly edified by your patient explanations.

Whereupon, our visitor would withdraw to his home planet to write a monograph upon the social customs of the earth dwellers, which would probably appeal to his associates as the report of a field trip among some primitive peoples does to us. He might also be struck by the similarity of our social behavior to the actions of certain young monkeys when trapped by a hunter with a bottle: The hunter puts a sweetmeat in a bottle attached firmly to a tree; when the monkey finds the bottle he reaches his hand into it, grasps the bait, and then cannot withdraw his doubled hand; so he remains until the hunter comes around and bags him.

Of course, no visitor would dare to offend us by remarking on this similarity. His visit and comments while here serve, however, to call attention to the peculiar character of social problems, for their solution apparently does not involve the discovery of a new technique or tool, nor the removal of obstacles in the way of applying known techniques and tools, at least as they are discussed; for what the discussion and the proposals made for their solution indicate is that a social problem is an enterprise in finding ways of getting something done or prevented, while not interfering with the rights, interests, and activities of all those who are involved in the failure to do, or the persistence in doing, what is the subject of the problem.

It is interesting to observe that each of these peculiar problems has a history which throws much light upon its nature. For, in the case of the housing problem, it appears that the construction of dwellings has heretofore proceeded, more or less *pari passu*, with population growth, under the institutions of private property, the "price system," and all the other social customs and laws which have seemingly fostered this construction. But that either gradually or suddenly there developed a shortage of housing (e.g., the period of the war in the present case), and somehow the old, reliable house-building operations, instead of relieving the shortage became, if anything, more defective and harder to work than ever.

This indicates that a social problem is addressed to the difficulties associated with an institution or custom which once was fairly adequate and efficient. It is probable, therefore, that the attempt to get rid of the difficulty, by seeking some device to make the formerly reliable institution or custom work again, as of yore, testifies to our general conviction that "you cannot change human nature." It is evident, however, that a social problem is indicative of a fairly considerable change in human behavior and social institutions, else these difficulties arising from reliance upon older customs would not occur. And it is also clear that, if we could manage to discover what those changes were, and whither they were tending, we should be able to discuss these situations, if not to act therein more intelligently, i.e., with reference to the consequences of our present behavior.

This suggests that the rise of a social problem is an augury of something better, or at least more effective, in the way of doing things, and that the bigger and more complicated the problem, the greater the change it portends. From such a point of view, we should look upon our social problems, with all the confusion and even suffering they involve, as incidents of transitions in our social life, wherein we are painfully giving up our old habits and learning new ways of doing things. And if we really want to do something in the circumstances, it would appear to be the part of wisdom to try to help along the transition and get over the agony of change. But since only the young can learn new habits, the old are caught in a situation of acute distress and apprehension. Such an attitude bespeaks a seemingly transcendent faith in human nature, but, in fact, it is merely what all our history reveals. Men will, barring a catastrophe, go on living and reproducing their kind, and, to do so, they must have houses, healthy infants, and all the other accompaniments, necessities, and luxuries of life. So, if the practices of our fathers are not sufficiently accommodating to the exigencies of the life we lead, we will come to terms with one another upon the basis of new practices. The sooner we do this the better, seemingly, for neither young nor old are happy while the transition is dragging along. And these new practices, which appeared outlandish, scandalous, subversive, and so on, to our fathers, will in turn be outlawed, scandalized, and subverted by our children, world without end. For neither our fathers, nor we, nor our children, can arrest the evolution of social life which is seemingly accelerated by the progress of science, or the discovery of new techniques for doing more effectively what we have severally tried to do, with less success.

We have a housing problem, while men are developing and trying out new practices and methods of combining the multitudinous efforts required, in a society of highly specialized industries and crafts for building dwellings. All the difficulties about financing, labor, prices, and so on are indicative of the fact that the habitual practices of men have broken down or are breaking down, which is the first step in the change to a new set. Bankers and moneylenders are blamed for their unwillingness or inability to finance housing, but they are merely the millstone of the god of change. Labor is scolded for not doing this or that or the other, but labor is merely a convenient term for a host of men who, like everyone else, are groping around for a new status and a new basis of operations. Producers of materials, railroads, and everyone else involved are blamed and threatened, according to taste. Those who despair of civilization, because the days of cheap mortgages and of dollar-a-day wages are no more, have merely forgotten how their fathers bemoaned the loss of the days in which their habits were established. We may, likewise, discount the fever of apprehension over the collapse of civilization in Europe because, forsooth, the prewar institutions of the "price system," private property, private industry, and so on are showing symptoms of obsolescence, at least in certain particulars, while those who cherish them are trying to arrest the inevitable, by all manner of antidotes, stimulants, and gestures of defiance. What is highly interesting is the disposition among those, who see war as a consequence of the greed of capitalists, and regard the late war, in particular, as a nationalistic, capitalistic holocaust, to point to the present confusion and distress in Europe as proof of the inadequacy of capitalism. In all fairness, one cannot blame capitalism for the conditions which accompany, or result from, the giving up of capitalistic practices, as is evidently the fact in the currency inflation, confiscation of capital, stoppage of trade, and sundry other political interferences with capitalistic enterprise and the private operation of the "price system" incidental to developing new customs.

2

ALL OF this discussion may appear as pure tommyrot and balderdash, and, if the reader so thinks of it, I shall not be disposed to quarrel with his good judgment. For I am not seeking to prove anything, least of all a point of view, taken merely as one undertakes any experiment, to see how phenomena look or behave under new conditions of lighting or through a different lens. And yet I cannot escape the notion that, in approaching these social problems uncritically, as genuine and valid scientific problems, as I fear we are frequently doing, we are diverting our time and energies to unproductive tasks. If the task of social science, as of any science, is to discover the sequence of events, then we might more profitably use the data of these so-called social problems in studying the direction and rate of social change and in revealing the sequences of behavior which make up social life. That is to say, if we took man's habit of behavior as the subject of a study, and sought to disclose the genesis, operation, and evolution of those habits, we should have *a* social science, even though, to many, it would not be *the* social science. It would be a science, addressed to a scientific problem of discovering sequences, in this case the sequences of behavior or antecedent stimulus and consequent response, the sequence of the learning process or of habit formation, in which the consequent response to an antecedent stimulus was established and was the consequence of that process of cumulative change in habits which we call social evolution.

And here it might be appropriate again to remark that the evolution of social life, or of the habits of behavior which give rise to social life as we find it, appears to be the product of scientific or technical development. In so far as science provides more dependable ways of conceiving and handling situations, they displace the older habits and institutions with which men met those situations when no dependable, or less dependable, techniques were available. Each new generation seemingly builds up its habits of behavior around the ideas, tools, and techniques which science provides, and since science is continually developing better tools and techniques, these social habits change from generation to generation, always in the direction of greater effectiveness of execution of the tasks addressed by those habits and techniques. This does not imply any mystical doctrine of progress, but merely that the same old tasks of nutrition, housing, begetting offspring, and slaughter are done with more and more finesse. As Clark Wissler remarked in *Man and Culture*, "What happens in an evolution of a culture is an elaboration and enrichment of these complexes, a process which we sometimes speak of as progress . . . One need not be surprised that such a bewildering mass of civilization turns out to be a matter of bulk rather than complexity, for we find in it everywhere the familiar trait-complexes, each fashioned upon the same general lines."

This relation between science and social change, if it be what it appears, carries the interesting suggestion that agitation and radical doctrines are harmless and impotent to bring change, for men do not change their habits under the spur of words and doctrines. The preaching of radical dogmas may, however, be a growing articulation of changes already effected or taking place; but, then, agitation is but the froth on the cup, and the technical advances producing changes are scarcely to be checked by repression of the leaders of these views. What is true of radicals who urge change is, likewise and by the same token, true of conservatives who loudly deplore change. The liberal dogma is so much the pride of the intellectuals that one dare not suggest its kinship with radicals and conservatives, it being another way of rationalizing one's habits and susceptibilities. Legislation, we may venture tentatively to point out, either accelerates or retards social changes, but seldom, if ever, does more than that. For, to pass legislation in a modern representative state, the habits of people must be fairly well changed before something new can gain sufficient support to be enacted, and, when legislation is used to postpone a change, as, for example, the anti-trust or anti-combination laws in the United States, it operates to hasten along the next further change, or state of evolution, as we see in the development of industrial integration. Aside from scientific or technical advance, then, nothing can long delay or greatly hasten social changes, despite the fears and hopes of those who see portents in every new movement to save mankind from its own folly. Yet it might be possible, by disclosing the direction in which scientific advance is carrying social life, to make the process a little less painful and surprising, and, if someone would discover a technique of habit-breaking, whereby the ancient customs and institutions cherished by the different social classes could be gently, but effectively, replaced by others more nearly alike and more congruous with the machine technique and its twentieth-century concomitants, it is indisputable that we should all feel happier and more neighborly. In other words, if we could invent a technique for more quickly sloughing off the habits of individual activity or of person-to-person relations, which we learned in the days of agricultural, handicraft life, and would readily learn the habits of *group* activity which the machine process demands, and which we are so hesitant about adopting (as witness the law), then we should perhaps develop a *social* life. Moreover, the specific social problems which now plague us would disappear, because the conflict of habits and customs which generate them would be abolished. But such discourses and discoveries would conform to the foregoing intimation that social change is produced by scientific advance, for they would imply the development of that for which we eagerly wait—a social science.

(FROM: *The American Journal of Sociology*, 30 [1925]: 462–73.)

THREE

The Cost of Competition

IT SEEMS clear that the advantages and disadvantages of competitive enterprise, private initiative, and the "profit system" are increasingly to be debated. Not only do our own economic perplexities and distress focus attention upon this question, but the experiments abroad in collective and in national socialist economic programs force us to consider alternatives to, and modifications in, our present scheme of things. In this situation, there is need for some further statement of the terms of the problem so that inquiry may go forward as well as argument. Accordingly, the following discussion is offered to direct attention to some of the social and individual costs of competition and profit seeking, in the hope that this attempt to state the problem may enlist the interest of those more competent to collect and weigh the empirical evidence.

1

THE LOSSES due to insolvency and bankruptcy and to uncollectible commercial accounts (and some individual consumer accounts) form one large category of costs of maintaining competitive business. It is worth noting that the reliable customers who pay their bills make it possible for the numerous "dead beats," often of good social standing, to buy freely from competitive stores eager for charge account customers. The larger the unpaid bills the better service they frequently receive, at the expense of the honest citizens. The costs of the merchant, in accordance with standard accounting practice, are covered so far as possible by adding a percentage to the selling price of all goods sold. Thus, every competitive business organization seeks to protect itself by passing these losses along to the customers who do pay their bills; eventually they are transferred to the ultimate consumers or to capital investment accounts.

For every such business failure, there are also capital losses, borne by the entrepreneur, his confiding family and friends, and the banks which have extended credit to the business. The banks endeavor to cover these losses by charging interest rates sufficient to provide a reserve for such losses. These losses may be considered a cost of maintaining competitive business, paid eventually by the ultimate consumer, or lodged in capital investment accounts. The capital losses of the individual entrepreneur or of his trusting stockholders are also to be viewed as costs of competition, but with the variety of ingenious incorporations now available, it is difficult if not impossible to trace the final apportionment or assessment of these capital losses.

Within recent decades, so-called legitimate failures have been augmented by fraudulent bankruptcies engineered by "bankruptcy rings" that have made considerable gains through such schemes. Thus we have the ironical spectacle of profit-making through deliberate fabrication of business failures, the costs of which are of course borne in the final stages by the ultimate consumer or capitalized as a basis for future earnings.

So long as any one person or group of persons is permitted, if not encouraged, to start a factory, distributing agency, or retail store, these losses are inevitable. Various studies have shown that the bulk of business failures are due to incapable, unskilled, insufficiently financed individuals who nevertheless are able to start up such foredoomed enterprises because there are so many competing manufacturers of machinery, equipment, and supplies, competing wholesalers, and competing banks ready to take these risks for which they are usually able to cover themselves by the accounting practices already described.

Fire losses due to arson form another large category of losses due directly to competitive business since it is common knowledge that a considerable portion of our huge national fire loss comes from deliberate firing of factories and especially stores which are failing. This device, illegal to be sure, but difficult to prove, enables the unsuccessful business man to recover his capital and pay off his debts. Indeed, it is possible for the merchant in these circumstances to eat his cake and have it too, by surreptitiously removing his stock before the fire, thereby saving his goods for another venture (or private sale) and collecting his insurance money. "Arson rings," like "bankruptcy rings," have been exposed frequently throughout the country as an organized business, devoted to making a profit out of losses that are really borne by the ultimate consumer. In so far as this deliberate destruction of goods and premises is covered by insurance, the cost is borne by every business enterprise and family in the country, for the spreading of risk by insurance means just this distribution of losses.

As a cynical observer has remarked, every family in the country is being taxed, through percentages on selling prices as well as higher insurance premiums and higher interest rates, so that Dick, Tom, and Harry may enter business and industry and prove their incompetence or dishonesty at the family's expense.

One of the conspicuous aspects of competitive business is the litigation it creates. With hosts of small business establishments seeking orders and selling goods on narrow margins to meet competition, it is not astonishing that breaches of contract and warranty are frequent. Much of this litigation arises from bad faith and sharp, if not shady, practices on the part of business men who have knowingly entered into agreements they cannot fulfill or have promised goods they cannot deliver. The desperate fight for existence against rivals who are equally desperate and unscrupulous inevitably evokes trickery and litigation.

But large-scale enterprises are equally engaged in litigation, as evidenced by their large legal staff and many highly paid counsellors. Indeed, litigation, or the threat of litigation, is one of the major weapons of competitive business, and legal battles between larger organizations, especially over patents, occupy no small share of the courts' time. The cost of this litigation is included in the general overhead expense that is loaded upon selling prices and the money damages assessed against the loser in turn are distributed through various channels to the ultimate consumer. In addition, the taxpayers bear the cost of maintaining the courts with all the variety of costs there involved.

The conflicts between highly competitive business have given rise to another activity that adds immensely to the costs of competition. Rackets have become rather well established in many of the retail trades and small-scale industries in which there is keen competition. The racketeer finds an inviting situation there since he can exploit the cutthroat competition among the numerous small concerns with small capital and limited capacity. Entering as a self-appointed regulator of competition, he becomes a powerful czar, who, for a regular tribute, will ward off newcomers and destroy the business of those not fully paid members of the "association." The tribute paid to the racketeers is of course a charge upon the business and is passed along to the consumer. Those who are wiped out, through intimidation or destruction of their premises or stocks, including their customers' property (as in laundries, cleaning establishments, etc.), help to swell the national total of business losses described above.

Mention here should be made of the Institutes and similar trade associations maintained by competitive business, the cost of which should be included in any adequate calculation.

The much discussed subject of advertising must be considered here. After making all possible allowances for advertising expenditures as socially useful methods of adult education, it is clear that enormous sums are spent upon purely competitive clamor and hokum designed to win buyers away from rivals whose goods are practically identical. These expenditures for purely competitive purposes and those for definitely misleading and deceptive advertising (the kind that keeps the Federal Trade Commission and Better Business Bureaus constantly occupied) make up another large fraction of the total social cost of competitive enterprise, ignoring for the moment the uncountable cost of the deceptions practiced upon consumers.

The cost of the idle equipment in competitive industry and business represents another large factor in the total price paid for competitive profit seeking. In most business enterprises, especially since the income tax procedure has been in operation, a definite charge for obsolescence and depreciation is made annually on the theory that the cost of production must include renewal of the capital invested in the business, either as interest on indebtedness or as profit. Since a considerable fraction, difficult to determine accurately, of plant capacity and distributive equipment is idle because there are so many competitive businesses, there is currently added to the price of goods bought a goodly sum for such unused plant and equipment. This item of cost of competitive business is, like the cost of bankruptcy, arson, racketeering, advertising, and litigation, spread over consumers' goods and capital

THE COST OF COMPETITION

goods but nevertheless is paid for in this indirect fashion. It is this withholding of production and services because they are not profitable that Veblen termed "capitalistic sabotage," likening it to the ca' canny and restricted output of labor.

Recently, this principle of charging the consumer for maintenance of idle capacity not capable of profitable use under competitive price conditions has been extended to agriculture. The processing taxes, levied upon processing of agriculture products so that the funds collected thereby may be paid to producers for withholding or destroying production, brought a new item into the total cost of maintaining competitive business. It represents the extension of business practices to the farmer who has heretofore been without the protection afforded by this device of charging the consumer for the plant and equipment that can not be profitably operated because of competition among such producers. As such, it signalizes the further logical development of a money and credit economy and its extension to agriculture.

The tariff imposed upon imported goods should likewise be considered as another cost of competitive business, especially those duties assessed upon imports to maintain prices in highly competitive industries which are thereby protected from their foreign competitors when they wish to reduce production.

International cartels to allocate markets and fix prices are a recent development, arising from the need of competitive industries in different countries to establish some control of production and distribution and price fluctuations arising from competitive struggles for markets, with frequent "dumping" at low prices. Cartels have restricted production in many commodities to maintain prices which will pay for the goods sold plus profits upon the idle plant and equipment.

In this connection some attention should be given to the large cost of governmental operations designed to maintain or raise the price of commodities which are produced by competitive growers, processors, etc., in excess of the effective money demand and hence must be kept off the market to protect those prices against collapse.

The enormous waste of natural resources of minerals, oil, gas, lumber, and soil fertility should come into the total reckoning of the cost of competition, since these wastes are largely due to competitive exploitation of such resources, and to their sale often at a loss in foreign countries. Efforts to halt or minimize such losses have not been very effective because they conflict with the doctrine of free enterprise and competition as set forth in the Sherman and Clayton Acts and therefore can be legally opposed by dissenters to any proposed agreement to restrict excessive and wasteful production.

With the assumption of unemployment relief by the federal, state, and local government, another addition is made to the costs of competition since obviously the lack of employment for able and willing labor arises from the inability of competitive industry and business operating under money prices to keep their equipment and working force profitably at work. No way of keeping men and women at work can be found without interfering with competition and free enterprise except through work relief on public improvements and noncompetitive services. It is not unfair therefore to consider the cost of unemployment relief as an item in the price paid for competition and profit seeking, a tax laid to preserve the competitive "system."

2

THE FOREGOING direct or obvious money costs of competition bulk large in the aggregate, but there are other costs, less apparent, yet equally important and burdensome. In a competitive money economy, competition is largely in terms of prices which can be lowered either by greater efficiency or by lowering quality. It is safe to say that lowering of quality, through cheaper materials, shoddy workmanship, and misrepresentation, is the major resource of small competitive industries. Indeed, it is notorious today that goods are produced primarily for a given price market, in accordance with the requirements of different classes of distributors. To get orders from these merchandisers, manufacturers must skimp quality and workmanship and adulterate the purity of their goods as specified by the buyers. What this production to meet competitive price markets means in various direct and indirect costs is difficult to say because the practice is so insidious.

It is clear that food and drugs are subject to adulteration and misbranding on a large scale, but what price is paid in health and welfare no one can begin to estimate. Consumers' goods generally are subject to this quality cutting to meet price markets because the consumer is so little able to protect himself. Manufacturers can, if they wish, institute rigid specifications and testing of supplies, and many of them do, always recognizing that they purchase substandard materials or adulterate them deliberately to meet competitive prices. Consumers generally, however, are naïvely credulous of bargains and are of course forced by low incomes to limit their purchases to the cheaper priced articles made especially for their trade.

Another method of meeting price competition is through reduction of labor costs which can be approached either through greater efficiency of management and equipment or through wage cutting, longer hours, and denial of wholesome, sanitary, safe conditions. Efforts to raise labor standards in the past have been met by the opposition of employers who plead inability to raise wages, reduce hours, or protect workers' safety and health because their competitive position would be jeopardized by the increased costs. Where repeated agreements to raise labor standards have been made, the operation of contract shops or sweat shops and the use of home workers have threatened and often destroyed the hardly won gains. How far strikes, lockouts, and other forms of industrial disputes may be assigned to competitive business will be answered in different ways by each observer. Nevertheless, the typical employer attitude toward labor is definitely that of a hard-pressed competitor who can not afford to be either generous or fair, as is shown by the reaction to the current attempt to limit hours and fix minimum wages.

Labor organizations have responded to the competitive situation of industry and business by attempting to set up the closed shop which is obviously a device to prevent or shut out the worker who is willing to compete for a job by accepting a lower wage or longer hours. Labor organizations have also enforced rigid limitation upon output per man or insisted upon "feather bedding" as another method of meeting the competitive situation and maintaining the price of labor, just as the manufacturer endeavors to maintain the price of goods by limiting production. In these procedures, labor has merely followed the business men who have tried by various devices to stifle or eliminate competition that has proved too much of a threat. Recently the emergence of competing labor organizations, each striving for control of the labor market has brought into this area what we have long seen in competitive business struggles.

Since our professional services are carried on under competitive conditions of each man for himself, some notice should be taken of the indirect costs of this competition. It is obvious that as a country we are inadequately provided with medical, dental, and other specialized services, and that, except for a few exceptional individuals, the majority of professional men are not working full time or making a very satisfactory living. Since any attempt to remedy this situation and provide much needed care for people generally conflicts with individual enterprise on a competitive basis, it is not unfair to consider some of the prevalent ill health, handicaps, and preventable defects as part of the cost of competition, as is the wasted time of many professional men waiting for patients or clients.

The greatest of the indirect costs of competition is in the rising costs of governmental regulation and control over competitive activity. The list of these agencies—federal, state, and local—is impressive, and the annual costs are enormous. Beginning with the Interstate Commerce Commission, which was formed almost fifty years ago to regulate competitive railroads, these agencies have multiplied so that today we have regulation and attempted control over competitive banks, insurance companies, building and loan and mortgage concerns, public utilities, commodity and stock exchanges, trade associations, labor organizations, building and housing construction and operation, food preparation and distribution —indeed, almost every existing form of industrial business and professional activity. It is difficult to realize the extent of this governmental regulation and control of competitive industry, business, and professions until one begins to check over the numerous and growing agencies. In addition to regulation and control, we also have government inspection to enforce observance of legislative standards of various kinds, including now wages and hours, in factories, packing plants, stores, restaurants, elevators, steamships, airplanes, other transportation equipment, and so on and so on.

All of these governmental regulations arise from the desire to permit competition but to avoid or limit the undesirable consequences of allowing free competition. In the aggregate, the number of persons employed in this regulation is very large and is growing, especially since the federal government has set up various emergency organizations for further regulation and control of competitive activities. The N.R.A. and the A.A.A. were primarily efforts to regulate competitive industry and business and agriculture and bring about through codes some regulation of the more glaring phases of free competition. The cost of this army of inspectors, examiners, accountants, and regulators, with their accompanying clerical assistants and expenses, plus the growing litigation over their activities, is a real addition to the indirect costs of competitive life paid in taxes by everyone directly or indirectly.

Another large category of governmental expenditures, some of which are recoverable, is the growing practice of subsidizing or otherwise supporting the prices of commodities produced by competitive business, such as silver mining and agricultural products. Likewise the federal government is engaged in the advances made by governmental agencies to banks, housing construction, business enterprises of various kinds, and so on.

In so far as competitive business enterprise is dependent upon foreign markets, foreign trade becomes an important factor in international affairs, if not the crucial factor in the foreign policy of the nation. The pressure of competitive business and finance upon the government for a vigorous foreign policy and increased military and naval expenditures to reinforce such a policy is indicated by the well-known slogan that "trade follows the flag." The dedication of national energies to this competitive struggle for foreign markets is one of the outstanding features of recent international developments. In any thoroughgoing calculation of the costs of competition, due allowance would have to be made for these governmental activities and costs, as well as the export of our minerals and soil fertility for foreign trade often at sacrifice prices to meet world competition.

In the current discussion of the rising cost of the federal, state, and local budgets, it would be illuminating to see how much of these rising expenditures might be attributed to competition and these various efforts to maintain competition and to protect the social life from competitive practices.

3

IF WE look realistically at the situation, it would appear that *laissez faire*, free enterprise, and price competition made possible the rapid exploitation of machines and natural resources, but that today the cost of continuing free competition under money prices is beginning to absorb an increasing share of the total national income and to engross our human resources. How much, in human terms, this costs in the aggregate, we cannot accurately reckon. We can, however, indicate the nature of these costs if we cannot compute their magnitude.

From a broad national viewpoint, we could say that all these money losses and money costs indicated earlier are but different ways of distributing income; in so far as they serve to maintain numerous persons who can not be allowed to starve, the diversion of income to such persons might be regarded as a form of overhead expense for maintaining a money economy. It is interesting to observe how often this point has been expressed recently by various persons who frankly say that relief, and social security provisions (old age and unemployment) are inevitable costs of protecting the profit system and must be so considered and borne by the beneficiaries of that system.

So long as our society has no clear aims or purposes but to grant individuals opportunity for self-aggrandisement, there is no reasonable basis for deprecating racketeering, bankruptcy, arson, unnecessary advertising, and a growing bureaucratic government control. We not only allow but applaud and socially dignify those who ruthlessly waste and destroy our natural resources, devitalize our human resources, and baulk our economic efficiency; hence, in fairness, we should not condemn the lesser fry who, with the same logic of calculated aggressiveness, try to "get theirs." In any event it keeps many people occupied.

The foregoing point is made, not to display the cheap cynicism so prevalent today, but to emphasize the necessity and inevitability of some scale of values in discussing any social situation and to introduce the discussion of the human costs entailed in a competitive, profit-seeking society.

Granted that our agriculture and industrial equipment could be operated under any institutional arrangements we might choose (collectivism, producers' or consumers' co-operation, capitalism, etc.) since the technological processes are independent of the controls, what standpoint or criteria of desirability should we adopt in assessing the human costs and gains of an economy? The question is relevant not only to the evaluation of our present competitive, profit-seeking society, but also in consideration of the various alternatives, actual and potential, now before us.

It is customary in such a discussion to refer immediately to the poverty and deprivations imposed upon the bulk of our population

THE COST OF COMPETITION

as contrasted with the wealth and income of the very few, and to stress the terrible price in human terms we pay for allowing people to live in such degraded, obscene conditions ("one-third ill-housed, ill-fed and ill-clothed"). This approach merely invites arguments over the rapidity with which the standard of living has been rising and comparisons with the town and agricultural laborer of a century ago. It is suggested therefore that we assess the human costs of our competitive, profit-seeking economy in the lives of the rich and successful. If we cannot find adequate justification for our economy in their lives, we need not rehearse all the misery and injustice of our times to demonstrate the point.

What price does competitive profit seeking impose upon the successful man and his family? The usual defense of "rugged individualism" is that competitive striving stimulates initiative and individuality. But it is evident that competition by forcing each competitor to engage in activities that are prescribed by the other competitors and are stereotyped by the rules of the legal-economic game actually suppresses individuality; the individual cannot vary or depart except in terms of intensity and magnitude, or lack of scruples, since competition means striving to defeat or outdo others *in a narrowly restricted pattern of activity.* The coercion of competition in business forces every man to watch his competitors with unceasing anxiety lest he fail to keep ahead of them or lag in adopting every device and trick they use. We need only reflect upon our business cycles to see the blind, sheep-like obedience to competitive standardization imposed upon business men who are unable to resist it, even when they realize the absurdity of the situation and foresee the destruction it will bring. Our banks and other pecuniary agents are peculiarly susceptible to this competitive coercion since the handling of money and credit is so largely a ritual that derives its major efficacy and its patterning from mass action and conformity to the prevailing beliefs and practices.

Any clear-sighted appraisal of competition must acknowledge that what it cannot do is to permit individuality, if that term has any significance and is to mean real distinctions among persons. The dominant urge of the competitor is first to be like others, but ahead of them in the race, and then to outrank them *in the terms of their own striving and goals,* so that after the original impulse to achievement has been expended in catching up, the competitor is forced to go on as if he were still racing. What competition has done economically has been to spur individuals to exploit our technology and resources in the process of striving to beat others. But to insist that economic advancement of a people can be insured only through competitive striving is to confuse process with purpose.

Not only does economic competition stereotype the economic activity, but it stylizes the life of the competitor and his family. Success in competitive striving necessitates a rigid conformity to the design for living that each competitive group has adopted as its ritual. The ambitious young man therefore finds a well-ordered scheme of life to guide him in almost all of our leading occupations. This scheme regulates not only his own dress, recreations, companions, speech, and ideas, but also those of his family so that of necessity his wife and children must also conform, in every minutia of life: house, domestic economy, cars, sports, entertainment, clubs, clothes, church, schools, colleges, vacations, and so on.

It is one of the ironic and yet pathetic aspects of our competitive life that with each step up in the ladder of success, the regimentation of the individual and his family becomes more intense and coercive. The goal of competitive striving is to be allowed to submit to these exactions and find fulfillment only in doing as faithfully as possible what others in one's competitive class are doing. Our leisure class lives a life of unremitting endeavor to keep within the enforced requirements of its leisure time schedule, and every "smart" resort offers this spectacle of anxious concern over one's orthodoxy.

The price paid then by the successful for attaining the higher levels of competitive rivalry may be the abandonment of individuality and the acceptance of fashion and style and "social" norms for living. This applies not merely to business life but to most professions as well, since the prevailing mode of a culture dominates all socially sanctioned activities therein.

But the more subtle and insidious phases of competition are to be seen in the influence upon personality. In a competitive society, the individual is from early years taught that his value to society and his worth to himself are to be judged by the measure of his achievements, not merely as his temperament and gifts may direct them, but as set by the prevailing patterns of the society. For the relatively few persons who do have the outstanding abilities to meet these competitive tests successfully, there are innumerable others,

THE COST OF COMPETITION

indeed the bulk of the population, who are doomed not only to failure in the competitive race but to self-accusations, guilt feelings, and the bitterness of defeat that leads to all manner of self-punishment and retaliation upon others. The cost in personality terms of the successful aspirants is perhaps more significant for our inquiry than is the examination of the failures.

There is, of course, a selective factor at work upon those who engage most actively in the competitive striving; not only ability but a need for the kind of pressure the competitive situation exerts is present, since the process is circular. The individual who in early life is personally insecure, who feels a strong desire to "get even" for his childhood unhappiness, or who is goaded by an inner feeling of inadequacy or guilt or hostility finds in the competitive game a release for these tensions and a further stimulus to increased tension. Each step forward in the competitive striving brings both the confidence for further effort and the incentive in the form of the more demanding requirements of the position ahead. Thus is set up that circular response that spirals up in intensity of activity paralleled by an equal or greater intensity of need for larger effort.

One of the significant aspects of competition is this inability to attain any security in terms of the competitive activity in which it is sought. The reasons for this are more or less clear since competition denies any status that can be considered terminal; hence the competitors, while always setting goals for themselves, are forced to a continual rejection of those goals when attained, in favor of a more remote goal. This rejection is necessitated by the onward striving of others who threaten each goal as reached, but more imperatively by the individual's own personality that has set that goal only as a symbol. It is indeed remarkable how naively we have looked upon the ambition to be wealthy, politically powerful, or otherwise highly placed, as if the wealth or position were really significant to the individual.

This gives some insight into the personality make-up and social philosophy of our captains of business and finance. They are insistent that only this unremitting pressure of competitive striving can insure our social welfare, and any relaxation of such pressure or interference will inevitably weaken out lives and destroy our culture. This viewpoint is of course a necessary one to those engaged in the competitive struggle since it serves to make reasonable the only kind of society that they can be at home in. Moreover, they exhibit an appetite for the pressure of their affairs that also becomes understandable as the necessary condition of their living: when individuals are driven by a feeling of personal inadequacy or guilt or anxiety or hostility, they develop such an avidity for strain that it becomes indispensable. Only when that strain is removed by forced retirement, as necessitated by ill health or sudden failure of a business, do we see the extent to which the individual has been driven and the pressure under which he has been living. The frequency of general collapse and of early death in such cases is so well known as to require no further comment.

The competitive urge then becomes comprehensible as we see it in terms of obsessional preoccupation with personal inadequacy and anxiety that has been projected out into a society, organized primarily to meet the needs of such persons. Not all inadequate and anxious persons engage in competitive striving, and so we must recognize a further characteristic, hostility and aggressiveness, that finds in the competitive scene a socially sanctioned area for its release. The combination of obsessional thinking, anxiety over personal inadequacy, and hostility requiring an outlet provides the energy of a competitive society and indicates the etiology of the "sickness" of a competitive society.

It is characteristic of each personality to wish for a world made in its own image; hence the successful individuals are concerned with the perpetuation of their own patterns and the formulae they have used to make them seem reasonable. Being successful and powerful, these individuals insist upon their own personal pattern in education, especially of their own children, and in social theory (economics, political theory, and sociology), whereby our society is kept true to the trends of their own make-up. Probably the most frequent "reason" given by the successful businessman for his constant striving for greater success is the necessity of "providing for my family." It has been suggested that the inability of an individual to meet the requirements of marriage and family life on a personal basis turns him to business success as a compensatory gesture to the family he has otherwise failed. The wives of successful men of affairs offer an interesting commentary on their "success." It cannot be said that the children, especially the sons, fully repay this parental concern and "self sacrifice," since in so many cases the successful man contrives to ruin his children. This is due, not so much to his success and wealth, as to the very quality of domineering aggressiveness that has made the father successful in business but a failure in human relations and especially family living.

Likewise it is important to recognize that the demands of competitive business will rarely allow an executive to be generous and fair in managing his business or dealing with others, especially employees. There is a premium put upon being "hard-boiled" and ruthless which contributes to, if it does not create, many of the social problems and bitter conflicts in our society. Those who may not initially have this ruthlessness and hardness are compelled to cultivate it, repressing any other tendency if they want to advance to the higher brackets of power and income.

To follow out the price we pay for this way of life into all the intricacies of social and personal life, the frustration and wastage of temperaments and abilities that do not and cannot conform to this competitive stereotype, the inevitable failure of the many who try to conform and fail, more often from lack of aggressiveness rather than absence of ability—these are some of the inquiries that we should and probably will make as time goes on. One of the major inquiries now needed is the extent to which our best brains and abilities are being drawn into competitive business and thereby impoverishing other activities; another is the damage and obstruction inflicted upon society by the failures who attempt to "get even" for their failures.

If we could demonstrate that the successful competitors, in the quality of their own personal and family life, justified the enormous social costs involved in a competitive society, the price we pay might be made to seem reasonable; but when those who come out on top must make such enormous sacrifices and gain so little, we can but add the human wastage of the successful to what we see in the mass of men and reach a staggering total of human frustration and defeat that is rendered more tragically poignant by the very unawareness of the victims.

4

The costs of competition do indeed need to be assayed as the foregoing sketch of the different varieties of costs indicates in order that we may more adequately assay the many merits and advantages of competition. It is unfortunate that the real issues are being debated, not illuminated, and that the polemics of the radical and the apologetics of the reactionary are confusing the minds of even the most discerning. Beneath the institutional framework of our competitive profit-seeking society are certain basic assumptions and beliefs that make that society more or less inevitable.

These same assumptions and beliefs are, to a large extent, tacitly accepted by those who are most vehement in attacking our present social life and by those who are engaged in setting up other social organizations abroad. Thus we have the ironic spectacle of apparent conflict among those who are basically in agreement, but have merely adopted different social schemes for perpetuating the same traditional conceptions of man and his relation to his society. We have only to examine critically the ideas of the upholders of democracy and capitalism to see how much they agree with the dominating ideas of communist and fascist states they so vehemently criticize; per contra, we need only scrutinize the organizing conceptions of the communists and fascists to discover that they are derived from the same cultural tradition as the capitalist democracies they so bitterly repudiate. They all agree upon the lack of significance and value in living, and agree in the belief that the individual must justify himself by achievement in the different fields of activity they favor; this view denies the value of the human personality as such and asserts the paramount necessity of sacrificing the individual to the state, but the competitive, profit-seeking society does it in the name of economic freedom and, ironically enough, "individualism."

(FROM: *Plan Age*, 6 [1940]: 314-24.)

FOUR

The Principle of Disorder and Incongruity in Economic Affairs

1

IN THE physical sciences, the basic conceptions have been those of order, regularity, and constancy as they were revealed in the earliest of scientific explorations, astronomy. With the aid of mathematics, itself a series of implications predicated upon postulates of order, the physical sciences made great progress with these conceptions in the fields of physics and chemistry, where confirmation was found on every side.

With such prestige and demonstrated success before them, it is not difficult to understand how the earlier students of social science set as their goal a body of organized knowledge in which the affairs of men would be revealed with the same elegant order, regularity, and constancy. The great conceptual system of celestial mechanics, derived no doubt, as Whitehead has suggested, from a prior formulation of the universe as divinely ordered and operated, had impressed itself upon thoughtful men everywhere as the very pattern of existence. Political theory, in the seventeenth and eighteenth centuries, searching for something permanent and secure upon which to rationalize the strivings and conflicts of a changing social order, laid broad conceptual foundations for the political state as a self-regulating system, predicated upon basic postulates as to the nature of the world and of man. In these labors both the hard logic of French rationalism and the equally hardheaded British empiricism were able to contribute to a common purpose, although differently expressed and weighted. Out of these efforts came the body of political theory which we have inherited in our political institutions as well as in our political speculations.

When, a little later, the time came for the political economists to take up the task of rationalizing the economic activities of men, they too were swayed by the great achievements of celestial mechanics and by the impressive use of its basic concepts in political speculation. They were therefore at pains to formulate a conceptual system within the framework of which economic events could find their predestined place. Economic thought was from the outset, then, a search for the underlying system of economic forces operating, like gravitation, to determine precisely what should and could take place. Economic wisdom, on the part of the statesman as well as of the entrepreneur, lay in discovering these economic laws and submitting to their guidance, since nothing permanent could be achieved except in accordance with these laws.

No doubt the attraction of this conceptual system of economic affairs was enhanced by the great confusion occasioned first by the agricultural revolution and then by the coming of the industrial revolution. Old traditions and guides to action were rapidly obscured. Novel situations presented unique opportunities. As soon as they could shake off some of the conflicting ideas of medieval economic thought against which Adam Smith labored so manfully, the business men of the late eighteenth and early nineteenth centuries and the political leaders who had already become familiar with that type of reasoning in affairs of state embraced the theories of political economy as a revelation of the universal purpose. It is to be noted that Adam Smith could so confidently urge the liberation of individual enterprise and the policy of *laissez faire* because he was convinced that economic affairs were governed by the forces of an underlying economic order or system, the "unseen hand" guiding men to social good in all their selfish efforts.

It is not our purpose to rehearse the tale of economic speculation during the nineteenth century. Sufficient to point out that, along with political theory, economic theory has clung to the basic conception of an underlying system or order to reveal which was its primary task. The *modus operandi* of the system has changed from generation to generation as successive theorists have offered new formulations of that system and its processes. With but little dissent, and that cavalierly ignored or logically refuted, the body of economic thought has kept persistently at this main task of revealing the regularity and order in human affairs, more particularly in economic activities. Even the radical assaults upon nineteenth-century economics and upon the *laissez faire* policies of government were patterned by preconceptions of an underlying order and system, as in Karl Marx, who employed the Hegelian logic to reveal the operation of a fundamental economic structure and to prove the inevitability of his forecasts. Within recent years this conception of an underlying system has found a new exemplification in the concept of business cycles, and investigators are industriously searching for the laws governing the rise and fall of industrial activity and prices, confident that such laws must be found because these cycles are the outward and visible signs of an inward and pervasive economic system.

After political and economic speculation had been well launched upon these paths, the break-up of the old agricultural, handicraft society, with attendant confusion and distress, directed attention to the problem of social organization and change. As was natural, the social theorist, true to the prevailing "climate of opinion," and in deference to those who had preceded him, essayed the task of framing a conceptual system of social life which would serve as a guide in urgent social reform. Thus the body of sociological thought was founded upon the tried and true principles of celestial mechanics as they had been adapted and refined to fill the needs of social speculation. Down to the very recent past, sociologists, like economists and political theorists, have been searching for the underlying social system, the forces of which must be discovered and understood as the very condition of intelligent social direction.

Seen in the broad perspective of historical development, the social sciences have been a search for the fundamental economic, political, and social systems which, underlying all social life, are more or less obscured by the naïve and conflicting activities of men. This search has been sustained by a faith in the ability of scientific method to disclose these systems of social forces as celestial mechanics so magnificently revealed the operation of our solar system. This faith has been buttressed by the assumption that social life, being a part of the natural world, must be orderly, regular, and constant, just as scientific investigation has shown the rest of nature to be ordered and lawful.

2

WE MUST recall that investigators in the fields of physical science may invoke certain governing principles of organization, coherence, interaction, continuity, and constancy with respect to phenomena under study. Thus they may, with a high degree of probability, proceed to infer the whole from the part and to impute to the part a determinate role in the whole. This is exemplified in anatomy, for example, and in physiology, to refer to the biological sciences in which these principles might be thought less coercive than in physics or chemistry. In chemistry and physics there have been progressive revelations of order and system, of regularity of behavior and constancy of relationships in every aspect of nature brought under study, so that, as in celestial mechanics, the physical sciences are studying an organized systematic whole. Because these principles are found in operation, it is possible to predict the future from the past in many fields and to infer the past from the present.

The recent skepticism over the application of these principles to the ultra-small world of electrons and radiation quanta is not immediately relevant here, but should be noted as an indication of a limitation upon these principles.

When we turn to human affairs and social life, we cannot invoke these principles because we are dealing with human behavior, which is learned or patterned by the individual through experience. The physical scientist is dealing with structures and events which are part of the very stuff of nature, the patterns of which were evolved and laid down aeons ago.

But man, and especially man's behavior, is not an event dictated by patterns laid down aeons ago. Of all organisms man has remained the most plastic and has escaped with the least structural limitation upon his behavior. As several observers have pointed out, every other species has advanced by differentiation of structure, but man has uniquely found the way to adjustment by modification of his habits and by the use of tools, rather than by alteration of his anatomy. In consequence, the history of man is a record of continual change and readjustment, of experiments and mistakes. He has developed what we call culture, patterns of conduct which govern his activities (especially his relations with other persons) and the exploitation of his tools and techniques. This culture has developed in an extraordinary manner, with vestiges and survivals of most ancient times continuing along with the most recent innovations and experiments. Some persons are living on one level, others on another; and the greatest possible discrepancies exist in the prevailing adjustments to the social life and also in the personal lives of the individuals. As we are discovering from the intensive study of personality, what the individual learns from the cultural life is never symmetrical and coherent, and rarely is it integrated. Man can, at one and the same moment, behave in the most incongruous and discrepant patterns, for within the framework of his elastic personality are conflicts and maladjustments that would utterly ruin and confound any other organism or energy complex.

With a culture or social life lacking coherency and uniformity, with individuals exhibiting all manner of asymmetrical development and warped adjustment, we have a complex that almost defies description or classification.

A glance over the past one hundred and fifty years will serve to show how utterly different is the situation in social life from that faced by physicists and chemists. With the introduction of machine industry came the rapid passing of the agricultural, handicraft society and its feudal codes. The process was assisted by legislation which repealed or modified many of the old patterns, so that man could freely experiment in discovering new modes more consonant with the use of the factory, and with wage-earning and competitive profit-seeking. Economic and social theory provided the rationalizations for the change, giving man the necessary reassurance while he was relinquishing the old and accepting the new. Then followed all manner of experiments in the organization of industry, in the elaboration of pecuniary and credit machinery to facilitate the newly created industry and consequently enlarged commerce, and in various other efforts to adapt social life to the new material culture. Sometimes a bold experiment or variation in the accepted mode was abruptly stopped by legislation. Again court decisions striving to bring the new industry and business into line with older precedents forced modifications, limitations, and evasions upon manufacturers, laborers, financiers, and others. Legislation would then be invoked to alter the legal decisions where possible or to curtail the activities sanctioned by the courts. Competition was fostered, but too rigorous competition was forbidden; monopoly or restraint of competition was officially banned, but not interfered with except when deemed excessive. Banking was authorized on one basis, which was suddenly outlawed in favor of another basis. Credit instruments were devised only to be refused recognition or sanction by the courts, and then were modified, revised, or patched up to pass judicial muster.

Production of goods was initiated everywhere by anyone who could manage to start a factory or workshop. Productive processes, formerly unified in the handicraft and putting-out system, were split up into various artificial divisions and stages, depending upon the amount of capital and available machinery collected into one factory; and all manner of business practices were devised to overcome these breaks and separations and keep goods moving along in the essentially unified productive process.

Distribution of goods was undertaken by various people with different ambitions, traditions, and irrelevant prejudices, leading to organizations and practices of varying character to which industry and finance of necessity adapted themselves.

The tale is endless but monotonously the same. Everywhere there was confusion, bold experiment coupled with reluctant conservatism, improvisation, and ingenious compromises. The material culture of machine technology was exploited through credit mechanisms and pecuniary devices that formed a crazy quilt of social survivals, judicial limitations, legislative mandates and interferences, business folkways and conventions.

It is a tribute to the courage of the earlier economists that they attempted to find some order and system in this complicated situation; and their ingenuity in devising theories which, abstractly at least, gave these discrepant efforts the appearance of a coherent whole, will ever be worthy of praise. It is difficult, however, in the face of the actual history of our present social life, to see how anyone can see evidence for believing that this amazing situation is an economic system, or for a faith in the operation of economic laws. Rather one is impressed by the very absence of any system, order, regularity, or constancy in the economic development of the nineteenth and early twentieth centuries.

What seems to have taken place is something like this: Under the influence of the rational tradition of the seventeenth and eighteenth centuries, economists constructed a conceptual system, expressive of a philosophy of social life which they, along with most others, believed to be most desirable and effective, especially by way of escape from the older economic order which they saw passing. Under the guidance of that conceptual system we have been attempting to shape the conduct of our industry and business, our pecuniary and credit operations, and our legislation and courts, ignoring the defects and difficulties and inconsistencies (to say nothing of the injustices).

So long as there was a need for such an economic philosophy it served an important social purpose. Indeed no culture can exist without a conceptual system expressing the dominant ideals and patterns by which the group life is to be regulated and the conflict and discrepancies reconciled. But within the past decade or so the social-economic situation has completely changed, and a new way of life has begun to emerge for which the existing economic conceptions are becomingly increasingly inadequate. In consequence we are becoming aware of the need for new formulations.

Indeed the situation today is very similar to that upon which Adam Smith reflected. Then the newly invented machinery was finding serious obstacles to full utilization in the historically developed scheme of legislative and guild regulations upon production and sale and employment. It was the office of Adam Smith to formulate a polemic against that inherited institutional complex and to preach the gospel of *laissez faire* under which the exploitation of machine industry could go rapidly forward. The theory of a system of economic forces, modeled upon the prevailing pattern of celestial mechanics, supplied the necessary framework of ideas to meet the need of a new social philosophy adapted to the early days of the industrial revolution.

In the present industrial and agricultural situation, the effective use of modern machinery and technology is being impeded by the institutional complex of free competition, bank credits, and fluctuating prices, with the concomitant social distress of unemployment and unnecessary poverty. We are endeavoring by all manner of expedients to avoid some of these difficulties and to remedy some of the defects, but it is evident that the onward march of technology will necessitate large-scale modifications in our institutional arrangements. Before we can accomplish such a social change as is involved in giving up free competition, credit control, and fluctuating prices, we must have a new set of conceptions and formulations to explain the surrender of the old and justify the acceptance of the new. What we await is another Adam Smith to rationalize the present stage of the industrial revolution as he did the earlier stages. In this service, social theory operates like mathematics: "if thus and so is the case, then . . ." In social theory we must make certain assumptions about the kind of social life we desire or think possible, and then develop the implications for action, just as nineteenth-century economists did for the assumption that a competitive social life was most desirable or as Russian economists are doing today for communism.

Before any such constructive formulations can be made, however, it will be necessary to emancipate ourselves from many older ideas and conceptions. This is where the recognition of the principle of incongruity and disorder in social life becomes important. At once it changes the focus of our thinking, directing us away from the search for the underlying economic laws and forces of a mythical economic system by which to guide and discipline our activities and conduct. Instead, we face a social life and a congeries of economic activities which are chaotic and disorderly, for which we must imaginatively create new patterns of conduct whereby some order, regularity, and constancy may be introduced. Just as Adam Smith and his followers, with the aid of the law and the courts, helped to create the *laissez faire* money economy out of the pre-existing regulated handicraft-barter economy, by reasoning from their basic assumption of *laissez faire* and free competition to the actual conduct of business, industry, finance, credits, etc., so the economists of tomorrow must create the new patterns for an industrial society in which poverty, hardship, and want will be eliminated through more effective exploitation of the available and growing machine industry and technology.

The principle of incongruity and disorder in human affairs is not a mere anarchic gesture nor an impertinent dismissal of present economic and social theory. Rather it is an acknowledgment of the tremendous role of theory in social life, where, like religious beliefs, it expresses the dominant conceptions and aspirations of the group and molds their conduct of life. Only in so far as we recognize that our social life must be patterned and directed by intelligence and imagination (because it is like all cultures, haphazard, disorderly, and more or less chaotic) can we realize the immense task awaiting economic and social theorists. So long as they accept the conceptions of an underlying economic system, of economic forces and laws inherent in the very nature of the world, they cannot undertake this creative task confronting them.

If and when they do accept the necessity of creating the new patterns of social order, they will find awaiting their use a number of new ideas and conceptions which will give their theories a very different cast from that of their predecessors. The changing conceptions of human nature, now being forged by students of behavior and personality, will perhaps foster the most far-reaching changes in social theory. Instead of the former belief in a fixed, rational, volitional, autonomous individual always seeking his own gain, we are learning that man is essentially irrational and plastic, not at all the creature pictured in the hedonistic calculus and traditional ethics. This is of immense significance for the future social science which will be concerned with man's behavior and its patterning into the social life we are to achieve. It has consequences for social science as far-reaching as the recent discovery in physics and chemistry of the basic similarity of all matter and energy and its differentiation through the organization or patterning it receives in various configurations and transformations.

Equally important is the changing conception of man's life. Since he has faced a precarious and ambiguous world from the beginning of his history, threatened always with hunger if not starvation, all his thinking and conduct has been of necessity acquisitive. Today he is in sight of a social life in which, for the first time, plenty will replace scarcity. There will be neither necessity for nor utility in the fiercely competitive patterns he has so long followed. His preoccupation with making or earning a living will flag with the collapse of the older institutional arrangements. Economic activity bids fair to lose its long dominant position in human life, as engineering replaces the uncertainties and hazards of competitive enterprise in industry and business. These changes will call for a radically altered viewpoint in the social sciences, for the latter, like mankind, are suffering from a hunger hysteria that even in the face of plenty acts like a neurosis to prevent intelligent adaptive behavior.

Economics somehow must escape from its traditional preconceptions and assumptions and adjust itself to a world in which a wholly new set of conditions prevails, for which only creative thinking will be useful. Perhaps, as has happened in similar situations before, a new group, unfettered by the traditions and conventions of the past, will arise to do this creative thinking. Thus far economists have not shown much fertility of thought in dealing with the present social situation, although their predecessors, as we have indicated, played a major role in the early days of the industrial revolution.

The great task of achieving an industrial society awaits the labors of some group which can replace the now sterile ideals of our inherited social science with those of a more dynamic, instrumental, and creative character. Such a group will start from the principle that social life, as a cultural artifact, is essentially and historically disorderly and incongruous, and that order, system, and regularity are not given, but must be achieved.

(FROM: *Political Science Quarterley*, 47 [1932]: 515-25.)

FIVE

The Emancipation of Economics

IN VIEW of the accumulating body of criticism of economics and the diversity of proposals for its reform, it is important to essay discovering where, in the scale of scientific evolution, economics at present stands. Such an enterprise demands an uncommon degree of detachment from contemporary interest, but, to the extent that we can discover our present position, we may anticipate some of the movement which is to follow and thus may forecast, however roughly, the next steps in scientific development.

1

IN ALMOST every field of inquiry the interests of its students are so focused upon various aspects of the subject that there appears to be a great diversity of problems and of solutions. Closer examination often reveals an underlying agreement or similarity of problems, masked by an ingenious multiplication of alternative positions upon the same subject matter and a set of conceptions common to all. Thus in economics, the various schools are concerned with seemingly different problems and offer a wide variety of solutions thereto; yet to the eye of the detached spectator, who is not too much confused by labels and formulas, economic theory appears to be a single enterprise, addressed to the problem of accounting for economic affairs in terms of two major or basic conceptions—an economic system and human autonomy.

That is to say, when we look, not at the points of difference (which, naturally enough, are emphasized by their proponents) but at the general characteristics of economic theories, we find that the diversity of economic problems and their proposed solutions are seemingly but variations on a single theme: the reconciliation of the antithetical concepts of a system of economic forces and of human volition or autonomy.

The explicit statement of these two conceptions appears but rarely in economic literature, because they are a part of our preconceptions or common sense. They are the verbal formulation of our attitudes toward economic affairs and give rise to the problems we study. For, since we can look at events only as our assumptions and conceptions discover them, necessarily our problems are generated by, and formulated in terms of, our conceptions.

Now it is not difficult to see how these two conceptions arise and find convincing empirical support. Observation of economic affairs discloses an astonishing regularity and constancy in economic occurrences, between which there are almost mechanical interrelations, so that it is impossible to overlook the systematic aspect of economic life. Moreover, it happens that economic affairs exhibit a separate and distinct variety of events called pecuniary, which could occur only in a system of economic forces where such phenomena as prices, for example, could be determined. This interrelated totality of phenomena is readily subsumed under the conception of an economic system which operates through a set of equilibrating forces.

At the same time it appears clearly that men are free agents in their economic activities; they engage in a wide variety of pursuits and enterprises, and they apply various amounts of effort to these activities. They are continually developing new methods of doing things, and they cease doing old things; among the many opportunities before them they are free to choose not only what they will avail themselves of, but how much thereof.

Thus this highly complex system operates through the free play of economic forces which produce the unique phenomena, pecuniary events. Among these phenomena and the forces which produce them, there are constant and uniform relations which presumably may be measured. We are confronted also in man with an autonomous, rationally volitional being, who pursues his own best interests as economic forces may permit.

The task of economic theory apparently is to account for the operation of economic forces and for the production of pecuniary phenomena, and also to explain the activities of man within the system, so that economic occurrences and pecuniary phenomena are presented as proceeding from a unified, interdependent whole,

THE EMANCIPATION OF ECONOMICS 49

while man, the economic agent, is left free and purposeful in the midst of this system. The diversity of types of economic theory arises from the several methods of approaching this fundamental problem and from the varying focus of interests of individual economists.

There has been a considerable amount of critical study of the numerous methods of attack upon this problem. If we start with these two conceptions and the premises and definitions to which they give rise, it is, of course, possible to carry on a speculative controversy indefinitely. It is not our purpose here to debate the validity of these conceptions, since we are concerned only with locating economics in the scale of scientific evolution. But, lest the significance of the antithesis between these two conceptions be overlooked, we may cite an analogous problem to illustrate the economist's difficulty.

Let us imagine an aquarium in which goldfish, snails, and plants are so judiciously combined with water that the aquarium is balanced, i.e., the activities of animal and plant organisms in the water medium are so well adjusted to each other that the aquarium may be considered a system operating by itself (except, of course, for the activity of the sunlight). Then the activities of any single goldfish may be stated in terms of the conditions of the system at any time. The consequences of those activities will appear as an effect of the total systemic causes and, in turn, as part of the subsequent systemic causation operating upon the other constituents of the system. Whatever is taken by an organism or given up by that organism (or by the water) may then be expressed as a determinate share of the systemic total of those substances (oxygen, carbon dioxide, and so on). The appropriation and liberation of oxygen, for instance, may be stated as a law, i.e., in terms of a general and constant process, with a mathematical formulation.

This aquarium system represents fairly closely the concept of economic life entertained by economic theory, the aim of which is to formulate the laws of this conceptual system, so that the occurrence of pecuniary phenomena and the participation or activity of every factor, human and otherwise, may be accounted for and predicted. Viewed simply as an hypothesis there can be no objection to such a conception of an economic system or totality, although empirical observation does not give it much support. But when that conception is employed simultaneously with the conception of human autonomy, economists face a difficult situation.

Reverting to the analogy of the aquarium, if the goldfish are conceived to be autonomous, free to engage in the symbiotic relationship with the other organisms or to refrain, to limit or expand their participation, then a problem arises—how to reconcile this autonomy with the conception of the aquarium system with which it apparently conflicts. For the freedom of the fish makes the "system" indeterminate and therefore scarcely a system at all. Any attempt to formulate the laws of the aquarium would seem foredoomed to failure, since one element, the activity of the fish, is not constant.

To review the various attempts to solve this problem would require a history of economic speculation. Roughly, these attempts have divided between the pro-systemic group, who, as notably in the case of mathematical economists, have sought to establish the operation of the system as rigorously mechanistic, and the pro-autonomy group, who have leaned heavily upon psychology and have been inclined to insist upon men's freedom of action and liberty of choice. Each member of these two groups has devised some individual concept or formula for mediating these antithetical concepts, and this has given rise to the several distinctive types of economic theories. In the main these formulas either reduce the concept of autonomy to a mere fiction, by granting men the liberty of choosing only in accordance with their best interests, rationally (and therefore almost mechanistically) disclosed; or they soften the conception of system to a set of determining "tendencies," which, in the long run, *caeteris paribus*, will mould and direct men's decisions. Both groups share the use of the concept of economic forces which makes it possible to move from the autonomous agent to the mechanistic system without a leap or break in the argument. And both assume that these forces are in free causal operation in all situations.

Likewise, both groups recognize a separate and distinct variety of events in pecuniary phenomena, which have their own order or sequence, in the explanation of which the concept of economic forces plays a large part. For an economic force is at once an expression of the operation of the economic system and a derivative of men's volitional activity, and therefore the participation of the mechanistic and autonomous elements in the production of pecuniary phenomena is simultaneously recognized. This, it need scarcely be emphasized, is highly important, since the individual man's use of money and credit is not to be denied, and his individual inability to control or direct pecuniary events is evident.

The conception of autonomy also raises the question of motivation, since, if men are free agents, their actions must arise from appropriate motives. As already suggested, the notion of rational choice is helpful in disposing of this problem of motives, since it provides a basis for action which is at once autonomous but uniform. This feature may lie behind the persistence of hedonism and of the calculus of utility in economic theory, for the problem of motivation cannot be evaded, if the conception of autonomy be employed, as seemingly it must.

It has ever been the historic role of speculation to deal with conflicting conceptions. It is illuminating, therefore, to compare this situation in economics with a somewhat similar condition in metaphysical speculation. There we find the problem arising from the conflict of two conceptions, appearance and reality, with two groups dividing in their efforts to reconcile those two conceptions. One group spends most of its energies upon the rescue of Appearance, while the other is absorbed in the pursuit of Reality or the Absolute (much as the two groups of economists favor autonomy and system, respectively). Both groups rely upon sensation-creating qualities to mediate between these conceptions, one emphasizing the deceptive character of these qualities and the other insisting upon at least their quasi-validity. Likewise, both groups recognize a distinct type of existence, the psychic, and a separate variety of phenomena of mental events, called variously perception, cognition, knowledge, and so on, which has its own order, in the production of which the qualities of things (arising from appearance and indicative of the workings of reality) are casually effective. The conception of deceptive appearance masking a controlling Reality or Absolute gives rise to the problem of epistemology or knowledge, very similar to the value and price problems of the economists.

This striking similarity reveals the orthodox features of speculation in economic theory, so that the question of scientific status of economics may be more closely approximated. It must not be supposed, however, that this method of describing economic theory is intended to be disparaging to economists or to portray economic theory as a worthless collection of speculation. Economists are the legatees of a philosophical tradition which they have carried on, and these comments are offered to show how and what they have done in that vein and by what steps they will probably develop a science. Most economists have, curiously enough, not permitted their concern for systematic theory to hamper them in the study of many specific social activities and concrete situations, from which they have brought forth empirical results of value.

Every science, apparently, must pass through a speculative, metaphysical stage, which is not wholly barren of results, since the discussion of any problem, however artificial, often serves to send men to actual phenomena for data, and in time this brings about a changed point of view. And not until the logic of this speculative stage has been thoroughly and completely worked out can the next stage of development come. The problems of the speculative stage need not necessarily be solved before further progress can be made, but rather will become obsolescent after men have exhausted their ingenuity upon them. So long, however, as each succeeding generation of economists accepts its problems from the preceding, the multiplication of these theories must continue.

It seems clear from the foregoing that economics is in that speculative stage which precedes the development of a science, when men are engaged in explaining or accounting for events by verbal symbols. And from the growing number of programs of reform we may infer that this stage is drawing to a close. The remedies proposed and the problems urged for study are in the main, however, specialized versions of traditional professional interests; that is, economists are variously invited to employ some one of the well-known methods exclusively and to concentrate upon some one phase of the above-described general economic problem. Thus we find appeals for better definitions and stricter logic, for a more modern psychological analysis (usually psychoanalytic), for the inclusion of institutions in the list of economic forces, and, finally, for the wider and more rigorous use of statistics, always directed by these preconceptions. These appeals for methodological improvement are coupled with more or less vigorous assertions that the problem of prices, of satisfactions or desires, of values, of wealth, of the measurement of economic forces, or some other such problem is *the* central problem. All this is quite normal and represents the initial stage of disintegration when the authority of tradition has begun to relax and men are seeking, by refining and purifying some fragment, to retain the virtue of the shattered whole.

The "old" economics is passing, amid confusion and conflicting counsel, and, while this may be viewed as a great loss, it may prove to be the necessary preparation for a scientific career. In this connection it may not be out of place to remark upon the lack of opportunity or provision for scientific training of economics students. The neophyte must look elsewhere for knowledge and training in scientific method, since academic economics does not provide them. It is true that courses in statistics are offered in most, though not all, graduate schools, but a course in statistics is not an adequate substitute for training in scientific method, however much persuaded thereof many economists may be.

The absence of training in scientific method and the almost exclusive dependence upon dialectics and logic for the investigation of phenomena is not unrelated to the speculative character of economic studies and their rationalistic bias. For, so long as the formulation of definitions and the development of logical consequences from a priori concepts are the ideals of economists, they must continue to use dialectics and to rely upon speculation. In this connection it is of interest to note how some economists have turned to mathematics as a better method of logical proof, much as metaphysics has adopted mathematical reasoning to establish the Absolute. It is obvious, of course, that no amount of refinement of logic can be a substitute for the investigation of specific phenomena.

What has been said of economics applies, on the whole, to the other branches of social science, in which much the same kind of conceptions are used, with the same undiminished confidence in logic and reason as tools of investigation, and where much the same kind of problems are debated. Moreover, there is no greater amount of scientific training to be found in these sister sciences, while all share the growing enthusiasm for the quantitative method or statistical study of non-experimental data. Thus there are no grounds for deprecating the backwardness of economics more than that of politics, or sociology, or history, or psychology.

The question here, however, is not one of assessing the worth of achievement, but rather one of seeing how and where social science finds itself today. To sneer at social science for not being equal in achievement to physics, or chemistry, or biology is to ignore the history of those sciences, which reveals a similar period at the beginning of their scientific careers. It is important now to orient ourselves in the social sciences, so that we may contribute, if possible, in some small way, to furthering the evolution which sooner or later will occur. To do this we must first attempt to understand the situation from which this development will move, which is the purpose of this essay. Needless to say, I am not concerned with criticizing economists or defending a conclusion, but rather with suggesting a point of view from which the future of economics may be discussed.

2

AS IN any other evolutionary development, the evolution of a science is a process of cumulative change, in which each stage of development grows out of the preceding and gives rise to the next further stage. That is why the foregoing attempt to "place" economics, however inadequate, may find some excuse, since it enables us to see, at least dimly, how far economics has traveled and what further transformations await. In the following discussion will be outlined some changes in economics which may, more or less confidently, be expected, although the time of their arrival is beyond conjecture. In this attempt at prophecy I am not urging these changes as the sole road to scientific salvation, but am merely pointing out what we may expect.

As we have already seen, economic speculation may be regarded as an attempt to deal with the problem generated by the conflict of two major conceptions: an economic system of equilibrating forces, and human autonomy. If this be questioned, the reader will doubtless admit that economic theory has been greatly concerned with the two aspects of economic affairs which we may conveniently call the systematic and the volitional.

Now it has repeatedly happened, in the course of scientific development, that we have discovered a way of solving our problems, not by finding a "solution" to the problem, but by showing that the problem was artificial, a product of invalid assumptions and misconceptions. This discovery has usually been accompanied by the realization that a very real problem of a different character lay hidden behind the phenomena which had been thus misconceived. And it has not been unusual to discover also that these misconceptions were a legacy from a much earlier stage of inquiry,

THE EMANCIPATION OF ECONOMICS

which had been carried over as indispensable terms, because no substitutes were available.

It is not difficult, when once we have begun to look for such legacies from the past, to see in the concepts of an economic system and of human autonomy, survivals from an earlier stage in human thought. For the conception of autonomy is, without doubt, an attenuated survival of the animistic tradition, which has given us the soul, psychic life, the ego, the reason, the mind, and sundry other psychic or supernatural entities. And the conception of a system of equilibrating forces derives from a later metaphysical stage when phenomena were seen as the products of special forces organized into various systems, such as chemical, physical, natural (biological), and spiritual.

In the earlier stages of thought, that is, men saw phenomena as manifestations of capricious spirits or the handiwork of the gods, or as the visible expression of an invisible, personalized power. Everything that happened, in the view of those who entertained these animistic beliefs, was willed by some deity. And somewhat later they saw phenomena as proceeding from the operation of the forces of nature, which existed over and above the events they controlled; men were then concerned with accounting for phenomena by describing the special forces of which they were the product. But whether events were attributed to unseen gods or to systems of forces, the really important aspect of phenomena was placed above and beyond man's reach and study. Now it is a commonplace that what modern science aims to discover is merely the order of events, finding in the sequence of the temporal and spatial order in which quantities of energy occur, not only all the explanation it needs but, more important still, the "know how" which we call techniques. Such an enterprise can dispense with animistic notions and metaphysical systems of forces and causes. Indeed, until we put aside such notions, we do not begin to develop much science, for these beliefs prevent us from seeing the repetitions and the sequences of phenomena necessary to a science.

Not all sciences develop in exactly the same mould or pattern. But, if economics is to become a science, it may be expected to pass through much the same sort of growth or change as all other sciences and to undertake the discovery of sequences as its problem. Fulfillment of that expectation would involve a number of changes which follow more or less inevitably upon the initial step of relinquishing the animistic conception of human autonomy.

While it is, of course, running counter to all our common sense to suggest that man's behavior is not autonomous, yet such a step gives promise of exceedingly interesting consequences. For, if we acknowledge that man's behavior is not uniquely volitional, but is a natural phenomenon, we see at once that it must be, like all other phenomena, a subject for scientific study.

If we ask how human behavior may be studied scientifically, we find that we have already begun to study behavior as a response to an antecedent stimulus. This does not mean that a stimulus (event, person, or thing) "causes" man's behavior, but rather that each person, from birth onward, develops a set of habits or patterns of conduct for responding to the stimuli of the environment he meets; these habits are "touched off" whenever the appropriate stimuli appear. Man's behavior then, like all other phenomena, is a consequent response which follows a specific, antecedent stimulus; but the character, quality, form, pattern, and so on of that behavior event is a product of past experience.

It is not difficult to see how the notions of volition and of motives arise and persist, for, if we do not know a person's habits or prior experience, his behavior in any situation can be accounted for only as something willed, the product of a specific motive. We may give up the conception of autonomy and the problem of motivation without embarrassment to social science if we approach the problem of human behavior as a sequence of antecedent stimulus, prior experience, and consequent patterned response.

If, then, we view human behavior as a learned response to a stimulus, we may go a step further and give up the conception of an economic system of equilibrating forces. For, just as the conception of autonomy is a way of viewing the variability of the responses among individuals, so the conception of system refers to the uniformity, regularity, and interrelation of the aggregate responses of a group, which give the appearance of a system of forces. In other words, the concepts of autonomy and system in economics are attempts to deal with the individual and the group aspects of human behavior. Since these concepts give rise to a problem which is more speculative than scientific, while the problem of behavior gives promise of scientific achievement, it is likely that the above-suggested changes in the attitude of economists will, sooner or later, take place.

THE EMANCIPATION OF ECONOMICS

3

WHEN WE get away from animistic survivals and metaphysical conceptions, the problem of the social sciences is revealed as that of human behavior. It would be rash to forecast the solution of that problem, yet enough is foreshadowed in contemporary developments to indicate the approximate course of events. At least we may essay a tentative exploration of the field.

Gradually, students of human behavior are coming to see that man's behavior is patterned by his prior experience in the group life of his parents; that to understand any specific activity we must discover how and when a person learned the habit exhibited; and that man's likes and dislikes, his wants and needs, are ways of describing his learned or acquired susceptibility to specific stimuli. Moreover, it is becoming apparent that the learning process or period of habit formation comes to an end after a varying number of years, and thereafter the individual's behavior is almost completely fixed unless, of course, something overwhelms and destroys his habits.

Now man's habits are not established by his bare contacts with events, but are, for the most part, learned under the supervision of parents, teachers, and other guardians of the young. It is they who, to a large extent, control and direct what he shall learn to do and learn not to do, or, as we have said, who see that he develops certain susceptibilities and certain negative susceptibilities. Under these auspices, then, the young develop habits of avoiding, or refraining from, the response to certain stimuli and of behaving in certain definite patterns to other stimuli. Since almost all objects and persons are involved in this supervised learning, man comes to maturity with an established habit of behavior toward all elements of his experience, derived almost wholly from what others have directed or permitted him to learn. These habits, of course, vary from person to person, but conform in the main to the approved and group-sanctioned patterns.

Looking at these learned patterns we find that the individual learns to refrain from a response to things (objects and animals) which belong to another; but he also learns that for every thing thus forbidden he may lift the ban by performing a ritual or by proffering symbols. Likewise he learns that every person is under a ban or number of bans, which may be similarly lifted. That is to say, each person learns the taboos on things and persons and the group-sanctioned practices for lifting those taboos.

Obviously we are dealing here with the familiar facts of social life, where we find large groups of persons living in close proximity who have much the same patterns of behavior, among which is the habit of inculcating these patterns in their children. When we speak of taboos we refer, of course, to private property in things and animals and to sexual and social taboos on persons, and when we mention rituals, ceremonies, and the use of symbols we have in mind marriage, voting, the "price system," and so on.

The situation appears to be something of this sort: With every object and person under a taboo, the failure to observe which is subject to penalty, all intercourse between persons is banned, except in so far as the prescribed practice or ritual is used. Hence the behavior of each person is necessarily like that of his fellows, since, to live, he must follow the group-sanctioned practices for private property and persons which protect them. The observance of these taboos is a varying obligation, since different social classes may be distinguished by the taboos which they must observe or may neglect, but the taboos of property and chastity are universally respected, at least in outward appearance. Both the taboo observance and the method of lifting the taboo are habits of behavior or learned responses to stimuli. When any situation arises in which certain habitual responses are made by one person, the same kind of response is evoked from a portion, if not the whole, of the group at the same time. For, sharing the same patterns and practices, others will behave in similar ways. Moreover, since man's behavior must be expressed in the prescribed practice, *which is always an act addressed to another person*, the behavior of one person acts as a stimulus to another, whose behavior in turn acts as a stimulus to another, and so on. Hence, when, as suggested, one person is stimulated to action, another is also stimulated, and the patterned behavior of one in turn evokes patterned behavior from all those to whom this behavior is addressed. Thus we observe a systematic order and regularity of social behavior, in which whatever happens to one portion of the group evokes a response which acts as a stimulus to the rest of the group in greater or less degree, just as if social events were controlled by large forces which the individual man was impotent to withstand.

In addition to these habits of behavior toward persons, as owners of things or of services, men also learn to make tools and to work out techniques and processes for making things and rendering services. Since these tools and processes and their products are covered by the property taboo, this means that the taboo practices have become more and more elaborate and important with the increasing specialization of skill and of property which these technical developments have brought about. It is necessary for each person to utilize his property and services as skilfully as possible, as stimuli to coerce others into responding with their property or services or pecuniary symbols. Thus have developed the habits of business, as we call this skilful manipulation of stimuli to elicit the responses with pecuniary symbols, which has become the dominant occupation of almost every person today. In these business operations, the practice is for each person or group having property or services for sale to demand the largest possible amount of pecuniary symbols it can obtain, except where this practice has been partially tabooed, as in public utilities. Those who develop the greatest skill (i.e., learn the habit most thoroughly) obtain the greatest amount of pecuniary symbols.

To attempt a description of the integration of these practices, their local variations, and the substitutes frequently used would far transcend the limits of this paper. It is sufficient to indicate here what the problems of a social science will probably be and to observe how the different aspects of the problem of behavior provide the several branches of social science with lines of attack more or less similar to their traditional interests.

The foregoing is not intended as a revelation of novelty, but rather as an attempted clarification and co-ordination of what is already under way in the study of economists, political scientists, and sociologists. As suggested at the beginning of this section, what is attempted is an outline of the developments now foreshadowed in many quarters, too numerous to permit citation of book, chapter, and verse. Hence this discussion is offered more to help along the change by trying to state its character, than to affect its direction or velocity.

It is not possible to develop a *social* life until we discover what new habits of social behavior are needed to replace the present and how to do the replacing. As intimated before, our historically developed practices are habits of person-to-person behavior in which mutual coercion is permitted and encouraged, whereas the machine industry and its concomitant activities call for group activities and habits of co-ordinated living. Sooner or later we shall have to learn how to live, work, and play as members of a group, but the learning process might be accelerated. For one thing, if we could stop the perpetuation of some of the most ancient habits, customs, and beliefs now recognized in our institutions and laws, so that we would all be living in the same century at least, it is obvious that some of our difficulties might be lessened.

(FROM: *The American Economic Review*, 14 [1924]: 17-38.)

SIX

The Significance of Industrial Integration

THE DISCUSSION of changes in the organization and operation of business and of industry is usually concerned with such questions as the relative economy, profitableness, and efficiency of various arrangements, when approached from the technical angle, or the legitimacy or menace of industrial combinations, if viewed from the social or economic angle. Integration of industry, as significant of a long-term trend in economic and social development, has received but little attention thus far, probably for the reason that these discussions are so largely concerned with the immediate situations to be dealt with. In order to obtain a better perspective, it is here assumed that questions of social policy, of legislation, and of ethics are irrelevant to the subject of long-term trend or evolution, which it is the purpose of this paper briefly to outline.

The organization and operation of a vertically integrated industry are not so familiar that we can assume them to be widely known. In briefest fashion, vertical integration may be described as the functional co-ordination of one or more units in each of the several successive stages of production, so that they are all operated as a single, unified industrial process. But such a brief description tends to confuse rather than to illuminate. We may perhaps gain a better knowledge of what vertical integration involves by approaching it genetically.

When the industrial revolution brought the machine techniques, it supplanted the handicraft stage wherein a single craftsman, or small group thereof, carried on the production of the various articles under a single roof, so to speak. There was differentiation of crafts, to be sure, but each craft apparently comprehended the production of finished goods from the initial preparation of raw materials. While some materials were prepared by one group for use by another group of workers, the usual arrangement was that just indicated, and one entrepreneur directed or carried on the complete industrial process. At least this is the impression one gains, and, if the foregoing statement be exaggerated, it is at least safe to say that, before the industrial revolution, the production of goods was divided into fewer steps and stages than after that great change, and that buying and selling in industry was fairly limited to the initial purchase of raw materials and the sale to final consumers.

It is customary, in commenting upon the industrial revolution, to emphasize the increase in production consequent upon the adoption of machines in place of hand tools. But it is equally important to notice, at least for our present purpose, that the machine process split up production into an ever-growing number of separate processes, separate because of the invention of new techniques and new machines for performing each step in the formerly unified handicraft operations.

Now it happened that these inventions came initially at a time when there were no large accumulations of money capital for investment in the new machines. This lack of large accumulations of capital (and of means for accumulating it from a number of small holders) made it more or less necessary for the industrial entrepreneur to change his methods of operation. Under the handicraft scheme the single individual, or partnership, undertook the direction and management of the complete process of production from raw materials to finished goods. It now became necessary for each of them to confine his operations to the conduct of one or perhaps two steps in this total industrial process, because the small capital of each limited the number and variety of the new machines which he could purchase. In some cases it appears that, having invested in the first machines available for use in their operations, these enterprising producers were unable to find additional capital to purchase the subsequently invented machines which were needed for processes antecedent or subsequent to their initially installed machines. Thus a separate group would set up

THE SIGNIFICANCE OF INDUSTRIAL INTEGRATION 63

an establishment to operate machinery which was technically allied to that of the first-mentioned group, but which, through this pecuniary or credit situation, was divorced both physically and functionally.

This situation with respect to investment capital merits considerable attention, for it throws light upon the development of the highly differentiated business and industrial situation of today, from the invention of separable machines and techniques and their exploitation by individual establishments. Also it may be remarked that the exploitation of the new machines, in the hands of individual entrepreneurs, as fragments, so to speak, of the total industrial process, was extraordinarily successful and profitable, and so we soon began to attribute these results, not to the inventions, but to the separate agents who exploited them. It is not difficult to see, therefore, how the nineteenth century became so generally persuaded of the efficacy of *laissez faire*, especially since the detailed regulation of the handicrafts, through pre-existing legislation, had to be overthrown before the new machines could be adequately exploited.

It was one thing, however, to seize upon the newly invented machines for the establishment of separately owned factories, each of which carried on one step in the sequence of technically allied and interdependent industrial processes; it was another thing to find means for overcoming the loss of unified direction of these separately controlled processes so that they could work together, for it is obvious that, with the multiplication of separate factory enterprises, each dependent upon the stage technically prior for obtaining its raw materials and upon the stage technically subsequent for disposing of its products, some sort of arrangements had to be elaborated for interrelating these separately owned and controlled establishments. Hence began the development of the modern art of buying and selling, for moving materials from the point of original production through the separately owned and controlled machines for finishing and on to the distributor to the final consumer or user.

At first this need was met by simple contract and sales, whereby the goods in the several stages of refinement or elaboration were transferred to the next subsequent stages for an agreed-upon price. But as the industrial equipment became more complex and more widely distributed among separate owners and geographical districts, there was a more or less concomitant development in the elaboration of pecuniary devices and operations and the organization of markets, as shown especially in loan credit, negotiable instruments, and similar instrumentalities for facilitating buying and selling, speculating in commodities, and the like. Only a cursory glance at present-day litigation is needed to discover how these pecuniary activities are working and how difficult it has become to observe all the necessary rules and limitations upon the use of pecuniary methods.

Thus it appears that the growth of individual enterprises, of the business practices of buying and selling, and of other related pecuniary operations were both a consequence (or concomitant) of the industrial revolution and the vehicles for its further propagation. Once the custom had been established of restricting a factory to one or only a few steps in the total industrial process, the further growth of any factory was largely confined to increasing the capacity in those steps. Not until late in the nineteenth century do we begin to see the expansion of separate establishments in the direction of adding additional subsidiary processes to the main operations of the plant.

But before this expansion really began, we had an exceedingly interesting development in the rise of industrial combinations. Under the prevailing scheme of separately owned establishments carrying on one or two steps of the industrial process, competition among the several producers of the same stage was provoked by the necessity of disposing of their product on a price basis. But this competition not only limited profits; it frequently prevented the producer from selling his goods at cost. Hence arose various schemes and arrangements whereby the producers in one stage of the total industrial process pooled their business operations of selling under the most capable business leaders. Thus it was possible to eliminate or reduce the activities of the less capable business men in that stage and so to improve the strategic business position of the combined sellers. It should be noted that these concerted operations were dependent in large measure upon the subordination of industrial activities and operations to the exigencies of the market, in the way of reducing output and even closing down plants; so that we find the practices of contract and sales, which were earlier used to facilitate the passage of materials

THE SIGNIFICANCE OF INDUSTRIAL INTEGRATION 65

through the industrial process, now giving rise to activities aimed to obstruct that movement.

These efforts at combination (or as it is sometimes called, horizontal integration) are not the only evidences of the difficulties encountered in the use of buying and selling as a method of relating these highly differentiated industrial activities. It is clear that, despite the fact of individual legal ownership and independent operation and control, no factory can run for long unless the production in the prior stage is sufficient to supply the needed materials and supplies, nor unless the factories or other users in the subsequent stage consume what it manufactures. This is the inescapable technical unity of industry in which all factories are involved and which they cannot violate for long. But with John Doe and Richard Roe and sundry other persons operating these factories, each of varying degrees of skill and ability technically, and with all manner of business capacities, it will readily be seen that the buying and selling of each establishment will approximate the technical needs of industrial operation only by the most fortuitous combination of circumstances—and then only for short periods. A priori, one would expect in a competitive economy that business men would periodically overbuy (and thus lead others to overproduce) and then stop all buying until they had used up their surplus, when again they would repeat the process. And, of course, this is what happens in these recurrent fluctuations in the magnitude of industrial activity and business operations which we call business cycles.

We may see in the foregoing how the progress of the industrial revolution through individual enterprise has placed an ever-increasing burden, not only upon the pecuniary operations or devices required to co-ordinate these separate establishments, but also upon the conduct of industrial operations within the separate plants. For the recurring periods of increased activity (expansion) make it difficult to obtain supplies in the quantity and of the quality required for effective operation and at a price necessary for business success. In the attempt to avoid these embarrassments of inadequate supply and of unprofitable price, the individual concern is led into so-called "legitimate" speculation in materials, that is, buying in anticipation of orders and sales so as to forestall the rise of prices and scarcity of supplies. This procedure, however, usually leads to undue inventory accumulations which, in the inevitable period of price declines, are the occasion for considerable losses that all too frequently wipe out the "profits" gained in the period of rising prices.

Moreover, when, in the course of the cycle, depression follows expansion, it is commonly found that the increased plant capacity, which the ever-rising prices and increasing orders made necessary, is not only useless for a time, but a source of further loss.

It is fairly clear, then, that despite the variety of efforts to make the money economy, or more precisely, buying and selling at money prices, serve both the needs of industrial operation and the quest for profits, the pecuniary mechanism is not entirely reliable and is subject to serious "backfiring."

Before we continue this brief resumé of business developments leading to the rise of integrated industry, it may not be amiss to comment upon the significance of this growth as revealing a recurrent process in social evolution. It appears that whenever a new tool or technique for meeting the exigencies of living appears in a group, it is usually seized upon as an instrument for greater production, comfort, or slaughter. But, since the pre-existing and traditional group arrangements of ceremonies, rituals, and symbols are group-sanctioned practices for exploiting the older tools and techniques, it frequently happens that the use of a new technique calls for some modification of these older practices. There follows a series of elaborations and refinements of the older group practices, designed to facilitate the use of the new tool or technique, but only too frequently acting as impediments and obstacles to that use. The increasing burden of these traditional group practices and their elaborations are accepted as unavoidable in the developing use of the new techniques and tools. Hence there is an increasing discrepancy between the needs of the technical processes and the possibilities and requirements of the institutional life of the group. To meet this situation there is, later, a bold attempt to rescue and even promote the institutional practices at the expense of the tools and techniques, which is the stage of outright ceremonialism or ritualism, when men cling tenaciously to ancient rites, symbols, and practices, at the expense of their industrial arts.

Out of this latest stage may come one of two divergent paths: either the group life is held to the institutional pattern and further change is stopped, as we see in so many primitive groups which have developed their techniques up to the point where the institutional limits, more especially of the religious life, make further exploitation and elaboration of their techniques impossible; or the older institutional life is relinquished and replaced by group practices and arrangements more in harmony with the needs of their technical equipment. Where further technical development continues, this revision of institutional life is almost inevitable, since the cumulative industrial changes render the customs of the traditional group life untenable.

Seemingly we are today at the point where this revision of traditional institutional life is beginning. In the attempt to develop the trust, pool, and combination, we see what is probably the last stage of elaboration of older institutional customs, for it is clear that these endeavors to promote pecuniary operations at the expense of industrial and vital requirements are, in truth, efforts to establish ceremonialism for its own sake. It should not be forgotten that ceremonies and rituals demand attendants whose advantages therefrom are not inconsiderable (but temporary) factors in the course of events.

If, then, we look upon the movement toward vertical integration of industry as part of the process of social evolution in which the older group practices and arrangements are giving place to a newer scheme of things, we will perhaps gain a better understanding of its significance and its operation. For undoubtedly vertical integration is an attempt to bring together under one management the separate stages of the industrial process which technically require unified direction and control. Since this technical requirement cannot effectively nor continuously be met through buying and selling of goods between separately owned stages, however ingeniously and elaborately those pecuniary operations be conducted, it has become both feasible and desirable to bring a number of consecutive stages of production under one managerial control.

Now this process of industrial unification is no simple operation of adding on to an existing factory building and organization a number of new wings and new departments. The inclusion of minor and subsidiary processes, such as repair shops, tool-making departments, and the like, in the factory scheme, began several decades before the end of the nineteenth century, but it involved no great change in managerial practice or social arrangement. Shrewd calculation showed that when these minor operations reached a certain volume, it was profitable to do the work in the plant, instead of contracting it out or purchasing at need. It was not, however, until late in the nineteenth century, probably first in the oil industry and later in the iron and steel industry, that real vertical integration began with the incorporation under one management of a number of different stages of production, carried on in separate plants at different locations. This, indeed, marked a new step, for at once it set a task for management, of how to direct and control the operation of several different industrial processes (or stages) so that they would function as one synchronized process, despite the differing time, techniques, and machines involved and the distance separating the several plants.

To meet the needs of this task, there has developed during this century an entirely new technique which is variously called cost accounting, administrative statistics, planning and control, or industrial engineering. This new technique provides a method of managing one or more factories by a system of controlling, whereby the advantages (or many of them), which seemingly were obtainable only by the individual enterprise and initiative of a factory owner, may be obtained fairly easily. For the method of planning and control is to plan in great detail what work is to be done and the machinery and personnel to carry out those plans, to delegate the authority to see that the plans are carried out, and then frequently and precisely to record and measure the results accomplished, the costs incurred, and the unfinished portions of the task. By such a technique it becomes possible to supervise one or a dozen organizations carrying on distinct operations at widely separated locations and to co-ordinate them into a single industrial process, so that materials flow from plant to plant, from stage to stage, as readily and as surely as they pass through a single machine or department.

The term "science of management" may correctly be applied to this technique which discovers the temporal and spatial sequences in the industrial process, and by planning and control directs operations of a given quantity according to those sequences. Planning, it should be noted, comprehends temporal sequence as well as spatial arrangements.

In the hands of a trained staff of industrial engineers, the operation of an entire industry, formerly conducted as separately owned and controlled plants in each stage, becomes a matter of bulk and detail, but not an impossible task, as may be seen in the

THE SIGNIFICANCE OF INDUSTRIAL INTEGRATION 69

Ford Motor Company, which has been integrated backward to most of the sources of its raw materials, such as iron ore, lumber, coal, glass, etc. The United States Steel Corporation may be cited as another conspicuous example of vertical integration.

With the several stages of the total industrial process brought under one managerial control, with each plant put upon a budget of performance and costs and the whole process directed to the production of the finished product, it becomes possible to achieve that technical co-ordination of process which the pecuniary operations of buying and selling could rarely approximate, except perhaps for brief intervals and then only with undesirable "booms."

It is obvious that the development of an integrated industry with such a scheme of co-ordinated operation calls for the ownership or control by some one organization of all other stages. The number of possible arrangements for affecting such ownership or control is limited only by the legal and pecuniary machinery to be used for that purpose. Thus, whether one plant buys outright the factory from which it has previously purchased its supplies or the factory to which it has heretofore sold its product, or whether it contrives to establish a control of their management through security ownership, makes little or no difference. Apparently, the growing number of corporate organizations, with control vested in a majority of the common stock, not only favors the method of financial or security control for effecting integration, but also renders the initial task of integration more easily accomplished than might otherwise be the case.

Just because integration of industry is so frequently built up by obtaining control through security ownership, its significance is liable to be overlooked. For, superficially, the separate corporation and the formerly independent plant are not in the least changed by these financial transactions: the individual corporate entities remain, goods pass from one to another by contract and sales, and all seems as before, except that the dividend recipients have been changed. Yet it is clear that this buying and selling and other pecuniary transactions are purely formal, merely the observance of the requirements for separate corporate entities and their appropriate activities. Beneath these formalities may be seen the central managerial control which is co-ordinating the activities of each separate entity and plant into a single process, more or less regardless of those proprietary rights which the law and custom demand. This means that the operation of any one plant and the activities of its owning corporation are governed, not by the exigencies of the markets for its supplies and its product, nor by its own expectancy of gain, but solely by the requirements of the entire integrated industry of which it forms but one functional part.

Buying and selling at money prices, then, give place to planning and control in an integrated industry as a means of industrial co-ordination. Thus integration implies much more than the superficial facts of ownership and security control indicate; it is not merely a scheme of pecuniary relationships, but a movement of technical development, taking effect through credit machinery so far as institutional elements (property, income, etc.) are concerned, but primarily an industrial methodology. That is why it is so significant as contrasted with combinations (or so-called horizontal integration) where the relationships between the constituent plants and the objectives sought were principally pecuniary. It is probable that the period of combination has prepared the way for integration, since the very magnitude of the combinations has made integration forward and backward both possible and desirable.

Integration does affect the pecuniary position of an industry, however, and usually to its advantage, although the business success or failure of integrated industry is not conclusive as to the real merits of integration. For so often the cost accounts and records of operation may be favorable, but the industry as a business enterprise is a failure, largely because, in the larger strategy of financial operations, the enterprise is being exploited for other ends. The income accounts and current stock quotations are not to be taken with too much faith by one who is concerned with the question of the efficacy of industrial methods.

The great advantages accruing to an integrated industry, which grow cumulatively with the extension of the integration, are found in the assurance of an adequate and dependable source of supplies, on the one hand, and a certain "market" for its product, on the other, for each stage in the industrial process. For, as pointed out above, the production in each stage of the entire industry is carried on in accordance with a budget, wherein are figured the requirements of each commodity in each stage. Hence the staff in each plant has a definite task to perform in a definite time, with

THE SIGNIFICANCE OF INDUSTRIAL INTEGRATION

the necessary raw materials and supplies and the disposition of its product provided for. To illustrate, the budget of production for an industry is prepared by working backward; thus one thousand automobiles will require one thousand engines, four thousand wheels, two thousand axles, and so on. Each of these parts will in turn require so many semi-finished articles, such as castings, forgings, stamped forms, and the like, which in turn will require so much iron ore, steel, wood, rubber, and similar raw materials. Production of these commodities and parts is then scheduled so that the various required amounts for each complete car will be produced with the necessary synchronization. Thus the production of iron ore, coal, and coke will be carried on at a rate sufficient to meet the requirements of the blast furnaces producing pig iron; this production in turn will be governed by the needs of the foundry for castings and of the steel-making plant for plates, rods, and bars; and so on with each item entering into the completed car.

It is instructive to contrast this method of co-ordinating the several stages of production in an industry with reliance upon the pecuniary relationships of buying and selling, where production is governed by fluctuating market prices, a multitude of individual contracts or orders subject to cancellation, the guesses and expectations of salesmen, and above all by the widespread practice of speculative purchasing which alternately overbuys and then refrains from buying while using up accumulated stocks.

It might be said that integration not only supersedes this variable personal relationship between producing plants, but indeed frees industry and industrial operations from direct pecuniary control.

Of course, it must be added that the full benefits of integration cannot be obtained so long as business and pecuniary operations are still controlling the economic life generally. But with the handicap of operating in a group life still predominantly on a business basis, the integrated industry obtains its supplies in each stage of production at a real cost which includes no margin of profit. It is true that on the corporate records the goods passing from one plant to another may be entered in the sales account at cost plus a profit, but since the profit, if any, goes to the integrated industry, in whole or part, this profit addition is merely nominal. This means that the final real cost of the product sold by an integrated industry will, ordinarily, be less than the final cost of a nonintegrated product, by the cumulative amount of these profit margins. In addition, it is possible in an integrated industry to reduce, if not to abolish, inventory accumulations in the several stages of production (goods passing from stage to stage uninterruptedly), thus reducing the amount of working capital required in the industry, or increasing the "turnover" (cf. the Ford operations). Again, with one plant feeding directly into another, the whole machinery of sales (except at the final stage) is eliminated, with a considerable saving on sales force, advertising, collections, and bad debts. Moreover, with the mobility of capital gained through centralized control of the cash and credits of a large industry, the reduced working capital required can be used to great advantage through rapid transfers, intercorporate advances, and the like.

The extent to which integration has developed is not known, since no systematic inquiry has been made. But from casual information it appears to be increasing very rapidly. Chain stores are growing at an amazing rate and these chains either are, or soon will be, integrated backward, since the very steadiness of their sales makes integration with the plants producing the goods they sell both logical and attractive. The growth of integration, or at least of its preparatory steps, may be seen indirectly in the situation among jobbers and wholesale distributors, who, in almost all trades, are being crowded out by direct selling, by purchasing groups of independent retailers (soon to lose their independence), and by sales agency contracts between producers and retailers (which foreshadow closer relations to come).

To one brought up in that article of faith that individual initiative and competitive private enterprise are the foundation of sound economic activity, these developments must indeed appear ominous. And yet, as the writer has repeatedly remarked, integration of formerly independent plants is an inevitable step in the evolution of machine industry. For it represents the coercion of the machine which demands functional co-ordination with its technical antecedents and consequents; that is to say, integration is coming about because, from the raw state to the final form, goods are "in process," whatever may be their legal or proprietary status; hence if buying and selling at money prices retards or interferes with the operation of the machine industry, which each year is growing larger and more technically complicated, then buying and selling will be eliminated. Integration, therefore, is the form in

THE SIGNIFICANCE OF INDUSTRIAL INTEGRATION 73

which the price system, in so far as it affects the conduct of industry at least, is being rendered obsolete.

Viewed with a little perspective, the movement toward integration is not so much a new departure as a return to the unified direction and control of production which obtained in the days preceding the coming of machine industry. As suggested earlier in this paper, the ownership and control of materials were usually held by one person who hired craftsmen to work them up through all the stages from the raw state to finished product. In the person of this entrepreneur, the various stages of industrial operations were unified and co-ordinated. Then came the splitting-up of production with the introduction of machinery and its ownership by separate individuals, each of whom bought his materials and sold his product to other entrepreneurs. We have multiplied and elaborated our pecuniary devices and methods to an enormous extent, in the endeavor to make buying and selling function adequately as a means of co-ordinating these individually controlled industrial operations. The number of accessory methods devised to help business men to direct these pecuniary operations, such as trade papers, market quotations, business forecasts, trade barometers, credit indexes and reports, and records beyond count, are truly appalling to the thoughtful observer, who remembers that scarcely any of these are necessary to the conduct of industry as such, but all and many more such aids are required to carry on buying and selling of goods, at fluctuating money prices, between separately owned and managed stages of industry.

It is usual to think of society as divided between producing and consuming interests, but we frequently fail to realize the magnitude of the pecuniary transactions (measured in sheer quantity of materials transferred) which occurs between business men as producer-buyers and producer-sellers or distributor-buyers and distributor-sellers, in which the final users of the goods do not participate. From the point of view of industrial management, these transactions are not only unnecessary but often a real obstacle to effective use of industrial equipment, as we see in the several periods of business cycles. When we detach ourselves from the traditional attitude toward business, it is obviously absurd that our industrial activities should be conducted by men who are intent upon deriving the largest pecuniary gain from their relations with other managers of industry through bargaining which is continually frustrating a well-balanced program of production in all stages of industry. But since this state of affairs has been historically derived, it is comprehensible, however absurd it may appear technically.

It may not be amiss to point out here that many business men, who repeat the classical notion of the "unseen hand" and extol the superior merits of production according to competitive profit-seeking, are in the van of those who are running or organizing integrated industry, wherein they are adding their bit to the obsolescence of the arrangements they praise.

It is probable that the increasing investment of funds by insurance companies, savings banks, and other fiduciary organizations (principally in bonds) is developing a large impersonal interest in industry which is more concerned for continuous, regular operation than in fluctuating profits; hence their influence will be on the side of integration, even though they exercise no direct control.

The growth of integrated industry is, however, much more than an industrial development; it is the continued sweep of the industrial revolution, completing, or rather fulfilling, that great change in industry and in social life. And it is not unwarranted to say that the further extension of integration in the twentieth century will probably entail social changes almost as great as those witnessed in the nineteenth century. For many of the characteristic features of an industrial money economy and its accompanying social life will pass away with the further growth of integrated industry.

For one thing, integration will largely reduce, if not eliminate, business cycles, for the simple reason that it will free industrial processes from business control, thus permitting that continuous, non-fluctuating operation which is the peculiar function of the machine. Even agricultural operations, which are so variable and seemingly beyond man's control, will be regularized so far as production is concerned, since the integration of agriculture with the industries using agricultural products will undoubtedly be accompanied by the development of mechanized agriculture with reserve stocks and storage for stabilizing crop yields from year to year, thus freeing industrial operations from the risk and uncertainty of fluctuating yearly crops.

A society in which production is carried on continuously and fairly evenly will be a society with no periodical unemployment crises and hence with less of those socially undesirable concomitants of unemployment. The large shifts of occupations from industry to industry, which occur in periods of expansion and contraction, also will disappear, along with fluctuating wage rates and earnings. The sudden rise of large fortunes and the impoverishment of others will decrease, since the rapid fluctuations of prices will not occur to make such changes possible.

Looked at in perspective, one might expect to see a return to the condition of social stability which prevailed from time to time in England before the nineteenth century (between the various upheavals of lesser magnitude than the industrial revolution). But such stability will be something rather new to western society, since it is probable that, under a so-called democratic government, with an income and inheritance tax, with a decreasing number of hours of work (capable of considerable reduction in a stable industry), and with a large reduction in the number of persons engaged in "pecuniary employments" (Veblen), our social life will be greatly altered. It is difficult to conceive of any part of our social life today which will not be changed by integration of industry with all that such a development implies.

Thus, as we see this onward sweep of the industrial revolution fulfilling its inevitable function of reorganizing man's industrial activities and hence altering, *pro tanto*, his social life, the significance of what we call integration appears very large indeed. Naturally we regard the development of integration as something rather daring and experimental, to be viewed questioningly and made to prove its right to usurp our accustomed life and pecuniary methods; but to our grandchildren or great-grandchildren, our doubts and hesitation and reluctance will probably seem highly amusing, much as we regard the early railroad operations where each shipper had his own car and where the ownership of the roads was limited to small local sections, and the movement of goods and passengers was largely at the mercy of bargaining between rival and connecting owners. The notion of transportation as an industrial activity, involving through movement, regardless of proprietary rights, has scarcely become established even now, as witness the current discussion of the merits of railroad consolidation. But integration of industry and consolidation of railroads and public utilities and the social changes they will necessitate will come; the command of the machine and the tool have ever been directive in man's affairs and probably ever will be. Social theories and philosophies, like all rationalizations, will arise to justify the new order of affairs after it has become a little more established and, no doubt, an economic theory will be developed in due season to minister to this new scheme, as Adam Smith and Ricardo, with their successors, have variously upheld the virtues and inevitability of the old.

(From: *The Journal of Political Economy*, 33 [1925]: 179-95.)

SEVEN

Social Planning and Individual Ideals

IT IS interesting to review the shift in our ideas and conceptions of economic life during the past few years. Beneath the familiar forms of business life and the old indices of activity, however, there has been a profound change which we are just beginning to realize. Everyone will recall the first response to the situation in the winter of 1929-1930. Like the British during the early days of the first World War, we adopted the slogan, "Carry on, the crisis will soon be over and we can then resume. Above all we must not lose sight of the essentials, nor allow our faith to falter." As the depression deepened and the easy optimism of the Hoover administration proved repeatedly fallacious, there came a rapidly growing flood of proposals for economic planning. Scarcely a day passed without some new scheme being launched to bring a revival of activity in industry and business through a well-formulated plan of action.

It is significant that in these early proposals for economic planning the major, if not exclusive, concern was with the plan of action. Only within the past year [1934] has there been a realization that planning without control is largely futile. So long as Dick, Tom, and Harry are free to operate their plants or stores, to expand their establishments or start a new factory, as they are impelled by private personal motives, an economic plan for an industry or for the country as a whole must remain a pious but ineffective exhortation that no one can, would, or should heed.

The Hoover administration was dedicated to the doctrine of rugged individualism, as we now term the older faith in Adam Smith's "unseen hand" that was believed to guide the selfish individual to work for the benefit of society. The Roosevelt administration, as indicated by the legislation upon agriculture, industry, and banking, repudiated this doctrine in favor of planning *and* control, invoking whatever sanctions are necessary to make the planning effective, if not coercive, upon individuals and organizations.

Thus, in the short space of four years, we witnessed a far-reaching change in our thinking and in our economic activities. It is evident, however, that these economic changes are only the beginning of our difficulties, for they will force us to consider a host of other questions, not economic but personal, that underlie the economic-social situation and largely control our economic thinking.

If we will look at our social situation with a little detachment, we will see that in business and industry we have been primarily concerned, not with strictly economic questions, but with the question of individual personality development. Free enterprise has meant the right of each individual to engage in whatever activity he chose in order to realize his own peculiar personality needs and adjustments. To this invitation the individual entrepreneur has responded in vigorous fashion, starting new workshops, factories, new distributing establishments, new service-rendering organizations, and all other forms of profit-making endeavor. Where fortune favored, he has enlarged and expanded his business, competed aggressively where it seemed advantageous, or connived surreptitiously to drive out or frustrate competition. The economic development of the United States has accordingly been conducted as a by-product of individual striving, wherein the really important factor was the realization by the individual of the aspirations and ambitions that impelled him to ceaseless, and often ruthless, endeavor.

The property acquired, the wealth gained, the power achieved, as well as the concrete economic goods and services created by this individual enterprise, were, and are, essentially symbols or indices of attainment of the personal goals sought. No one can seriously maintain that our great captains of industry or our petty shopkeepers have been impelled by the desire for wealth, power, or success itself. Their public careers plainly contradict any such superficial interpretations, while their utterances and their official biographies testify to the burning ambitions that flowed into their actual business life.

What we are prone to forget is that each individual constructs a picture of himself as he would like to be, an ideal self, which expresses his aspirations and ambitions and also marks out for him the direction and character of his future strivings. Just to the extent that he projects a career of business success, he creates for himself the major problems of his personality development and raises constant threats to his security until he has achieved that success. In this the business man differs not at all from the politician, the military man, the professional man, the scientist, or the artist, each of whom proposes for himself a career involving the attainment of certain objectives and standards. Business life has been exploited for individual ends more frequently, perhaps, because it was so easy of access and the dominant social patterns all pointed thereto.

With a continent to exploit and a rapidly growing population to feed, clothe, house, and otherwise serve, the lure of business has been extraordinarily strong. An immense apparatus of industry and agriculture has been created which is far in excess of our social needs or our export markets. The cost of all this has never been reckoned and, indeed, may never be computed because the ramifications are so many and so involved. What army of accountants could estimate the approximate costs of competitive business and industry if we really attempted to assess in those costs the losses due to bankruptcy, uncollectible commercial accounts ("bad debts"), fire losses resulting from arson, tributes to racketeers, business litigation, labor disputes, bank losses, and the indefinite but poignant human costs of anxiety and worry over business affairs. Most of these losses and costs arise from competitive industry and business run by incompetent individuals who should never have been permitted to start a business, or from sheer surplus capacity and facilities, the overhead on which has been appalling.

We have paid a stupendous price, mostly concealed in indirect charges and insurance premiums that are borne ultimately by the consumers, in order that ambitious individuals might express their individuality in business enterprises. While it may sound a bit far-fetched, nevertheless it is precisely true that our economic life has been a sort of out-patient clinic for restless, unadjusted individuals who found in competitive striving some sort of alleviation of their acute personality problems that otherwise might have driven them "insane." Our social and economic life has been at the mercy of anyone who had the desire to exploit it for his own personal needs and satisfactions, regardless of his ability or competence or the cost to society. The justification offered for this scheme of things has been the great benefits which individual enterprise has presumably brought to society, although it has become clear that, like the classic case of roast pig, we were burning down the house unnecessarily. Moreover, it is difficult to evade the question of whether individual competitive enterprise has not been just an accidental accompaniment of the basic technological advances which are really responsible for social gains.

Today we face, in the new legislation for regulating agriculture, industry, banking, and transportation, the beginning of restriction upon this freedom for the individual. Planning under adequate control will no longer permit the use of social capital to start a new business or expand an old business when no increase of facilities is necessary or desirable. Instead of leaving it to the judgment of private investors and the banks to decide upon the basis of possible profit, the operation of business will be directed by some sort of planning and scheduling to meet social necessities. In the modern technique of planning and control, cost accounting, budgeting of production, and management engineering, we have the necessary methods for operating a controlled economy, as the Soviets, borrowing these methods from the United States, are rapidly demonstrating.

Here, then, enters the problem of personal adjustment which may prove more difficult and perplexing than the purely economic problems, however complex and far-reaching. In place of business success through competitive striving for profit, individuals must find other channels into which they can pour their energy and enthusiasm. There will be need for new ego-ideals that look toward non-pecuniary goals and avoid the exploitation of society. Can such goals be created and will they prove sufficiently compelling to capture the imagination and zeal of American youth?

When the American Indians of the plains were put on government reservations, many suicides of young braves occurred, because they faced a world in which the avenues to worth-while achievements—hunting and warfare—were closed. When the age of chivalry was ending, many could see nothing worth living for if the older tradition of knightly deeds disappeared. Even our own pioneer ancestors in America felt life was losing its zest and value

as the frontier life was displaced by organized community living.
Every generation that faces the passing of its favorite symbols and dominant occupations is harassed by doubts and beset by fears that life will be worthless if those cherished patterns are lost. It is interesting to note that the nineteenth-century *laissez faire* economic life came to fill the need for engrossing activity just as the older ideologies and religious faiths were beginning to feel the impact of the new science of the seventeenth and eighteenth centuries. The nineteenth-century economic expansion rescued Western European culture from an abyss of skepticism and acute *Weltschmerz*, as indicated by the literature of the early 1800's. It provided avenues for human energy that saved man from thinking while he feverishly produced goods and wealth. Now, at long last, he must return to the questions he has evaded for a hundred and more years and attempt to formulate some new ideas and conceptions, some new faiths and aspirations by which to live.

Whence will come the new patterns that will serve to displace competitive free enterprise and how will they be introduced against the weight of tradition? Mr. Hoover and those who stood for rugged individualism indicated their inability to conceive of a life in which competitive business enterprise had been removed. Yet it is pathetically absurd that many should cling so tenaciously to gainful economic activity as the only satisfying and worth-while activity for their personal development.

Anyone who reflects upon this fierce determination to perpetuate competitive economic activity of the kind we have for so long pursued, must wonder at the truly remarkable character of human personality. For it is obvious that the individual entrepreneur lives a most miserable life of worry and anxiety over prices, expenses, contracts, sales, and the ever-present threat of competitors. Preoccupied with these cares, he often neglects his family and children, or loses the full richness of intimate life while he plays the game in which only a few can win. Those who do win and arrive at the heights of power and wealth usually do so by renouncing all that is humanly generous and valuable, transforming themselves into the "hard-boiled" executive or "tired business man."

It is as if our social life were overshadowed by a major social psychosis, a *folie sociale*, that seizes upon our young men and women (who aid and abet the process) and makes them mad, driven by a consuming frenzy that devastates their own lives and those of their children. Meanwhile, society in a thousand ways pays for the maintenance of such a scheme of things and doggedly refuses to concede the possibility, let alone the need, for change. None so fiercely resents the deliverance from burdens as he who is most heavily laden, as any student of personality and mental disorders will testify. The resistance to any change in our competitive economic life is tremendous because it arises from those who are most acutely, but unconsciously, the victims of the whole process. They will fight a "New Deal" or misuse it if they can, to perpetuate individual enterprise whereby their patterns of life may be preserved and transmitted to their children.

But the problem cannot be evaded long, since no amount of argument or scheming can still the doubts let loose in the world, and now reinforced by Soviet Russia and by the many other countries in the midst of social economic revolutions. Somehow we must acknowledge that our naïve faith in the sufficiency of economic achievement is tottering, and as it goes it reveals the immense void left by the loss of religious conviction, involving human destiny and social progress. These empty places, as already indicated, were becoming apparent to the more sensitive minds of the late eighteenth and early nineteenth centuries. The democratic dogma, the belief in social progress, and the engrossing exploitation of the machine process and pecuniary symbols, swept our predecessors along and comfortably concealed their dying faith in the ideas of the past.

Thus we come to the essentially moral, ethical, and philosophical questions that underlie the new culture that we or our children must attempt to build. They are, indeed, hard questions to formulate, let alone answer, for they require the highest order of creative imagination and artistic insight to penetrate to the essentials involved. But, even if we cannot yet discern whence our deliverance is to come, it would help to clarify the situation and prepare the way if we would recognize that our economic perplexities and conflicts are but disguises for these basic problems of human conduct.

This recognition would have important consequences, for at once it would show that our educational needs are not exclusively for the social studies, more knowledge of economic conditions and political programs, but rather for clarification of the individual's personal development. It is conceivable that a plan for life-guidance in our high schools and colleges, whereby individuals could be helped to explore the full implications of vocational choices and careers, might prove more efficacious in bringing to pass much-needed social, economic changes than any amount of didactic instruction in social aims and social needs. At least, a wisely conceived program of counseling and guidance, oriented to the development of saner, more wholesome personalities and their enrichment through art, science, and the fuller enjoyment of the world and human relations, would undoubtedly contribute greatly to this purpose.

The outlines of the new culture are still dim and uncertain, but it is probable, as Ortega y Gasset has pointed out in *The Modern Theme*, that the new culture will be directed toward an increase in "vital sensibility." If this is to have any definite meaning, it must imply the testing of the old and of the new institutions and cultural patterns by their influence upon the quality of human life and personality. This same point was expressed in the following quotation from the *Report on Recent Social Trends* which may well serve to conclude this discussion:

The immense structure of human culture exists to serve human needs and values not always readily measurable, to promote and expand human happiness, to enable men to live more richly and abundantly. It is a means, not an end in itself. Men cling to ideas, ideals, institutions, blindly perhaps even when outworn, waiting until they are modified and given a new meaning and a new mode of expression more adequate to the realization of the cherished human values. The new tools and the new technique are not readily accepted; they are indeed suspected and resisted until they are reset in a framework of ideas, of emotional and personality values as attractive as those which they replace. So the family, religion, the economic order, the political system, resist the process of change, holding to the older and more familiar symbols, vibrant with the intimacy of life's experience and tenaciously interwoven with the innermost impulses of human action.

The clarification of human values and their reformulation in order to give expression to them in terms of today's life and opportunities is a major task of social thinking. The progressive confusion created in men's minds by the bewildering sweep of events revealed in our recent social trends must find its counterpart in the progressive clarification of men's thinking and feeling, in their reorientation to the meaning of the new trends.

(FROM: *The International Journal of Ethics*, 45 [1934]: 81-9.)

EIGHT

Apology for Irresponsibility

IN HIS book, *The Road to Serfdom,* Friedrich A. Hayek tells us that national economic planning in Italy and Germany led directly to totalitarianism and that in Russia it was the chief instrument of state regimentation. With these examples as evidence, he warns us that the current efforts and proposals for national economic planning in England and in the United States will, if we persist, lead to the same fate, of a totalitarian government, the loss of human freedom, and the cessation of all progress—hence the title, *The Road to Serfdom.*

Dr. Hayek assumes that what has appeared in one country or national group, with its cultural traditions and its predominant character-structure can be naïvely applied or transferred to people with other cultural traditions and a different way of life and character-structure. We need to be reminded again and again that each cultural group has developed its peculiar traditional beliefs, patterns, and institutions which are the source of its strength and also its weakness, of its self-created social problems and likewise of its attempts to find the only solution it can or will accept for those problems.

What Dr. Hayek says seems less plausible when we remember that the national economic planning and the totalitarian governments he cites occurred among peoples who had no traditions of self-government and political freedom, and who have never accepted the conception of individuality and the kind of social ethics which are characteristic of England and the United States. In each of the countries described by Dr. Hayek, the individual has historically been an instrument of the State, to be ordered, forbidden, and used ruthlessly by the State and the governing group for its own purposes. In all the dictator countries people have been reared to accept authority, both secular and theological, and to submit to regulation of their lives, as in the dictator countries which Dr. Hayek does not mention, e.g., Portugal and Japan. National economic planning in the dictator countries, like all the other forms of state control, continued this well-established practice of domination and exploitation of people, technologies, and resources for the State or those controlling the State. Those policies and the coercion and regimentation of all activities were accepted by the people generally (a few dissenting) as an expression of their ideals and traditions and as necessary to the way of life they believed in.

Proposals for economic planning and governmental action in England and in the United States arise from a different set of traditions and express other beliefs and intent. In both of these countries there is a well-established tradition of the place and rights of the individual as paramount over the government, which is conceived not as an authoritarian power but as an agency for the common good, to be invoked when people need help, protection, and assistance.

Economic and social planning in England and the United States has long been familiar. Jeremy Bentham, from whom economists derived many of its basic assumptions, urged national planning over a century ago in England. In the United States national planning was early recognized as desirable and promising for promoting the general welfare and was advocated by Gallatin, Adams, Jefferson, and Alexander Hamilton.

National planning as now urged in England and the United States expresses the belief in the exercise of intelligence to guide our individual and group life toward the goals which the people have chosen for attainment. Such planning is not the coercive control by the State over passive citizens nor a cover for a ruthless minority, exploiting a nation as we have seen in European countries. Planning in England and the United States is the way people seek the help and protection they need and the advancement of a free democratic society, through governmental action when necessary. (See "The Possibilities of Planning," by Charles E. Merriam, *American Journal of Sociology*, March 1944.)

To understand this conception of planning and the legislation which attempts to regulate, control, and forbid various practices in England and the United States, it is necessary to recall the social-economic-political context and problems to which planning and legislation are addressed.

When the guilds were succeeded by the enterprising producer-businessmen toward the end of the eighteenth and beginning of the nineteenth centuries, little or none of the guild tradition of responsibility (very inadequate according to present-day social standards) survived the passing of the handicraftsman—petty trader. Thus Thomas, Richard, and Henry, who started up factories and business activities as independent private enterprises in the hope of profits, refused to recognize or to accept any responsibility for the consequences of their activities for their employees and families, their customers, or social order. They had no traditions of responsibility, and they claimed immunity from any ethical considerations except those of pecuniary profit and loss. These early enterprisers and their successors justified their stand by an appeal to economic theories and economic laws (e.g., the iron law of wages so firmly upheld by Ricardo) and rationalized what they did by attributing everything to the "forces of competition."

Social legislation designed to regulate and forbid what businessmen were doing was later enacted in response to repeated and prolonged protests and after interminable delays, in order to curb these activities that threatened various groups. Beginning with the Interstate Commerce Commission and the Sherman Anti-Trust Act about 1890, there has been a series of such acts and commissions, each provoked by the necessity of curbing or regulating the irresponsible activities of industry and business and professional practices, as, for example, the Securities and Exchange Commission after 1929. In England the record of social legislation is similar but usually it has come two or three decades ahead of the United States, as Mrs. Lynd has shown in her recent volume, *England in the Eighteen Eighties*.

Legislation earlier sought to regulate employment, to forbid hazardous and dangerous occupations and later to provide compensation and medical care of injured employees; more recently, to provide social security against unemployment and old age, for those who, in the face of an urban, money economy, are helpless to meet those exigencies unaided.

Every such step has been bitterly opposed, by fair means and foul, by those whose practices or negligence made such legislation necessary. Much of the legislation has failed of its purpose because of opposition, evasion, or sabotage, but such failures do not diminish the meaning and significance of the intent and of the methods employed. Social legislation is the effort, on the part of people themselves, by constitutional means, to obtain needed protection and assistance in those areas or fields where private enterprise, individual and corporate, has refused to accept responsibility for the human and social consequences of its decisions and its activities.

Within recent years there has been a growing realization of the need for national planning, as shown by the organization in England of P.E.P. and the National Planning Association in the United States, in which many prominent business men are active. The organization of the Committee on Economic Development for postwar economic planning is another indication of the growing acceptance of national planning by business men, and by religious, labor, and other groups. All these groups are convinced that we must find something more effective than blind competitive struggles and the "higgling of the market" to articulate our complex and diversified economic activities.

The more forward-looking business men are recognizing that business must accept the social and human responsibilities which accompany their economic power and freedom of action. They realize that we must curb the irresponsibles and "chiselers" whose activities continually provoke the extension of governmental regulation and control. (See *Tomorrow's Business* by B. Ruml.)

Thus we are seeing some business men seeking co-operative planning by business and government because they realize that business decisions today have such far-reaching consequences in our technological society and therefore must be planned and articulated.

Looked at in this perspective, it would appear that the proposals for economic planning in England and the United States are expressions of our ethos, the ethical-moral traditions of a people who for many years have regarded their government as their instrumentality for whatever action was necessary to ward off the threats to their life, liberty, and pursuit of happiness and to protect the freedom they cherish. This is quite a different tradition and setting from the people who have long been committed to Statism and accepted authoritarian governments to which businessmen have been largely subservient, if not partners in regimenting the lives of people.

The foregoing is not offered as a plea for, or a defense of, social legislation and economic planning. Those who have closely observed what was attempted in 1917–1918 by the War Industries Board and other war boards, again in the middle 1930's with the National Recovery Administration, and during World War II with the many war agencies and controls, must agree that national economic planning, even for war, is a prodigious task. Our efforts have not been too successful, partly because of the difficulties of the task, but also because of passive or active resistance and especially the calculated sabotage by irresponsible individuals and groups.

Anyone who reflects upon the situation will realize that proposals for national economic planning are not only in our tradition but are encouraging signs that the English and American people believe that something can be done through popular, free government to protect themselves against the threats of unemployment, the fear of want and disaster, by planning how to utilize our resources, our technology, and our manpower and womanpower for the general welfare. The belief that many of our businessmen have not yet learned to be responsible will be confirmed by the very acclaim given to Dr. Hayek's polemic against English and American planners and his reiterated statements that we must trust our lives and our national welfare to the "forces of competition."

It is not my purpose to defend national economic planning against which a more devastating criticism may be directed, namely, that *national* economic planning may fail completely to recognize the necessity for *world* economic planning if we are to achieve any world order. National economic planning may be a vehicle (and in the minds of some planners it is so regarded) for a self-sufficient nationalism or autarchy which even in a free society can be a massive obstacle to world order. Moreover, *national* economic planning may, like other nationalistic groups, fail to recognize the necessity for redirecting business enterprise and technology to the larger world tasks for which they are now ready, but blocked by diplomacy, military policy, and similar nationalistic survivals.

As Mrs. Langer's article in the March (1945) *Fortune*, "Make Your Own World," so cogently explains, businessmen must assume even greater responsibilities. We cannot today tolerate the "irrational forces of competition" to continue the international anarchy that periodically erupts into war as another expression, not of the deliberate intent by businessmen (peace to the writers of 1929!), but of the irresponsibility for the consequences of their competitive trading and business and financial activities.

Dr. Hayek's book merits study not merely as a controversial piece to be defended or attacked according to the sympathies and interests of the debaters. Whatever uses the book may be put to, there is no question about Dr. Hayek's sincerity and personal integrity. His volume is important because it raises the central question of our times—the nature of social order and the place of the individual in that order. It attempts to answer that question by using concepts and a way of thinking that are not *merely* obsolete but, in the new climate of opinion today, are almost archaic.

If we will look back in our intellectual history, we will see how the Newtonian conception of a system maintained in equilibrium by the operation of large-scale forces, acting at a distance, captured the imagination in the seventeenth and eighteenth centuries. It provided a concept which could be used, both as a polemic against the existing order and as a pattern for new theories and arrangements which would supersede the older scheme of things.

Thus, when the political theorists began to attack absolute power and divine right and to demand political freedom, they invoked the doctrine of natural law and proposed a scheme of government on the Newtonian model. In place of royal and ecclesiastical authority, they asserted that a government of political rights and duties should be established, as a self-regulating, equilibrating system. This was the model which early in the eighteenth century was adopted by the English. The full expression of the Newtonian concept appears in our own Constitution with its system of checks and balances and three separate branches of government (which England gave up after a brief trial, as President Lowell pointed out).

Later, toward the end of the eighteenth century, when new inventions and expanding opportunities for trade made the historically developed parliamentary regulations and guild rules no longer desirable because they hampered production and commerce, economic theorists likewise invoked the Newtonian model. They conceived of economic events as arising from an economic system, operating through economic forces which controlled all economic life and so kept the system in equilibrium.

Thus, in 1776, Adam Smith, wishing to displace the established economic order and to inaugurate the new arrangements, pleaded in *The Wealth of Nations* for freedom of enterprise to exploit the new machinery and to enlarge foreign trade, unhampered by parliamentary regulations and guild prescriptions. He denounced these survivals of the older order as interfering with economic progress and invoked the guidance of the "unseen hand," because he was persuaded that there existed an economic system, with economic forces which would automatically regulate all activities, maintain equilibrium, and bring social benefits from selfish strivings.

Succeeding economists accepted this Newtonian model and skilfully developed a coherent body of theory explaining everything that happened as the result of these economic forces and economic laws. They ignored the few dissenting voices or explained away any reservations or contrary beliefs, even when expressed by such leaders as Jeremy Bentham or John Stuart Mill, as Mrs. Lynd has pointed out.

In the same tradition, then, sociologists accepted the Newtonian conception and explained social life and social order as a natural system or mechanism operated by large-scale social forces. In the hands of Herbert Spencer these ideas dominated social theory and provided an explanation and a justification for whatever existed.

The nineteenth century was committed to the Newtonian conception and viewed social order as a part of nature, a system or mechanism, existing somewhere between the earth and sky, operated by large forces, political, economic, and social, which governed all social events. Thus, everything that happened, for good or evil, was natural and inevitable and beyond man's reach or even understanding. Indeed, it was impious and destructive to attempt to interfere with these forces. When later in the century the cumulative misery and degradation of the "satanic mills" was beginning to undermine this faith in the beneficent operation of economic forces, the Darwinian conception of the biological struggle for existence served to reinforce the waning belief in the efficacy of unrestrained competition. Newton and Darwin were joined in the doctrine of social Darwinism (See *Social Darwinism in American Thought*, by Richard Hofstader) to maintain these earlier beliefs and economic practices.

These concepts have been the basic ideas in our classic economic theory. Their coercive role in thinking is shown by the way the opponents of the classical school accepted much the same concepts and likewise assumed the existence of an economic system, only they asserted that the system was not entirely beneficent or beyond human interference. Even Karl Marx was influenced by Newton and Darwin, whose concepts he fused into a powerful polemic against classical economics and things as they are, asserting the inevitable operation of economic laws and forecasting the evolutionary development of the kind of society he championed.

Now it has become evident that these basic assumptions and the organizing conceptions of economic and social theory have become obsolescent in the light of the emerging new climate of opinion, with the concept of the "field," of space-time, of relativity, of quantum and nuclear physics and the reformulation of the ideas of a force (space rate of energy) and of power (time rate of energy). These shifts in thinking show that most of our classic economic theory is but an elaborate metaphor and the assumption an economic system as a part of nature, is gratuitous and misleading. Moreover, the cumulative observations on other societies, built upon different cultural traditions, with their peculiar assumptions and values, show that each society has its own economic "system," its historically developed institutions and practices and arrangements. These differ markedly from our own "money economy" of free enterprise, as shown by Margaret Mead in *Competition and Co-operation Among Primitive People*.

The political, economic, and social theories based on these Newtonian concepts served as a useful polemic to release us from the surviving institutions and practices of medieval life. They rationalized the explosive outburst of energy and fertility in the nineteenth century which brought an amazing productivity but also an appalling misery, exploitation, and degradation. It would appear, however, that these theories are predicated upon the ancient belief in man's helplessness in the face of superhuman and supernatural powers and forces.

From the early days of man's reflective thinking he has been essentially defeatist about human life and social order. All through history man has been told (or has told himself) in his religion, his philosophy, his law, and his art, that he was a weak, helpless, impotent creature, subject to these superhuman and supernatural powers and controls and that social order was divinely ordained or inherent in nature. Whatever happened was, therefore, inevitable and unchangeable, and man must be resigned to accept whatever happened as necessary and, could he but understand it, as desirable. Wars, plagues and epidemics, natural catastrophes, the tyranny of rulers, and the exploitation of the many by the few have been explained and justified by these theories which always tell man he is abjectly helpless. Indeed, these disasters and oppressions are often interpreted as well-merited punishment for his lack of piety or as necessary trials to strengthen his character.

As Mrs. Lynd shows, economic theory in the nineteenth century was the instrument for justifying God's ways to man and for making the misery and degradation of the poverty-stricken mill and mine workers appear as both inevitable and desirable. Likewise, Herbert Spencer asserted with all the authority of his position that no one should attempt to interfere with the automatic self-regulating social laws and forces which beneficently operated to eliminate the unfit.

In the context of nineteenth-century thinking, these ideas and teachings were reasonable and acceptable, but today they appear as utterly defeatist and cynical. When Dr. Hayek tells us that we can enjoy freedom only by "submission to the irrational forces of competition" and that "the only alternative to submission to *impersonal* and seemingly irrational forces of the market is submission to the arbitrary power of men," he preaches the ancient doctrine of human helplessness and defeatism which has been utilized so long to compel man to submit to every and all indignities and exploitation in the name of superhuman and supernatural authority, power, or forces. The tragic irony of the situation is that these doctrines of man's impotence have been utilized throughout the centuries by those who knew what they wanted and were determined to get it at whatever cost to others. These doctrines are the mainstay of the cynical who today wish to continue their historic role but who seem unaware of the new hopes and growing beliefs in the dignity of man now stirring in the minds and hearts of the common man.

As indicated earlier, these are the arguments of the irresponsibles, those who want to do what they please in business and industry and professional practice and be permitted to ignore or evade the consequences of their actions and decisions, their negligence, and their chicanery. In the name of human freedom they claim immunity from any ethical, moral, or social values and assert that only competitive struggling must determine our lives. It is indeed surprising to read Dr. Hayek's invocation of Milton, Locke, and Hume in defense of freedom of enterprise and the irrational forces of competition since those ideas were unknown to those men. Those writers were concerned with human rights and *political* freedom and would have been incapable of understanding what is meant by *economic* freedom, since that idea was not developed until almost the end of the eighteenth century.

But we need not pause to debate these issues. The important, the central problem of our time is how to establish and maintain social order, without invoking authoritarian control, whether human, superhuman, or supernatural, and how to recognize and protect the dignity of man and, if you please, of woman also.

As the evidence increasingly shows, social order is not given as a part of nature; it is not a system or mechanism out in space. Social order is in man; it is that which man himself creates and maintains by what he believes and assumes, what he has selected in nature and human nature for cultivation and elaboration (and has rejected or ignored). Social order is man's self-chosen design for living; what he values and how he feels toward himself and other members of the group direct his conduct and so constitute his social order. Social order is not given; it must be achieved. It can be maintained by authority of the ruler, the state, or the church, or it can be maintained by self-disciplined, responsible conduct of each member of society who can and will respect the rights and needs of others. This is what we mean by a free democratic society which for its continuation demands the highest standard of individual and group ethics, not submission to mythical forces or powers. If individuals are to be accorded freedom of action, speech, and belief, the power to contract and to engage in self-chosen activities, then, of necessity they must observe in their individual and group activities, in their personal relations and professional practices, the ethics which will make such freedom compatible with social order and our enduring human values and our persistent aspirations toward human dignity.

Today the older conceptual apparatus of classic social and economic theory has become obsolete. Also, the older legal and religious sanctions invoked to maintain social order with its injustice, misery, and degradation have been losing their credibility. With the rise of new sensibilities and of aspirations, largely due to the more recent trends in our literature, drama, and art, these changes have combined to make our time a period of confusion, disorder, and conflict. But this very confusion and conflict are indicative of the potentialities of the future as we grope forward to a social order in which not only equality of opportunity but the basic equality of human needs will guide our social philosophy.

In this transition from the older and now obsolescent ideas and practices to the new, perhaps the most influential ideas will be those derived from our new understanding of individual personality and the new insights into the dynamics of human conduct. We are learning to recognize how the growing child and adolescent takes over the cultural traditions transmitted by his parents and teachers and develops his highly idiomatic version of what he has been taught, with a persistent way of feeling toward people and himself. Thus, we may view the individual as a unique personality engaged in the multitudinous activities of life, as he participates in social order in his peculiar, personal way, with often warped, distorted conceptions of our cultural traditions, and impelled, if not driven, by his persistent feelings, frequently of anxiety, guilt, or resentful hostility.

We are beginning to recognize that the individual who ruthlessly strives for power, prestige, and property and utilizes our legally sanctioned patterns of competitive rivalry in business or politics for these strivings is usually an unconscious victim of his own personality make-up and "forgotten childhood." Thus, he is driven to sacrifice not only others but himself for achievement of his ambitions, as he attempts to "show them" or "get even," or releases his otherwise intolerable feelings in his interpersonal relations or various psychosomatic disorders. (See Karen Horney, *The Neurotic Personality of Our Times*, and Henry B. Richardson, *Patients Have Families*.)

So long as individuals are so driven, coerced, or self-defeated by their own personality, they have no freedom, however freely they may appear to be living, conducting their business, or carrying on their political or professional activities. Nor can such unhappy, internally conflicted individuals participate in creating and maintaining a social order dedicated to human needs and values because of their distorted personalities. We are just beginning to recognize that an even more crucial task than winning the Four Freedoms is to achieve freedom for the personality, without which all other freedoms are of little avail.

When Dr. Hayek bids us submit to the "impersonal forces of competition," he is telling us to submit to the irrational and often neurotically distorted individuals whose aggregate economic behavior makes up what he calls the "forces of competition." While he offers competition as a bulwark against the "arbitrary power of man," his doctrine delivers us into the irresponsible powers of the men who, at whatever cost to social order and human values, must dominate and exploit social life for their own personality needs. Dr. Hayek assures us that if ambitious men are encouraged to struggle ruthlessly against each other with no interference by legislation, we may escape the slavery he sees coming from our attempts to develop some economic planning.

But this remedy, which Dr. Hayek offers, is of little avail for, as he himself points out, not only the misguided economic planners, but the businessmen themselves, through devious methods of controlling production and prices, dividing markets and otherwise preventing competition, as in cartels, are also interfering with the "forces of competition" which offer our only hope for escaping serfdom. It would appear that we are indeed lost.

It is a curious doctrine which some of our editorial writers, businessmen, economists, and professional groups are asking us to accept as the only guide for facing the problems of tomorrow. But the cynicism and defeatism of its implications (of which apparently Dr. Hayek is unaware) apparently have not escaped its apostles. Perhaps, as has been suggested, Dr. Hayek's book is being promoted as their *apologia* by the irresponsibles.

The bewildered and sometimes panicky individuals who are unable to muster the courage and the imagination to face the problems of an evolving technological social order, are but repeating the attitude and performance of those who in every previous generation have resisted the new ideas and practices upon which our present liberty and freedom are based. Today we must remember that we can pay our debt to the great figures of the past only by trying to do for our day what they did for theirs.

This means repudiating the archaic doctrines of man's helplessness and defeatism, reasserting the moral and ethical imperative of achieving a free, but humanly decent, social order as we recognize the dignity and worth of every human personality. For this task we can command the amazing new resources of science and technology, but they must be directed by self-disciplined individuals who will use those resources for human conservation.

Here it is important to realize that democracy is more than voting and representative government, more than freedom of action, speech, and belief, precious as they are; democracy is an aspiration toward the recognition and conservation of the individual personality. A society merits the term democratic, therefore, when it is prepared continuously to assay its government, its business, industry, its professional practices, its education, its religion, its law, its family life, indeed all its traditions and practices, in terms of what they are doing to and for the individual personality.

We do indeed face fateful decisions in our economic and political life. As we critically examine the various proposals now being offered for our guidance, let us not be misled into thinking that we have but two roads to follow—the "road to serfdom" and the road down which "Sammy runs."

(FROM: "The Rising Stock of Dr. Hayek." *Saturday Review of Literature*, May 12, 1945.)

NINE

Social Legislation and the Police Power

THE PROGRESS of social legislation has been attended by a difficulty which, in point of obstinacy, has been more formidable than any class interests. That is the legal difficulty. Our courts have been confronted again and again by legislation designed to promote the good of society, but which they were at a loss to sustain under the powers of our several state constitutions, as they interpreted those powers. Of late such legislation contains almost specific reference to the police power of the state as its basis. But here again the courts have had difficulty in ascertaining the scope of the police power. Almost every court has refused to essay a definition of that power, and many frankly confess to a fear of so doing, lest the definition prove too broad or too narrow.

This same dismay in the face of proposed social legislation has been felt by our legislators. The increasing participation of philanthropic, economic, and research organizations in the production of legislation, designed to improve social and industrial conditions, has made each session a trial of soul to the conscientious representative. How far should he go in supporting this legislation, and will it be constitutional when passed? The sponsors of these laws have based their appeal on two grounds—to some humanitarianism has been paramount, while with others the scientific element has weighed more strongly, but the purpose of both has been the promotion of the public weal.

To most courts humanitarianism alone is no basis for legislation, and to many scientific research appears irrelevant. The improvement of society, being debatable, may or may not be sufficient justification for a law, so that the support a law brings is usually of no moment. So, also, with many legislators. They are unmoved by an appeal for the betterment of society and unconvinced by the results of research. Humanitarianism may be a motive to legislation and scientific research a warning of evils to come, but neither is a legal justification for legislation. The police power, undefined and unlimited, alone can justify social legislation. What, then, can be said of the police power which will outline its scope and purpose?

In the case of Health Dept. v. Trinity Church (145 N. Y. 32, 45 Am. St. Rep. 579, 39 N. E. 833, 27 L. R. A. 710), Peckham, J., said: "It (the police power) must be exercised subject to the provisions of both the federal and state constitutions; and the law passed in the exercise of such power must tend, in a degree that is perceptible and clear, toward the preservation of the lives, the health, the morals, and the welfare of the community, as those words have been used and construed in many cases heretofore decided . . . It must not be exercised ostensibly in favor of the promotion of some such object while really it is an evasion thereof and for a distinct and totally different purpose, and the courts will not be prevented from looking at the true character of the act, as developed by its provisions, by any statement in the act itself or in its title showing that it was ostensibly passed for some object within the police power . . . Laws and regulations of a police nature, though they may disturb the enjoyments of individual rights, are not unconstitutional, though no provision is made for compensation for such disturbance. They do not appropriate private property for public use, but simply regulate its use and enjoyment by the owner. If he suffer injury, it is either *damnum absque injuria*, or, in the theory of the law, he is compensated for it by sharing in the general benefits which the regulations are intended and calculated to secure."

This discussion is affirmative in a general sense and negative in a particular way. It establishes, however, the right to regulation, subject to property rights, of any activity when such regulation will inure to the general or public good.

Thus it may be seen that the police power is regulative, if not prohibitory, in character. It does not, however, appear to be appropriatory except where the appropriation is incidental to destruction of property as a nuisance.

Leaving the theory of the police power, consider the manner of its application. One of the earliest forms of social legislation in this country is found in health laws, such as the quarantine regulations against disease. The health authorities have been vested with power by the legislature to prescribe almost any and all activities of the citizens. This power at present may transcend all other civil power or rights solely to protect the community from danger. Another early exercise of the police power is in the laws regulating factories and conditions of labor. Not only have factory acts established certain sanitary standards for factories, but they have prescribed the maximum hours which children, women, and even men may toil. Lately, in New York state the question of fire prevention has been enacted into certain regulative statutes. And for some fourteen years the construction of tenement houses has been subject to rigid requirements. By these various forms of social legislation based upon the police power of the state, a man's home, place of work, manner of living, and care of his property, are brought within certain limitations of free action for the benefit of the community.

The existence of these limitations and the method of their enforcement are, when considered historically, indicative of a change in government. All of these regulations are enforced by a corps of inspectors whose duty it is to seek out violations of the laws. When such violations are found and the accused is adjudged guilty, a fine is laid upon the individual for the misdemeanor. In a word, the violator is guilty of a crime. What he may have done to incur such a penalty varies from running a machine without proper guards to a negative act such as refusing to clear his premises of rubbish. In another case an individual may have rented and maintained a room lacking a window, for which he is likewise held guilty, and is fined. The functions of government have surely changed when a man can be held guilty of a crime who merely has kept rubbish on his premises or has not guarded machinery. And no one can claim a precedent for the act that prohibits windowless rooms and adjudges the renting of the same a crime. Yet the courts have held valid such laws because they promoted the common good. In each case it was demonstrated to the court that such regulations were desirable and necessary to the well-being of society.

The theory of the common law regarding torts or wrongs done to an individual has been that for every demonstrable wrong there was a remedy by an action at law. It was necessary to establish the wrong and the relation to the tort feasor, and the action was clear. Violation of the right of privacy, in using a person's photograph for advertising, has been held a tort and actionable. Conspiracy resulting in injury to an individual, where only the injury was proved, has been sufficient ground for an action, so that apparently the law of torts is potentially able to right all wrongs that can be proved and which are measurable. Thus, when John Doe, having legitimate business to transact, passes across the iron grating in the sidewalk before a man's building and is precipitated into the cellar, he may sue the owner for the injury and the time lost in recovery. There the wrong is apparent and the feasor is clearly negligent. The relation of cause and effect appears in no uncertain light.

Now enter circumstances and situations wherein there is much to ponder. An owner of property rents several rooms, one or two of which have no windows. In the course of several years the tenant or some member of his family develops pulmonary tuberculosis. Or again, a property owner permits rubbish to accumulate in his building whereby a fire is propagated and fed, so that despite the efforts of the fire department the building of his neighbor is destroyed or his employees are endangered. Or a youth enters a factory, and after four or five years of work at a machine that has no device for removing the dust, he is stricken with pulmonary tuberculosis. In each of these cases an injury has been done to an individual and research has demonstrated the cause of it. But the element of time has entered in to obscure the causal relation. The injured party will seek in vain for redress in a court of law. There is no remedy for his wrong. These injuries occur in large numbers and many suffer thereby. The state, through its accustomed procedure, can give no aid until the legislature prohibits the renting of windowless rooms, forbids the accumulation of rubbish, and compels the use of "blowers" with grinding machines.

These three instances are typical of many cases where wrong is done for which no remedy at law exists, and of conditions detrimental to the community which must be changed. The point to be made is that these wrongs are not always capable of individual demonstration, but are known to exist, though the law offers no redress or course of action against the author of the wrong. Legislation which is designed to eliminate the possibility of these wrongs and to benefit the public as a whole is called, and clearly is, an exercise of the police power of the state. Thus it may be said that the police power of the state is that power which permits the state to regulate those practices or acts which may result in injuries to individuals, but for which there lies no private right of action. The test of the validity of such exercise of that power is the demonstration of the injury generally.

By the application of such a test the court deciding the question must concern itself primarily with matter of fact, rather than of law.

This definition of the police power will permit the acceptance of every form of constructive social legislation excepting insurance and compensation laws, which are of a somewhat different character. Under such a definition class legislation is scarcely possible. By it scientific knowledge of industry, of housing, of practically all human activity, will be stimulated and be recognized as the proper ground work for drawing up legislation. Accepting such a definition, no court can refuse to admit the researches into the nature of fatigue poison as evidence in support of laws limiting the hours of employment. Briefs will be written in cases testing the constitutionality of social legislation by men of science and their investigators, rather than by lawyers alone.

To those who look askance upon any such departure in the law, it is well to recall to their minds the development of equity and the function it had to perform in English law. In a larger sense equity, before it crystallized, and social legislation are closely related. One intervened to soften the rigor of the existing law and sought to bring into harmony conscience and legal procedure; the other seeks to better society where conscience is absent and legal procedure is powerless. Both are instruments of progress disturbing the established order as all progress must, but making for the betterment of society and the conservation of human rights.

(FROM: *Case and Comment*, February, 1916, pp. 747-749.)

TEN

Social Change and the Family

IF WE ARE to understand the rather bewildering situation in family life today, we shall have to go behind the social and economic situation and attempt to reveal what is happening to men and women. It is not enough to repeat the catalogue of economic and industrial changes if we do not go further and ask what they imply for the conduct of men and women generally, and more especially in the association we call marriage.

From many discussions of the home and the family, one might gather the impression that there were grave difficulties in altering our traditional domestic economy over to the new. It is frequently suggested that living in a multiple-family dwelling, buying bread, cooked food, and canned goods, sending out the washing to the laundry, using gas and electric power, riding in automobiles, using rapid transit, and otherwise utilizing the manifold conveniences and comforts of urban life were so baffling that the home and the family could not cope with them.

Again, it is often asserted that technical changes in industry and business, the growing size of establishments, the use of power machinery, the operation of chain stores, and other aspects of the contemporary industrial development have revolutionized social life; but just how those changes react upon the family is less clearly indicated.

MATERIAL CHANGES EASILY ACCEPTED

If one reflects upon the situation and reviews his own recent experience, it is readily seen that no great difficulty is encountered in adopting modern ways of living with their conveniences and inconveniences, their gadgets and their refinements. Indeed, it is so easily accomplished that a family or an individual from the backwoods may come to the big city and be thoroughly urbanized in a few months' time, so far as acceptance of modern urban living is involved.

What we are prone to forget or ignore is that the material culture—as the anthropologists term this array of tools and equipment, techniques and skills—is readily changed, but the nonmaterial culture, of custom, tradition, codes of behavior, ethics and morals, and the *mores* or folkways of behavior, is less plastic. Long after the material culture has changed, the patterns of conduct which governed man's behavior in that former material culture will still be observed, producing confusion and dismay and often misery and distress as he struggles to reconcile the old with the new. An illustration of the cultural lag can be found in the industrial situation. The introduction and widespread adoption of machinery and modern technology in factories displaced the older handicraft; yet the customs of the older culture persisted in the law of master and servant and in a variety of traditions and ancient standards of conduct which we see today in many problems of industrial relations.

If we are to gain some insight into family life and the marriage situation today, we must address ourselves to these less apparent aspects of the situation and, if possible, discover how far the traditional folkways and patterns of conduct for men and women, for parents and children, are being frustrated and distorted by these changes in the material culture we are witnessing. In other words we must attempt to reveal the impact of the changing economic life upon personality and mating.

EARNING A LIVING

Perhaps the most direct evidence of the effect of the changing social-economic situation upon the individual is to be seen in earning a living. At the outset it is well to remind ourselves that today it is largely a question of *earning* a living, while a few generations ago it was a question of *making* a living. Then, the individual man and woman was for the most part engaged in agriculture or handicrafts in which strength, skill, patience, and endurance bulked large. Money, as income and as expenditure, played a relatively small role, as the following extract from the diary of a New England farmer clearly shows:

"My farm gave me and my whole family a good living on the produce of it and left me, one year with another, one hundred and fifty silver dollars, for I never spent more than ten dollars a year, which was for salt, nails and the like. Nothing to eat, drink or wear was bought, as my farm produced it all."

The family was the industrial and economic unit, and to make a living a man had before him the example of his father and his neighbors, with a body of lore and custom to guide him in growing food and raw materials and fabricating them into needed articles. The young woman also had her guides and teachers in her mother and other older women, who taught her the arts and crafts needed in her activities as a housewife or a spinster.

Today the situation has changed completely, and even in the rural sections, few farmers are engaged in *making* a living; for the most part they are occupied in raising cash crops to sell in order to *earn* a living. Moreover, where formerly only the most enterprising and courageous (and perhaps also the black sheep) went out to seek new occupations and livings, today, with the increasing mechanization of agriculture and the growth of industry, almost everyone is being forced out to seek a job and to face new and unfamiliar conditions. Thus we see how, for the majority of persons, no longer are there safe and comfortable refuges of traditional occupations and ways of life; all are faced with uncertainty, often anxiety, and are called upon to exert themselves in strange surroundings with few guideposts and traditions. How much this has to do with the current mood of anxiety and restless uneasiness, we can only speculate.

Money income is the focus of endeavor and the only means to a livelihood, in earning which not only men but increasingly women, unmarried and married, are engaged. The conditions affecting gainful occupations are therefore of prime significance for the family life and the home, since the individual man or woman is subject to their governance.

INDIVIDUAL HELPLESSNESS

The helplessness of the individual is perhaps the outstanding characteristic of these conditions. Whatever may be the individual's capacity and skill, his employment is subject to abrupt termination or limitation by business depression, which closes down not only his place of employment but also others, to a greater or less extent, thus preventing him from seeking another job in a different location or in another industry or business. When times are good, he is subject to loss of his job through technical changes which render his work obsolete or his particular factory uneconomical to operate. The person who escapes these threats may be laid off or discharged because he is too old—at forty.

These large and intangible factors creating the worker's helplessness are reinforced by more direct limitations upon his activities. The control of wages, hours, and output by trade unions and other forms of collective bargaining has deprived the individual of any but an indirect participation in determining his earnings, whatever may be his capacity or skill.

Again, the growth of large-scale industrial processes, demanding ever larger capital investment; the rise of chain stores and other forms of productive or distributive activities, requiring incorporation, strong resources, and connections increasingly beyond the reach of the individual—all have conspired to close the former avenues to personal enterprise and initiative. Earning a living is being restricted to wage earning and salary earning under conditions but little amenable to influence or modification by the ordinary worker.

Within the larger corporations, promotion is fairly slow and restricted, and the routine demands a conformity that gives little room for individual activities except for a few at the top. In the professions—law, medicine, and engineering—the overcrowding is notorious; and for one or two brilliant successes there are thousands who barely earn a living in the practice of their professions, while many, after undergoing the prolonged training required, enter upon other occupations as the only way to earn a living.

With the growth of child-labor laws and compulsory school attendance, the age for beginning to earn an income has been progressively postponed. In this present [1932] period of acute unemployment, the school authorities are urging pupils to continue their schooling and to defer seeking a job.

The foregoing description of the economic situation is intended to show the direction of social change. In some sections of the country the old conditions still prevail, and many small shops and factories are still in operation; but it is clear that the drift is away from those former conditions, and impending changes are already at work upon the attitudes and beliefs of men and women. Lest the reader be led into despondency over this seemingly gloomy picture, he should be reminded that the introduction of the factory system and the elimination of handicraft, a century or so ago, brought as great if not greater changes of a similar character to the artisan and craftsman. The industrial revolution is still in process.

While the individual has been rendered ever more helpless in this matter of earning a living, he has also been progressively relieved of the frequent claims upon him for immediate or future contingencies. Through widows' pensions, old-age pensions and retirement allowances, accident compensation and often sickness allowances, industrial or governmentally supplied medical care and the succor of family welfare societies, a large portion of the former responsibilities and anxieties has been lifted from the shoulders of the wage earner. These provisions reflect fairly accurately the helplessness and inability of the individual today to make provision for such contingencies, and the disappearance of the older practice of mutual aid by family and neighborhood assistance.

TRANSFER OF HOME FUNCTIONS

When we turn to the question of what is this living for which an income must be earned, we again see a large shift in process. The functions of the home upon which the family life was focused are being transferred to other agencies and organizations. Food, as we know, is to be found increasingly in restaurants and cafeterias, and that which is consumed in the home is prepared by canning factories, bakeries, ice cream factories, and so on.

The care of the sick and the mentally disordered has become institutionalized in hospitals, sanatoria, and clinics, aided by visiting nurses and related personnel who render the care formerly given by members of the family, including care of the aged.

Childbirth is increasingly taking place in hospitals, and the care and nurture of the child is likewise moving outside of the home to clinic, nursery school, kindergarten, school, summer camp, playground, and youth organization. The young adult who formerly lived at home is now living in dormitories and bachelor hotels, leaving the family group as soon as wage earning begins, instead of waiting until marriage. With the prolongation of schooling, however, the economic dependence of the child is continuing into

SOCIAL CHANGE AND THE FAMILY 107

the years when the maintenance of the child is probably most costly.

The making of clothes for men and now for women is being industrialized, as is their cleaning and laundering, which marks another transfer of home functions.

For recreation and leisure-time activities, the home has already yielded to the theater for plays and moving pictures, to clubs and associations and commercialized amusements of all kinds. On the other hand, the radio is bringing entertainment into the home, with the possibility of television as a further addition to home life.

The provision against the proverbial rainy day, as already discussed, is being cared for by social and governmental schemes of annuities, pensions, allowances, and tax-supported services.

In the religious sphere, the home and the family are becoming an increasing object of concern on the part of the church leaders, while the old-time intimate religious life of the family appears to be fading out or losing much of its former importance and significance.

These transfers and losses of home functions are being met by changes in housing. We are rapidly becoming residents of congregate dwellings, or apartment houses as we call them, where we live as tenants, paying rent. The home as a secure haven and as a symbol of solid achievement and status, is passing, so that we may in truth refer to the homeless millions, who occupy a house or an apartment only so long as the rent is forthcoming. This homelessness is reflected in the frequent moving from one apartment to another, since our complete lack of responsibility or concern, save for the rent, prevents the formation of ties to the particular dwelling we inhabit. In this connection it should be remembered that by paying rent we are provided with all the services which members of the family once performed, such as maintaining the heating and hot water, removal of garbage and trash, cleaning the premises, repairing equipment, and the like, not forgetting the use of gas for cooking and electric power for lighting, and the innumerable household chores they have wiped out.

Family life, which has long been a by-product of housekeeping, is now being freed from some of the incessant chores and burdens. This is creating new problems of developing a design for family living that will bring fulfillment of what men and women so strongly desire in intimacy and shared living.

FORMER GOALS ARE PASSING

Thus stripped of its functions and responsibilities, the home no longer is a major focus of human endeavor and interest, but is becoming rather a place at which various services are rendered, for which the payment of a money income is necessary. Home ownership is ceasing to be the goal of striving it once formed for the family; houses are purchased or built for financial reasons, and mortgages are not reduced except when required.

Other goals are being relinquished in this shift of home functions. To own property, especially land and a house, was once the chief aim of a family and the mark of its solid worth in the community. Various furnishings also occupied a special position in the family aspirations and were objects to be sought through thrifty saving. But installment purchasing has changed that, and as the automobile and the radio have superseded the piano and other prized items of furniture, the need for waiting and saving has passed. The car and the radio are not goals, they are necessities and are purchased as such, to be paid for "on time."

Status in the community has long been the goal of endeavor, but today has a limited appeal. The restrictions upon small enterprise and industry have closed the door to the usual route to respectable competence and a dignified position in the community, and the frequency of moving about in large cities has rendered the neighborhood of little account except to the children. The prestige of the competent housekeeper and mother of a family has diminished with the simpler function of the household and the decrease in number of children.

Children have been both a goal and the focus of family endeavor; but with the declining birth rate they are playing a somewhat altered role in the family. Today economic insecurity and conditions of urban life unfavorable to child care are both to be considered before childbearing is undertaken. When and if a couple has children, the number is less frequently four or five, as formerly, and more often one or two. The multiplication of child-caring techniques, each calling for additional expenditures of energy and money, has enhanced the cost of child-rearing for the conscientious parents who are anxious to provide the best available care and treatment for their children.

THE CHANGING WAY OF LIFE

While we rapidly note the passing of these different goals and enumerate the loss of home and family functions, we cannot too much emphasize that the disappearance of these various activities and strivings marks the passing of a *way of life*. To marry, have children, acquire property, gain a position of respect and dignity in the community, share in the common body of beliefs and affirmations about the universe and man's place therein—these made up a way of life to which the teachings of family, school, and church and the sanction of government and religion were all directed. Young people grew up in a society where the patterns appropriate to this way of life were ready-made, and, while they often criticized their stodgy parents and revolted against their demands, middle age found them more or less settled into the ruts of conformity, since there were no socially sanctioned alternatives.

The traditions of this older way of life remain, but the social-economic situation to which they were addressed has altered. Young men and women face either frustration in their efforts to conform to the older patterns, or confusion and anxiety as they explore for new patterns of conduct. These frustrations and anxieties are the dominant aspect of home and family life today.

The young man who would fulfill the older conception of a competent male, ambitious, enterprising, prepared to support a wife and family, faces a most perplexing situation. What kind of a job shall he seek, what career shall be undertake, what scale of income shall he adopt as his goal? The young men of today, coming out of high school or college, are beset with such questions, since they must have some program or aim by which to guide their efforts and to measure their achievements. No less is the young woman bewildered and adrift or acutely miserable under the authority of tradition and the impulsion of present-day movements.

There are a few fundamental patterns and needs which determine in large measure the conduct of the individual and his mating. These touch his security, his reassurance, and his sex functioning; and if we are to understand how social and economic changes are affecting men and women, we must seek some illumination on these fundamentals and their fate today.

THE PERSONAL GOAL

Security for an individual is relative—not absolute; it is defined by the reach of the individual's aspirations and ideals. As he pictures himself, as a man, as a worker, as a husband, as a father, in the various other roles which as a male he must play immediately or in the future, he creates an ideal self—the kind of man he would like to be. This is compounded of all the images and experiences he has had of real and imaginary men, in books and plays, and it becomes the secret goal and ambition of his life. To the extent that this ideal self is congruous with and sanctioned by the social-economic life around him and is within the reach of his real abilities and talents, it may be thoroughly realistic and desirable, giving to the man who cherishes it an admirable purpose and stability. Until he does achieve those purposes and fulfill those ambitions, he must remain anxious, apprehensive of check or defeat—in a word, insecure.

This insecurity, however, is of the man's own making, for it represents what tasks he has measured off for himself against the world. To his aid he may summon mighty forces of religion to give him a feeling of relatedness to the visible and the invisible universe and a belief in his own importance to whatever power lies behind the universe. He may invoke the strength of his family position and status to reinforce his own immature prowess and win for him the opportunities to show his ability. He may call upon his age and sex mates for assurance of his fitness and comparative capacities. Within himself he may find a large resource of quiet confidence in his readiness to meet life and its demands, if he has been fortunate enough to grow up in an atmosphere favorable to such inner peace. Beyond these ministrations to his security he may have access to affectionate intimacy in the love of his parents and later of his own mate and children, which will give him the most potent of all reassurance to meet the world.

But if one builds up for himself an ideal that is beyond his actual abilities, that is torn with internal conflicts or is irreconcilable with the actual social, economic, and political life in which he must live, then his aspirations and ambitions will betray him into endless anxiety, leading him into vain endeavors for a security he can never achieve. The resources of religion, of family status, and of contemporary regard will avail little in this struggle, for he bears within himself the real source of his insecurity, for which no external reassurance will avail.

THE YOUNG MAN'S OUTLOOK ON LIFE

This is in large measure the situation of the young man today, for the discrepancy between the patterns offered him by a tradition (an older way of life) and the changing social-economic conditions, gives rise to acute anxiety and perplexity. There is no security either in himself or in the social life around him, and the sources of reassurance have been depleted if not eliminated through the very process of change, undermining religious beliefs, family status and position, and the power of contemporary associations. This anxiety and dismay have infected the older men and women too, so that their affection is troubled and they can give little intimacy to their children.

What, asks the young man, can I do? What should I do? What is worth striving for, amid all this confusion and turmoil? What picture of myself can I construct as an ideal to be achieved with all the abilities and energies I can command? To these questions the young man receives dubious answers, since the old patterns are not applicable to the new organizations, the new operations, and the new set of economic, pecuniary arrangements now emerging from our obsolescent institutions. As yet, the new patterns which will guide the young man of tomorrow have not been created. In endless experiments and many futile efforts this generation is seeking them, but it has not clarified or stabilized them nor found the sanctions needed for authoritative use.

According to the once popular view, a man's love was "a thing apart" from his work and position, and his marriage and family life were quite removed from his occupation. But this view will scarcely survive against the contrary evidence today. The man looks to his wife for recognition of the man he hopes to be, seeking from her the reassurance he needs to achieve his ambitions. He must have aspirations and ideals to lay before her as an earnest of the true self he hopes to attain and as a touchstone of her faith and love for that self. If his ideals are shaky or dubious and he is filled with anxiety, he has little to offer or to gain in his mating. Or if his ambitions are high but incompatible with the new conditions of life, then he is threatened with heightened anxiety from without and from his wife's too trusting faith in him. If he has overrated his prowess before marriage, he faces his wife's reproaches or her silent disappointment, even when he has fought the good fight against overwhelming odds—changed conditions making that kind of success impossible. If he has too modestly pitched his hopes, while another succeeds, often by fortuitous circumstances, he may feel inferior and lose her esteem. These mischances and dismays are not so much the failing of the man as they are unavoidable situations of a changing social life, wherein the young man can find no unequivocal patterns to guide him.

There is no need for elaborating upon this theme. Any one with insight and awareness can see on all sides the tragedy of marital discord engendered by this insecurity and the lack of a compelling way of life.

The ego ideal, or *persona*, of an individual, the picture of himself as he hopes to be, is the most important aspect of an individual, and when it is confused and weakened, his whole self and all his relations are disturbed. Especially are his marital relations disturbed, since the need for recognition of the ego ideal and for reassurance are as important as sex needs, if not more so. Indeed, sex compatibility is scarcely possible unless a man and a woman have faith in each other's personality and integrity. Moreover, the man who lacks security is scarcely able to fulfill the role of a competent husband, for which psychological potency is as essential as physiological potency.

New patterns in mating, especially for the male, are imperatively needed, since successful mating has become so much more important in marriage faced with the loss of family functions and responsibilities. Men and women require more affection and fuller sex realization to compensate for the loss of other activities and satisfactions, and to sustain them under strain and anxiety.

THE WOMAN'S PERPLEXITIES

Woman, in these changing social conditions, is not less insecure and troubled with doubts. Her traditional goals and patterns are going, and she faces the necessity not merely of finding substitutes, as does the man, but also of discovering patterns for new activities and functions never before attempted by women.

Child bearing and rearing have been devalued, robbing woman of one of the major channels for her energy and interests and compelling her to seek others. Moreover, to have a home and children today, more and more women must find jobs to supplement the man's earnings.

The conflict of competing loyalties is acute, and her sources of security are more depleted than are those of the man. Indeed, parents, education, religion, and literature have only intensified her problems by their conservative refusal to recognize these changes or help her to find some way of life compatible with her needs and new responsibilities.

It would take several volumes to outline the perplexities of the woman today, their source, and the frustrations they are imposing upon her. In the field of gainful employment into which women have been entering rapidly, various obstacles and the disillusionment about men are productive of attitudes and emotional conditions of serious import for marriage, especially marriage of the old pattern. We can but indicate here how woman is fumbling for ego ideals in which she can employ her immense energies and capacities; how she might clarify her aspirations but dare not because men are not ready to accept her vision and her hopes—not prepared to receive the new woman who will displace the creature of masculine tradition.

We have today the high tragedy not only of bewildered men and women unable to find their way through these novel situations and circumstances, but of tortured personalities yearning for reassurance and intimacy and full mating, but doomed to rend each other through lack of insight into themselves and their mates and the patterns of conduct needed for their realization.

What men and women are doing to each other, they are doing to their children, but in different ways. The child, above all, needs security, reassurance, and the warmth of affection and peace which his parents, preoccupied with their anxieties and frustrations, can scarcely give him. Nor can the father and the mother who are apprehensive over their own way of life offer tolerance and sympathy for the child's bewildering experiments.

THE FORWARD LOOK

We cannot stand still nor go back to the older ways of life, since belief in their authority and sanctions is gone. We must go forward in faith and hope, trying to gain some real insights and a more sympathetic awareness of the personality needs of one another. No one is untouched by these situations, and no one is free from the anxieties and the poignant need of reassurance and intimacy. Perhaps the largest step in the working-out of the new home and family life will be taken when men and women realize their mutual uncertainties and needs, and together face the task of working out the future.

When we seek to understand the influence of changing social and economic conditions upon the home and the family, let us remember to go behind the housing, the conveniences, and the thousand-and-one changes of material culture. Let us try to envisage the groping man and woman who, amidst these changes, are seeking something stable and effective for those enduring human needs that will some day, we hope, find a new fruition in the good society which will emerge from all this turmoil and confusion.

(FROM: *The Annals of the American Academy of Political and Social Science*, 160 [1932]: 94–102.)

ELEVEN

The Management of Tensions

THIS PAPER is an outline of a theory of personality development viewed as a product of the learning process. More specifically, it is an attempt to sketch the personality as the outcome of the individual's learning how to manage his physiological tensions, under the tutelage of parents and other adults who present him with various tensional problems, in their efforts to mold his behavior into the socially sanctioned patterns.

This theory is offered, not as an explanation or rationalization, but as a program for research, a plan for the further study of personality development. For the sake of brevity and clearness the exposition will be made rather dogmatically, and will follow the order of the child's development, showing chronologically the kind of tensional problems he faces, the several varieties of "solutions" he may work out, and the operation of the learning process in this development. It is hoped that the meaning of the terms "tension," "tensional problem," "solution," and the nature of the learning process, as understood by the writer, will be made clear in the course of the discussion. It may be desirable to state here, however, that the writer's conception of learning is not limited to the memorizing of verbal symbols or the acquisition of overt behavior patterns; learning is to be considered as the process of structural and functional modification wherein the organization of internal process and of overt behavior is achieved. Growth may be viewed as the process of changing dimensions, while development is the molding and patterning of that growth into specific structures, functions, and activities through the operation of maturation and the learning process.

An organism may be viewed as a structure engaged in the capture, storage, and release of energy. The human organism at birth is probably the least organized functionally of all the mammals, and this deficiency is exhibited not alone in its helpless condition and inability to execute movements beyond a few reflexes, but more significantly, in highly unstable physiological processes or functionings. Literally speaking, the human infant is not yet organized, in the sense of having its various structural and functional units or parts integrated into a co-ordinated structure or unvarying sequence. The relatively stabilized organism of maturity is something which the child, during its prolonged infancy, must achieve. And as we shall have occasion to point out later, this prolonged infancy, exhibited physiologically in fluctuating processes, is paralleled by a prolonged infancy exhibited psychologically in varying reactions and intermittent behavior. Whatever the child learns implies a dual modification of physiological factors (structure and process) and of overt behavior, for the overt activity is instrumental to the physiological conditions, and vice versa.

The infant is confronted with his first tensional problem shortly after birth, when physiological hunger appears, in the rhythmic contractions of the stomach accompanying the fall of blood sugar. These contraction tensions are usually relieved by the maternal ministrations at recurrent intervals, but the child must learn to sustain these tensions or to diffuse them (by crying, fretting, or other overt activity) until the feeding period arrives. This problem demands a physiological adjustment, with a regularization of nutritional process, uniform utilization of blood sugar over the period between feedings, and the concomitant functional adjustments, as well as the learning of the overt activity described. To a considerable extent the child must also learn the unvarying sequence of processes involved in digestion, at least to the extent of developing a straightforward sequence of metabolic processes, a task not so automatic as many assume, as any mother will testify, since only the sucking and swallowing reflexes are prepared.

The frequency of regurgitation, of intestinal disturbances, and malfunctioning of the sphincters and valves of the digestic tract are evidences of the unorganized situation in the young infant. And it is clear that he learns to handle his food by repeated trials in which he frequently develops various idiosyncrasies of digestion. The achievement of competent digestive functions is a matter of

THE MANAGEMENT OF TENSIONS

organizing the several structures and their processes into a coordinated sequence of operations.

Indeed, the regularization of the nutritional processes and the management of hunger tensions is a major problem for the infant and young child. The number and variety of "feeding problems," both physiological and psychological, exhibited by young children is ample evidence for this statement and for the importance assigned it in the development of personality.

The hunger tensions and their management are usually made more acute for the child at the time of weaning and of the introduction to solid food. For then the infant is faced with the necessity of learning to use novel stimuli to relieve his hunger tensions. If he is wisely handled at these times, he may achieve a wholesome solution, but the clinical records reveal an astonishing number of children who have made the transition with difficulty. This problem is more or less a prototype of subsequent tensional problems, in that the child, who has learned to use a certain stimulus to relieve his tensions, is now required to relinquish that stimulus and to learn to use other stimuli. This substitution of a novel stimulus for the customary (or biological) stimulus is, of course, one of the essential features of learning, and it describes the physiological learning as well as the psychological. For in substituting a new situation, stimulus, or event, the child must learn how to establish a new sequence, or, to put it in another way, must make his functional or behavior response a consequent to a new antecedent. Moreover, the new stimulus may be not only different in kind, such as one foodstuff for another, but also different in order of time, i.e., the new stimulus may be the antecedent of the original stimulus, and the learning will then be in the nature of getting ready for the response to the more remote or deferred stimulus. The whole process of development is conditional upon the capacity to make these substitutions, or, as we have said, to learn to make a given functional or behavior response to a new structure or event, either within the organism or in the environment.

This process of substituting a new for an accustomed stimulus is difficult largely because the period of learning involves a prolongation of the tensions, the release of which is the focus of the child's activity. In starting a child on solid food, for example, he is offered substances which he has no learned method of handling;

indeed, he scarcely has learned to swallow non-liquid food, and so is inclined to reject it. While he is tentatively tasting and trying to swallow the solid food, the unrelieved hunger tensions increase his irritability toward the strange food and also his efforts to obtain the customary liquids. He must sustain these tensions until he has learned to swallow the solid food and discovered its use as a stimulus to relieve his hunger tensions. This learning can be greatly facilitated by wise handling which assists the child in meeting this trying situation, by giving him such soothing and reassurance as will enable him to endure these prolonged tensions.

We cannot here describe the variety of "solutions" the child may offer to these problems of hunger tension, or the manner in which the child's other learning is affected by his hunger tensions; it is enough here to note their occurrence during the early life of the child and their importance in his later development.

The elimination of waste through the urine and faeces occurs as a reflex in the young infant, when the accumulating pressure tensions release the bladder sphincter or the anal sphincter. Sooner or later the parents attempt to teach the child continence and so present him with a new set of tensional problems: he must learn to sustain these accumulating tensions until the appropriate time and place for their release is presented. This learning involves a gradual raising of the threshold of the sphincters so that they will hold against the increased pressures and, more difficult, also learning to use these intravesicular pressures as a stimulus to the overt activity of seeking the appointed place for their release. The child must also learn to regularize his eliminations to a large extent.

We cannot pause to detail the variety of "solutions," the frequent delays in learning, and so on, associated with the problem of managing these pressure tensions. We should take note, however, that again we have a prototype of later problems in that the child is called upon to learn to use somatic events and their accompanying tensions as cues to specific behavior. Moreover, he must learn not only to respond to these cues when they occur, but to prepare for their recurrence and so organize his activities to make provision for the future.

In hunger and pressure tensions we have situations in which the child must learn to respond to present situations by preparing for their consequences, which means again that he learns to manage his recurrent organic tensions by definitely working out the se-

THE MANAGEMENT OF TENSIONS 119

quence of his functions and his behavior to make provision for their later adjustment.

As we shall see later, the child is increasingly faced with this problem of learning to respond to present situations in terms of their consequences, which means that his behavior must become increasingly instrumental, or, in other words, he must learn to sustain tensions while he is achieving the duly sanctioned opportunities and means for their release.

In early infancy, if the processes of nutrition and elimination are not troublesome and no pathological process disturbs normal functioning, the infant will, when slightly fatigued, go to sleep, thereby achieving the release of accumulated muscular tension and the restoration of the depleted physiological processes. As the child grows older, however, this almost automatic slumber may, and usually does, disappear, largely because the child cannot readily get rid of the tensions accumulated during waking hours. The child then may have to learn how to release his muscular tensions for sleeping by developing a method of relaxing when put to bed. Not all children do learn this release, especially those who are allowed to become too fatigued. Even when they do sleep, they fail to achieve a wholesome relaxation. We must, therefore, include sleeping in our inventory of tensional problems facing the child, since the less desirable "solutions" will largely influence the child's general condition.

One process in the child which is functionally complete and efficient at birth is the organic reaction or so-called "emotional response." Under stimulation, such as shock and the blocking of activity, the sympathetic division of the vegetative nervous system is stimulated into action, thus initiating a series of physiological changes: a quick visceral spasm, followed by a progressive relaxation of visceral tone, accelerated pulse and respiration, alteration in circulation from visceral to peripheral, and release of glycogen from the liver into the circulation. All of these changes are in the nature of preparations for the exertion of flight or fight, and they operate to raise the tonicity of striped muscle and to make available the energy resources of the organism. This condition of "panic," however, is inhibitive of any discriminative or adjustive reaction to a situation, and so is rarely useful in social behavior where learned patterns of response must be employed.

The liability to this "panic" and to the release of the suddenly available energy in activities such as retreat from contacts with other persons, violent attacks upon persons or things, and so on, gives rise to tensional problems which we may group under the term "emotional reactions." The essential features of this problem, considered from the viewpoint of the child learning to live in group life, are, first, to inhibit the progressive development of the sympathetic reaction beyond the initial visceral spasm, so that he may escape that cumulative "panic" and its expression in non-sanctioned behavior; second, to learn some form of motor activity more or less adequate to such emotional-producing situations, so that he can deal with those situations whenever they recur. Whatever increased tonicity may be evoked by such situations will then be channeled into some form of overt activity specifically addressed to the requirements of that situation.

This problem of emotional management is exceedingly difficult because the sympathetic reaction is both primitive and powerful and so resists modification. Moreover, the child does not ordinarily learn either to inhibit his sympathetic reaction (or panic) or to develop an adequate motor pattern, such as a technique addressed to the situation, except with the aid and collaboration of others. For if, concurrently with the emotional stimuli, some soothing or reassuring stimuli, either auditory or tactual or both, are received, the progressive development of the sympathetic reaction may be checked and, with further practice, inhibited or at least restricted to the initial visceral spasm or "start." Then if the child is helped to acquire a motor pattern for dealing with such situations, he can face their occurrence with some show of adequacy. Such motor patterns, in early infancy, may be of the simplest, such as learning to shout when exposed to a shock, provided they offer to the child some overt reaction to the situation and thereby give him both an outlet for any sudden rise in tensions and an alternative to the "panic." Of course, the general physiological condition of the child will play a large part in such learning, since many children find it exceedingly difficult to sustain their tensions long enough to permit the acquisition of motor patterns into which those tensions can be diffused.

The importance of this problem of emotional management arises from the fact that failure to inhibit the "panic" reaction may operate to compromise the child's future learning in situations of the same or similar character as the panic-producing situation. For

THE MANAGEMENT OF TENSIONS

after a child has once been thrown into panic, a recurrence of the original situation (or portion thereof) will revive the panic and to that extent render learning of motor techniques impossible. So again the intervention of other persons appears necessary to enable a child to escape from his emotional reactions. The threshold to emotional stimuli can be raised by practice, as we see in the various occupations and professions where individuals are taught to handle emotion-producing situations with a specific technique, such as soldiers, firemen, butchers, undertakers, surgeons, nurses, and so on. What we call the secularization of life (or progress) is just this development of techniques for meeting situations which previously evoked reactions of an emotional type.

The overt expression of an emotional condition in the patterns termed fear, rage, anger, etc., appears to be the product of learning wherein the organism establishes those patterns as its response to specific varieties of situation. In support of this view we may refer to the similarity of physiological disturbances in each of these emotional reactions and to the displacement of emotional reactions by learned techniques or other patterned responses for diffusing the physiological disturbance.

Another variety of tensional problems facing the child arises from the physiological instability of the human infant which is exhibited in recurrent conditions of general bodily hyper-tonicity or hypo-tonicity. It seems probable that these conditions and their alternations are generated by the fluctuations in the balance between the sympathetic and para-sympathetic (vagus) divisions of the vegetative nervous system; as one or the other is dominant, it will set the tone (mood) of the whole organism and to that extent render it tensionally disturbed.

What takes place apparently may be described in this way: The infant undergoes these fluctuations which leave him tensionally disturbed, but he is restored to more or less of an equilibrium by the tactual stimulation received from the mother. In this respect the human infant is like the young of all land mammals in requiring cuddling and mothering (cf. the licking of cubs). This tactual stimulation is obtained from close contact with the mother's person, especially during breast-feeding, when the infant receives both nutritional and tactual stimulation. It should be noted that the mother usually accompanies these tactual ministrations with soothing auditory stimuli, thus providing the essentials for conditioning the child to use auditory stimuli in place of tactual stimuli as sources of adjustment. Thus when the infant is weaned and more or less suddenly deprived of access to the mother's person (although her mothering may be otherwise continued), he is partially prepared to use the auditory stimuli of approval and reassuring words as substitutes for tactual stimuli. If he is successful in meeting this problem, he will learn then to use auditory stimuli as sources of adjustment and to accept them from an ever-widening number and variety of persons. Concomitantly he will develop a susceptibility to auditory stimuli of a disapproving and threatening character. In this process we see the beginning of the individual's dependence upon the verbal reactions of others to his behavior, which plays so large a part in social relationships and the personality development of later years. Gestures and facial expressions of others are likewise implicated.

If the infant is denied mothering and breast-feeding, or is upset nutritionally so that the equilibrium between the two divisions of the vegetative nervous system is unduly disturbed, he may then be unable to achieve "complacency" and so have his learning of other tensional adjustments profoundly compromised. He may also learn to use various forms of tensional diffusing, such as thumb-sucking and masturbation, or "tics," under these conditions. If he is not freed later by the parents, especially by the mother, he may fail to learn the use of verbal approval and disapproval by others and so escape this preparation for living in the group. As we shall see later, the ability to deal with other persons is essential to life in a group, and in all probability may be traced back to the manner in which the child "solves" this problem.

It may be remarked that what is termed a "mother fixation" is probably just this continued dependence upon the mother as the unique source of these auditory, if not tactual, stimuli for adjustment. It may be further noted that in adult mating there is a revival of the susceptibility to tactual stimulation, dormant or suppressed since childhood, which may thereby become one of the principal sources of tensional adjustment in both the male and female. It seems clear that this tactual susceptibility plays a large role in the achievement of satisfactory sexual relations. *Per contra*, tactual idiosyncrasies are frequent among those with personality difficulties, which suggests the possibility that they are initiated by the failure to make this substitution in early childhood.

THE MANAGEMENT OF TENSIONS

To a greater or less extent, then, each child will have to learn to use auditory and visual substitutes for the tactual intimacies of infancy, and thereby will be directed to the world of things and people around him, wherein his increasing strength and mobility favor an ever-widening exploration. Thus he gradually learns to use these new opportunities for achieving adjustment and so begins the process of his socialization.

Before we discuss this socialization, however, we should consider in more detail what the terms "sustain," "diffuse," and "release" tensions mean as used in this context. The child who is learning to endure progressively longer intervals between feedings is learning to sustain hunger tensions, just as is the child who, instead of urinating in his diaper, calls for assistance and retains the urine by sustaining the increasing pressure tensions in his bladder. Not infrequently, he will attempt to diffuse his tensions by crying, kicking, or other overt activity. At present the neurological pattern is obscure, but it is clear that the tensions of smooth muscle can be, and are, diffused to striped muscle, while at the same time the sensorium is apparently rendered more acute (i.e., has a lowered threshold to possible tension releases). This is evident in maze experiments with animals, where hunger is used to render the animal tonic, alert, and actively responsive to stimuli.

Sometimes the diffusing of tensions or achievement of general tensional adjustment is accomplished by setting up a countertension, as is seen in infantile masturbation, or by using a semieffective substitute for tension release, as in thumb-sucking. If the method of diffusing tensions is purely auxiliary, as in the child's hopping up and down to help sustain and diffuse bladder or rectal pressure until his clothes can be removed for elimination, such aids are wholesome expedients. But if they become established as surrogates for the more difficult tensional adjusters, thus relieving the child from effort, we may have a short-circuiting of activity which bodes ill for the personality, for the wholesome development of personality lies in the direction of achievement by the individual of receding or remote goals. ("A man's reach should exceed his grasp, or what's a heaven for?"—*Browning*.)

We may, then, say with some confidence that the period of childhood and youth should be occupied with active achievement of ever more remote tensional releases, since the period of adult life demands the capacity to work for deferred goals if the individual is to meet the requirements of earning a living, mating, and family life. In other words, the period of growth is the period for learning tensional management, or the ability to sustain, diffuse, and, when necessary, to defer the release of tensions according to the exigencies of social life and the tasks of maturity. Not a little of this tuition is received in play or games where the youth learns sustained exertion and increased capacity for deferred consummations. Indeed, pleasure appears to be just this heightening and prolongation of tensions (to a critical point), so that the release is enhanced through the postponement or summation. The quality or intensity of a consummation appears to be a direct function of the preparatory activities essential to its achievement. But, as in all other features of personality development, the individual may become engrossed in the tensional management and so renounce the consummation or release.

Since the naïve response of the infant is to release his tensions at the first opportunity, the ability to sustain tensions and to diffuse them into overt activity must be learned. Moreover, this learning requires the active participation of another person, usually an adult, who can interpose between the child and the immediately available tensional releases, or otherwise persuade him to defer such tensional adjustments. The process of release of tensions, however, is itself subject to modification by learning, for not only does the child, in releasing tensions according to adult requirements, become conditioned to very specific stimuli and situations, but he also learns to vary the degree of tension release upon such occasions. Thus he learns to hold his pressure tensions (bladder and rectal) and to release them only when a particular situation is present (specific vessel, retired place, and so on); further, the degree of evacuation and of tension release he achieves will also be learned as a specific mode of response to such situations.

Again, in eating the child will learn to use certain foods and no others as a means of relieving his hunger tensions, and so will build up food idiosyncrasies. Also he will learn to eat at certain intervals and to consume a greater or less quantity of food, and so build up a highly individualized appetite.

With sleep, emotional reactions, and the use of tactual and auditory stimuli, we may observe the same process of individuation of tensional adjustment, so that these physiological processes are all modified and readjusted to a definite regime of living, as set by the tensional releases established for the child by his learning experiences. In all probability, the endocrines or ductless glands dominate the physiological processes involved in the rise of tensions, but they also are modified by the learning process.

It must be clear that the manner in which a child responds to these incessant attentions from adults, submits to the frustration of immediate consummation or tension release, "sublimates" or "diffuses" his accumulated tensions into overt motor activities, and adapts himself to the specialized regimen of life which is his family portion is a total organic modification making demands upon all of his resources. The strain and stress of this tuitional program are both continuous and severe, and any constitutional or physiological deficiency will soon become apparent. Unless the child can muster sufficient physiological energy to meet these demands he must compromise in some way in order to survive. It is this process of individual adaptation to the demands of the family which gives rise to the idiosyncrasies of the personality as revealed in the child's patterns of tensional management. And it must be remembered that these "solutions" are all begun in early childhood, when these problems are first encountered.

It is customary to remark upon the formative influence of the child's early years, but the precise manner in which this influence is exerted has not been made clear. There is no doubt that the early motor patterns disappear, as in the use of a bottle, or creeping and the like, so that this remark cannot imply a persistence of the pattern or activity itself. In the writer's view, the essential process may be described as follows: since the young child reacts to the world of things and people as obstacles to, or sources of, tensional adjustment, each such reaction or response will bring a tensional change which thereby becomes established as the recurrent response to all subsequent appearances of that situation or stimulus. Thus every experience will leave the child in a specific tensional condition. Consequently, the child necessarily will approach all new situations with the tensional condition arising from immediately prior experiences in other situations or from the already-experienced stimuli present in that novel situation to which he has learned to respond with a given tensional condition. It follows, then, that he will learn from a novel situation in accordance with his then tensional condition, which means that he will respond selectively to that novel situation, ignoring therein whatever is incongruous with the tensional condition he brings to it. So experiences are cumulative, and each tensional change learned by the child operates to condition his subsequent learning, thus giving the personality development that appearance of inevitable direction and trend which is so difficult to interrupt or divert.

Thus it is that the early tensional solutions of the child continue to dominate his approach to all subsequent situations unless some definite reorientation is given him through shock or the intervention of others. Our previous comments upon the significance of the child's early reactions to the several kinds of tensional problems may, therefore, be understood in the light of this selective characteristic of the learning process. Moreover, it seems clear that any temporary or prolonged failure to maintain these tensional "solutions," as previously learned, will largely influence the child's ability to continue his learning at that original tensional level. So an illness may initiate an entirely new trend in personality, while the escape from some physiological handicap may bring a new energy, and with it the beginning of a new trend of learning.

It seems necessary to enter upon these points in some detail before discussing the management of the sex tensions, since these other tensional "solutions" will so largely condition the adolescent's approach to the sex problem. This is not intended to imply that sex stimuli do not occur or are not used before puberty, but rather to assert that, until puberty, the problem of specific sex tensions as such does not ordinarily arise. Before puberty the child may employ various forms of stimuli upon his or her genitalia as modes of tensional diffusion and may establish these patterns as dominant forms of activity which serve as substitutes for, or as releases from, more difficult situations. But in these pre-pubertal experiences it does not appear that the child is under the same kind of tensions as occur with the beginning of adolescence. What is called infant sexuality is probably the effort to obtain tactual stimulation for adjustment of the hyper- or hypo-tonicity, as discussed earlier.

When adolescence does arrive we have not merely the appearance of a new kind of tensional problem, but also the beginning of a new period of growth with an accompanying loss of physiological stability. Thus the adolescent is faced with new demands just as his painfully acquired resources of established physiological rhythms are being disorganized preparatory to the attainment of adult stature and functions. So adolescence is indeed a period of storm and stress, wherein the previously developed personality is to be seriously tried.

The specific problem presented to the adolescent is to learn how to sustain and diffuse the accumulating sexual tensions, definitely refraining from using the otherwise available stimuli to their release, either in the person of others of like or unlike sex or in autoerotic practices. At least this is the problem formally set by Western European society, although in the Orient and in primitive communities the period of deferred consummation may be much shorter. The rationale of continence for youth has been the necessity of restricting mating to the adults who were competent to fend for themselves and their families, since otherwise there would be an increase in the number of dependents (infants) upon the group resources, with no increase in the number of contributors. It is apparent that by damming up the sex tensions in the youth he is put under the greatest possible stimulus to new activity, achievement, learning, and other forms of diffusing his tensions.

It is pertinent here to remark that the social life is primarily a patterning of behavior and of human relationship so that the individual is forced to achieve something as a preliminary or mode of approach to his tensional releases or consummations. This, as we shall see later, is brought about by the establishment of obstacles to immediate approach to tensional releases and by the exaction of concomitant or consequent obligations and efforts when such consummations are used. The social life, therefore, is a method for accumulating tensions in an individual person and then directing those tensions into some achievement as a price for the permission to release those tensions in some consummation. As we have said earlier, the major emphasis of the child's preparation for adult life is upon the learning to defer tensional releases and to deal with present situations with reference to their consequences, in the way of achieving remoter tensional adjustments and minimizing the price or penalties, natural and social, incurred by using such tensional releases.

The operation of this restriction upon sexual release is different in the male and in the female. Moreover, the female, with the additional physiological organs and functions of menstruation, gestation, lactation, experiences tensions and their adjustments which the male entirely escapes. So we should expect, and we do find, that the female learns from her life experiences very different lessons from those acquired by the male. Moreover, the female, unlike the male, must face the possibility that the sexual consummation may be not only a goal, but the beginning of the achievement of another objective, in conception, childbirth, and lactation. The male sexual tensions are apparently more exigent in their rhythmic recurrence than those of the female, which seemingly are more pervasive and physiologically more diffused. Our ignorance of sex functions, however, must make every statement we make a purely tentative guess. It is difficult, for example, to reconcile the prevalent notion of a lesser sexual interest in woman with the greater capacity for the orgasm if and when she does achieve it.

We must be content here to point out the tensional problems of sex as nearly as we can at present reveal them. In so far as there are sexual tensions which are denied release by parental oversight and teaching, the youth and maiden must learn to sustain those tensions and to diffuse them in the myriad "sublimations" and diffusings of adolescence. The problem is, in its outlines, not unlike that of hunger tensions, where the child must learn to refrain from taking the food freely exposed to his gaze. In so far as the parental tuition in sexual questions is liable to all manner of overemphasis and distortion, the lessons learned by the youth are not infrequently quite complicated and unwholesome; for, as we shall see later, when the child's naïve approach to a tensional release is thwarted or blocked by the adult, there is a possibility of establishing a negative conditioning which will be permanent and incapable of being removed in adult life by the recognized social sanctions. Moreover, if the blocking operates to turn the child into the use of some substitute, as in homosexual or autoerotic practices, or in the various forms of sexual vicariates which become established as permanent patterns for tensional release, we may see the youth turn aside from other activities and forego the achievement of a mate, with all the consequences and concomitants of this atypical adjustment. What the so-called normal, adult solution offers is the opportunity to obtain tensional release in a person of the opposite sex who will find reciprocal tension release in the mutual relationships and responses of mating. But to achieve such a normal, wholesome adjustment calls for sustained efforts and abilities and a plasticity which is not common.

In their adolescent learning the young man and young woman

acquire their basic patterns of response to the opposite sex and thereby prepare themselves, well or ill, for the adult mating. In their efforts to enforce continence upon the adolescent, the parents frequently resort to the practice of deprecating sex relationships altogether, with the result that they create a most unwholesome shrinking from the opposite sex, thereby rendering the achievement of adult mating exceedingly difficult, especially for the woman. In this problem of sex tensions the child receives his introduction to adult life, and in most cases experiences for the first time the enormous pressure to conformity of which his parental instruction has been but a foretaste. The greater frequency of failure in the management of sexual tensions is to be considered as arising from the fact that the achievement of "normal" consummations involves direct, personal relationships which, as we shall see later, are the most difficult art the child must learn.

This brings us to the process of socialization which the child must undergo as preparation for life in the group. Toward this all the problems of tensional management are directed, for the essential characteristic of group life is found in the group-sanctioned patterns for tensional management. That is to say, social life is congregate living which concentrates all the various stimuli to tensional releases, such as food and sex, within the group; but this very abundance of such stimuli has made necessary the establishment of prohibitions upon the direct approach to, and use of, these stimuli, since otherwise the members of the group would be continually interfering with each other. Thus there has developed what the anthropologists call culture or group patterns of behavior, whereby each group regulates the activities of its members and imposes upon them the observance of certain taboos and the use of prescribed practices for raising, setting aside, and transferring those taboos in order to attain to the tensional adjustments.

These taboos, which we call private property, the sanctity of the person, and so on, are not things or qualities of things and persons, but learned ways of behaving toward things and persons. The learning of these taboos occurs principally through the parental tuition of the child, and is part of his schooling in the management of tensions. As the child goes out into the social life he finds the stimuli to tensional adjustments, or the means thereto, on all sides, in the persons of other individuals and in their goods; and just as he was taught to sustain, diffuse, and release his infantile tensions by being deprived of immediate release and made to wait for the duly appointed times and the stimuli supplied by his parents, if not forced to forego their release entirely, so he is blocked, repulsed, frustrated, or punished when he attempts to approach and seize these freely exposed stimuli to tensional adjustments.

Under this parental instruction, reinforced by the reactions of others whom he approaches, he gradually learns to refrain from making unsanctioned approaches to, or from appropriating, such stimuli, and thereby learns to observe the taboos on things and persons. At the same time he learns to use whatever means are provided by the family to relieve his tensions or to diffuse them into various activities. Such observances and habits of living, as we have noted, call for the sustaining of tensions and their diffusing into overt or other activity, which means that the blocking of the naïve response dams up the tensions and so makes available the energy for other activities.

Again we see that just as the child learned first to sustain his infantile tensions and then to use certain prescribed patterns and manners for their release, so, as he grows older, he is gradually inducted into the group-sanctioned institutional practices of contract, barter, buying and selling, courtship and marriage, political activities, and so on. These practices provide the ceremonies and rituals whereby one person may approach another whose goods or services (behavior responses) he seeks as direct or indirect means to his tensional adjustments. By employing these group-sanctioned patterns and proffering the stimuli to which the other person is susceptible, one individual may prevail upon another to raise, set aside, or alter the taboo which bars his approach. It should not be overlooked that whether an individual seeks a thing or a personal response, his address must be made to another person, since the control of the taboos on things as well as persons is in the hands of individual persons. This means that life in a group is primarily a question of person-to-person activities or relationships, even when the tentional release sought is a substance or thing, such as food. Moreover, these person-to-person relationships are always affairs involving mutual stimulation or reciprocity, as in the exchange of goods and of services or the proffer of some recognized token or symbol (such as money or credit symbols) carrying a definite stimulus potency in the group.

From the problems of tensional management in infancy, where

THE MANAGEMENT OF TENSIONS 131

the main difficulty is one of physiological adaptation to the regimen imposed by the parents, the child as he grows up is increasingly exposed to new tensional problems which require him to deal with the world of things and people. He must learn to refrain from an immediate response to these tensional stimuli around him, through the same process of sustaining, diffusing, and releasing his tensions according to adult requirements. But the new problems introduce the factor of personal relationships, both as they arise in the child's activities toward others and in their activities toward him. Thus he must learn not only to achieve his tensional adjustments within the limits of the social patterns, but, more difficult still, he must learn to participate in activities where he either withholds or supplies the tensional adjustments sought by others. Frequently his ability to achieve a tensional adjustment, obtainable in the goods or services of another person, will be conditioned largely by the skill he has acquired in the art of ministering to the tensional needs of other persons. For the give-and-take of social life is largely a matter of playing upon the tensional susceptibilities of individuals in accordance with the socially sanctioned taboos and privileges.

We might interrupt here to remark that these learned patterns of behavior which focus a person's activities upon other persons are what make the group life social. To live in a group one must learn the social patterns of taboo and institutional practices or be debarred from obtaining the means to life. Institutions are to be viewed, then, as the patterning of the behavior of the group members into more or less uniform practices and observances. When so regarded we can study social life and human behavior without invoking the various conceptions of "group mind," "like-mindedness," "instinct of gregariousness," and similar ideas, since the learning process serves to reveal the genesis of these acquired patterns and to show how both the similarity of group patterns and the individual differences in tensional management are imposed upon persons.

The socialization of the individual is, then, to be viewed as a continuation of the parental and other adult instruction under which the child learns to observe the various taboos and acquires an ability to use the institutional practices as the group-sanctioned patterns for tensional management. If the social life were characterized by a few simple taboos of general applicability, this problem might be fairly readily solved. But in most social groups we find that this problem is exceedingly complicated, since the taboo observances are differentiated by a great variety of criteria and the institutional practices are, within certain limits, highly elastic and devious.

Thus each person in a group must learn the precise degree and kind of taboo he must observe in his approaches to every other person with whom he has any dealings. Specifically, this means that he must learn all those distinctions we associate with the terms "status," "class," "rank," "position," "kinship," "authority," and so on, with the behavior appropriate to the individuals so distinguished. In any activity either directly or indirectly offering approach to a tensional adjustment in the goods or the person of another, the individual must employ the mode of address and the group-sanctioned institutional practice duly established for approaching that specific person. In addition to these distinctions of taboo observance there are also distinctions in the use of institutional practices demanded by the mores of the group.

But the situation is further complicated for the young individual learning to live in the group, since he is also the focus of approach by others, seeking his goods or personal responses as instrumental to their tensional adjustments. To each of these he must learn to offer submission or repulse according to their rank, position, authority, etc., thereby enjoying in his goods and his person the differential taboo protection to which he is entitled by his position, rank, etc.

Thus the child is taught by parents and others the operation of the group culture, the rules and codes and cues to which are expressed in laws, customs, conventions, and their enforcement by interested individuals and by their surrogates duly appointed to these tasks.

Out of this tuition he develops his social behavior or the group-sanctioned patterns he uses to achieve his tensional adjustments, as found in the goods and activities of other persons which offer immediate tensional adjustments or the means thereto. With this learning he acquires a status, compounded of all these various personal relationships toward others and by them to him. He also obtains a varying degree of skill in the use of the several institutional practices, so that by the time he has reached maturity he

THE MANAGEMENT OF TENSIONS

will have worked out a highly individualized adaptation to these social requirements.

It is obvious that these lessons in socialization present difficulties and complexities of no mean order, and because of these very difficulties and perplexities each individual will achieve but a modest degree of successful adjustment in all of them. We may, however, classify some of the varieties of adjustment made to these social lessons.

If we take the problem of taboo observance, first, we may note the frequent occurrence of overconditioning against the approach of things and persons, so that the individual develops a permanent inhibition of response to things or persons or both. This overstrong conditioning is commonly established by the strong reproofs or blocking of response by parents when the child shows any sex interest in others, so that he develops an inability thereafter to approach other persons as sources of adjustment to sex tensions.

Again, we may observe the contrary cases where, through parental neglect, illness, or incapacity for such learning, the individual fails to learn the observance of the taboos on things and persons. Since he may not learn to respect private property nor the sanctity of the person, he will have no bar to appropriating what he sees as obstacles thereto. Such persons may, however, learn to practice evasions and subterfuges to escape detection and punishment.

The bulk of the population in a group will learn to observe the taboos with greater or less fidelity, at least to the extent that their experience of social life permits. Thus they manage to "carry on" with little conflict or difficulty from unsanctioned approaches to things and persons.

Just as the individual may learn the taboo observances in one of the three ways just described, so he may learn to use the institutional practices with little or no skill, with exceedingly great skill, or sufficiently to get along in the position and status for which experience has fitted him.

Using these classifications for taboo observance and for institutional practices, we may assess the social competence of any individual, at least to the extent of his overt activities. But if we are to gain a real insight into personality development we must consider what lies behind these social adaptations and examine the tensional situations involved.

The essential feature of all these learned behavior patterns is the predominant role of other individuals in the various learning situations. In childhood the parents are actively present when the child is learning his tensional management, and later on the parents' efforts are supplemented by teachers and the individuals whose property or person is approached by the child. Moreover, the child soon finds himself being approached by coevals, as well as by adults, intent upon coercing him or using him as direct or indirect means to their tensional adjustment.

All these experiences with other persons, in situations of more or less ambiguity for the unskilled and often helpless child, may give rise to acute anxieties and strains. Early in this tuitional process the child begins to show his individual reaction to such experiences: either he develops a progressive competence to meet these personal encounters, or he fails to do so, and thereafter his learning of the various varieties of tensional management is compromised by this continuing strain in his personal relations.

If we follow the sequence of events in these second cases we find that such individuals, by reason of this very difficulty in facing other persons, become increasingly focused upon the issue of their personal encounters. Their approach to other persons or their reception of others' approaches become ordeals for which they must "nerve themselves," and naturally they begin to stress in their behavior the carrying off of these encounters more than the pursuit of the objectives which lead them to other persons. That is to say, repeated experiences of stressful dealings with other persons will raise the problem of future personal relations with all other persons, because the individual, by those experiences, will develop a stressfull (heightened tension) response to other persons. And just to the extent that he has this initial difficulty in dealing with others, his ability to achieve the tensional adjustments to be obtained from others will be compromised. Moreover, the urgency of these stresses arising from personal relations will begin to compete with the organic tensions, for the adjustment of which the individual initially undertakes these personal encounters. This competition may become so effective that the pursuit of organic consummations will begin to flag, while all the energies and efforts of the individual are concentrated upon meeting the problems of dealing with others. Thus there is created a type of personality intent upon the questions of his status in every meeting with other persons, for status involves, as we have previously stated, relationships a person bears toward the persons around him, as gauged by the varying degrees of immunity he enjoys from their invasions of his person or goods and by the differential taboos he must observe in his approaches to the person or goods of others.

The learning process operates in these cases of stressful human relations in a manner similar to the animal experiments where a food or sex stimulus is guarded by an electrical shock; after the animal has had several such shocks, he will cease his efforts to obtain that food or sex stimulus. So an individual who has had a number of difficult encounters with others will become, if not wholly conditioned against further approaches, at least wary and alert to the risks of such encounters. The selective operation of these early lessons upon subsequent learning will then foster an increasing emphasis upon the question of status as it may be affected by these personal relationships.

This concern for status may appear either in an aggressive or submissive guise, depending upon a variety of factors, such as available physiological energy, character of parental tuition, and so on. When aggressively exhibited it is seen as a continual effort to assert one's status, by always exacting due observance from others. Such a person will eagerly seize the rich opportunities offered in business, politics, the military establishments, fraternal organizations, and any other organized groups of persons among whom one can attain a position of increasing prestige and power over the activities of others. The purpose or objective of such organizations may be a matter of indifference to such an individual, as seen by the successful man of affairs who attains to high position but may be totally uninterested in what he has achieved, objectively, while gaining that position. Since various symbols and tokens and regalia offer tangible means of reinforcing one's efforts in this struggle for status, the accumulation of money and titles, the use of clothes, and so on, are all a part of the total personality. Moreover, the personality which has difficulty in personal relations will turn to the acquisition of power or money, through which he can more easily manipulate others.

If a person becomes focused upon the question of his status but lacks the aggressive qualities, he will be equally intent upon finding opportunities where he can assert his status by submitting himself to coercion and invasion of his immunities by others. He thus obtains an affirmation of the status which others will accord him in various kinds of organizations where a secure position is afforded to those who will permit the agressively inclined to climb.

It must not be forgotten that where there are aggressors there are usually persons who will submit to such aggressions. Thus any form of human association with definitely established positions and ranks offers opportunities both for the aggressively and the submissively inclined. Today we see business organizations attracting these two kinds of personalities and providing opportunities for their activities which were in previous ages found in politics, military life, or religious affairs.

If the difficulty of sustaining personal relations is too severe, especially when there is no skill in the institutional practices of business and politics, a submissive individual may seek isolation from others, turning to the study, laboratory, studio, or the open-air occupations in which he may preserve his status through avoidance of personal encounters or by indirect claims upon the group. In so doing the underlying endeavor may be aggressive, as in the creative artist or scientist, or submissive, as in the celibate or hermit type, each of whom, in his own way, attempts to elicit a social response.

It should be noted that the same fundamental difficulty in facing other persons may give rise to seemingly unrelated varieties of individuals, the aggressively and the submissively inclined persons. Both the aggressive and the submissive, however, may find the occasions for their peculiar interests in the same kinds of occupations and situations. This indicates the dubious validity of the many occupational criteria now used in classifying personalities. This also suggests that what is called an "inferiority complex" in all probability is an expression of this dominant preoccupation with status and the difficulties of personal relations, for it appears both in the aggressive and the submissive forms. But what is of the greatest significance in all the individuals of this general class, however characterized by other terms and labels, is this predominant concern with the status they can create or sustain with others, even at the sacrifice of the consummations deemed most important. This sacrifice is all the more remarkable because the relations of one person to another, as prescribed in the social taboos and institutional practices, are primarily instrumental to the achievement of tensional adjustments and consummations. Yet the

THE MANAGEMENT OF TENSIONS

evidence from business, politics, domestic relations, indeed every field of human endeavor, repeatedly shows these individuals foregoing such consummations and the means thereto in favor of this dominant concern for their status.

The writer, therefore, is inclined to regard this status type as a major category of personality development arising from the individual's inability to master the initial phases of personal relations involved in the tensional problems set by his family and by the group life generally.

By contrast with this class of personalities we have the individuals who have little or no difficulty in facing these personal relations and who are, in consequence, able to go on to learn the management of their tensional problems in accordance with their capacities and their opportunities to learn. In a sense such persons are unaware of personal relations, for they are never much troubled by them. Even in childhood such persons, while exhibiting some timidity toward strangers, are never made anxious by their encounters with others. Being therefore free of this preoccupation, they may pursue their tensional adjustments as skilfully and persistently as their physiological energy and learned abilities will permit. Since they do achieve their tensional solutions fairly readily, they will employ their energies in whatever occupations and pursuits they may find congenial to their talents. In these activities they will be primarily concerned with objective goals and the means or instruments for achieving them, finding it rather easy to adapt themselves to situations and to people, as factors to be dealt with objectively in reaching their goals.

The very ease with which they can take life may prove their undoing, betraying them into a comfortable routine from which neither internal tensions nor external events will ordinarily disturb them. If, however, they are energetic and happen to come to the direction of other persons or large affairs, they may become extraordinary leaders, for their very absence of self-seeking wins the loyalty of others to the disinterested enterprises they foster. When placed in contact with the status type, however, they may be unable to understand or sympathize with such persons, finding it difficult to allow for the preoccupation with status, prestige, and the continual seeking for credit which mean so little to them. Nevertheless these objective types may be found in the same organizations and callings as the status types, since they find therein the opportunities for the various objective achievements they favor. They may also undertake the more solitary labors, at least for a time, if in that way they can bring about the objective results they seek. Occasionally one meets an individual of the objective type who has become engrossed in the achievement of status, not because of this personality trend, but for the fun of the game and the pleasure of the chase.

The status type in its genesis and its mature expression may be likened to the schizoid type described by Kretschmer and others. When such individuals become markedly disturbed by these difficulties of personal relations, they exhibit the characteristics of the clinical cases grouped under schizophrenia.

The basis for this internal "conflict" or "split personality" is to be found in the difficulties of personal relationships. In so far as these individuals have normal physiological processes they experience the usual tensional needs of mankind, but since they can achieve the "normal" release of these tensions, especially of sex, only by approaching other persons (who will supply the required stimuli of goods or personal responses), they are, by reason of their incapacity for such personal encounters, in the position of urgent need but acute anxiety over the approach to the satisfaction of that need.

If the foregoing description represents the situation more accurately, we might substitute for such conceptions of "conflict" or "split personality" the following notion of the situation: The individual has the organic need or "desire," but has never learned how to approach other persons; he has, therefore, never succeeded in establishing a sequence of preparatory activities leading to a consummation. Instead of addressing himself, then, to the persuasion of others to meet his needs, he must first and last consider his position or status in relation to others, and by so much fail to evoke from them the desired response. Thus these individuals must fall back upon the coercive power of status, as expressed in position, rank, authority, and other concomitants of status to obtain their tensional adjustments or the means thereto. It appears probable that the status type begins to seek position, rank, etc., at an early age when he first discovers that status will bring him what his personal address to others fails to achieve. If such persons cannot obtain these extrinsic aids, which are necessarily limited to a few, they must compromise upon whatever "solution" they can

THE MANAGEMENT OF TENSIONS 139

achieve. It is apparently these various compromises, with the frustrations they involve, which give rise to the mentally disordered persons who exhibit the "conflict" between organic tensions impelling them forward and the inability to use the socially sanctioned approaches they must employ in reaching the tension release. The liability of such persons to overconditioning in the learning of the taboo on approaching others for sex adjustment may be the clue to the frequency of the sexual factor in such disordered personalities.

When a person of the status type does not experience the normal organic tensions, he not only misses the energy for diffusion into overt activity, but also the susceptibility to tensional adjusters through which he is stimulated to seek releases. These losses not only deprive him of the tensional problems, but they also handicap him in his dealings with others as seekers of his goods and services. That is to say, in so far as the "normal" person, in pursuing his tensional adjustments, meets with others similarly occupied, their encounters usually lead to some form of reciprocal activity or of avoidance, in accordance with their susceptibilities, institutional skills and status, and available energies. But the person who lacks these vital interests is necessarily at a disadvantage in meeting these approaches and activities. He finds himself, therefore, either exploited as an easily obtained tensional adjuster, or ignored as lacking the qualities which make individuals attractive to others. In a person who is already troubled by the question of his status, either of these two positions or roles will create anxieties for which some resolution must be sought. Of necessity, this resolution will be outside of the group-sanctioned patterns and practices, and thus thrust upon the individual new difficulties and problems for which the group life offers no assistance.

Whenever a person employs an unsanctioned method of tensional adjustment or engages in some activity which is not socially approved, he must be constantly alert to disguise his activities or to escape detection and exposure, if not punishment. Thus he learns to anticipate attacks or interference and to shape his activities with those apprehensions ever in the foreground. From cautious subterfuge and evasion to the preparation of ever more elaborate defenses against anticipated attack is a road of easy transition leading to the so-called paranoid conditions. Delusions of persecution and of grandeur alike revolve around the questions of personal status and the individual's inability to achieve tensional adjustments in the approved social patterns.

Under the stress of these perplexities arising from frustration of tensional adjustment, from preoccupation with status, or from failure of the organic tensions which send the individual forth into the world, the individual may begin to relinquish his learned patterns of tensional management, such as continence in eliminations, table manners, etc. To the extent that these learned patterns involve the sustaining and diffusing of organic tensions, they will have to compete with the more acute problem of tensional management, and so may lose out. The sloughing off of these learned patterns of tensional management in the mentally disordered or perplexed is what we call regression.

If, as the students of the constitutions and types appearing among the mentally disordered are now suggesting, the status or schizoid type is found in the asthenic habitus, the interesting question is raised whether the long, thin individual is physiologically unable to meet the situations arising from personal relations. Such incapacity may be exhibited in an inability to maintain equilibrium, in a lack of physiological energy adequate to the demands of these personal encounters, or in a deficient capacity for learning to sustain and diffuse tensions in accordance with parental and group requirements. Whatever may be the limiting factor, it usually appears in early childhood, and, as we have noted before, by its participation in the early stages of learning becomes dominant in all subsequent learning, especially in the adolescent problems of sex tensions.

The objective type may be compared with the circular, cyclic, or syntonic type, which is prone to fluctuations of activity, and, when too pronounced, appears as the manic-depressive type. Such persons, as we have said, ordinarily have no tensional problems because their ability to deal with persons gives them an initial advantage in achieving tensional adjustments through others. But they are subject to fluctuations in the energy they bring to their activities, probably because their very freedom from prolonged tensional maladjustments had deprived them of opportunities for learning sustained effort against obstacles. If, therefore, they are checked or thwarted, they may be easily diverted into other endeavors or thrown into a condition of reduced activity until they accumulate new energy for other attempts.

We may illustrate the difference between the status type and objective type by describing their behavior as in a game: The status type learns the rules and plays for points only so far as he can do so while intent upon the question of his personal status with all the other players. His whole style of play is therefore fashioned into a series of personal encounters about his status in the eyes of the other person; his activities, therefore, are devious and frequently inscrutable, since they are guided by these much-prized factors of status, as interpreted by him alone. The lack of more objective goals and stimuli in his conduct, and frequently the apparently unnecessary sacrifice of the game for the sake of his status, render the status type always difficult to understand.

The objective type, on the other hand, learns the rules and plays the game in a thoroughly hearty pursuit of points which makes his behavior relatively easily understood. When energy flags or the tensions fail to furnish stimuli to activity, his cheerful play may cease for want of goals or consummations to be won.

Curiously enough, the objective type will cast the blame for his failures upon himself usually, while the status type will ordinarily attribute his defects and failures to the interference or blocking by others, thus maintaining his status and prestige if only in reverie and phantasy.

As the foregoing discussion indicates, the usual criteria of occupation, interests, and so on used to classify personalities are of dubious worth, since they ignore the different modes of performance in those occupations and interests. Instead of the introvert-extrovert categories, the more recent efforts to distinguish personalities by their more fundamental reactions to the same life-situations appear more promising. The writer's suggested categories of status and objective type are offered as an attempt to refine upon these efforts and to focus attention first upon the kind of interest or susceptibility (organic tensions) a person brings to life, and then upon the way he learns the social rules for achieving those interests or adjusting those tensions. It does not matter especially whether or not the foregoing descriptions of these types are adequate and consistent throughout, since they are offered as a statement of the problem to be studied, not as its solution.

The advantages of approaching the development of personality through the study of tensional management lie in the inclusiveness of the problem they present. In the physiological tensions arising in the child we have the energy necessary to learning; in the child's gradual achievement of tensional management by learning to sustain, diffuse, or release his tensions to stimuli, in accordance with the prohibitions and the sanctions of the group life, as inculcated by the parents, we have a clue to the personality development and the socialization of the child. This enables us to see the problem in terms of a process of modification in which a wide variety of factors, somatic, experiential, and cultural, participate. Moreover, in viewing the learning as a process of alteration in the tensions of the learning organisms, which cumulatively control future learning, we have a clue to the integrative aspect of experience and the selective characteristic of individual learning and behavior. If time and space permitted we might elaborate upon the theme of tensional management and show how these several tensional problems and their solutions interact upon each other; how individuals turn to religion, art, mythology, and other values for help and comfort in meeting their tensional problems; how the "solutions" which lie outside of the group sanctions create anxieties for the individual, since to utilize those atypical "solutions" he must contrive substitutes for the socially sanctioned institutional practices. In contriving such substitutes the individual foregoes the assurance and approval of his activities granted to those who conform, and this intensifies his problem. We might also dwell upon the role of language, not only as the institutional practice of the most flexible use in approaching others, but also as a mold or pattern for thinking and rehearsing activities. This would lead us to consider the need to bring one's thought as well as one's activities into conformity with the group norms, and the anxiety (unresolved tension) which the failure to achieve such reconciliation creates.

But all these fascinating topics must be postponed until another occasion since here we can merely state the problem and outline an approach to its solution. If we can make clear the participation of the culture complex in the individual personality development, and substitute for the various mystical conceptions of personality and its manifestations a process open to study and experimental investigation, we may perhaps help to further the study of personality and carry on the work of the many students to whom the writer is so obviously indebted.

(FROM: *The American Journal of Sociology* 33 [1928]: 705-36.)

TWELVE

The Concept of Inviolability in Culture

THE CONCEPT of inviolability in culture is essentially an extension of the taboo concept which is familiar to all students in this field. Perhaps it would be more correct to say that the taboo as described in anthropological literature is one form or instance of the principle or practice of inviolability which forms the basis for the larger part of the non-material culture.

Approached in the most direct and explicit fashion, we may say that each person in a cultural group is taught, with greater or less effectiveness, to respect the inviolability of persons, things, and animals, and frequently certain kinds of situations in which they may be congregated. That is to say, the education or training of the young individual is focused upon establishing in him a respect or observance of (a) the sanctity of the person of others, (b) the inviolability of private property, and (c) the general taboo on animals or places.

The manner in which this training is given, of course, varies, but in general it consists in thwarting all attempts to approach or appropriate or violate the sanctity of the person or private property or taboo situations, or in punishing such actions if surreptitiously or defiantly carried out. Since these persons and things are usually biologically adequate stimuli to action by the young individual, this thwarting or punishing serves to condition negatively such naïve responses until the young individual learns to refrain from further attempts.

About the time these lessons of observance have been learned, at least in a general way, the young individual is introduced to the institutional practices which provide a duly sanctioned pattern for dealing with persons and things protected by this inviolability.

That is to say, he learns to use contract, barter, sale, various forms of etiquette, and later courtship and marriage, as the group-sanctioned ways of approaching persons to obtain their services or their property.

If we undertake a more detailed examination of the practice of inviolability in culture, we shall readily see that the young individual who undergoes this tuition, usually at the hands of his parents and immediate family, faces a most complicated task. He must learn at once to observe in his behavior all these restrictions or prohibitions upon his approach to persons and things and at the same time learn how to behave toward others who approach him as a person or owner of property. He is at once an actor and a recipient, an aggressive subject and a defensive or acquiescent object, depending upon his role in the group and his individual personality.

If we look more closely we shall discover that for his activity toward others and their property, and for his reception of others' activity toward him and his property, there are a variety of highly differentiated patterns which he must observe, frequently under severe penalty for omission or infraction thereof. Let us canvass these distinctions in his behavior.

AGE

The first and most obvious aspect of an individual's socially patterned behavior is his age, since what is demanded of him by way of observance of the inviolability of other persons and of private property is so largely dependent upon his age. That is to say, the younger he is, the less vigorously are the prohibitions laid upon him, and, conversely, the less he enjoys the protection of any inviolability to his person or property. Also, the older a person, the more protection and privileges he may enjoy. Practically, this works out in the group life in a nicely graduated severity of imposition and of punishment for infraction or neglect of the established patterns and likewise a rather ill-defined and often incomplete extension of the usual inviolability over the immature individual. There is no time here to give examples of the age differentiation, but we can refer in passing to the different treatment of children who transgress against private property, the almost complete lack of protection of the child's person against parental invasion, except perhaps sexually, and finally the toleration of breaches of etiquette

THE CONCEPT OF INVIOLABILITY IN CULTURE   145

and of legal rules in the young child. Decidedly, then, age is a most important factor in the operation of the inviolability practices.

SEX

Next to age, the differentiated observance of group practices of inviolability according to the sex of the actor or of the person acted upon is most significant. The sanctity of the person usually has a different meaning for males and females, and even the property of males and females calls for different observances, when they are both permitted to possess property.

Under this heading of "SEX" we must pay attention to the relationship sustained by an individual to others, especially the kinship or marital relations. As we shall see when discussing institutional practices for dealing with otherwise-inviolable persons, the relationship of the individual gives rise to privileges and restrictions in the observance of the sanctity of the person and of private property.

MENTAL STATUS

The capacity for intelligent behavior, as measured by the group norms, and the degree of sanity, again as measured by group norms, are also to be noted as affecting the operation of inviolability, both as regards what is required of the individual whose intelligence or sanity or both are abnormal, and what is demanded of others who deal with such a deviated individual.

PHYSICAL CHARACTERISTICS

A variety of physical characteristics are frequently invoked as the occasion for differentiated observance of the practice of inviolability. The possession of some unusual color or feature may entitle the possessor to unusual protection or subject him to all manner of approaches since the ordinary inviolability of the person and property is withheld from such a deviate. Again, it may operate to release the possessor from observing the inviolability of other persons or property.

RELIGION

Membership in a religious group, or in a family so embraced, also modifies the operation of the practice and observance of inviolability, especially when there are various sects. An individual of one sect will be faced with one set of prohibitions and of observances which a member of another group, living perhaps in the same community, may largely ignore or neglect. The presence of a dominant or "state" religion may develop sharply drawn lines of demarcation in this regard.

POSITION OR RANK AND CASTE

It is possible to describe position, rank, and caste wholly in terms of the kind and degree of inviolability enjoyed by individuals of each such category, and of their obligation (or lack thereof) to observe such prohibitions toward others. Indeed, it is difficult to see how we can avoid or neglect this approach in studying position, rank, or caste, since they are so largely matters of privilege with respect to what an individual must observe or others must observe toward him, and differences in the use of the institutional practices, such as contract, barter, sale, marriage, and so on. A group hierarchy rests upon these differentiated patterns of behavior appropriate to each position, rank, or caste in their dealings with other persons and with things and animals covered by the property classification and with those "situations" which are generally taboo.

Under this broad heading of position, rank, or caste we must recognize all kinds of social status even when not specifically designated by a title or membership in a formal group. Thus we have citizens and non-citizens or aliens, distinguished not alone by their participation or exclusion from political actions, but also by the differentiated application of the inviolability practices which they must observe or others observe toward them and in their privilege to use the institutional practices of contract, marriage, and so forth.

The great gulf between the free man and the slave may be clearly and specifically defined in terms of the inviolability of the person, of property, and the use of institutional practices. What the jurists are fond of saying, after Sir Henry Maine, that social progress is marked by the transition from status to contract, reflects just this emergence from a fixed, unalterable position respecting inviolability or lack of it to a position where an individual may dispose of his person and property by agreement and for a consideration or reward.

OCCUPATIONAL CLASS

Both the membership in an occupational group and the possession of special skill in its arts serve to modify the operation of the practice of inviolability. A particular profession may violate the ordinary sanctity of the person of another or enjoy additional and peculiar immunities in his own person, such as a physician today who may more freely manipulate the person, also of the opposite sex, or claim exemption from military or jury duty and violate the speed laws, just as the magician, medicine man, etc., of more primitive groups has his privileges and immunities. Again, special skill or competence in an occupation, such as is found in a great hunter or a famous artist, may confer privileges and immunities in the sphere of inviolability and the institutional practices.

PROPERTY

The possessor of property, measured either in quantity or in quality, likewise has a different code of observances respecting inviolability of his own and others' person and property. The special privileges accruing to the property-owner have been the focus of social conflicts second only to the revolt of slaves in severity and fervor.

In the foregoing categories, to which additions may and will be made, we find the more obvious differentiations in the operation of the inviolability principle respecting the person and property (things or animals). Animals occupy a place between the person and property, since they are protected not only by the property concept but also by the sanctity of the person, especially when they are invested with religious and social significance as in the sacred animal cults, the prohibition against slaughter of particular wild species, etc. Over and above these specific categories of differentiation we must observe the broad modifications based upon periods or occasions when a specific cycle of inviolability followed by non-inviolability obtains, or when a particular time of the year or season governs observances, or when inviolability has a limited duration consequent upon some antecedent or anticipated event. We may illustrate the periodic variations by reference to the custom of suspending sexual taboos during certain periods of group celebration, e.g., Saturnalia, the seasonal variations by reference to open and closed seasons for hunting, fishing, and the like, and the operation of specifically limited duration in the prohibition of sex intercourse until a specified time after menstruation or parturition.

Location also enters into the inviolability practices in that specific places may operate to suspend all rules or impose restrictions over and above the usual rules. Thus the church or sacred edifice may confer unusual protection upon the person of those who repair there for sanctuary, or a particular designated place may be recognized as free from the operation of the usual group prohibitions against violation of the person or property.

With every person and almost all things and domesticated animals, if not wild animals also, covered by this principle of inviolability which each member of the group is taught to observe toward others and to maintain in his own person and property, always according to the differentiated applications just described, it is obvious that group life can be carried on only by practices which permit individuals to violate the sanctity of the person and private property in duly sanctioned patterns. Thus in every group we find, as an accompaniment of the inviolability principle, a well-defined set of institutional practices for this purpose, with specific rules which legitimize approaches to the property or person of others. Language as a conventionalized symbolism is, of course, the primary institutional pattern for approaching others to negotiate for the shifting of these inviolabilities. Along with language we should note the group patterns of gesture and ritual generally in all institutional practices.

Since each person enjoys a highly differentiated inviolability in his person and property, he may, and indeed is expected to, demand observance of that inviolability from all others according to the rights, titles, obligations, and immunities of his case, and to defend himself from unwarranted invasion. In approaching others he must likewise observe their specific condition and refrain from any unsanctioned invasion. But if he is moved to obtain another's property or services (being their behavior responses to him or whatever he designates as the focus of their behavior), he may open negotiations looking to an agreement or contract, or to a sale if not an exchange by barter.

The essential features of these negotiations are the offer and the acceptance thereof. This is not the place to review the law of contract in its various forms, but it is appropriate to point out that the acceptor waives his inviolability, as regards his person in

THE CONCEPT OF INVIOLABILITY IN CULTURE 149

agreeing to work or serve or limit his ordinary freedom of action, or usual immunity or as regards his property, in allowing the offerer to use his property or to take possession of it as new owner. It should be noted that the offer and giving of a consideration, as the legal phrase has it, is essentially a stimulus designed to evoke the response of waiving this inviolability, and the acceptor is deemed to be the best judge of what is an adequate stimulus in the absence of fraud. The other point is that in waiving his inviolability the prohibition is not set aside generally; rather, the operation of inviolability is changed so that the offerer is now privileged to violate the prohibition for his own purposes and the acceptor is ordinarily bound not only to acquiesce but to defend against all others, including himself, that privilege which he has granted. In other words, he has divested himself of his former inviolability and bestowed it, either partially or wholly, upon another in the case of property, or removed it in regard to his person so far as that other is concerned. Thus the whole law of contract revolves upon the concept of inviolability and the shifting observances thereof so far as the protection it gives and the privileges it confers. The former owner must ordinarily defend the title of the purchaser and may no longer approach or use the property transferred; the individual who lifts the prohibition upon sexual approach to his person in favor of his wife or her husband must not only refrain from such action toward another but resist any other's sexual approach.

The complexity of legal rules regarding marital relations, property, real estate, contract, torts, and so on are all to be viewed here as so many attempts to recognize these differentiated operations of the principle of inviolability and the use of institutional practices addressed to these inviolabilities. The intentional or unintentional trespass or invasion of another's immunities or privileges gives rise to legal remedies, involving compensation and redress or punishment as in the criminal law.

For each application of the inviolability principle there is a code or systematized declaration—legal, ethical, religious, moral, or what is called etiquette—accompanied by a more or less well-organized scheme of explanation or rationalization and a kind of sanction appropriate to the enforcement of the code.

A tentative generalization might be offered here, that the development of inviolability of the person and of things with highly differentiated observances has come with the decline of the generalized taboo binding upon all persons, which is another way of describing the secularization of life in which the growing material culture has fostered the practices of inviolability and diminished the general taboos.

Since the biological significance of the principle of inviolability is in the interposition of a pattern between the individual and the normal focus of his behavior (nutrition, sex, shelter, self-protection), it is obvious that the peculiar manner in which these patterns are imposed upon the individual and the fashion in which he learns to use the group-sanctioned institutional patterns will give rise to this quality or aspect we call personality.

Culture may be regarded as just this intervention of patterns between the individual and the world of other individuals and things whereby, instead of a purely native or reflex response to a situation, there is a pause and a patterning of behavior so that the pattern may often become more significant than the situation or the original biological focus; thus culture, both material and nonmaterial, as Lowie (*Culture and Ethnology*) has so cogently put it, is neither wholly psychological nor biological nor geographical but a complex such as only human behavior can comprehend in an activity.

Thus it is suggested that a careful, detailed exposition of the concept of inviolability, in its multitudinous ramifications and implications, will provide at once a basic scheme for the study of comparative culture, comparative law, and indeed all the social studies and a peculiarly significant program for investigating the development of personality as it arises in and through the impact of culture upon the individual. For what we call personality appears in the individual's manner of behaving toward others in observing the code of inviolability as it affects them and his own person.

(FROM: *The American Journal of Sociology*, 36 [1931]: 607-15.)

THIRTEEN

Social Order and Psychiatry

A STATEMENT of what psychiatry ideally might contribute to alleviate national and international difficulties, that is, to foster social order and international peace, must rest upon certain assumptions.

Psychiatry, as a therapeutic agency, has the responsibility for the diagnosis and treatment of individuals in need of psychotherapy. This responsibility is paramount and apparently will increase, but obviously psychiatry cannot hope to treat all individuals, young and adult, who threaten social order and impair group relationships. There are too many such individuals—there are too few psychiatrists, and treatment is necessarily long and, unless other conditions are favorable, not always effective.

What is of special significance is that so many of the individuals who threaten or block social order are acting with full social sanctions in politics, in business, industry, finance, professional life, in education and religion, and in marriage and the family. At present neither the individuals engaged in these activities nor the public generally are prepared to regard these as in any sense in need of psychiatric treatment, since they represent to a very large extent what is regarded as wholly normal.

While we may speak figuratively of "society as the patient," it is obvious that psychiatry cannot *treat* society; there is no mysterious entity called "society" to be treated as a sort of superorganism. Society is merely a convenient term for designating a group of individuals whose patterned conduct and feelings make up the group life. While we may observe certain large-scale statistical uniformities and regularities in the behavior of these individuals and note the use of highly stereotyped, institutionalized rituals and practices, such as voting, contract, buying and selling, litigation, courtship and marriage, and the like, nevertheless, it seems clear that these are but the aggregate expressions of individuals, acting, reacting, and inter-acting through the patterns of established group relationships.

Here it may be appropriate to suggest that we recognize how much our thinking about society is colored by the traditional conception of a social organization or system that is supposed to exist somewhere between earth and sky, operating through large-scale social forces believed to be a part of the cosmic process. Our prevailing social theories either explicitly or implicitly are built upon this concept which was derived in large part from the Newtonian conception of celestial mechanics, with the belief in large-scale forces acting at a distance. This conception of a social organization or a system has fostered the belief that our social life is something more or less fixed and inevitable, to be patiently studied, like astronomy, in order that we may learn how more effectively and obediently to submit to its exactions. To challenge such a belief, with all the authority and sanction it now carries, may indeed seem foolhardy and unjustified but, nevertheless, it may be asserted that the growing evidence from studies of other cultures and a more critical examination of the historical development of our own Western European culture, renders this traditional conception of the social sciences exceedingly dubious. It begins to appear that what we call *organized society* represents an historic endeavor to achieve social order in accordance with certain basic ideas, conceptions, and beliefs that are the basic dimensions of a culture. In accordance with the assumptions about the nature of the universe, of man's place and function, the relation of the individual to his group, the basic beliefs about human nature and conduct, and the image of the self, each of the different cultural groups throughout the world has attempted to establish a social order, more effectively to use and exploit the environment, to organize group living, and to regulate individual conduct. Social order as thus seen is not something that is given, as a part of the cosmos, but is always that which is sought. Social order, therefore, has to be achieved and the nature and quality of the social order sought will be governed by the basic cultural assumptions and beliefs and by the quality of sensibilities which that culture fosters in the individuals composing the group.

Moreover, it begins to appear that each cultural group, guided by these basic assumptions and beliefs, has developed a process for inducting each generation into the group life and rearing them to be participating members of the society and carriers of the cultural tradition. These beliefs and this process foster a predominant character structure or personality in and through which the members of the group attempt to carry out their life careers. But it is also apparent that the preferred character structure of a group may be neither congenial to, nor supportable by, some members of that group who thereby find themselves at a disadvantage or in conflict with their social life. Moreover, many, if not most members of our group, suffer greater or less warping and distortion with persistent affective reactions as a consequence of the very process of induction into our society and culture. It begins to appear that those who threaten or defeat social order are the individuals who have been warped and distorted by their nurture and rearing. Dictators of today are the most recent of a long line of destructive power-seeking personalities.

The foregoing very brief and inadequate statement of what may be called the *culture and personality viewpoint* is offered as a basis for discussing what psychiatry might contribute to the alleviation of national and international disorders and conflicts. It views psychiatry as offering not only the psychotherapeutic technics for diagnosing and treating individuals but, what is more important in this context, the insights, understandings, and awareness with which we may critically examine and assess our cultural traditions and the character structure and personality of individuals which that culture and, more especially, the educational process, foster in our society.

Here let us point out that, while the current discussion of democracy is concerned chiefly with questions of voting, representative government and freedom of action, speech and belief, it is evident to more thoughtful observers that democracy is essentially an affirmation of the value and worth of the individual personality. A society therefore may be said to merit the designation "democratic" to the extent to which it is prepared to assay or evaluate all of its traditions, beliefs and practices in terms of their meaning for the personality. This would involve a critical examination of all our socially sanctioned practices, in government, business, industry, agriculture, professional life, education, religion, and the family, to see what they are doing to and for the individual. With the further development of our knowledge and skills, and especially of our sensibilities toward human needs and values, we can and must undertake a progressive reorganization of our social life and reconstruction of our culture to further that democratic aspiration. This reconstruction must be undertaken because our historic culture has become progressively archaic. It is our major task from now on.

Assuming, therefore, that we share this democratic faith and hope, it would be appropriate to suggest where and how psychiatry may bring its professional concern with, and understanding of, personality development to bear upon the exigent task of achieving a social order dedicated to human values, more especially the protection and conservation of the human personality. How can these insights and understandings of the psychiatrist be made effective instruments in this process? As indicated earlier, what psychiatry can do through the diagnosis and treatment of individuals is necessarily limited. While there have been numerous and promising experiments in the direction of group procedures and therapies, it is difficult at the present time to say how much and how far further efforts in this direction will yield on a large scale. The critical question then arises: how far can psychiatry undertake to modify and redirect the already existing processes for the perpetuation and transmission of our cultural traditions and the procedures for the education of children?

One of the first steps in such a direction would involve a critical examination of our cultural traditions in terms of what they mean for the individual personality and for the group life. Surely there is no other professional group better prepared to conduct such an assay, since the psychiatrist is uniquely aware of the full consequences of our legal conceptions and rules, our religious beliefs and ethical teachings, our educational programs and procedures, and the thousand and one other formal and informal declarations and activities through which our culture declares and perpetuates itself. Here it may be appropriate to recall that the perpetuation of cultural traditions unchanged enjoys in our society, as in most other societies, the highest social approbation and sanctions; yet, as we look back and attempt to see some meaning or trends in human history, it would appear that every significant human advance, including all those we now cherish so highly, came into being only because some imaginative, courageous individual or small group dared to question tradition and propose some new belief and some new institutional practices more consonant with the aspirations and values they cherished. Indeed, it begins to appear that the primary task of a democratically inclined society is to develop ways and means of interrupting the continuity of cultural traditions in those areas where it is evident that the ideas and beliefs and practices of the past are working to the disadvantage of human welfare and threatening or destroying the integrity of the human personality. As F. J. Teggart pointed out in *Processes of History* (1918), wars, migrations and invasions have been the great occasions of human advance because in those troubled periods a few individuals escaped from the cultural traditions and so were able to see and think creatively. Can we not devise an educational equivalent of war to free us from our group past, as the psychiatrist frees the individual from the coercion of his personal past history?

This indicates one of the tasks to which psychiatry can contribute, to assist or to create the agency through which our society can continually evaluate its culture and its social institutions in the light of developing insights and understandings concerning the personality. Just as organized scientific investigation self-consciously undertakes to question and examine its concepts and theories, and improve its methods and procedures, we likewise need a professional group, competent to undertake the same task with respect to our inherited culture and our organized social life. It would seem to be especially appropriate for psychiatry to help us understand how our cultural traditions and practices produce the dominant figures in our political, economic and social affairs, who so frequently threaten social order and seek to exploit others in pursuance of their personality trends and needs.

This presents a situation for psychiatry somewhat similar to that which confronts clinical medicine as it attempts to face the task of health care: how to translate its knowledge of the innumerable ways in which human functioning can be disturbed or diseased, over into a constructive program of redirecting the many aspects of human living, city planning, housing, nutrition, recreation, working conditions, and the like, not only to prevent disease, important as that is, but to foster vitality and well-being throughout the population. Such a proposal may appear so remote and perhaps so fantastic that many will believe it utterly Utopian and absurd, but if the new understanding of man's origin and development, of his immense capacities and, above all, of the amazing flexibility of human nature and its patterning by social life and culture, have any social significance, they point to the realization that, despite the age old belief in man's complete helplessness in the face of superior forces and powers, he can, if he will, take charge of his destiny and begin to create the kind of culture and the kind of group life that is dedicated to human needs and values.

Let us turn then to some of the more immediately concrete areas in which psychiatry can contribute directly to the conservation of human personality and indirectly to the furtherance of this larger goal of cultural and social reorganization. It is now becoming evident that the process of early education of the child, which ordinarily takes place in the home and family, gives rise to the basic character structure as a persistent way of organizing and interpreting experience and reacting affectively toward life. To the extent that both clinical and experimental studies are showing how various cultural traditions and certain time-honored methods of rearing children tend to foster distortions of the personality and persistent affective reactions, destructive to social order and to the individual, it would appear that in this area of early childhood education we have one of the most significant opportunities to modify the predominant personality difficulties and distortions characteristic of our society. More specifically there is a need for critical scrutiny of the traditional ideas and beliefs about human nature, about human conduct, our ethical and moral teachings, and an exposition of how these either block or actually threaten integrated personality development. Likewise, the prevailing practices of education of children call for similar examination and exposition of their consequences. It might be suggested that the psychiatrist is uniquely competent to tell us how to practice the Christian injunction to love little children.

Again, in the publicly supported programs of education starting from the nursery school, through high school and college, there are also large opportunities for translating the psychiatrist's knowledge of personality development and personality distortions into a going program that might serve to minimize, if not to eliminate so much of the damage that is now being inflicted upon children and adolescents. Specifically, it may be urged that psychiatry might provide for the preparation of teachers a formulation of the insights and understandings concerning personality development of children and adolescents that could be utilized by teachers in place of the rationalistic, intellectualized concepts and beliefs they are now taught. Here it may be appropriate to say that the task we are discussing may be viewed as chiefly one of superseding the historic conception of human nature and conduct by the insights and awareness which psychiatry has developed. Not, be it emphasized, to foster amateur psychiatrists, but to provide psychological equivalents for the archaic ideas and beliefs they are now using in their educational work. For example, it would make a difference if teachers were to view social adjustment, not as if it were a reaction to something outside, like gravitation, but rather as the way an individual has come to terms with his own past experience—that how he has learned to live with himself will govern how he can live with others.

A careful scrutiny of all the cultural agents, children's welfare organizations, youth organizations, and the like, engaged in socializing children and adolescents and young adults, will show how each of these socially sanctioned agencies and practices bears upon the development of the individual and either accentuates or modifies the trends of our culture and the individual distortions and disorders of the personality. The question then may be raised: how far is psychiatry prepared to organize its resources of professional knowledge and insights and understandings in an attempt systematically to modify and redirect these many different activities, realizing that in each case these activities are directed by a body of ideas, beliefs, and practices which are derived from our cultural traditions. In addition, psychiatry could help us to realize that individuals with unique, idiomatic personalities, expressing their unique life experience, are engaged in carrying out those ideas and practices. The question of how and to what extent psychiatry can effectively contribute to the modification of these traditions which are tenaciously held by these individual personalities cannot be answered by any superficial formula, as recent experience so well has shown. But it is suggested that psychiatry might, from its clinical experience, generalize to the extent of indicating what ideas and beliefs in our culture are productive of the major personality distortions and social disorders. The development by psychiatrists of what has recently been called clinical epidemiology may be likened to the emergence of a similar concept in public health, with the recognition of the necessity of eliminating persistent sources of infection, e.g., typhoid fever and infected milk and water supplies. It does not seem unwarranted to suggest that the persistence of certain ideas and beliefs, and especially of conflicting traditions that foster personality and social disorders, might be approached on this broader community and epidemiological basis.

Equally important to recognize are the various professional groups and institutional practices, such as the law and courts, and journalism, to mention only two, which continually reiterate and confirm the very concepts and beliefs which now appear to be most questionable. The question, therefore, may be raised: what can psychiatry contribute toward a reorganization of the assumptions and beliefs of the law and of journalism as two outstanding procedures that have been relatively untouched by the insights and understandings of psychiatry. If the schools of law and of journalism are not beyond possibility of being influenced, they constitute two important, highly strategic agencies in any such program. Theological schools also should be mentioned, especially since we face the ironic situation in which many of those most concerned professionally with ethical and moral issues are seemingly most resistant to the insights that are most significant for understanding human misconduct and distortions.

It is neither appropriate nor desirable to attempt here any exhaustive or detailed examination of all the possible ways in which psychiatry might contribute to these situations; rather it would seem more important to try to clarify the major issues and possibilities of which the modification and redirection of our cultural traditions and of the processes of educating the child would appear to be of major importance. At least they would seem to deserve careful consideration to see whether any organized, deliberate activity by psychiatry might offer possibilities of alleviating national and international difficulties.

At this point it would seem appropriate to ask whether psychiatry itself, as a professional group, or a discipline, faces internal difficulties which make it hard for the individual psychiatrist to feel that discussions of this kind have much substance or meaning. As already suggested, it may be that many psychiatrists, because of the very nature of their clinical training and their preoccupation with concrete individuals, feel either indifferent to, or baffled by, any proposal of this kind. Like many internists, their way of thinking and their major preoccupations with diagnoses and treatment of specific disorders and illnesses, make the concept of preventive medicine and health care more or less unreal, if not fantastic. It involves a concern for the larger cultural and social environment, out of which their patients emerge, with which they are relatively unacquainted and in which they are uninterested. Such attitudes and feelings on the part of individual psychiatrists are not subject to reproach, because it is quite possible that clinical ability must, to a very large extent, preclude these other interests and concerns. The only unfortunate aspect of this situation is when such clinically minded individuals, in a perfectly legitimate endeavor to maintain their own professional position and interest, feel it necessary to decry or destructively attack any proposals made in this direction as wholly unsound and futile. Some professional group must be concerned with the larger problems of health care, of mental health, and of social welfare, and if the professionally competent psychiatrists are not ready to assume their full share of responsibility in this area, then it is clear that we will be at the mercy of all the self-constituted doctors of society of which there are far too many today.

Just as we are beginning to ask whether the scientists whose scientific conscience is highly developed may not need to develop a social conscience and an awareness of the immense responsibilities which development of seientific knowledge and techniques imposes, so we might likewise ask if the psychiatrist whose professional medical conscience is highly developed does not need to develop a more active social conscience and especially a greater concern with human values and sensibilities. Is it enough to release an individual from his conflicts and distortions and offer no help in finding some aspirations and values that will make his emancipation meaningful to himself and his society? This situation again may be likened to the operation of scientific research which is progressively freeing us from the terrors, the superstitions, and the limitation of our cultural past, but offers little help in finding the purposes, the human values and aspirations in and through which our newly won freedom and our newly acquired tools and technology can find any meaning. Surely the psychiatrist needs no reminder that man cannot live on a level of physiological functioning and organic impulse, but must have aspirations and goals to give life any tension and significance. Perhaps the psychiatrist needs to join hands with the artist, the poet, the dramatist and novelist who can create the new aspirations and values we need for reconstruction of our culture, illuminated by the insights which psychiatry can contribute.

Again, the question may be raised of how far any proposals in this direction will be rejected by many psychiatrists because, for various reasons wholly understandable, they are firmly convinced that human nature is more or less predestined to be antisocial and destructive, if not by original sin, by other innate and unavoidable characteristics. Reading some psychiatric contributions one cannot help feeling that Calvin would be much at home with the ideas of human nature that are sometimes expressed. It is possible also that some psychiatrists are committed to a conception of society and of culture as a part of the cosmos, as something fixed and unchangeable, to which man must passively submit, as to gravitation or the climate, and therefore any suggestion that human intelligence might attempt to reorganize social life and reconstruct our culture must appear as a Promethean fantasy. This viewpoint seems to be implied frequently by the way in which the term "facing reality" is often used, as if there were some permanent, fixed reality which the individual had to face and accept with the implication that one of the major human virtues is to learn to "take it," regardless of the defeat and degradation involved. In this viewpoint psychiatry would seem to share somewhat the same defeatist attitude that is so implicit in much of our social science and our religion. How often have we been told that war and human destruction and suffering must be regarded as a part of the divine plan which man must obediently accept, just as we are told that the so-called price system, which has been historically developed within the last three or four generations, is a basic feature of the cosmos.

Perhaps we should explicitly recognize that psychiatry is a convenient term for designating a body of professional knowledge, skills, and techniques that finds its locus and expression in discrete individuals called *psychiatrists;* that each of these individuals is himself a product of this culture, of this society, and has developed a personality and a way of interpreting and organizing experience and feeling toward life that involve, like all the rest of us, the same distortions and affective trends that our culture so prolifically produces. It would be both absurd and unfair to reproach psychiatrists on this account, but we might ask whether it is unreasonable to expect that, out of their wealth of clinical knowledge of the human personality, and with the insights and understandings they now have, they give us some vision of what human nature and the human personality might become if freed from the distorting and defeating experiences now so common.

This desire on the part of many individuals for some constructive program looking to the future does not necessarily imply a fantastic hope for a Utopia in which all human problems will be solved; there is a growing realization that the individual cannot "solve" his personality problems, which arise from his unique personality as his way of organizing and interpreting experience and feeling toward life; so society cannot "solve" its problems which are, so to speak, created by its cultural traditions and group practices. Every group must face the persistent tasks of group life which each generation must take up anew in terms of its knowledge, its understanding, and its sensibilities. With intelligence and the techniques contributed by science, with insight and awareness into the human personality, and with sensibilities and aspirations, it should not seem Utopian today to hope that succeeding generations could meet these persistent tasks with courage and, above all, with the friendly, co-operative attitudes and feelings which the human personality, when not too badly warped and distorted, can bring to life.

(FROM: *American Journal of Orthopsychiatry*, 11 [1941]: 620–27.)

FOURTEEN

Freud's Influence on Western Thinking and Culture

ONE WAY of assessing the contribution of an individual is in terms of his influence upon the basic organizing conceptions with which his culture attempts to order and interpret events, to organize its group life, and regulate its conduct. In the long run only the reorganization of this conceptual basis of the culture upon which the social life is built may be said to have any permanent significance, however strongly contemporary society may acclaim individual achievements in various other areas of activity or thought.

If we attempt to see the contributions of Freud in this perspective we must first recall that Western European culture has been built upon the following four organizing conceptions:

1. The nature of the universe; how it was created; how it operates.
2. Man's place in this universe, whether in nature or outside nature.
3. The relation of the individual to his society, or "Who is to be sacrificed for whom?"
4. Human nature and conduct, and the image of the self.

These four organizing conceptions, as expressed in religion, law, philosophy, and the thousand and one socially sanctioned institutional practices through which they are put into effect, have for the past four hundred and more years been undergoing a progressive disintegration. Beginning with the early work of Copernicus and Galileo the geocentric conception of the universe and its creation, as depicted in Genesis, has been becoming progres-

WESTERN THINKING AND CULTURE   163

sively incredible in the light of the findings of Western science. Later, the conception of man's place in the universe as an individual, specially created outside of nature, has likewise come under critical scrutiny from students of paleontology, biology, and especially the medical sciences, which have increasingly revealed man's origin from the same mammalian ancestry as his fellow primates whose functional needs and capacities he shares.

During the nineteenth century the historic conception of the individual's relationships to his group and the firm belief in the coercive and unchanging character of what is called "organized society," were exposed to an increasingly critical revision based upon the reports of other societies and cultures and a better understanding of the historical development of the earlier stages of Western European society.

Despite the growing awareness of the changes in these three basic ideas and conceptions, faith in the validity of the older conception of human nature and conduct, of man as a rational, volitional, autonomous individual whose conduct was governed by reason, continued more or less unchallenged.

Freud's illuminating studies of personality and his elucidation of the emergence of the human personality out of the processes of being socialized and culturized in childhood brought the final step in the disintegration of this conceptual basis of Western European culture. We are still so close to the event that it is difficult for us to see the larger significance of his contribution, or to realize its far-reaching implications both for our traditional culture and for our ongoing social life.

While it may be said that the collapse of the first three basic concepts of our culture made inevitable the abandonment of the fourth conception, of human nature and conduct which depended upon these ideas and beliefs for its validity and its sanction, nevertheless it must be recognized that Freud's contribution was both a demonstration of the invalidity of the older conception of human nature and at the same time a formulation of a new and replacing conception. This newer formulation, although tinged by the older ideas and beliefs, is largely in accord with the new climate of opinion and the newer conceptions of the universe, of man's place therein, and of the relation of the individual to his society that are now emerging from contemporary scientific explorations. If we can, therefore, see Freud's achievement in terms of this historical perspective we can gain a better understanding of the larger significance of his contribution to Western European culture as ending the older traditional concepts of human nature and conduct, and providing the new idea with which we are gropingly trying to reconstruct our thinking and our society.

Once this new conception of human nature and conduct has been grasped, we will begin to see that it completes the full cycle of cultural change that has been going on for nearly four hundred years, and brings us face to face with the immense and unavoidable task of rebuilding our culture upon the firm conviction that man can and must take charge of his own destiny because now he can, with knowledge, understanding, and especially insight, begin to create the kinds of human personalities essential to the development of an orderly human society. It is curious that so many of those who have been closest students and coworkers of Freud are essentially pessimistic in their attitude toward human nature and its expression, as if they still clung to the ancient belief in man's innate wickedness and perversity so long proclaimed by theology. Indeed some of their views on man's original nature would be highly approved by the old Calvinists.

Perhaps we may see here another illustration of how the prevailing climate of opinion affects even the most adventurous thinker. Just as Newton, concerned with theological questions, was seemingly unaware of the full implications of his own work, so much in the same way it may appear that Freud and many of those associated with his work are equally unaware of the implications of his work and are particularly unable to realize the immense liberation which is coming from the newer conception of human nature and conduct that Freud has given us. The important and culturally significant achievement of Freud is in opening the door to the newer ideas of human personality. As we are progressively emancipated from the older beliefs about human nature as fixed and unchangeable, as innately wicked, sinful, and antisocial, and begin to realize that the process of socialization creates the warped, twisted, and distorted individuals, and that this process of personality development can and will be changed, then it would appear that the present pessimism, and in some cases defeatism, will be replaced by a broader and more balanced viewpoint with a longer time perspective.

Moreover, as we understand more clearly the relation of culture and personality and see how "culture coerces the individual and by that coercion distorts the individual who in turn changes the culture so far as his opportunities and capacities will permit," then we will realize that the nature and quality of a society are determined by the personalities who make up that society and these in turn are created by what the family and other agencies of child rearing and education do to and for the child. Thus it will be apparent that the many and diverse "social problems" with which we are confronted are symptoms of the distortions of personality fostered by our culture and our society which frustrate so many human needs and create these warped and twisted personalities who exhibit these many varieties of individual and social defeat.

The ancient dichotomy of the individual and society will sooner or later be resolved as we understand that society is in each individual and what we call "social adjustment" is essentially the individual's relation to himself.

One of the curious and ironical aspects of Freud's work and its reception is the widespread inability or refusal to recognize that in his portrayal of the process of personality development in infancy and childhood he has provided the most effective support for the ethics of Jesus: the injunction to love little children, and the historic assertion of the supreme importance of the human personality, find their strongest support and confirmation in Freud's studies and teachings. Preoccupation with his clinical findings on neurotics has obscured these implications for education and the conservation of mental health which, in the longer future, will have far-reaching consequences.

Until we have had one or two generations of individuals who have not been driven by the acute anxieties, guilt, resentment, and hostility from which we all suffer, it will be difficult to look forward clearly and courageously to the future which Freud's contributions to Western European culture have made possible.

(FROM: *American Journal of Orthopsychiatry*, 10 [1940]: 880–82.)

FIFTEEN

Cultural Coercion and Individual Distortion

THOSE who are concerned with the development of ideas and especially the new climate of opinion that now is emerging are faced with the task of assessing, so far as they can do so today, the significance of the new ideas and conceptions that are increasingly engaging attention. Such a task is difficult because the vehemence of apologetics and polemics always emphasizes the purely contemporary service of ideas to current conflicts and by so much obscures the more important question of their larger roles as organizing conceptions of life.

The rational, intellectual tradition which we have inherited in Western European culture also creates further difficulties for the student of ideas since that tradition has for so long fostered the belief in permanent absolute Truths (with a capital "T") that exist as entities to be discovered by rational means and when so revealed, become enduring, unchanging, and coercive realities.

To the loyal followers of this tradition, ideas and conceptions are possessions to be fought for and against, as real things or entities that have no taint of possible obsolescence or of instrumental quality. To such devoted loyalty we owe the intellectual battles so familiar to the historian of ideas and also the sterner conflicts of racial and international war, as we see people today repeating the same passionate self-sacrifice that their ancestors gave to the Truths of their day.

For those whose only interest is apologetics and polemics, it is idle, if not exasperating, to invoke the conception of a changing climate of opinion with which to evaluate ideas. Such a conception imposes upon its user the necessity of viewing his favorite symbols and beliefs in a context, as instruments or means with which to order events and experience, and to give meaning and significance to the welter of life and the complexities of the environing world, social and natural. Such instruments have both a history and a functional efficacy, the neglect of which only too often leads to grotesque, if not tragic results. Today, especially, we need the illumination given by the conception of a changing climate of opinion upon the perplexing questions of our personal and social life where there are so many candidates for Truth.

There is nothing esoteric or recondite about the conception of a changing climate of opinion. It need not now be rigidly defined to be understood as indicating that, at any one time in the history of a culture, there are prevalent ideas and conceptions about the nature of the universe, of man's place therein, of man's relations to his society, and his conception of the self. These ideas and conceptions give order and meaning to experience, to social and individual action and belief, and provide the criteria of credibility and the principles of explanation used in science and the common life. These ideas and conceptions and the tools and techniques through which man establishes and sustains these relations and preserves his own biological continuity, make up the culture. In a very real sense they may be said to prescribe what the individual will be aware of, how he will interpret it and respond to it, and what he will believe.

Now it has been the office of religion, art, philosophy, and science to clarify and apply these ideas and conceptions to the goverance of life and to find, if not create, the sanctions that give these patterns their coercive quality over the impulsive life of man. The history of ideas and the study of comparative religions and cultures indicates the extraordinary diversity and often the fantastic character of these creations.

What is of immense importance is the clear record of a succession of these climates of opinion in most cultures, a succession not unlike the geological succession of our own earth's history, with its advancing and retreating land and water areas, its alternating ages of warmth and cold, humidity and aridity. No less significant is the equally clear record that in those several climates of opinion, when once established and accepted, men of all degrees, with rare exceptions, found the world, as pictured by these organizing and ordering conceptions, as a reasonable, desirable, and necessary world, to question any aspect of which, however painful or destructive, was impious in the highest degree. When in the course of time the climate of opinion began to lose its clear and coercive authority, men became troubled and unhappy as they groped for new Truths or sought some way of bolstering up the old sanctions and reestablishing their cherished beliefs; conflicts ensued between those who clung with nostalgic longing to the past, and those who were fired with the light of new beliefs, new conceptions and techniques, because both the conservatives and the radicals, to use contemporary terms, built their lives upon those organizing conceptions and so must live or die with them.

The climate of opinion that was ushered in by the men of the sixteenth and seventeenth centuries (building, of course, upon the daring ideas of their predecessors) has gradually established itself throughout Western European culture and has been elaborated into every phase of so-called modern life. Only recently, however, has the cumulative influence of these major shifts in man's organizing conceptions become effective upon the common life. Astronomy, geology, paleontology, the biological sciences, and, more recently, anthropology have undermined almost every feature of the older conceptions of the universe, of man's place therein, his relations to the group life, and the image of the self, all of which were taught and sanctioned by revealed religion as the Truth and as the essential framework for human conduct. The limited time span of the earth and of man, the anthropocentric universe and the coercive sanctions of eternal rewards and punishments have all been shaken, if not largely overthrown, as a consequence of scientific investigations, while the older belief in the inevitable nature of government, society, and human nature has been disintegrated by the findings of comparative culture and of psychology.

The beginnings of this disillusionment and the dismay it created can be traced back for many generations among the more intelligent and sensitive, but the full impact of the loss of faith and the resultant bewilderment were received by the mass of people during the present generation.

Just as we have begun to realize that this older conceptual world was shattered by the scientific advances of the past three hundred years, we have been confronted with a new set of ideas and conceptions that will probably constitute the climate of opinion of the near future. The amazing changes in the basic ideas and conceptions that have come since the turn of the century are not only a revolution in the climate of opinion but a revolution that may, so to speak, end revolutions, for these newer ideas and conceptions now emerging in philosophical and scientific explorations carry a novel, if not unprecedented, meaning. Instead of a new set of Truths, of authoritative beliefs with fearsome or awful sanctions, we are invited to accept a set of conceptions for ordering experience that make no pretense to finality or absolute quality. Indeed, we are asked to view our conceptions as temporary, relative, and purely instrumental ways of seeing the universe and giving answers to man's persistent search for certainty.

Here we can gain some insight into the remarkable situation today when we may, with approval from philosophy and science, regard any idea or theory as a tool or instrument, a way of ordering experience and giving meaning to so-called "facts," as a perspective on a world that must forever be regarded in this relative manner, a world that man himself patterns by the character of the organizing ideas and conceptions with which he approaches it, asks questions of it, and "explains" it.

The older absolutes, the certainties, the all-embracing laws and generalizations are not repudiated, but shifted from their formerly high position of unchallengeable Truths, to the more genial role of human creations to serve the human need of understanding and manipulation. Moreover, it is evident that the individual philosopher, scientist, and artist, by the very make-up of his own personality, his emotional bias and needs, is the agent who makes these conceptual patterns and bends and twists them to serve his personality needs. Emotional congruity rules the scientist and philosopher no less than the folk life in their acceptance and rejection of knowledge.

Thus, by a devious path we come to Marx and Freud, about whose teachings controversies have been raging these many years and probably will continue. If we can see their contributions in the light of the foregoing we may gain some understanding that is denied to apologetics and polemics and the preoccupation with specific points of doctrine. Where in this changing climate of opinion do Marx and Freud stand and what is the relation of their teachings to these more recent revolutions in our thinking?

To answer this question adequately will demand more scholarship, daring, and perspective than anyone today can probably muster; but pending a more competent and definitive treatment it is permissible to indicate how these seemingly disparate and conflicting theories may be viewed in a context that gives to each a complementary role in the contemporary drama of ideas and of social change.

For this present inquiry it will be helpful to recognize that the Marxian interpretation of history in terms of dialectical materialism is another statement of this conception of a climate of opinion and how it changes. It implies, where it does not explicitly state, that the ideas and conceptions and beliefs of any time are essentially relative products of the knowledge and the instruments of production available to the people of that time, and are developed, if not created, for the very purpose of ordering their individual and group experience and making their lives appear reasonable. Theories and beliefs therefore are instruments that arise from the contemporary social context, or as we are coming to realize, out of the culture.

The influence of the rational tradition is to be seen in the sharp dichotomy of instruments of production (the material culture, as ethnology and anthropology have termed it) and the ideas, beliefs, and theories (non-material culture) which, in accordance with that rational tradition are given a functional character distinct from the instruments and technique of production. This attempted distinction reflects the climate of opinion of the nineteenth century and was adopted by Veblen in his writings. But as the introductory remarks indicate, it is becoming increasingly difficult to maintain that distinction today when we are being forced to recognize that ideas and conceptions, like the tools, machines, and techniques, are instruments for organizing and manipulating the world or directing human behavior.

What this means more explicitly is that behind every tool and machine and technical process is an idea, a conception, a theory or belief, that gives the concrete material instrument its efficacy and purpose; but in turn these material instruments for manipulating the world give these ideas and theories a sanction and an efficient validation that serve to uphold and perpetuate them. This distinction between instruments and theories becomes less useful as we gain a better understanding of culture and a perspective upon culture change, since we see that the concrete material instruments are patterned by the ideas and theories that dominate man's thinking and behavior, and that in turn man is dependent upon the efficacy of his instrumental applications. Moreover, our growing understanding of culture is revealing how at any one time the prevailing culture of instruments and ideas is differentially used and accepted by various sub-groups of the larger cultural area, so that we see a broad culture with its general patterns and within that culture we can discern sub-cultures of more or less discrete groups and the sub-culture of individuals.

Thus we are led to a view of culture as those organized and sanctioned patterns of belief and conduct prevailing among a people and coercing them because only in those patterns can they think and behave.

Culture coerces and dominates the individual, through the ideas, conceptions, beliefs and patterns with which he orders and explains his experience, directs his efforts, and guides his conduct. But culture is not an entity, nor a force, nor anything superhuman and cosmic; it is merely a term and a concept for the totality of these patterned ways of thinking and acting which are specific modes and acts of conduct of discrete individuals who, under the guidance of parents and teachers and the associations of their fellows, have developed a way of life expressing those beliefs and those actions. Thus within the larger group life that exhibits these more or less uniform patterns of conduct, there may be and usually are numerous smaller groupings of individuals whose beliefs and conduct conform to the general pattern but exhibit a definite deviation peculiar to themselves; this deviation of pattern is included within the larger cultural context in that it shares some of the more generalized features, such as language, morals, religion, use of money and so on, but it has its own peculiar and restricted observance. Within these sub-groupings, then, individuals will find their way of life and its explanations, which they take over because they must have some patterns for living and these are given to them or imposed upon them.

It becomes clear then that culture coerces the individual into conformity to patterns, duly sanctioned and rationalized, so that with rare exceptions, he can think, act, believe, and aspire only in accordance with the dictates of his culture, which, as we have observed, is a relative, changing aggregate of individual beliefs and conduct. The historically developed "organized" society, with its legally sanctioned patterns of conduct that we call institutions (private property, money, marriage), with its religious and scientific beliefs and conceptions, with its various tools and the skills needed for their use, together with all the many other aspects of a so-called high civilization, is to be seen in a time perspective that reveals the slow process of cumulative change, punctuated by occasional reversals or sudden changes in trend, as the individual's patterned conduct is modified by and with the changes in the culture. But these culture changes are to be seen as the cumulative reflection of individual deviations from the previously established pattern.

This conception of culture and the individual as two aspects of the same process or event is itself a recent deviation from the historically developed pattern of thought about society and the individual which treated the society as an entity, a superhuman organization, operating with cosmic forces and sanctions under mysterious but potent controls such as sovereignty, etc. Today we can begin to free our thinking of these older patterns and see culture and the individual much as we conceive a gas and an electron.

In contemporary thinking it is found useful to think of a gas as an aggregate of molecules, atoms, or electrons which exhibit a statistical uniformity of behavior; that is, the gas, with its pressure and its other characteristics, is constituted by the patterning of many discrete activities within a field. The aggregate of these individual patterned activities (energy releases) gives rise to the aggregate event we call the gas, and in turn the individual energy release or activity of the discrete electrons is patterned by the gas field in which they occur. The same electrons in a different field would release energy in other patterns and constitute a different gas or liquid or solid. The significance of this analogy is in its clear indication of the dual aspects, individual and aggregate, of physical events and also of human behavior which the individual exhibits within a cultural field of patterned conduct. In another culture the same individual organisms would behave in accordance with the culture patterns at their disposal, since human behavior is a biological process that submits to these patternings.

It is this conception of the cultural coercion of the individual which, as suggested earlier, promises to be one of the major features of the emerging climate of opinion, and in this conception, it is submitted, one of the enduring contributions of Marx will be expressed, whatever more exigent purposes Marxian theory may serve now and later. Once it is realized that the individual's conduct, both in overt behavior and in beliefs, reflects the cultural impact of his time and of the sub-culture (economic, social, political, or religious grouping) to which he belongs, then we can begin to see more clearly what we mean by culture without perpetuating an artificial dichotomy of material and non-material culture. We can also approach more confidently the question of the role of the individual in culture and again relinquish the many confusing conceptions and beliefs about the relation of the individual to society that encumber our social theory and studies. Moreover we may view a culture as essentially a human creation, transmitted by parents and teachers to children and thus perpetuated in patterned behavior, thereby escaping from the older beliefs in "organized society" as something superhuman, sanctioned by various mystical and supernatural forces and powers.

This then brings us to the second major theme of the new climate of opinion, a theme we may attribute to the insight of Freud, whose theory of human conduct has been so confused by apologetics and polemics that his enduring contribution is not really understood even by some of his most ardent disciples. Here it becomes necessary to disclaim any superior wisdom or desire to make a pronouncement; the intention is to offer a perspective that may be helpful to an understanding of the conceptual reorganization that now is taking place amid great confusion.

No better illustration of this confusion today is needed than the mutual distrust and dislike of most of those who follow Marx and those who follow Freud in their thinking. It will be seen, as we go further, that in Marxian theory we have a most fruitful conception of the role of culture in human life and of the process of cultural change, while in Freudian theory we find illumination upon the behavior of the individual personality that has been subject to this cultural patterning.

It must be re-emphasized that culture is not an entity, or force or other superhuman agency that mysteriously organizes and dominates social life and individuals, like a superior imposing control over an inferior; nor is culture the whole which organizes the parts by some mystic power resident in wholes. Such conceptions derive from a prior climate of opinion that viewed all existence in terms of a hierarchy, like the feudal society and the monarchial society and the patriarchal family in which it flourished, and so imputed to all events the same kind of relationships and the same kind of obedience of a lesser or an inferior to a greater or a superior. Our social theory and much of our biological theory are permeated with survivals and vestiges of earlier ideas and beliefs, including animistic conceptions of specific powers resident in organisms, such as the Will that guides and directs them. It is therefore difficult for us to escape the influence of these pervasive ideas and to discard these older conceptions of something that organizes, rules, or controls and of the individual as rational, autonomous, and volitional. But it is the very crux of the emerging climate of opinion that is superseding these older beliefs, to view organization and structure as the patterned activity of constituents in a field, wherein the field is seen as arising from the interaction of the constituents which in turn are patterned by that interaction, without invoking any mystic entities or powers or forces.

The discrete individuals, whether electrons, atoms, or organisms, exist and act on, and are acted upon, by impinging other individuals, and out of these impinging reactions arise the fields which define or pattern the range of the individual behavior. If there were only one individual atom, molecule, or person, we would not have a gas or a culture, since the gas and the culture imply or necessitate patterned interactions. Even a single cell ceases to function according to its specific pattern when isolated from other cells that constitute the field of cell functioning.

What we need to recognize as the essential feature of a culture is that the adults attempt to impose the culture patterns upon their children, who, to a greater or less extent, accept these patterns because they are young, dependent, and helpless and need guidance and patterning of their behavior. We have then the human energy of individual organisms, released in patterned conduct toward other individuals, as the dynamics or energetics of a society, and thus we may discard the notions of social forces used by earlier theorists to explain the changing events of social life. But when we examine more closely the process of transmission of culture from parents (and teachers) to the child, we find that it is not a mere moulding of passive clay into the shapes required by the culture and preferred by parents. Rather it is a dynamic process of interaction, of stress and strain, of coercion and persuasion, of love and

CULTURAL COERCION AND INDIVIDUAL DISTORTION 175

hate, of acceptance and rejection, and the gradual constellation of a variety of conduct patterns that the individual child selectively incorporates into his individual personality. Just as we are discovering that within the atom a varying number of the basic electrical charges of enormous energy are constellated into a pattern of behavior unique to each element, so we are learning how the fundamental physiological processes and needs of the human organism are repressed, inhibited, frustrated, and released in the patterns that the culture, as interpreted by the parents, requires or permits, and as the unique individual child has adapted them idiosyncratically to his life career.

The drives, urges, impulses, needs, and similar terms we use to designate these basic organic functions are the dynamic energy that moves the organism to react upon the world that impinges upon him. But those reactions, it must be emphasized, are interactions between the prescribed pattern of the parental expectations and requirements and later group prescriptions, and the energetic needs of a child to whom that pattern may or may not be wholly appropriate and to whom the parental mode of application may or may not be satisfying. Deprivations and frustrations are active interferences with biological processes which they obstruct or divert but cannot, without destroying the organism, eliminate. As in physical processes, so in organic, there occurs a conservation of energy through transformation into other modes of release. The dammed-up functional needs of the individual are diverted by parental training into other channels or converted into activities that eventually bring release as a reward for the effort of achievement.

More important, however, is the affective or emotional disturbances that these patternings, especially the deprivations and frustration, arouse in the child who resents this interference and feels the blocked expression as tensions we call anxiety. These affective reactions become part of the learned patterns of conduct so that every repression and every expression is more or less warped or distorted by these feelings of resentment and the tensions that accompany them. The individual child thus receives the culture and develops his unique constellation of feeling and behavior in a highly idiomatic manner so that his conduct is of necessity a deviation from the socially prescribed pattern. We may, therefore, speak of the individual distortion of the culture as an inevitable reaction of unique individuals to that which is forbidden and required. This individual distortion of culture faces the limits of tolerated deviation beyond which it evokes the socially sanctioned restraints applied to the criminal and the insane.

But this warping and twisting of the culture patterns by the individual's affective responses would be relatively insignificant, merely deviations around a mode in accordance with the usual distribution of organic characteristics, if they were only deviations. The cultural patterning in deprivation and frustration often gives rise, however, to persistently affective conditions or states in the organism which permeate every action and color every situation, so that the individual's resentment toward parents for deprivation or blocking his desires becomes an organic drive or urge, of equal or greater potency than the primary physiological needs, the blocking of which apparently supplies the energy for such resentful, retaliatory impulses and reactions. Such resentment may then blossom forth in hostility and aggression openly expressed or appear in disguised fashion as distorted performances of the required cultural conduct, wherein the hostility is only partially released because of fear of retaliation or punishment.

The child's early lessons in these deprivations and frustrations and the performance of prescribed acts under coercion involve an adult to whom the child reacts affectively as he complies or refrains from acting, as the adult requires. To the coercion or persuasion, then, of the adult, the child responds with an emotional or feeling tone that is just as much an organic reaction as the motor response it accompanies. These affective reactions to the adult give rise to the child's generalized pattern of response to authority wherever he encounters it. Authority, then, is not an entity or power, but the way situations and persons evoke learned affective responses to situations and persons that enter into all patterned conduct. If the child's experience has been with adults who have mitigated the severity of deprivations and have administered frustrations benevolently, his feeling toward authority will be without resentment; he can repress what is forbidden and perform what is demanded with little conflict between the learned behavior and his emotional response. If, however, the child has been cruelly and harshly deprived and brutally frustrated with little or no affection and emotional security, his persistent feeling toward the parents and all adults will be acute resentment toward authority;

he will repress what is forbidden, feeling hostile toward those who deprive and frustrate him; and he will perform what is demanded reluctantly, so that every act is in conflict with his feelings.

Let us pause here briefly to note that what we call private property and the sanctity of the person as defined and enforced by the law are not entities or mysterious emanations; they are the generalized concepts we apply to the learned behavior of not touching, using, taking, or invading objects, places, and the physical person of other individuals. This conduct toward objects and persons that gives rise to what we call private property or sanctity of the person is established in the child by the parents' repeated blocking and frustration of his naïve reactions to things and persons until he learns to repress those responses and learns to tolerate exposure to things and persons without an adult to block his behavior. He learns to inhibit, and only those inhibitions make private property and sanctity of the person possible, because, without them, only constant watching and guarding with physical force would make things and persons inviolate. The diversity in different cultures of things considered private property and the variety of the immunities enjoyed by the person give ample corroboration for this conception of property and sanctity as a learned response. Moreover, the enormous variations within our own culture in the prescribed observance of inviolability, to be seen in different social and economic classes and regions, likewise support this conception of learned conduct.

Likewise we must recognize that the immense accumulation of manners, of etiquette, of morals, and ethics, are all dependent upon this learning of repression and inhibition of naïve response and of conformity to prescribed modes of conduct that one generation transmits to the next with utmost fidelity to tradition except when the cultural continuity is interrupted or modified.

But the cultural patterning of conduct is not all prohibitive and negative. In each culture there are rituals and symbols taught to the growing child as the duly sanctioned practices for dealing with other individuals in the approach to objects and persons which are protected by the learned inviolability which we call private property and the sanctity of the person. These practices we call barter and sale, contracts by which agreements to waive or set aside or transfer inviolability or permit use, are made possible and enforceable; courtship and marriage; inheritance and bequest; and the whole complex institutional framework in which living is carried on, with infinite gradations and differentiations for each class, rank, status, and for vested interests, privileges, and persistent disabilities.

The use of these socially sanctioned practices is learned by the child who grows up to accept the symbols, such as votes, money, and credit as more real and compelling than natural events of the environment. In and through these practices he seeks, then, his life fulfillment according to the personality trends that his early training have established, with the distorted patterns of the culture that his individual experience of life has given him, and always with the persistent affective or feeling tone toward the prohibited sources of his desires. To the individual, his way of life appears usually as admirable or desirable or wholly unsatisfactory irrespective of the actual conditions in which he lives, since he projects upon these surrounding circumstances the feeling tones of his personality, thereby transforming them in meaning, significance, and value. Moreover, to the individual the focus of his desired happiness appears always in the environing situations and people, since he cannot, without insight, realize that his own affective relation to life gives, or prevents his finding, happiness. With this emotional orientation and these projections, the individual faces his world, assessing each encounter by the peculiar affective meaning it has for him, and reacting thereto with the cumulative affective load that his experience has given him. Since for many individuals in our culture there has been predominant deprivation and frustration, unmitigated by love and affection, the prevailing attitude toward life is that of anxiety and fear, resentment and hostility, and a strong drive for retaliation.

These individuals find, in the institutions of private property, of barter, sale, contract, money and credit, and the intricate manipulations to which they are subject an unlimited field for retaliatory expression, directed to acquisition of property, exercise of power, and attainment of prestige. Thereby they discharge their resentments and hostility, with full social sanction for the aggressions otherwise prohibited, and in the symbols of their achievements they find solace for the feelings of guilt and worthlessness derived from the scoldings, punishments, and humiliations of their childhood.

Many individuals, with the same desire for retaliation and aggression, are too weak, too incompetent, too fearful to struggle against others, and so they must nurse their grievances and find release in sly, underhand, obstructive activities that appear to others so senseless and futile but bring a wry satisfaction to the defeated individuals practicing them.

In the area of sex expression the full impact of the cultural training is to be seen most clearly, for the biological functions of sex are so pervasive and energetic that their repression and patterning, according to the prescribed rules, create highly diverse outlets for the affective load they carry. The early training of the child in the repression of all genital activities, the teaching of the inviolability of the person of others and of himself, are sufficient to build up a considerable affective meaning for all sex interests. But this is imposed upon a strong feeling of guilt about sex experiments and desires, anxiety over the efficiency of the genitals, and fear of discovery of one's peculiar idiomatic sex desires and practices that together make a persistently dominant emotional focus for the individual. He may try to resolve this complexity in the overt fashions approved by society or in a variety of vicariates, surrogates, diversions, and perversions (so-called), including the legally forbidden but widely practiced alternatives to monogamous marriage.

For our present purposes the significance of sexual repression and of the almost universal distortions inflicted upon individuals is in the clue it gives to the immense energy released or expressed in the institutionalized practices of acquisitiveness, and the struggle for power and prestige by individuals who can attain no fulfillment of their sex functions and needs in marriage or the available alternatives. So many individuals, more especially men, are filled with resentment and hostility, aggressively competitive and retaliatory, having had little or no experience in receiving or giving affection and love, so that in marriage they find only a minor and subordinate focus for their lives, a purely genital functioning that brings a physiological discharge but no affective release and no assuagement of the corroding anxiety, fear, and guilt they carry within them. Such individuals are psychologically impotent, however strong their genital functions, because they can approach a sex partner only as a sex object to whom they give no intimacy or affection and from whom they will accept none.

These are the individuals who live compulsively in and for their business, their professions, their careers, to which they sacrifice themselves like slaves under the lash, only the lash is now in their own personalities and is never withheld, so that they cannot relax, nor play, nor enjoy but the briefest and often the crudest of recreations until later life when, secure in possessions and power, they may, with waning genital functions, begin to cultivate other interests. The concern with philanthropic giving of their property is perhaps the clearest evidence of the purely symbolic value of their acquisitiveness and the persistence of guilt feelings that their gifts will, they hope, expiate. Acquisition of property, and more important today, of income is a symbol for the aggressive competitor who no sooner obtains it than he turns to prestige for satisfying his personality needs. Prestige involves personal recognition and acceptance and depends upon performance of those ritualized acts — recreation, leisure time, manners and etiquette, and conspicuous waste (Veblen) which only property-income permit.

With such strong aggressive drives, reinforced by sex frustration and guilt, such individuals cannot abide by rules and laws but must always push beyond that which is permitted and obeyed by others. Every aspect of culture they touch is distorted, warped, redirected, or destroyed and replaced by practices and arrangements more satisfying to themselves, even when the destruction brings no tangible gain or advantage. Such conduct is not the rational, hedonistic calculation of social theory; it may be grimly planned and coldly executed, but the drive and the focus are derived from the twisted personality that moves emotionally and converts everything into symbolic representations of its needs.

Thus we face the dual aspects of personality and culture. The culture, in the active efforts of parents and teachers to enforce conformity to the group-sanctioned patterns of ideas, beliefs, and conduct, imposes upon the individual's behavior its direction and form and instrumentation in the institutional practices for personal relations. The personality that emerges from this cultural tuition, with the affective tones, meanings, and drives that the individual develops from the way the cultural training has been imposed by parents and teachers, is always a variant from the ideal or model patterns and is always uniquely constellated so that it must bend and distort that culture.

Culture coerces the individual and by that coercion distorts the individual who in turn changes the culture so far as his opportunities and capacities will permit. The most ideal governmental, economic, and other social arrangements, including those for mating, are at the mercy of the twisted personalities who must compulsively reject them in order to project their own idiosyncratic symbols and meanings and needs which they aggressively assert, or submissively retain, with consequent alteration, if not defeat, of the social scheme. The individual, except when uniquely endowed, cannot escape from his culture and the peculiar climate of opinion of his age; he is immersed in it, like the fish in water, and as unaware of this surrounding medium. Nor can the individual, unless aided by skilful re-education that may bring some insights, escape from the personality that he has become through development in this culture and in the particular family constellation of which he was a part; he is that personality, and all his biological functions and physiological needs are structuralized by that personality, which is just that uniquely patterned organism that acts and feels in and through these modified functions and needs. These are the inescapable and unchangeable aspects of human life and human society about which there is an immense body of folklore, rationalizations, imposing verbalisms, documentary pronouncements, and other crystallized group apparatus.

Most poignant of all is the overwhelming unhappiness, misery, and personal defeat that characterizes Western European culture, regardless of social and economic status, or privileges and power, mitigated by various consolatory religions, by anodynes and sedatives of varying potency, and by hopes that from generation to generation are rekindled from the ashes of recurrent despair. As Otto Rank has expressed it, "man everywhere seeks happiness — but only gets success — occasionally, and then at the cost of many others who must be defeated or destroyed to win that success."

Our material culture of tools, techniques, and skills, which could with increasing adequacy meet the basic needs for food, clothing, shelter, the care of the sick and disabled, is, like our governmental and our professional organizations, manipulated by individual personalities for these highly personal, emotional needs and can therefore minister to social needs only incidentally. As Veblen pointed out, it is not so much the share of income and goods and services taken by the owners that is so significant socially, but the subordination of these instruments and productive capacities to the personal aims of the owners striving to solve their personality problems in business and politics.

Our present day "capitalism," underneath the imposing façade of its rituals and symbols and behind its ruthless, antisocial exploitation of instruments and men, appears as one more, in a long succession of socially sanctioned practices whereby the accumulated resentments, the urgent desire for retaliation, the drive for discharge of hostility and aggression, and the imperative need for release of tensions have been institutionalized. Each generation in this "capitalistic" society creates in its children the basic emotional needs that, depending upon the rigidity or mobility of stratification, insure perpetuation of that society: each group or class, with varying emphasis, implements its children with the ideas, beliefs, values, training in skills, and share of power and control that it cherishes. Class interests, like their learned patterns, are inculcated by parents in their children to become an integral part of the personality and its expression, so that no one usually questions them. Occasionally, however, an individual fails to conform to his class or family background. In the United States the opportunities for competitive striving have been, until recently, so varied that many, through acquisition of property, power, or skill, have moved to another class, in the standards of which their children have been reared. This hope for economic advancement has been, until recently, a persistent consolation and also a spur to competitive struggling.

We can observe the same personality expressions in the preceding social arrangements of our Western European culture where aggressive individuals used the prevailing institutions, as in feudalism, monarchy, or military and other dominating practices to coerce, defeat, or exploit others.

The question that then demands examination is, how far can we find differences in the cultural patterning and parental attitudes among the several more or less differentiated social classes that would give clues to the differences in personality constellation and in conduct that we see in our present social life. Or to put the question in the terms of this discussion, how far can we find differences in cultural coercion and in personality distortions that bend and twist the culture, which will illuminate the social situation we face today with the acute social conflicts and increasingly sharp class struggles?

Needless to say the evidence for any definitive answer to this question is not now available, largely because such questions have not been asked by those interested in social studies, and when asked by the students of personality they have been put to only a limited number of cases and predominantly among the better favored classes. It is necessary, therefore, to rely upon indications and inferences that must be validated later by intensive research.

The most illuminating approach to the question of differences in child training is through the conception of stages and modes of response in the personality development in children. The significance of that scheme for this discussion is in its revelation of how certain persistent modes of behavior are established in the child by the way the parents handle the various functional activities of the infant and young child. There are three early modes—the receptive or taking in, the retentive or holding, and the releasing or extruding, with a later fourth mode, the penetrating or intrusive. In sucking and in being mothered and cuddled, the infant receives or takes in; in accumulating urine and faeces the infant retains or holds; and in evacuation of the bladder and bowels the infant releases or extrudes. These functional processes are the focus of parental training, since the mother is concerned with regularization of food intake and weaning and with toilet training, wherein by the timing of these cultural patternings and the manner of their application she will emphasize and often fixate one or more of these modes of behavior so that the receptive or retentive or extruding mode will be carried over into all later learning and adjustments. Moreover, it is to be noted that the infant will react both to deprivation or curtailment, and to indulgence or the prolongation of these functional processes, with persistent modes of response to his subsequent life experiences that we characterize by the usual terms for motives and dispositions.

Thus it appears that the infant who has had generous breast feeding and a benevolent weaning will face life with a benign, generous, and optimistic attitude or disposition, while the infant who has been denied adequate nursing and mothering and has been abruptly weaned will feel deprived, suspicious, and fearful and bear resentment that may be crystallized into active hostility and aggression.

Again it appears that the child who has been trained in continence of urine and faeces slowly and without pressure or punishment will yield control over his eliminations without anxiety or resentment, learning to release without conflict; but a precocious or harshly coercive training that forces the child, before physiologically ready, to release in response to the outside demands, will set up resistance, accentuate retention as a defensive response, and focus the child's behavior upon acquisitive and niggardly activities as symbolic or compensatory outlets for the denial of possession of his own eliminations.

These three modes of behavior—accepting, retaining, and releasing—are the primitive or elemental organic responses upon which the earliest cultural training is focused. They are also the three dominant modes of behavior that throughout later life give the individual's conduct its characteristic personal configuration and impulsion, since the child meets the successive steps in his socialization with these basic modes of response that create his selective awareness of, and idiomatic adjustments to, this cultural patterning.

The learning of the inviolabilities that, as described earlier, constitute private property and the sanctity of the person (of others and of the self) is to be seen as taking place with these earlier acquired modes of behavior response as fundamental in such learning. The child who feels deprived, fearful and suspicious, if not resentful, will receive the training to respect inviolability, with its continuous frustration and necessary inhibitions, with a different attitude or meaning from the child who feels that life is good and generous and that frustration of these later impulses is not a cruel and exasperating deprivation. The child who is concerned with retaining and acquiring will accept private property with a different attitude and meaning from the child who is not fixated upon those activities.

What we see in these early childhood personality trends is of great significance for the understanding of a culture and the differences in conduct observed in the several social classes in a culture, where the generally observed social patterns of inviolabilities (private property and sanctity of the person) and the generally available institutional practices of barter, sale, contract, employment, and other ritual-symbol procedures are differentially employed by members of each class. The most promising clue to these differential uses of the available social practices is in the differences of early childhood experiences which, as we have just indicated, will focus the individual's life interests and activities into various modes of behavior that enter into his later adult conduct in the institutionalized patterns.

From what is now known we can say that the prevailing folk patterns of child rearing among the proletarian class are: breast feeding with much indulgence and little of the rigid time scheduling prescribed by the pediatricians, deferred weaning except when a succeeding pregnancy forces the issue and a large amount of cuddling, handling, and attention, not only by the mother but by siblings, kin, and neighbors. Toilet training is usually casual and unforced, so that no great pressure is put upon the child to learn continence and no harsh punishment is administered for slow learning.

In the better favored classes where nurses and pediatricians set the patterns, where maternal care of the child is subject to much competition from social interests and is often transferred to a nurse, and where the women are less adjusted to their feminine, maternal roles, there is less breast feeding, less mothering and cuddling ("doctor says baby must not be played with"), and earlier weaning; also rigid training in toilet habits is started at an early age with continuous pressure to learn continence.

The contrasts, with many exceptions to the general class practices, indicate a greater indulgence and toleration of infantile functioning among the proletarian children than among the middle and upper class children who are more deprived and frustrated and earlier and more strongly regimented, often by nurses who provide little or none of the affection the child always needs, but especially requires, to make these deprivations tolerable. There is, therefore, a marked difference observable between the folk-proletarian class and the middle and upper class with regard to the prevailing practices of child training in feeding and eliminations and expressions of attention, affection, and mothering.

Let us examine other aspects of child rearing that have a profound influence over the life career of individuals because they establish the basic affective or emotional orientation of the personality and so supply the energetic factor or drive that, channelled by the modes of behavior, flows into the socially sanctioned practices of the culture. Every deprivation and frustration imposed on the child sets up tensions and evokes resentment that may be mitigated by affectionate mothering but, if not so alleviated, may be fixated as a persistent feeling tone toward life. The child thus treated will be fearful, tense, anxious, and resistant and, as increasing age makes possible the overt expression of these affective or feeling reactions, he will show them in resentment that with further provocation may become hostility. The world appears to such a child as an unfriendly and hostile world because of his own inner discomfort and distress, which he therefore projects upon the whole world and releases in resistance or active retaliation. By contrast, the child who has been indulged (not "spoiled") will feel the world as a genial, comfortable place, to be accepted and enjoyed with little resistance or resentment, despite the many prohibitions and requirements, and as offering opportunities for giving and receiving affection. It is the same common or public world but it has a different meaning and value and presents wholly contrasting aspects to these two personality configurations.

Every mode of behavior response is therefore expressed with the tension of these affective reactions that together make up the individual's world; in a very real sense each person "structuralizes his life space," imposing upon the surrounding situations and persons, the specific configurations and meanings that his life experience has given him as his design for living.

But there is another aspect of this childhood training that enters into the personality make-up and trends that is of major significance for our present discussion, namely, the child's basic attitude toward authority that emerges from his experience of deprivation and frustration, and which conditions his acceptance and conversion of outward prohibitions and requirements into inward inhibitions and compulsions. This development is to be viewed as a naturalistic event, involving no mystical entities or powers in the child nor implying any pre-potent force in the environment, but rather to be seen as the persistent modification of human behavior as experimentally demonstrated in animals.

Thirty years or more ago Triplett showed with perch that persistent frustration and blocking of their attempts to get at and eat minnows, by interposing a glass partition in the aquarium between the perch and minnows, would establish a learned response of not attacking those minnows when the glass partition was removed; moreover, the perch would swim to and along the line where the partition had been placed but would not cross such an imaginary line. The inviolability of the minnows was established in the learned behavior of the perch.

Every frustration and prohibition imposed upon the child (not arising from natural events) is the act of a person who directly

CULTURAL COERCION AND INDIVIDUAL DISTORTION   187

interposes between the child and the situation to which he would respond some form of barrier or blockade, thereby preventing the child's response. Continued repetition of this interference has the cumulative result of setting up an inhibition within the child who then may be exposed to the stimulus but will not respond (just as Triplett's perch learned to inhibit their response to the freely accessible minnows). This, as previously described, established observance of the inviolabilities of things and persons, known as private property and sanctity of the person, and establishes the basic repressions of impulses, rage, anger, and sex. It is evident that the observance of these inviolabilities is a learned form of inhibition, just as the performance of the required acts of manners and etiquette and duties is a learned form of compulsion, since the situations and persons evoking these forms of conduct are not themselves the natural, biological stimulus to such behavior but become effective stimuli when presented by another person who defines situations culturally and directs those responses.

What makes the child conform by inhibition or by compulsive response is the personal intervention of the parent or teacher who defines the situation and exacts the prescribed conduct, using either persuasion and affection that the child wants, or coercion with greater or less physical pain. If the tuition in these required patterns of conduct is administered with gentleness and reassurance the child learns the required conduct without a feeling of resistance, resentment, hostility, or aggression; authority for that child becomes an unquestioned aspect of all orderly patterns of behavior. There is little or no conflict between the required action (positive or negative) and the feeling tone or effective response that the parental demand evokes, since the child wants and receives affection from the parent who requires that conduct. If, however, the teaching is given harshly, with scoldings, punishment, and other means of arousing fear, anxiety, and resentment, and if no affection is offered as consolation for the deprivation or reassurance for the required conformity, then the child may exhibit the required conduct (refraining from acting or performing what is demanded), but he does so with a feeling tone or affective response that conflicts with his actions. The powerful overbearing parent becomes the symbol of an external authority that threatens and coerces, to be questioned, challenged, or evaded, while every situation arouses a conflict that makes life precarious and disorderly. The child under such tuition may become overtly hostile and aggressive or restrained only by immediate or threatened punishment, or consistently cowed and submissive, yielding through fear but inwardly rebellious.

It is evident that in these experiences of authority the mother may and often does play the role of affectionate teacher while the father plays the role of coercive controller, offering little or no affection or reassurance but demanding unquestioned and unrewarded obedience, or punishment for disobedience. Thus authority is essentially the affective power of situations, projected thereon by the child from the experience of parental training. If that training is alternately affectionate and coercive or if the demands made by the parents are inconsistent and capricious, the child's response to authority may be confused and intermittent, although it may happen that the indulgent affectionate mother may so effectively balance the stern, demanding father that the child can apportion his conduct between the two phases. When both parents vary from day to day in what they demand and in tenderness and severity, the child lives in continual perplexity and uncertainty and cannot adjust to authority.

The authority response then is of basic significance for the adult's social life, since he brings to his mature years the feeling tone or affective reactions established in his childhood, and these enter into his responses to all the authoritative relations he encounters, toward teachers, leaders, supervisors and employers, police, courts, government, and the many informal but meaningful hierarchal relationships of recreation and social life.

The predominant authority response of the proletarian is submissiveness, with characteristic outbreaks of delinquency, disorderly conduct, and futile but symbolically meaningful rebellions that reflect the lack of consistent demands in his early training. This we see arising from the stern, often brutal prohibitions and punishments applied to proletarian children, with awful sanction of religion to strengthen the parental hand and force submissive acceptance, with only occasional revolt in early years but general antagonism toward parents later. Aggression appears only when safe, that is, when immediate restraint is absent or the gang support dispels fear of punishment. The variations in the parental demands and their enforcement also are shown by the child's selec-

CULTURAL COERCION AND INDIVIDUAL DISTORTION 189

tive obedience to some requirements and ignoring or flouting others.

Because the child, in crowded homes, is less sheltered and curbed in sex curiosity and practices, sex is less of a source of conflict, but also less of a focus of life endeavor than in the individual who has been shielded and filled with repressions. Also the proletarian child has greater freedom to express emotional responses to life at the moment of impact and hence carries less pent-up affect for discharge elsewhere. The proletarian child, therefore, is less liable to be a neurotic, suffering from repressions that seek outlet in disguised fashion, but is more disposed to submissive conduct so long as directly supervised, with misconduct whenever released from adult supervision. He is also more inclined to use sly and indirect, obstructive actions or sabotage, to express his hostility because he dare not show aggressive behavior openly. Moreover, not being dominated by the acquisitive, retentive mode, he is not inclined to those activities of money-making, property getting, and the prudential calculations of the business man. In so far as he has had generous breast feeding and mothering that have given him a persistently receptive mode toward life he is inclined to accept life without feeling anxiety about tomorrow or an eagerness to strive competitively for advantages; life comes and brings its fruits and God will provide.

To this characterization there are exceptions because only in a highly stratified society is there a consistent pattern of child rearing and parental attitudes. The important point to note is that from the viewpoint of personality development and expression, a uniformity of class conduct and feeling can exist only in so far as there is a uniformity of child rearing and authority responses, with one or more of the modes of behavior predominating. Adult life experiences such as living in the same neighborhood with similar housing, working under similar conditions of hours, effort, pay, and discipline may generate a group uniformity of conduct; but without the basic emotional or affective reactions to life, derived from early childhood, that alone can give unity to a group, there can be no class consciousness and hostility to another class unless the latent but repressed hostility in the individual can be aroused and evoked into aggressive group behavior. Lacking this stimulus and without the protection of a group of like-feeling individuals who will react together and thus permit the repressed hostility to be exhibited, the characteristic submissiveness to authority and acceptance of limitations, of income, and possessions, will be the prevailing conduct, largely because the underlying feeling tone toward life, derived from breast feeding and mothering will prevent any strong resentments and will foster an attitude of cheerful acceptance. The occasional individual who rises from the group and becomes an economic or political power has found a way to express his hostility to authority by aggressive, competitive striving within the framework of the socially sanctioned institutional patterns.

In the middle and upper classes the retentive, acquisitive mode of behavior is frequent because of early toilet training, and inadequate breast feeding that makes the individual feel he must strive for life; the feeling of resentment is common because of the denial of breast feeding and mothering; the attitude toward authority is ambivalent because the frustrations and compulsions have been administered by the otherwise preoccupied parents with indulgence that has undermined or tempered their occasional stern discipline. This ambivalent attitude toward authority may be seen in later life as the individual initiative and enterprise of "rugged individualism" that challenges the existing arrangements and obstacles that others of equal ability but less aggressiveness accept. Moreover, this ambivalent attitude toward authority gives the individual the opportunity for independent activity that others who are either openly hostile or submissive dare not take alone, but only when accompanied and reinforced by their group.

This individual initiative and independent striving are, however, channeled by the retentive acquisitive mode of behavior into property getting and control so that it necessitates defeat and exploitation of others whenever possible.

It is significant that the leaders of social life come so often from this middle group that has escaped from the submissiveness of the lower group and has been untouched by the complacence of the upper group, which instills rigid obedience to its authority but with equal emphasis upon its superior status and freedom from the necessity for achievement except in fields such as sport, where aggressive competition can be displayed without tangible rewards.

The upper-class group maintains its class position upon the basis of its freedom from the coercive necessities of life that compel others to work, strive, and struggle; hence they rarely furnish leaders for other than the sport, scientific, and artistic pursuits. Their concern is with protecting the privileged status and vested interests that support their superiority and, having property, they are concerned with questions of prestige that continually reinforce their class consciousness but do not arouse rebellion against authority.

The dynamics of social life and change may be seen in these several group attitudes and reactions to life. So long as the proletariat are submissive to authority, they accept their limited share of property and income and their limitation of opportunity. So long as the middle class has the ambiguous attitude toward authority, it will furnish leaders and strive for individual achievement against existing arrangements. So long as the upper class accepts authority but by its superior status and prestige teaches its children to exercise authority over others, it will show little submissiveness, few leaders, but many arrogant displays of complacent direction over the submissive and skilful manipulation of the rising leaders.

There is a subtle but pervasive change in the individual who finds himself no longer struggling against authority but in a position to compel or forbid others' behavior. The life experience of authority may prevent him from utilizing that authority except in arbitrary exhibitions that satisfy his previous hostility toward the authority he has reluctantly obeyed. It has been frequently remarked that the self-made man, who has risen from the bottom to the top, is usually harsher, more rigid and demanding, than those who have exercised authority longer; but occasionally, when the acquisition of property and income have been sufficient, he learns that prestige is desirable and can be bought by using his wealth for connoisseurship in arts, sports, and other fields for patronage.

Any attempt to attribute uniform patterns of child-rearing to the economic groups in this country is more or less futile because here the economic groupings do not conform to cultural groupings. Among the wage-earning, proletarian group, there are to be found representatives of diverse ethnic stocks, different religious faiths, and contrasting local traditions and environmental circumstances. The middle-class groupings are likewise heterogeneous, and while the upper class are more or less homogeneous they have been so largely recruited from the middle class and so recently that their homogeneity is limited to fashions in dress, sports, and style of living, except for a uniformly stubborn defense of their property, income, and privileges. But here again this defense is provided by the professional group who, as executives, bankers, lawyers, and politicians are employed to guard the position of the upper class against attack, and who do so because such employment is the most profitable and the most effective route upward.

What has escaped notice is the progressive extension of the middle class methods of child rearing to the proletariat through prenatal clinics, well-baby clinics, the supervision and teachings of mothercraft, home nursing, and other health programs. As these teachings, by pamphlets, lectures, public health nurse visits, and clinical advice are spread into the families of wage earners, the older traditions are replaced by practices of the middle class: reduced breast feeding and early weaning, earlier and more rigorous toilet training, less mothering and cuddling, and in general a trend toward more fixed routines and discipline of this early behavior with a beginning neurotic anxiety over health; but this is followed in childhood by more exposure to disorganized neighborhood life, with gang activities, deliquency, and sex offenses as the older community, moral training disintegrates with the passing of common neighborhood life. The mothers in wage earning families are employed more frequently than before, and this also is producing a change toward less baby care and mothering, so that the formerly receptive mode toward life is being displaced by a trend toward the retentive and acquisitive mode, and the feelings of resentment that approximate the middle-class configuration. Thus we see a change in child-caring methods, initiated in the name of child welfare, bearing unexpected fruit in the altered personality trends it fosters.

Perhaps the most important question to be faced is, what are the possibilities of changing our social life through modification of early child-rearing in the home and in nursery schools to minimize the personality distortions that now prevent social order.

(FROM: *Psychiatry,* 2 [1939]: 11-27.)

SIXTEEN

Freedom for the Personality

THE PROBLEM of freedom is one of the persistent perplexities that face every generation. As we look back and observe the gradual emergence of our present concepts and beliefs about freedom, it appears that freedom must always be relative to the climate of opinion, the sensibilities, and the immediate occasions which have stimulated both reflective thinking upon, and overt activities toward, the extension of the freedom enjoyed by individuals.

It is especially appropriate today to stress this evolutionary and relative aspect of freedom because we are now passing through one of the more acute phases of the continuous process of transition that has characterized Western European culture, and we need, therefore, the benefit of a long time perspective with which to see our present situation in its due proportions, and, above all, its scarcely revealed promise for the future. It is not intended, however, to essay an historical examination of the ideas of freedom for which others are more competent, but rather to indicate a way of approach to the discussion of human freedom and to emphasize another dimension to that problem that has been largely neglected, namely, the meaning of freedom for the personality.

We may perhaps gain the needed perspective for such an enterprise by rehearsing somewhat briefly the conditions that generate the problem of freedom for man, more especially for man within Western European culture.

We may therefore begin with a consideration of man and his culture, to use the term by which we designate the ideas, concepts, and beliefs, patterns of conduct and of feeling, and the many different kinds of signs, symbols, and rituals, together with the tools and techniques, that have served man as instruments for his uniquely human modes of life. It is only very recently that we have become aware of culture as these historically developed patterns which man has attempted to impose upon nature and himself in order that he might survive biologically and, more importantly, organize group life and regulate his conduct so that he could have what we call "social living."

As we have learned of other cultures and discovered how the same geographic world of nature and the same basic activities and functions of man have been so variously conceived, patterned, and ordered, we have become more keenly aware of our own culture, and have slowly begun to realize that we can see, think, speak, act, and feel only as our culture has given us the awarenesses, the concepts, the symbols, the patterns, and the sanctions. Our efforts today to understand what culture does to and for the individual are still handicapped not only by this relative unawareness of culture, but by the ancient idea of society as some mysterious, cosmic organization operating through superhuman, if not supernatural forces to which man must obediently submit; moreover, we have the long-established, historical tradition, carrying the most venerable and awful sanctions, that our basic concepts and beliefs and our culture derive from some supernatural origin which therefore renders them inviolable to inquiry or critical examination. We might hazard the suggestion that the twentieth century, and perhaps the major portion of the twenty-first century, will witness prolonged conflicts over the exigent questions concerned with culture: whether it is supernatural or humanly derived; whether it is susceptible to modification; and by what criteria the coming reorganization of Western European culture shall be directed.

Pursuing our immediate inquiry, we may say that man gained freedom from the demands and limitations of a primarily biological existence by and through the development of his culture: instead of being controlled by physiological functions which insistently drive all other species to pursue their fulfillment, man has learned to emancipate himself to a greater or less extent from the more exigent control of hunger, of eliminations, and of the acute emotional reactions which, if left unregulated, would leave him at the mercy of functions and impulse. Moreover, man has found through culture a way of enjoying a degree of freedom for his person and for his belongings by observing the inviolability of others, called

FREEDOM FOR THE PERSONALITY

the sanctity of the person, and of things called private property. This inviolability of the person has been of special significance because it has made possible man's freedom from the coercion of his own sex impulses and from exposure to unrestrained sex exploitation by others.

But culture has served not only as a way of managing man's own organic functions and impulses that would otherwise rule his existence with their imperious biological demands; culture has also provided man with the patterns of conduct whereby he could manage to live in groups, respecting the inviolability of the person and the property of others, sharing in that division of labor which tools and techniques make necessary, and, above all, finding in the use of group accepted and group sanctioned symbols, rituals, and institutional practices—such as contract, barter, courtship and marriage, and voting—the common modes of communication, negotiation, and person-to-person relationships. This human organization and group living should be sharply distinguished from the animal aggregations and communities which arise, as in the insects, from highly specialized, organic structures and capacities, which not only provide for the differentiated activities necessary to an organization, but likewise forever prevent any modification of that specialized form of community living.

This amazing service of culture to man is not limited, however, to his organic functioning or his group organization, but goes further in providing him with a way of conceiving and dealing with the world of nature that presents itself, precariously and problematically, offering the only resources for living, but at the same time threatening man directly by its own order, regularity, and complete disregard of values. Faced with such a world of nature, man has sought to allay his anxiety and find both reassurance and the more concrete patterns and sanctions for his relations to that world through the basic ideas and concepts that he has created for his commerce with nature. Through these ideas, which have at once recognized the enormity and seeming ruthlessness of nature, yet have given man both the courage and the approach to wrest his security from nature, we see how culture has enabled man to come to terms with the universe, not by accepting and submitting, but by creating his own realities.

At this point many of the discussions of human freedom have either paused or stopped, having shown that culture has enabled man to achieve a degree and range of freedom enjoyed by no other species, but only by accepting the exigent demands and coercive requirements of his culture that necessitate the surrender of his physiological autonomy, the regulation and modulation of impulse, and the observance of those innumerable restrictions upon conduct through which alone the inviolability and freedom of members of the group life become possible. These points cannot be too often reiterated nor too strongly emphasized because there is a persistent nostalgia for a mythical Golden Age when man was believed to have been completely free and unrestrained. As Santayana has acutely observed: "A passion for the primitive is a sign of archaism in morals," which, less felicitously, may be restated that those who have been bruised and distorted by culture yearn neurotically for a freedom that neither they nor others could ever enjoy, because it would mean a return to an infra-human level of existence and a denial of all aspirations and values which man, especially representatives of Western European culture, cannot repudiate except in the psychoses.

Thus we can not only support the foregoing position but perhaps strengthen these contentions with the further observation that the very conditions of human life, under the guidance and direction of culture, involve the acceptance of these persistent tasks of life, these recurrent responsibilities and burdens, and the continuing efforts to reach for that which is sought in human conduct. In the contemporary discussions one finds repeated exhortations to strive for an ever more rigorous objectivity as the only possible method of dealing with the confusion, perplexity, and conflicts of social life. Those who counsel such objectivity are seemingly unaware that it implies a return to a purely biological mode of existence, where natural processes and events present themselves as demands for biological responses that ignore all regulation, patterning, values, and aspirations, through which alone human life becomes significant. Moreover, no one who has grown up in an organized social life and has been inculcated with the selective awareness and the conceptual framework of his culture, could achieve complete objectivity if it were desirable. We can direct, and progressively we are mastering, the technique of scientific investigation, whereby we may reveal the order of natural events, of how spatial, temporal, and energy relations arise and reveal themselves through ongoing processes; but it must be evident, upon reflection, that

FREEDOM FOR THE PERSONALITY

our most rigorous scientific procedures disclose only the relationships of events to each other and cannot, and should not, attempt to determine what the meaning or significance of those relationships or that order of events should be for man himself.

Culture is an imaginative creation, a deliberate attempt, like the work of the artist, to give form, proportion, meaning, significance, and value to experience. It necessitates rearrangement, suppression, selection, and all the other discriminating activities with which the artist works in order to give dimensions and proportions, thereby helping us to become aware, not merely of the natural world surrounding us, but, more importantly, of the aesthetic configurations which come from the artistic imagination and sensitivity and, above all, the courage and daring to create something that is more meaningful than nature itself.

If the foregoing offers a valid basis for a discussion of human personality and conduct, we may point out some of its major implications for the question of freedom for the personality.

The historic conception of human nature and conduct has always stressed man as a rational animal, as one who can and does use reason as a guide to conduct, weighing situations and alternatives and choosing among them in accordance with various criteria, among which has been predominantly recognized that of self-interest. This psychological theory of motivation and of conduct has received its fullest expression and elaboration in theology, in law and the various social theories where the autonomy of human conduct is assumed as a basis for ethics—the legal rules regulating the individual's rights, titles, obligations, and interests—and as an explanation for the observed behavior of man in his economic, political, and other social activities.

As we look back over the historic development of the Western European cultures, as expressed in the different ethnic or nationalistic groupings that make up the shifting political units of Western Europe, it is evident that in different periods and in different countries there has been a continuous struggle among different groups within the populations over the limitations that might be imposed upon the individual's action, speech, and belief. Our major preoccupation has been, therefore, with these overt aspects of individual activity and the guarantees against restraint upon or interference with action, speech, and belief. The underlying assumption has been that rational man, given the opportunity and left unfettered by social constraints, can and will exercise his right to act, to speak, and to believe in such ways as will bring him individually what is essential to human life and dignity, and will insure a social life that will foster a rational human mode of existence.

To say that the foregoing represents the basic assumptions upon which the Western European societies have proceeded for many generations is not to offer any pronouncement but rather to indicate a way of interpreting our historical development and of revealing the preconceptions with which many of our present-day discussions of freedom are conducted.

These statements will also serve as an effective background for further discussion of freedom that contrasts sharply with this official, rationalistic conception.

If we recall the process of culturation and of socialization through which the child is made a participating member of his culture and of his society, it will be remembered that at every stage in this process adults are engaged in the systematic interference with, and redirection of, the basic biological or mammalian pattern of functional activity and the inculcation of the amazingly complicated beliefs and concepts and patterns of conduct and feeling with which the young individual is enabled to live in the common public world that his culture has selectively organized for the guidance of its members. The surrender of physiological autonomy by the young infant occurs when he accepts these interferences and, above all, the deprivations required by him in weaning, toilet training, and management of impulses and emotions. Moreover, the basic social patterning of his conduct necessitates his learning to inhibit his impulsive behavior toward other persons and things so as to respect their inviolability and also learning to perform the many prescribed actions deemed essential to his or her sex, class, rank, status, and other social obligations. These deprivations and frustrations, these inhibitions and coercions, beginning at birth or shortly after, arouse anxiety which colors the private idiomatic world which the child constructs from such experiences. If these early experiences make the child feel the world is threatening and hostile, he can only build his private world accordingly; if they are reassuring and comforting he can develop confidence in the world as hospitable and benevolent and create his private world with those meanings.

FREEDOM FOR THE PERSONALITY

What is of greatest significance is that these lessons in socialization create persistent affective reactions or feelings toward life which direct the child's subsequent experience and control his later learning. So long as we think of human conduct in terms of rational processes and volition and recognize only the so-called conscious memory of what can be verbalized, it is difficult to realize how coercive these early experiences are and how these initial feelings toward life dominate the individual's whole life career. When we see human conduct as arising from the selective awareness, the persistent affective set or expectation toward life, then we can better understand the dynamic process of human personality and conduct.

Just as we have learned in physics and chemistry, and now in biology, that the previous experience of any energy complex continues to operate in the present because the past experience is not out in some mysterious realm, but is just this persistent modification of the energy complex that continues to operate in the present; so in the consideration of human conduct we are beginning to see that these early experiences of childhood, when the infant is just beginning to construct his private world and to organize those patterns of feeling that will be coercive over subsequent experience, continue to operate in every attempt the child makes to order events, to organize experience, and to learn to regulate his conduct.

We may point out here how the traditional concept of man as a rational animal, whose every action arises from deliberate volition, stands in the way of our accepting this viewpoint towards human conduct, but we shall see that, without a conception of the coercive role of early experience, human conduct remains inexplicable and continues to baffle every effort to achieve any measure of the social order we so desperately need.

If we recall, therefore, how these early experiences initiate a continuous process wherein the child meets every new situation with the expectation and the feeling engendered by his past experience, then we may see how not only this early physiological training, but all the subsequent lessons in learning the inviolabilities, in accepting the socially required compulsions, are but a continuation of the same process of coercive and often distorting experience to which the child submits because he must, but which gives rise to a private world of inner thoughts, beliefs, and feelings that rarely if ever become apparent. We need only pause to recall how our own personal lives are led in terms of this inner monologue and that constant interplay of feelings which, with adult years, we have learned to hide so adroitly behind the outer mask of adult conformity and seeming poise.

Where these considerations lead is to a progressively clearer conception of the personality as this dynamic process of organizing experience, so that every situation, person, and event is fitted into the patterns which the official culture and the social requirements have prescribed, but always with that bias and distortion, that selective awareness and those peculiar feelings that our individual life experience has made the basic dimensions of our private world. We spend our days preoccupied with the effort to maintain this private world, like the spider, carefully repairing its web after each shock or invasion, and never relaxing our vigilance in every personal encounter, which we assess either as reinforcing or threatening this inner, private world. Caught in this private world we can only rarely understand the private world of another or fumblingly communicate. As Thomas Mann has so well expressed it in *Joseph in Egypt:*

The world hath many centres, one for each created being, and about each one it lieth in its own circle. Thou standest but half an ell from me, yet about thee lieth a universe whose centre I am not but thou art.

Here it becomes appropriate to point out that whatever the social life may afford in the way of opportunities for the individual to think, believe, and act, are of necessity either limited or extended by this highly individualized and personalized acceptance and utilization of such opportunities. Again the historical tradition of rationality serves to obscure what is so clearly shown in all our conduct as we see individuals in little groups accepting and rejecting what their society and their communal life offer, always in terms of the very idiomatic patterns of their special orientation. For each of these cultural and social variations there is usually a well articulated statement of justification, often expressed in the form of a vigorous polemic against those whose patterns of life differ, and always with the invocation of whatever sanctions are utilized by that group from among the many available in their culture.

FREEDOM FOR THE PERSONALITY

It has been the boast of the so-called democratic societies, and it has been a special characteristic of Western European culture, that between the recurrent periods of oppressive intolerance, it has offered the widest range of variation to individuals and to such subcultural groups; when heresy hunting has been rife, Western European culture has been torn by internal conflicts over these variant sects, but there is still discernible a long-term, secular trend toward the progressive toleration of deviants.

When we consider, however, the personality aspects of this situation, our perspective on this historical process and our approach to the present-day perplexities and conflicts are shifted rather sharply. What we begin to realize is that however much a society may offer the possibility of individual variation, and, more specifically, may guarantee what we call "freedom" of action, speech, and belief, nevertheless, each individual, with the personality process he has developed through his life experience of socialization, can utilize that freedom only as his personality organization will permit. Instead, therefore, of interpreting human conduct in terms of rational considerations and the exercise of freedom, we are called upon to see each individual as engaged in doing what he must, because his life experience will permit him only to be aware of and to act as that past requires. We are, to phrase it tautologically, what we are, because we have been what we have been.

Yet even this statement of how the individual is coerced by his past experience so that he can only think, believe, and act as it dictates yields but a partial insight into human conduct and personality expression, because more coercively than the patterning of action by past experience is the pervasive distortion of all human conduct by those persistent, affective reactions that arise in childhood and continue to operate throughout our whole life careers. As the individual has been reared in early childhood, so will his personality process and his affective reactions to life operate, and will continue to operate, scarcely modified by any process of reason or other control so long as the individual has no awareness of how these affective processes are operating in his personal life.

We can see how this takes place by looking at the concrete situations in our lives today. Thus we are confronted with the pathetic picture of individuals who in their early childhood have been unnecessarily deprived, frustrated, and coerced and so have built up a private world which is forever insecure and threatened; hence they must react with resentment and hostility to every experience. Within their own private world are continually operating these strong feelings of resentment and hostility, which may be expressed in overt reactions against people or may operate as a subtle distortion of everything they do, leading to constant sabotage and destruction, always within a range that protects them from retaliation or official punishment. Again we see how the early childhood experiences of being socialized by those who exercised their authority brutally have created a persistent resentment toward all authority, so that throughout the life of the individual so humiliated there is a constant endeavor to thwart, if not to challenge, everyone in positions of authority or control. Again all through the early experiences of childhood, the young child, who is striving to meet the demands made upon him, is under constant tension which is crystallized into a persistent anxiety about his own competence and functional adequacy, so that he goes through life obsessed by anxieties that may become focussed upon the most extraordinarily irrelevant activities and events or upon his own bodily functions; he acts as one who is compulsively directed to perform actions that are either absurd or obstructive to the common life or are disturbing to his physiological processes. Perhaps the most frequent of all these personality distortions are the persistent feelings of hostility that become channelled into a constant endeavor to "get even," to prove that one is not as worthless or as wicked as one has been made to believe, or to retaliate for all the humiliations and brutalities of the past. Then too there are the individuals who, in spontaneous exercise of those activities common to all young mammals, have transgressed the moral code of their elders, and have been overwhelmed with reproach and punishment that have established a persistent feeling of guilt, for the atonement of which they spend their adult lives.

Thus we might go on enumerating many different forms of persistent, affective reactions that color and distort the personality, driving the individual to engage in the most astonishing varieties of activities that bring little or no satisfaction of basic human needs and aspirations but nevertheless are exhibited by the individual because this coercive past experience forces him to their performance. If the recital of these seems to be predominantly unwholesome, destructive and, to use the term that has become

FREEDOM FOR THE PERSONALITY

progressively meaningless, "abnormal," it is not to signify that human nature is, in accordance with the theological tradition, innately wicked, sinful, antisocial, and destructive, nor is it to ignore or deny the acute hunger of every individual for love and affection, to be accepted and cherished as a person of some worth and consequence to others. The insistence on these distorted and destructive affective reactions is only a recognition of their greater frequency, eloquent testimony of what Western European culture does to and for the personality of the growing child who is terrorized, humiliated, and often brutalized while being socialized. There are other cultures in which children are not terrorized, humiliated, and brutalized, are not filled with persistent feelings of anxiety and guilt, of hostility and resentment, because the process of acculturation and socialization is conducted with affection, tenderness, and benevolent patience that recognizes that the young human mammal can be brought within the range of social requirements only through a warm, cherishing nurture; and it is to be observed that in those cultures where the socialization of the child is conducted in this manner, the social life is not disrupted by the aggressive, destructive, exploitive individuals from whom Western European culture has suffered for so many centuries.

In every culture the individual is of necessity "cribbed, cabinned, and confined" within the limitations of what his culture tells him to see, to believe, to do, and to feel, the limitations which man can never escape because he can only live in a cultural world which he himself creates and imposes upon himself. But within the range of these limitations the individuals who have been benevolently reared and wisely and patiently socialized may and apparently do possess that freedom which only the undistorted personality can enjoy.

It is becoming evident that every culture fosters a dominant character structure or socially preferred pattern of life and of expression, in and through which the individual expends his energies and finds some release for his own anxieties and guilt. Likewise each culture creates the peculiar distortions of personality which the group sanctioned methods of socialization produce in the child. The bearers of this official character structure and of these personality distortions are the active agents in the social, economic, political, and other activities of the group. We may therefore regard the social conflicts and disorders as essentially symptoms of the cultural traditions of the group and of the character structure and personality expressions of its members.

This discussion has led us rather far from the present preoccupation with forms of government, laws, and the innumerable complications of contending groups and individuals. As we have examined the process of acculturation and of socialization and attempted to trace the emergence of the personality as itself a dynamic process of organizing experience and of reacting affectively to life, these contemporary issues have become progressively attenuated from their positions as major foci of interest, and have become symptoms of the basic, underlying conflicts of Western European culture and of the unhappy, distorted, and perverted personalities it fosters. We begin, then, to realize how our need for social order and our aspirations toward the enduring human values are continually frustrated and destroyed by these distorted personalities who are driven by their private worlds to seek release for their intolerable feelings and warped ideas and beliefs.

So long as we were at the mercy of supposed, coercive social organizations, viewed as a part of a cosmos operating through mysterious social forces, above and beyond man's reach or control, to which he must submit, and so long as we viewed our culture as having been given us from supernatural sources and therefore to be accepted without critical inquiry or questioning, and so long as we conceived of human nature as innately predetermined according to theological tradition, and expressed through conduct rationally directed, just so long did the fate of man appear tragically determined. In the face of these cosmic immensities and these unchangeable verities, what could man do but cherish the wisdom of the past that taught him how best to protect himself in a world of that construction? Even though modern science has banished many of the larger terrors and superstitions which had for so many ages dominated man's thinking and beliefs, it has still left him at the mercy of these cultural and social and psychological beliefs that have so completely governed his attempts at ordering group life and individual expression.

Today we are faced with the prospect that is so extraordinary in all its implications that we have scarcely the courage to examine them. We now begin to see that culture is an historical creation of man himself—not a supernatural structure imposed on man, but rather the product of his own efforts to order events, organize group life, and regulate conduct in accordance with the sensibilities and the aspirations which he himself has created for the guidance of his own life. Social life, instead of being a cosmic organization, operating by inexorable laws and forces, likewise is being revealed as an historical creation, arising from man's efforts to meet the persistent tasks of life to which each generation addresses itself in terms of the ideas, conceptions, beliefs, patterns of conduct, and, above all, the sensibilities and feelings that are operating in their lives. Finally, we are beginning to see that the human personality emerges as the individual's way of life, his peculiar, idiomatic way of ordering events and organizing experience, and reacting affectively to situations and people as a direct consequence of how he has been acculturated and socialized. Thus the conception of human freedom becomes not mainly an issue of overt action, speech, and expressed beliefs, but rather freedom from the personality distortion and the destructive affects which make this overt freedom an ironic tragedy, since the individual may be compelled to use those possibilities not only for destruction of others, but for his own frustration and defeat. The acute irony of this situation is in the incalculable damage inflicted upon human life by these unhappy personalities whose warped, twisted lives are derived from their childhood when love, affection, patience, and understanding of human needs would have made different personalities.

So long as we are coerced by these persistent affective reactions of anxiety, of guilt, and of hostility we do not enjoy freedom, however much we are unrestrained by external limitations upon our actions, speech, and belief. We are not only dominated by these feelings which we rarely recognize or acknowledge, but we are at the mercy of those who, by playing upon these feelings, can use and exploit us as they wish. We can see this more clearly in the dictator states, but also in the democracies where we are becoming aware of how the citizens are skillfully manipulated by political and other leaders, who cynically provoke these repressed feelings in order to control their voting. Indeed, political strategy is based upon the solid expectation that the individual will always sacrifice or forego his own advantage and even his basic requirements in order to express his warped personality distortions and release his otherwise repressed feelings.

In the light of these considerations and insights we may begin to reformulate the problem of freedom as more than freedom to act, speak, and believe, as we recognize the imperative necessity of freedom for the personality from these distortions and destructive affects which so coercively dominate the individual's life, compelling him to utilize his freedom of action, speech, and belief so largely for self-defeating and socially destructive expressions.

We can and must undertake this reformulation and accept the new tasks it sets because we are, somewhat reluctantly, realizing that the democratic aspirations cannot be realized nor adequately expressed in and by voting and representative government; democracy, or the democratic faith, is being reformulated today in terms of the value and integrity of the individual, not as a tool or means, but as an end or goal for whose conservation and fulfillment social life must be reoriented. Indeed, democracy reveals its essential meaning only as we see it as a continuous assay of our culture and of our society in terms of its human consequences — of what they do to and for human life and personality. Thus freedom for the personality may be viewed as the crucial issue of a democratic society, for which we must seek to develop individuals who can accept all the inhibitions and requirements necessary to group life, without these distortions and coercive, affective reactions. Only then will we discover what human freedom means and how to achieve the persistent human values we have for so long vainly sought.

(FROM: *Psychiatry*, 3 [1940]: 341–49.)

SEVENTEEN

Two Tasks of Education

WHEN we turn to the task of refashioning the educational process into a means for developing intelligence, we are faced with a temptation that has frequently brought reformers to grief. If the existing practice of educators fails lamentably to develop more than a regimentation in obsolete ideas and beliefs, let us create a new set "nearer to the heart's desire." The effect of this substitution is to establish a new pantheon of educational gods against which later reformers will in their turn revolt. Thus the merry game goes on, and every movement toward emancipation is compromised and perverted into a scheme for perpetuating what is, at the moment, satisfying.

The path of educational development is strewn with obsolete panaceas, and we can scarcely hope to escape from contributing to the same intellectual refuse heap. For even our most rigorous thinking is all too subtly infected with the preconceptions of our age, which, like the unseen eggs of the parasite, ripen with time into agencies of destruction. If we be aware of this danger, however, we may somewhat diminish its potency by a sort of mental prophylaxis, for which nothing is more effective than the historical perspective.

When we consider the fairly recent development of science or, more particularly, of applied science and engineering, we cannot fail to be impressed by its extensive activities in what we loosely term the control of nature. This control has been the product of a continuous effort to bring what was a desultory, intermittent occurrence into the realm of occurrence at need. The movement from Franklin's kite, tapping the irregularly recurring electrical energy of a storm, to the ever ready light upon my desk, is a movement from the spasmodic and fitful to the continuous and dependable.

Somewhat the same task confronts the educator. At intervals in the history of man intelligent behavior has made its appearance, painfully circumscribed by the inherited culture of the day, but nevertheless, within the limits of its activity, addressed to the actual world or the portion thereof with which it was immediately concerned. To make intelligence a dependable and steadily functioning activity is the goal of education. But how shall we approach such a task and what means shall we employ to accomplish it?

But first we must make our peace with the psychometrists whose assertion that intelligence is born, not made, we can scarcely deny. Though we grant their contention, we may still maintain that native intelligence may be, and is, hampered and thwarted, chiefly by social life and the process of formal schooling, and that it is the office of education to assist in the emancipation of intelligence.

Some help may be obtained from a consideration of the nature of thinking, of reflection leading to intelligent behavior, which is generated by difficulties, troubles, and doubts. When habit and custom no longer suffice to carry us through the exigencies of life, we are forced to take stock of the situation, to consider its possibilities, to rehearse various responses with a view to discovering a way out of our troubles (see Dewey's *Human Nature and Conduct* and his earlier *How We Think* for an exposition of this instrumental logic). But difficulties alone will not engender thinking; all too frequently they but foster a genial phantasy which only allays our incertitude. Man has been faced with a precarious world since he first was man, yet only occasionally has he made an advance in the solution of his perplexities.

When we inquire into the circumstances which attended those advances, the situation, in the words of Professor Teggart (*The Processes of History*), appears to be thus:

> The conclusions arrived at so far may be summarized in the statement that definite advance has taken place in the past when a group, forced from its habitat, ultimately by a change in climate, has been brought into collision with another differing from it considerably in culture, and has remained upon the invaded territory . . . In short, the change that leads to advancement is

mental. What, then, is of importance to notice is that when enforced migration is followed by collision, and this by the alien occupancy of territory, there ensues as a result of the conflict the breaking down or subversion of the established idea systems of the groups involved in the struggle. The breakdown of the old and unquestioned system of ideas, though it may be felt as a public calamity and a personal loss, accomplishes the release of the individual mind from the set forms in which it has been drilled, and leaves men opportunity to build up a system for themselves anew. This new idea-system will certainly contain old elements, but it will not be like the old, for the consolidated group, confronted with conflicting bodies of knowledge, of observances, and of interpretations, will experience a critical awakening, and open wondering eyes upon a new world . . . human advancement follows upon the mental release of the members of a group or of a single individual from the authority of an established system of ideas. This release, in the past, has been occasioned through the breaking down of previous idea systems by prolonged struggles between opposing groups which have been brought into conflict as a result of the involuntary movements of peoples . . . throughout the past, human advancement has, to a marked degree, been dependent upon war. From this circumstance, many investigators have inferred that war is, in itself, a blessing—however greatly disguised. We may see, however, that this judgment is based upon observations which have not been pressed far enough to elicit a scientific explanation. War has been, times without number, the antecedent of advance, but in other cases, such as the introduction of Buddhism into China, the same result has followed upon the acceptance of new ideas without the introductory formality of bitter strife. As long, indeed, as we continue to hold tenaciously to customary ideas and ways of doing things, so long must we live in anticipation of the conflict which this persistence must inevitably induce.

From the above, the suggestion stands forth that more intelligent behavior has appeared fortuitously and fitfully, as electrical energy is generated and emitted from the clouds. But if the analysis be sound, the way is indicated for producing intelligent behavior more consecutively, for evidently the process is one we can control and produce at will. We need not, like Elia's mythical Chinaman, burn down the house for our roast pig, nor rack the world with mischief-making war to evoke intelligence and human advance. But we may plan our education so that the ideas, conceptions, and beliefs which shackle intelligence are subject to the same devastating effect that war so meagerly and at such a cost brings to pass. We may, in brief, construct an *educational "equivalent of war."*

It is one thing to devise a solution for our difficulties; it is another to discover the means for its execution. And however appealingly the new may summon us to its support, we still must live and operate in a world of established institutions and fixed habits of behavior buttressed by the idea systems we would destroy.

And yet the situation is not entirely lacking in possibility of change. Just as the Supreme Court assumed the office of interpreting the Constitution and thus became an agency for perpetuating the ideas of the 18th century, so the schools and colleges have become the bulwarks of our institutions, the deliberate instruments for a social coercion of intelligence. While this condition is not peculiar to our times, the necessity for divorcing the schools from this institutional safe-keeping is, perhaps, more urgent today than ever before. The world has need of intelligence far beyond the possibilities of its occurrence, and we must insist upon the schools' undertaking the work of emancipating whatever intelligence exists. As the President of Edinburgh University has remarked, "The history of human intelligence is a record, not so much of the progressive discovery of truth, as of our gradual emancipation from error."

The technique of this emancipation requires some consideration. Too frequently it is assumed that men may be freed from their beliefs by a process of logical refutation. This assumption ignores the nature of beliefs, as disclosed by their origin. For most beliefs are generated by the impact of circumstances with which we cannot deal; they are the attitudes we assume in the face of the unmanageable and unknown, which, given a verbal expression, we use to sooth our fears and quiet the doubts of ourselves and others. They are, in brief, things we live by which salve our frustrations. Often they operate, like martial music and war cries, to keep us tonic under misery, strain, and uncertainty. While ordinarily we apply the term psychosis only to certain forms of mental disorder with which the individual seeks to neutralize the acid of reality, yet it is only our solicitude for the normal or modal which blinds us to the fact that many of our political, economic, social, and patriotic beliefs, and our speculative social "science," to say nothing of our "culture," are genetically the same.

To dispel ideas of such a character no dialectical skill will suffice; we must supply the technique of dealing with the world and its difficulties for want of which the individual has recourse to beliefs; or, failing that, we must "psychoanalyze" the person, so to speak, whose idea systems we would disrupt. For such a treatment, we must show him the genesis in specific past situations and conditions of his ideas and of the social conceptions and beliefs which he shares; we must point out how his and others' earlier ideas were relinquished, not because they were refuted, but because they no longer were needed, and we must lead him to see that most of his personal difficulties and those of society are produced by these beliefs and assumptions, not by the actual events.

Unfortunately we have no tested practice or technique for the process, and until these have been experimentally developed, we can make little progress. Something, however, can be done in this direction by exposing the institutional factors in social conduct, by disclosing the role of archaic ideas in current thinking and speculation; and a great deal can be accomplished by pointing out how so many difficulties and problems are generated by mythical assumptions and conceptions. But the process to be employed is chiefly that of breaking down established habits and building up more intelligent behavior.

The most formidable obstacle to the inauguration of such an educational procedure is the almost universal desire to guard the young against a knowledge of their elders' ineptitude. To this may be ascribed that unformulated wish that a child be "a cross between an angel and an idiot," for we insist upon stunting the young and budding intelligence with the most preposterous ideas about human nature and rules of social conduct. While this is understandable it is, nevertheless, deplorable, since, to a world more than sufficiently complex and baffling as it is, we add the impediment of these special myths for children.

Adult education, being divested of its appealing novelty, appears quite simply to be an enterprise directed to the undoing of juvenile education, that is to say, re-educating the products of the existing school industry. This indicates that its proponents suspect the inadequacy of the orthodox school mythologies, but melancholy to relate, they propose, in large measure, merely to substitute the more recently invented fairy tales.

While it is an historical platitude that "the heresies of today are the orthodoxies of tomorrow," few realize that, in seeking to bring the schools up to date with the latest heresies in ideas and beliefs, they are but guaranteeing more surely the orthodox sentiments of the future. In the very nature of things we cannot discover the password to a future of final significances, since futurity implies significances and meanings yet to be wrought out by intelligence. The major social difficulties turn not so much upon the discovery of new facts as upon the disputed meanings we severally ascribe to the already familiar facts. Meanings are the consequences of activities and events, which our ideas and beliefs, being generated by ignorance, prejudge in the interests of our deficiencies. How then can an education, which is a preparation for a better future, thrive upon the exposition of our compensatory ideas?

So again we return to the point that the responsibility of education is for the emancipation of intelligence from the anachronistic beliefs we cherish and, on the positive side, for the teaching of those meanings, significances, and processes which our science has experimentally verified. When anything whatever is to be accomplished, processes have to be invoked that can be depended upon. To put into operation processes that will generate specific results is the method of intelligence.

To recapitulate, a reform in education that is to transcend the pathetic fallacy of viewing the present *sub specie aeternitatis* will envisage at least two tasks: first, the emancipation of intelligence from obsolete ideas, conceptions, and beliefs which, by their very nature, hamper intelligence in dealing with the world, and, second, the teaching of science as the method of intelligence whose cumulative findings give the major promise of a better future through a better knowledge of its control.

(FROM: *School and Society*, 15 [1922]: 655–59.)

EIGHTEEN

General Education

GENERAL education today is giving rise to considerable discussion and much controversy. Many of those engaged in educational work are almost openly resistant to proposals for the development of general education which they regard as a threat to professional purposes and standards. Others are attempting to channel the demand for general education into the support of their special interests and designs. In this situation there is need for some clarification of the aims and purposes of general education, as contrasted with the training that is usually provided in educational programs.

If we are to gain a better understanding of general education, we must see the need and the opportunity as arising from our contemporary cultural situation and its effects upon the growing individual. Thereby we can begin to realize that the demand for a program of general education is more than a desire for modernizing subject matter and pedagogical methods.

Formal education in the schools has been dominated largely by ideals of scholarship and scientific endeavor which have, so to speak, been pushed down from the graduate schools into the colleges, from the colleges into the secondary schools, and from the secondary schools into the elementary schools. Every step in the lengthening period of education, from the elementary school through to the university, has been regarded as essentially a preparation for the next step. The emphasis has been upon the mastery of subject matter and of skills, including the procedures known as scientific methods and the apparatus of scholarship. The imparting of knowledge that could be tested by examinations and standardized tests has naturally developed along with this emphasis upon mastery of subject matter. In consequence the changing interests and needs of growing students have been deliberately sacrificed to an ever-receding future competence which they were supposed to be approaching. In such a scheme of training, there has been no consideration of how these various subject matters might be integrated; indeed, the intent of most subject matter teachers has been to capture the student as a disciple for their particular fields and interests. In consequence, departmentalism has had precedence over the student's needs and so has increased his confusion.

The foregoing description of the educational situation is fairly familiar since it has been repeatedly stated by many educational critics. Their questioning of this process of training has, however, been regarded by those who are primarily committed to scientific or scholarly work and whose institutional position and personal security are bound up in the preservation of that program of training, as an attack on scholarship and academic standards and a threat to the maintenance of sound educational procedures. Therefore, so long as every critic of our educational tradition is regarded as an opponent of sound scholarship, the value of his criticism is necessarily diminished. It is imperative that those who are interested in general education should clearly distinguish their concerns from those that are embodied in a program of training for scholarship and scientific work. To do this, it is necessary to understand how the present urgent need for a program of general education has arisen.

The emphasis upon mental discipline and training in formal education has been fairly satisfactory because the general education of youth until recently was carried on by the family, the church, or the community, through which agencies the young received their introduction to the accepted ideas and beliefs, customs and practices of our culture. These cultural agents—family, church, neighborhood, and others impinging on the life of children and youth, are no longer able to provide the older general education, nor would it be of value if they could, since we are in a changing climate of opinion involving a far-reaching shift in the conceptual and ideological framework of our lives. This shift is so all-embracing that few, if any, aspects of contemporary life can escape. Because this involves the fundamentals of our thinking and values, it is of much greater significance than the more obvious social changes we so often discuss, such as urbanization, rapid transpor-

GENERAL EDUCATION 215

tation and communication, and the many other technological alterations in our industrial and living conditions. These physical and technological changes are modifying our habits of daily living and working, but the readjustments they demand are of minor significance as compared with the basic reorganizations necessitated by alteration in the climate of opinion, arising from our scientific and artistic exploration. To understand both the need for general education today and the major task of such a general education, we must seek a clearer understanding of these changes in our basic ideas and conceptions and realize how urgent is the need for illumination in the areas that are now so greatly confused.

In any culture, we find that the basic conceptions that underlie the whole framework of man's life are concerned with the nature of the universe, man's place therein, his relations to his society or group life and to other individuals, and finally his conception of human nature and of the self. The content and the sanctions of religion, of morals and ethics, as well as the fundamental character structure developed by a culture, are built upon and in turn express these conceptions. These ideas and conceptions may be said to constitute the world in which man lives since, under their guidance and patterning, he learns to see and think of the world of events and people. In a very real sense, they organize life for him by imposing upon the world of people, objects, and events a "structuralization of the life space," as Kurt Lewin has so well said, which gives his life its meanings, significances, and values and so controls his conduct.

At any one time in the history of a people there is a body of such ideas, beliefs, and meanings shared by almost all members of that culture, with minor variations and divergencies. These traditional ideas and beliefs may be regarded as the climate of opinion in which the people live, for they are immersed in them and are subject to them just as they are in a meteorological climate of their geographical region, looking upon it as normal and inevitable until travel or visitors teach otherwise. Throughout the world we find groups of people, each living in its cultural world built upon the locally held conceptions and beliefs of its climate of opinion. The existing records of comparative culture and studies of comparative religion provide ample evidence of how divergent are these cultural formulations.

The climate of opinion in which we live today is confused and disorderly, for we are witnessing the cumulative disintegration of the basic ideas and conceptions upon which Western European culture has been built. For over three hundred years astronomy has been undermining the older conception of the universe in which were embodied the idea of man's place in the scheme of things and the time perspective of Judaic-Christian theology. During the past hundred years, geology and, more recently, paleontology have accelerated this disintegration and have prepared the way for evolutionary biology to complete the destructive process.

Astronomy, geology, paleontology, and biology, jointly and severally, have rendered untenable the cherished cosmology and time perspective of our inherited religion and have undermined the traditional ideas of man's place in the universe and his destiny, with far-reaching consequences for the stability of our culture and for the character structure of our personalities. But this is only one aspect of the changing climate of opinion in which we live. Cultural anthropology has made us increasingly aware of our parochial conceptions of the individual's place in and relations to his society and group life and has revealed many other kinds of social order and different forms of family and social relationships. Through these studies of other cultures, we are beginning to see that the ideas and beliefs we have accepted for so long as the true and final statement of man's relation to his family and social group and therefore have cherished as the basis for our government and law are, indeed, only one variety of many such ideas and beliefs, and not necessarily the most humanly desirable. Thus we have sustained a terrific assault upon the fundamentals of our individual and group life from those cumulative scientific developments. In themselves they are sufficient to account for much of the widespread and growing confusion we see everywhere in Western European cultures.

But the crumbling of these foundations of belief about the world and extra-human sanctions is only one part of the disintegration we are witnessing. The ideas of human nature and conduct that have for so long governed man's relation to other individuals, especially within the family, and have formed his conceptions of the self, are being replaced by new insights and understanding provided by students of personality and mental hygiene. The ancient conviction of man's inborn wickedness or fall from grace and the belief in the depravity of human nature that necessitated

GENERAL EDUCATION 217

stern discipline and harsh, even terrorizing punishment to make him fit for society is being challenged from many sides. The belief in human volition is undergoing extensive revision as intensive studies are revealing the coercive role of past experience in the individual's conduct and his naïve unawareness of the needs, impulses, and desires that so largely impel him. These insights are providing an illumination of the persistent perplexities and aspirations in husband-wife, parent-child, and sibling relationships that are bringing far-reaching revision in our traditional ideas and beliefs. The increasing knowledge of man's own body and its functioning, as derived from his mammalian ancestry, has also rendered untenable the older ideas of a mind and a body and by so much have shown the inadequacy of previous conceptions of man's behavior, disease, and organic needs.

With these recent developments impinging upon our inherited body of ethical-moral beliefs and sanctions, it can be understood how bewildered youth is today. No longer can he with confidence and surety project goals and aspirations, nor create an ideal self that will resolve his conflicting needs and impulses and provide the guidance and sanctions he seeks. His impulses and aspirations are receiving a reorientation for which there is little historical precedent, and accordingly he is tragically confused and often self-defeating.

If we reflect upon these far-reaching shifts in our climate of opinion and consider what they signify for the immediate future of the individual and our society, we may begin to realize the nature of the educational task that we face. Scientific research for many generations has been largely destructive of the traditional ideas and beliefs upon which man's world and conduct have been built. This was inevitable and on the whole desirable, but we can and must consider what is to replace this older framework of ideas that scientific research is destroying. If we look back to the origin of these older conceptions, we will see that they were the products of the ideas and speculation of their time and as such were both valid and tenable. The Ptolemaic conception of the universe and of an anthropocentric world was founded upon the best evidence and clearest thinking then available. The conceptions of man's relation to his society and of his relations to other individuals and his conception of the self were developed by long and arduous reflection, as we may plainly see in the Old Testament and in Greek speculations. It seems almost axiomatic, therefore, to say that the scientific work that has destroyed the older framework of ideas must provide the basic ideas and beliefs for the new.

Thus, we come to the essential task of general education, which is the formulation and communication of the emerging new ideas and conceptions already implicit in our sciences and arts today that are to direct our future culture. This calls for an imaginative presentation, not of scientific facts or laws or methodologies, but of the larger meanings and significances of scientific research and of artistic insights.

For reconstituting our ideas of the universe we must draw upon astronomy for an enlarged and more awesome picture of the scheme of things, with an immensely greater time perspective for the past and for the future. The newer conception of an enlarged universe must also be viewed in the light of the ideas, now coming from modern physics and chemistry, of relative, contingent, and approximate understandings, that are replacing the older absolutes and certainties about nature and events. From geology, paleontology, and biology will come the newer ideas of the earth upon which we live and of the slow process of evolution through which have emerged the various organisms including the latest arrival, man. Here general education faces a fascinating but almost unique task, since it is not detailed knowledge of facts and figures, nor skill in using sources or techniques, nor mastery of current methodologies as in training future scientists. The essential task of general education is to convey the general ideas, meanings, and significances of these sciences to those who are in need of a new framework of beliefs and assumptions to replace those that have become obsolete. The need of youth and of adults is for coherent, interrelated ideas, conceptions, and meanings, a new frame of reference drawn from and solidly supported by scientific research, but presented so that they are meaningful and congruent. Without a firm conviction of the nature of the universe and man's place therein, human personality can find only a precarious foothold for the life career. Today especially we can see the devastating influence of doubts and confusion over these cosmological and biological beliefs as man is striving to reach a new conception of his place in an evolving world, as a late comer upon the scene, with an immense heritage of mammalian capacities and functions that he need not be ashamed of nor can ignore.

GENERAL EDUCATION

These altered views of man's place in the world must be accompanied by a revision, drawn from our growing scientific findings, of man's relation to his society and to other individuals, especially in the family, to provide a coherent basis for his conduct. The development of personality is dominated by now archaic ideas and beliefs which seriously imperil the stability of the individual's personality. Moreover, the conception of the self that forms the matrix of personality is now distorted and obscured by the conflict of older ideas and beliefs with more recent conceptions, thereby creating an urgent need for general education to help clarify these vital concerns with the help of the newer insights and the newer meanings coming from scientific and artistic explorations.

Here it is appropriate to point out that general education has the responsibility, not only of communicating the general ideas, conceptions, and meanings of recent scientific advances, but also of deliberately interrupting the continuity of the cultural tradition in these vital areas of belief and feeling wherein the individual needs to be emancipated from loyalty to archaic beliefs. We have accepted the necessity of freeing individuals from the ancient cosmology and non-evolutionary biology, but we are either indifferent to or timorous about the acute need of emancipation from ideas of human nature and conduct surviving from most ancient times that are now revealed as the source of most mental disorders and personality conflicts.

General education faces the task of rebuilding the older conceptual world (that is being destroyed by modern science) upon the emerging scientific ideas, conceptions, and beliefs of today and tomorrow. General education also must reconstruct the areas of ethical belief and conduct that have likewise suffered disintegration.

It is not unwarranted to say that the social, economic, and political difficulties of the next generation or two will be generated by the conflicts over the fundamental questions of man's relation to his group and the ideas of human nature and conduct that dominate his conception of the self. The conflicts and discords within nations and between nations, however expressed in terms of specific, practical, economic, and political issues will be essentially struggles over these ideas, some holding to the ancient doctrines, or their equally obsolete alternatives, others espousing one of the many emerging beliefs of today. Here we see the urgent need of a general education that will attempt to release men from the coercion of dead tradition and the confusion of blind groping for values.

Factual knowledge and scientific methods, in and of themselves, are largely useless for this general education, as we may plainly see in present day scientists and scholars themselves. If exact knowledge of scientific findings and procedures or training of the intellect were the answer to our educational needs, we would not find our scientists and scholars showing the same confusion and dismay as the non-scientific individuals. The man engaged in scientific or scholarly pursuits may be as incapable of understanding the meaning and significance of his discipline for human life as the untutored layman, because the very habit of mind and training in techniques needed for present day detailed research usually precludes such creative and reflective thinking. Moreover many of the tools of thought for reflective thinking come largely from the past which to a large extent we have to reject if we are to face up to the exigent questions presented by the new climate of opinion.

The historical parallel that suggests itself is the situation in Greece in the sixth and fifth centuries B.C., when the traditional ideas and beliefs of nature, government, and human conduct became increasingly unacceptable to the critical questioning that we know today as Greek philosophy. As a result of this criticism and exploration for new ideas and conceptions, the common life became increasingly disorderly and conflicting as older patterns lost their former cogency. Plato and Aristotle endeavored to meet the social and individual crisis by advancing new conceptions and beliefs and by projecting a new way of ordering events and conduct. Their labors introduced a climate of opinion that persisted until the beginning of modern times. Now we face the same task of reconstituting our conceptual world and of creating the new patterns of reflective thinking needed for that purpose, since we can rely neither upon the Greek ideas and conceptions nor their methods of thinking, but must courageously and imaginatively attempt for our time what they did for theirs. The persistent perplexities and aspirations of human life that were familiar to them confront us, but we must not evade our responsibilities by a nostalgic return to their formulations and procedures. As Santayana once remarked, "a passion for the primitive is a sign of archaism in morals," and, he might have added, of regression of intelligence and failure of nerve.

The sterility of our present educational programs for contemporary society is to be seen in the light of the foregoing, since it is just this insistence upon loyalty to the past and upon specific training in scientific and scholarly techniques and intellectual exercises that blocks a fruitful approach to general education. Training in scientific methods and scholarship requires a basic orientation in general education; indeed it is probable that until we provide this general education as a foundation, our future scientists and scholars will continue to be handicapped by conceptual confusion and frustrated by personal perplexities. Once we see clearly this *educational* task, we can undertake the *training* of scientists and scholars for their vocational tasks more realistically and effectively, thereby freeing general education from these dominant vocational concerns.

The general education for today must start with the science of today (not the science of the nineteenth century nor of the third century B.C.) and elaborate the conceptual framework that is the core or matrix of such education. But this is not purely an intellectual task, either in constructing or communicating that framework of ideas. It is primarily a task of creative imagination to interpret the human *meanings* of this new climate of opinion and the emotional significance of these new ideas, not the abstractions and quantitative results of scientific investigation. Thus we cannot rely upon a purely rational, logical procedure that didactically imposes these ideas and conceptions upon students. For this larger task of general education wherein ideas and beliefs and insights are to be communicated with an emotional tone, we must employ actual and esthetic experiences as the chief instrument of general education. Only through living, and the vicarious experience of art, can we communicate meanings and insights and develop new sensibilities.

If we will reflect upon the history of the older conceptions and beliefs we have held so long we will see that they were always presented in an emotionally toned setting, as in the family, church, and the neighborhood life from which they derived their great power and their emotional significance. Esthetic experiences are doubly important and necessary in general education because teachers generally do not and cannot show any genuine emotional interest in pupils who are so much in need of reassurance and emotional responsiveness, especially for this conceptual reorganization of general education. Esthetic experiences may provide for the pupil some of the missing emotional tone in his education.

The use of esthetic experiences as an educational procedure is so novel in pedagogy that most teachers are not only puzzled by the situation but emotionally disturbed by it. Their professional training and experience have been concerned with the explicitly verbal, rational type of learning in which their own emotional bias and responsiveness have been ignored and denied. It comes, therefore, as a shock to many to be confronted with the proposal to use novels, plays, poetry, moving pictures, radios, and such activities as projects and out-of-school trips, as the most important tools of general education. Yet in many of the experimental elementary schools and in nursery schools and a few colleges, exploratory work of this kind has been under way for some years.

Since the most crucial areas for general education are concerned with human relations (the individual's relations to others and his ideas and beliefs about himself and his conduct) it is especially important that novels, plays, "movies," and poetry be utilized, for only in the esthetic experiences they provide can we communicate the newer insights and the sensitivities so much needed by young people today. Only the artist, with his sensitive awareness to human perplexities and aspirations, and with the power of imaginative presentation, can speak effectively to the groping personality of the bewildered youth of today.

This points to one of the larger obstacles to the acceptance of such a program of general education. The scientist, the science teacher, and the scholar are trained to eliminate, so far as they *consciously* can do so, all emotion and feeling from their research; and hence in their teaching they strive to inculcate an objective and impersonal interest in their fields. Rarely do they realize (nor could they acknowledge it) that their own objectivity rests upon a prior, and usually unrecognized, emotional loyalty to their science, its teaching, and to certain basic concepts or postulates which few ever question. Moreover there are large numbers, perhaps the bulk of our population, who have neither the intelligence nor the temperament needed for detached, impersonal, and scientific thinking.

It will be evident, upon fuller reflection, that for our present needs we cannot rely upon science alone. Only too clearly are we

GENERAL EDUCATION 223

seeing today that science, because of its very objectivity and impartiality, can be the instrument of destruction of human values as well as their servant. Social and human problems must be recognized as value problems which involve not objective, detached processes but emotionally toned beliefs and aspirations and goals to which our sciences are and probably always will be instrumental. The plea for objectivity and purely scientific detachment as the sole resource in handling social difficulties is essentially a neurotic defense against the emotions and feelings that individuals have been unable to manage in their own lives and is as much of a defeatist program as the retreat into the cloister. Thus we must guard ourselves against the plausible schemes of social study programs that assume we can make all students into amateur social scientists, capable of "solving our social problems" by patient, "objective" examination of the facts and impartial weighing of the conflicting issues and solutions. Not even our trained social scientists, or the austere physical scientists, can exhibit such capabilities as we can plainly see in the professional and lay journals today.

Even if we could overcome some of these professional difficulties and obstacles, the task of general education would present a formidable and unique enterprise for education because of the very position we occupy in this changing climate of opinion. We are emerging from a past of stable ideas and beliefs into a present of almost universal skepticism, of increasing relativism in all areas, and continuous revision of scientific thinking and procedures. We cannot hope for any early attainment to stability in our ideas and conceptions, since future scientific work will inevitably remake even the most solidly established findings of today (a point often ignored or slurred by contemporary scientists). As the implications of recent shifts in the pattern of our thinking (relativity, discontinuity, uncertainty, operationalism, and non-Aristotelian logic) are realized, we will undoubtedly face increasing confusion and uncertainty in science, especially since some recognized branches of science have scarcely been touched by the new climate of opinion.

Thus we cannot project a program of general education with a fixed and unchangeable content. Rather we must plan a program that deals in relative and provisional substitutes for the older absolutes and certainties we are losing. Our inability to offer another set of finalities makes it imperative to envision an educational program that will change with every year and yet be conceived in the largest and most significant terms and enriched with emotional tone and meaning. This indeed is "education for living," but for the real life that is managed by feelings rather than reason and for life in the precarious, provisional world of today. This is the education that youth is hungry for, and if we do not provide it, youth will evoke its own teachers, as we have seen abroad.

This need for ideas and conceptions that will organize our world and help to build our personalities are persistent concerns from early childhood to old age. The same perplexities and curiosities, the same anxieties and aspirations run through the whole life span; and as the individual grows up and matures, he continues to seek answers to these same questions of life import. Adult education has its largest opportunity in providing for adults the help needed in gaining new understandings, at an increasingly mature level, of these basic, enduring curiosities, perplexities, anxieties, and aspirations of childhood and youth. As Dr. James Plant has so cogently remarked, we do not *solve* our personality problems; we only restate them on a different level of maturity and experience. Likewise we must recognize that we cannot *solve* our social problems; we can only restate the persistent, unavoidable tasks of group life in new terms more consonant with changing technology and new insights, understandings, and sensibilities.

In truth we are concerned here, not merely with an educational program but with a program for the organization of our future culture. Every idea and conception, every belief and meaning we offer to children, to youth, and to adults must be viewed in the light of its relevance to, and fruitfulness for, the culture and the social order they or their children must build, since the culture that will eventually replace our own will be organized upon these new ideas, conceptions, and beliefs that we are striving to clarify and unify today. A culture is constituted essentially of awareness, sensitivities, and values that are reflections in the personality of the way man conceives the universe, his place therein, his relations to others, and his conception of the self. How to build up the new sensibilities we are striving toward, to establish the new scheme of values and meanings that alone can bring the resolution of our many social, economic, and political perplexities, is the crux of general education and the key to our future religion. For such a program we must learn to assess the efficacy of our educational procedures, not merely by subject-matter examinations, objective tests, or skill in the use of techniques, but rather by the individual's personality and conduct of life as revealed in daily conduct and human relations. Only in so far as there is an alteration in sensibilities and in personality make-up and expression can we hope for any substantial gains in meeting social, economic, political, and international problems. There is already sufficient evidence to show the symptomatic character of our social problems.

It is obvious that we of today can do little more than make a tentative beginning on the immense task of creating a general education for the future. But if our efforts are to be fruitful for that future, we must strive for a larger and more general view of this task so that we can rise above the all too prevalent preoccupation with the minutiae of the subject matter fields, with questions of mental discipline and of training, and with the mechanism of pedagogical practices. The opportunity for educational philosophy, as John Dewey so long ago pointed out, is unlimited.

(FROM: "The Task of General Education." *The Social Frontier*, 3 [1937]: 171–73; 209–11.)

NINETEEN

Mental Security

THE QUESTION of mental security obviously cannot be considered apart from the other social-economic goals to be sought through education since there is a continual interaction among all of these. But in a very real sense mental security may be said to be primary and to a large extent a controlling influence over all the others, because our existing social-economic life and any changes sought therein are, and must be, expressions of the individual's emotional make-up and anxieties and his search for mental security.

If the discussion of mental security is to rise above platitudes and pious exhortations for mental hygiene, it is necessary to recognize at the outset that the individual in any society is faced with certain unavoidable life tasks set by the very process of growing and maturing in a group life. The way in which he meets those life tasks is conditioned by hereditary capacities, nutrition, health, and the physical environment, but the specific character of those life tasks and the way he faces them is governed by his interpretation of the culture of his group. This group culture, in turn, reflects the historic outcome of the efforts of previous generations of individuals to meet these same life tasks and to cope with the persistent problems of group life.

Every culture of which we have any record shows, with greater or less elaboration and refinement, how the group has attempted to order life by erecting certain ideas, conceptions, and beliefs about the nature of the universe, man's place therein, his relation to the group life, and finally a conception of human nature or image of the self. These beliefs and conceptions, transmitted from parents to children, and incorporated by the children into their personal adjustments to life, make up the mental world in which each individual really lives. They also define the life tasks he must face and prescribe the socially sanctioned answers he will make to those demands.

It has been the historic role of religion to provide man with these basic ideas, conceptions, beliefs, and patterns of conduct. The crisis that now exists in western European culture arises primarily, not from economic changes and political disputes, but from the disintegration of the organizing ideas and beliefs of our traditional religions. For over three hundred years these ancient ideas and conceptions have been undergoing a slow but steady loss of prestige under the cumulative impact of modern science. First astronomy, then physics, chemistry, geology, paleontology, biology, and, more recently, anthropology and psychology have rendered untenable the older ideas about the nature and extent of the universe, man's place therein, the make-up of so-called organized society, and the nature of the self, especially the ideas of human nature and the process of personality development. Thus far, there has not appeared a body of coherent, integrated ideas and beliefs, consonant with recent scientific findings and theories, to replace the older beliefs. Our basic, mental insecurity then arises from this cultural situation for which it is idle to expect any early and simple remedy. We cannot now find any certainties or any absolutes to replace these that were so comforting. Rather we must prepare ourselves to live in a precarious, changing world that promises to continue indefinitely to be precarious, uncertain, and constantly shifting. Probably our most acute need today is for a formulation that will give us a view of the changing world and of changing man that is at once in accord with scientific knowledge and also humanly, emotionally satisfying. Until we are provided with such a scientific, philosophical outlook everyone, in greater or less measure, depending upon how much he has been influenced by modern science, must suffer from a profound feeling of insecurity, often acute anxiety, because he can find no coherent view of life and of the world that will help him to order his conduct and beliefs.

What this means, more generally, is that we are living in a changing climate of opinion wherein traditional ideas and beliefs are being superseded by new ideas, similar to the crisis in Greek culture initiated by the inquiries and speculations of the natural philosophers and sophists of the sixth and fifth centuries B.C.

When the inherited body of beliefs about the nature and constitution of the universe, about the gods and their control of human life, and the basis for conduct were questioned by those inquiring minds, there was at once a quickening of life, of speculation and investigation, but also a rapid disintegration of manners, morals, and customs that became cumulative. The individual needs a solid framework of ideas and beliefs to order life for him, to define his relationships, his duties, and his privileges so that he can live without the constant anxiety and guilt that uncertainty and confusion over these basic questions engender.

We today are living in a changing climate of opinion that began with the challenge of astronomy and physics over three hundred years ago and has become acute with the more recent scientific developments and the new insights into human nature and conduct that challenge the older ethical, moral, and legalistic conceptions of conduct, just as astronomy upset the older conceptions of an anthropocentric universe. Thus we are in all stages of transition from the old to the new today. Probably never before have so many individuals faced the responsibility of finding security for themselves instead of receiving it in the traditions and customs of the group. With so many conflicting ideas and beliefs, so many divergent moral and ethical codes, the individual is continually forced to make decisions and to endure the tensions of uncertainty because there are few, if any, clear-cut, unequivocal guides to conduct. These tensions are almost unbearable and create the most profound insecurities that drive men and women and adolescents to seek escapes thru incessant activity or thru anodynes such as alcohol, drugs, and stupefying entertainment. In any discussion of mental security we must not neglect this social background of uncertainty and confusion in the lives of everyone, especially of children, to whom we can give so little of the certainty they crave.

There is also the problem of individual mental security that must be faced by the child, always against this larger background of cultural confusion, but more directly focused upon the intimate life of the family and home. Again we must recognize that each individual child faces certain inescapable life tasks that no program of education or social change can fundamentally alter, since those tasks arise from the process of growth and maturation in group life and the inevitable dependence of one human being upon other human beings, in early life for care and nurture and security and in later life for intimacy, affection, and·sex fulfilment. What we are beginning to realize today is that the inevitable process of socialization is indeed essential for the child who needs help in organizing and regulating his life and finding his or her place in the group, but that there is an extraordinary opportunity to foster mental security and wholesome personality development in the parental handling of this socialization. When it is realized that weaning and toilet training involve the most acute stresses and strains and emotional disturbances, and that these anxieties may become persistent characteristics of all the rest of the individual's life, we may begin to see what the problem of mental security really involves. It is becoming clear from recent studies of personality in young children that this surrender of physiological autonomy and acceptance of cultural control over bodily functions is usually accompanied by anxiety. This anxiety may be purely temporary and slight, or it may be intense and devastating, with all manner of disturbances, physical, mental, emotional, and social, depending primarily upon how the child is handled. If a child has a feeling of being wanted, of being loved, and of belonging to the family, the stresses and strains of this early training will be slight and transient; but if the child is denied this reassurance and affection, is made to feel wicked, worthless, and unwanted or guilty, the anxiety and fear may become persistent and dominate his life. Here we find the roots or genesis of mental insecurity in the personal, intimate relations of the child to his parents, especially to his mother and his siblings. Once this feeling of insecurity has been established, the child becomes a prey to feelings of guilt, of loneliness, and of fears that may poison his whole life and compromise all his human relations.

There is, for a variety of reasons, a considerable resistance to the consideration of these basic aspects of personality development. Part of this resistance derives from the traditional conception of man as a rational, logical person, a conception that sees all behavior as an outcome of willed conduct and denies the emotional, alogical, and often irrational character of most human conduct. This illustrates the predicament we are in because the older conceptions of human nature and conduct are venerable beliefs buttressed by law, ethics, and religion but now being challenged by experimental and clinical studies of behavior. On the one side we have those who assert that all human behavior is a question of individual, moral judgment and will, and any deviation from socially sanctioned conduct must be punished. On the other side we have the cumulative findings of students of human conduct who tell us that delinquents, criminals, prostitutes, homosexuals, sex offenders, and the mentally disordered and others who violate the laws or customs, or who find themselves in mental and other conflicts, are really the victims of the distortions and anxieties inflicted upon them in early childhood. From this viewpoint there is only a limited opportunity for cure of these deviants, but the possibility of prevention is clear, through a saner, wiser, and more affectionate child nurture and a revision of our ideas and conceptions of human nature and conduct.

To assert that the conflict over these two opposed conceptions of human nature and conduct is the central problem underlying all our other social, political, economic, and educational difficulties may, at first sight, appear like the ill-considered and prejudiced opinion of a fanatic. But sober reflection upon this view may give occasion for pause before it is summarily rejected. It is well to remember that scarcely a generation ago the theory of disease from microbes and bacterial invasion was also regarded as absurd and was resisted not only by laymen but by medical men as well. Without drawing too close a parallel, it may be said that many perplexing aspects of individual and social life become clearer when the newer conceptions of personality and conduct are used in approaching them.

One of the most important ideas coming from the more recent psychological studies is that the conduct of an individual is dominated largely by these feelings of hostility or guilt which, largely unconscious, drive the individual into all manner of behavior antagonistic to family and social welfare and peace, which he does not understand but for which he invents various and sundry explanations or "good reasons." Thus it would appear that the ambitious strivings that mark our political and economic and professional life are derived from these basic personality characteristics, these feelings of not being wanted or loved, of inadequacy and guilt and hostility that are channeled by a competitive economic society into "rugged individualism" and the behavior that gives rise to our many social-economic problems. Similarly, the ambitions that appear in politics and the striving for power may be viewed as efforts to overcome a feeling of inadequacy and guilt and release feelings of hostility. These same emotional disturbances, especially the feeling of guilt and anxiety, are found in many patients suffering from illnesses, for example, gastric ulcer and various forms of cardiovascular disease, and they appear quite frankly and overtly in those who suffer from mental disorders.

What this viewpoint implies is that a given individual who, because of early childhood and adolescent ill-treatment, has these feelings of inadequacy, anxiety, and guilt will develop hostile and aggressive impulses that may be discharged thru physical illness, mental disorders, the various forms of crime, delinquency, and sex offenses, or in the socially tolerated forms of competitive striving, wherein by achievement, by acquisition of property or income or exercise of power over others, he may find some release or forgetfulness of his profound insecurity and unhappiness. This insecurity and unhappiness arise, in large part, from the lack of affection and "belongingness" in early childhood and from corroding fears and distorted ideas in early training.

To say, therefore, that our social, economic, and political problems are largely the symptoms of intense mental insecurity and unbearable unhappiness that drive individuals into aggressive, anti-social conduct which they cannot understand or explain except in terms of older ideas and rationalization, is to give these social problems a new orientation in terms of mental insecurity and emotional disturbances that are rarely, if ever, recognized in the currently accepted formulations of social science and social philosophies. Such a transformation of problems from the realm of large, speculative issues over so-called "social forces" and ineffective moralizing to the concrete arena of personality development and culture change is not unlike the shift in biology from concern with mass fertility rites to the concrete and manageable processes of fertilization of egg or seed, nurture of the embryo, and development under genetic control.

If such a proposed transformation appears to neglect the historically developed ideas and theories of social science and of ethics, such neglect is and has always been essential to any fundamental advance in knowledge. The history of ideas is, as Dr. Kemp Smith of Edinburgh University stated some years ago, "a record not so much of the progressive discovery of truth as of our gradual emancipation from error." It is difficult and painful to give up cherished ideas and beliefs, as we have seen in the ancient ideas of cosmology that modern astronomy and geology have superseded, but it is not unwarranted to say that a similar renunciation of traditional beliefs about human nature and conduct impends, with far-reaching consequences for individual happiness and for social welfare.

Here it is appropriate to point out that these more recent views of human nature and conduct are in no sense contradictory to the basic ethical and moral teachings of Christianity. The New Testament sets forth essentially the same view of man's conduct as the most recent conceptions of psychiatry: both agree in denying the guilt-punishment theory and accepting the view that the individual's conduct needs to be understood in the light of his personal history. Moreover, modern psychological insights give full confirmation to the doctrine that affection, toleration, and love are indispensable to children and to adults. It is indeed probable that recent studies of personality will reinstate the Christian beliefs that have for so long been distorted and perverted by later teachings.

If the conception of our social, economic, and political (including international) difficulties is accepted as essentially the outcome of the individual's desperate striving for escape from inner insecurity and unhappiness, then our social-economic goals and the proposed education and other means thereto will require critical scrutiny. Otto Rank, in his penetrating book *Modern Education*, has pointed out that "man everywhere seeks happiness . . . but only finds success." So far as our social philosophy and education accept uncritically the operations of individual ambitions and foster individual striving, they may be helping to perpetuate the very social ills they wish to diminish or abolish. Again, so far as an educational program relies upon verbal exhortations to be socially-minded and co-operative, it may be aiding the most ruthless and aggressive to exploit the others who take that teaching seriously. What is apparently controlling in the situation is the sensitivity of the individual to human values and his respect for the personality of others. Sensitivity and values cannot be taught as so much subject matter or rules; they can only be communicated by warm personal human relations and the esthetic experiences of drama, novels poetry, and movies.

Here the issue becomes acute since the preoccupation of formal education with intellectual training, with achievement of subject-matter competence, but with neglect of the emotional, personal, human needs and concerns of students results in the schools and colleges having little or no real influence upon the motives and impulses that control our individual and social lives. If the need for mental security is recognized as one of the essential social-economic goals of America, then active steps must be taken to meet that need. The preparation of boys and girls and young men and women for marriage and home life and for child-bearing and rearing becomes an insistent duty of education, especially today when it is evident that we must release the next generation from the beliefs and theories and practices regarding sex, marriage, and children that create so many of these human conflicts and personality difficulties. Parent education offers another large opportunity for education to help along in the transition from these older, devastating ideas of human nature and conduct to a more wholesome, sane, and humanly desirable understanding. The need is primarily for insights and awareness, for affectionate understanding and toleration, not merely information, skills, and technics.

With so many children, young and older, especially adolescents, suffering from a profound sense of isolation, of inadequacy and guilt, preoccupied with their anxieties and worries, much of our educational effort is sheer waste, if not worse, because of its fundamental irrelevancy to the students' acute personality needs. This refusal or inability of teachers to see the pupils' needs may, and often does, create a hatred for knowledge and a blind resentment to education. It is as if we had hospitals in which doctors and nurses carried on an elaborate routine of daily work, wholly indifferent to and unconcerned with the agonizing pains that the patients dared not reveal, except for occasional outbreaks of disorder and efforts to escape. Such an analogy is not fantastic, as the clinical evidence so plainly shows, since children sit in classes and daily endure anxieties, fears, and unhappiness that they dare not reveal nor does the teacher ever suspect, until some symptomatic outbreak — misconduct, delinquency, truancy, or other overt act — compels attention.

As Dr. James Plant has repeatedly stated, the real question for education to face is what does the school *mean* to the child. If education is to be concerned with mental security, that question must be asked in the light of the child's basic needs for affection, reassurance, toleration, and understanding of the burdens he bears within. Education and youth organizations must recognize the child's constant worry over his status and position in his family, among his contemporaries and in the school or group life; his preoccupation with questions of his own physical and physiological normality; his perplexities over sex differences and sex functions and the role of mating in life; and his concern over the adequacy of his conduct to meet the standards set by society and by himself.

Education must learn to see beneath the intellectualisms, the verbalisms, the asceticisms, the varied forms of seemingly absurd and irrational behavior or disagreeable, aggressive hostility exhibited by boys and girls, and realize the ever-present worry and timidity and loneliness of the individual that hides behind these disguises until, if nothing is done to help, they become permanent forms of adult maladjustment for which our whole social life suffers.

Early childhood and adolescence are the two crucial periods for the individual's mental security. Education must rely upon the home, supplemented by nursery schools and parent education, to make its contribution to mental hygiene in the earlier years. For the adolescent boy and girl, education must assume a much larger responsibility, since then the youth and maiden are confronted with serious perplexities that threaten mental security. During the teens the schools have an opportunity to meet these needs of adolescence in terms of the acute life tasks that then confront boys and girls, but to do so the school must go beyond questions of training to the more difficult problems of the individual life: clarifying the masculine or feminine roles and the function of sex and the opportunities and responsibilities they carry for men and women, clarifying the aspirations and ego-ideals that are to guide the individual life and either foster social values or create social problems, and resolving the persistent, infantile interest and desires into acceptable adult conduct. To use the formula of the psychiatrists, the adolescent tasks are: to achieve a heterosexual adjustment with a sane, wholesome attitude toward sex and mating, to emancipate himself (or herself) from the parents and family so as to grow up and mature, to face reality by coming to terms with oneself, accepting the tasks of life, and seeking a design for living compatible with oneself and social requirements. Adolescents need a tremendous amount of reassurance, of sympathetic understanding and personal help to meet these tasks adequately, especially since the parents so often cannot or will not help, but actually oppose the adolescent's efforts in these directions. Inability to meet these tasks effectually is apparently responsible for most adult maladjustments and mental breakdowns and for the persistence of childish and neurotic behavior that continually frustrates our social and individual needs. It is significant that as the period when boys and girls are most concerned with efforts to make these life adjustments the schools put on the greatest pressure for academic achievements and threaten the child with failure, disgrace, and expulsion, thus intensifying his insecurity.

After a number of years of clinical service and study it is becoming clear that all adolescents, not merely a few problem cases, need help in this period, help that presumably the schools and colleges must give if it is to be provided. The signs and symptoms of anxiety among young are growing, aggravated by social-economic insecurity and the growing cultural conflicts and confusion. If this anxiety is not met by education, youth will seek and find its own outlets and releases, as we may plainly see abroad, where young people are turning to leaders who provide a mass treatment for their mental insecurity and anxieties. In our preoccupation with the figure of the individual dictator-leader, we have forgotten that he derives his power from the urgent needs of mentally and emotionally insecure individuals who crave an authoritarian rule as a release from their unbearable uncertainty and tensions. Men cannot tolerate freedom unless it is based upon a common body of ideas, beliefs, and standards of conduct that make freedom possible and bearable. When the traditional basis of a culture disintegrates, as we are seeing today, men no longer are concerned with freedom because of their greater need for mental security.

Adult men and women today are assailed on every side by anxiety and apprehension. Workers must face questions of conflicting loyalties to their fellow workers, their employers, their families, and their communities for which there are apparently no adequate ways of reconciliation. Employers likewise are torn by divergent interests and claims and find their social interests continually frustrated by the economic pressures they are under. Women are in a constant turmoil over their economic interests and their biological and psychological needs and are beset with insecurity within and without, so that they can give but little reassurance and comfort to their husbands and sons. No better indicators of this widespread and acute mental insecurity can be found than in the advertising and propaganda that is daily poured out in publications, movies, and radio, all designed to exploit this personal insecurity and intensify these anxieties in order to sell goods and services and influence behavior, to the ends sought by those who wish to profit from human unhappiness and distress. Evidence of general mental insecurity among men and women is also to be found in their leisure-time activities and amusements that are so largely escapes and anodynes. But the most important signs of mental insecurity among adults is the growing tendency to violence and brutality and willingness to surrender their freedom to the leaders who promise relief, no matter how fantastic and destructive their programs.

In formulating the social-economic goals for the United States, the goal of freedom is most in need of critical and penetrating reflection. So long as freedom is conceived only in terms of liberal laws and non-authoritarian government, the essential elements of freedom are neglected. There can be no freedom so long as individuals are dominated by fears, anxieties, blinding superstitions, and corroding doubts, since this inner emotional distress renders the individual helpless in the hands of any leader, fanatic, or demagogue who chooses to exploit his mental insecurity and unhappiness.

There is a tremendous amount of latent idealism and altruism in youth seeking expression that is now being wasted or exploited or brutally destroyed but could be used as the motive force for remaking our culture and creating a more humanly desirable society. This idealism cannot function unless it is guided and patterned into a design for living that is functionally realizable and freed from the all too prevalent mental insecurity. Today the young man and increasingly the young woman are guided and counseled educationally and vocationally but not often in terms of a life career that is both socially and individually desirable. Nor are they accorded the sincerity and respect they need if they are to mature as adults capable of and ready for adult living. Moreover, young people are being taught to study social problems in terms of everything but the human personality expressions and needs that create those problems, so that they see social improvement only as questions of legislation and propaganda, court decisions, economic "forces," and other large, distant conceptions. From the viewpoint of mental security our social problems are not purely economic or political questions, but rather the results of distracted, unhappy personalities who are driven by their inner insecurity and guilt, like small children, to dominate, destroy, and otherwise prevent the creation of a decent social and economic life. Men cannot be socially-minded so long as they are mentally insecure, emotionally immature, and hostile. Man must accept himself and learn to live at peace with himself before he can be generous, tolerant, and altruistic.

Perhaps the nearest approach to a formulation that will embrace the many aspects of the question of mental security is to say that every individual is threatened with mental insecurity by uncertainty or confusion over the basic philosophical questions of life and his own status in life and by anxiety and guilt arising from his childhood experiences. Man has to feel he belongs in the world and belongs to something bigger than himself—family, nation, or race. Lacking a sense of belonging, of being wanted, and feeling guilty and unhappy, he is driven to hostility and aggressions that create most of our social problems because he must express somehow his inner distress and fears at whatever cost to society. As we begin to accept these views of human nature and conduct, to see how distortions of personality give rise to antisocial behavior, to much illness and most mental disorders, a hopeful attitude toward the future becomes possible. We are not at the mercy of a human nature that is innately wicked, sinful, and destructive, but rather we suffer from the consequences of failing to provide affection, tenderness, reassurance, and toleration to children, adolescents, and adults, and freeing their aspirations for a better life. If we can and will provide affection and recognize each individual as a distinct, different person and foster his temperamental differences instead of frustrating them, most of the worst distortions and social conflicts will be relieved, if not eventually abolished. In this endeavor the schools should play a major part, but this step calls not so much for change in subject matter and pedagogical devices as for a warm, human concern and respect by teachers for the personality of the child and a recognition of the life concerns of the student as his most urgent educational need.

This does not imply a desire for a sloppy sentimentalism on the part of teachers but rather a kindly, understanding concern for human personality, an acceptance of individuality and temperamental differences, and for insight into the emotional needs and difficulties of children and youth. Perhaps if teachers received such treatment in their own training they could and would be able to offer it to their pupils, especially if formal education recognized and approved such non-academic concerns and abilities as much as skills and competence in subject matter. Only teachers can cope with this immense social need since there never will be enough psychiatrists and psychologists for all children nor can increased diagnostic and therapeutic treatments substitute for the need of daily interest and help by understanding and well-disposed teachers.

If we can and will lessen man's mental insecurity, perhaps we will find our social-economic goals will be changed. Today so much of our endeavor is to prevent or avoid what are apparently symptoms of personal insecurity and unhappiness that we have difficulty in envisaging a social life wherein constant struggle and worry are reduced, if not eliminated.

In the larger perspective of history the revision of our conceptions of human nature and conduct and the development of insights into personality will probably appear as more significant than all the other achievements of modern science and technology, since they will bring, we may hope, the key to man's ages-old perplexities and social conflicts.

When we have learned to recognize man's insistent need for mental security and to provide for its fulfilment, we may then discover what human freedom means.

(FROM: *Implications of Social-Economic Goals for Education* [ch. VIII]. National Education Association, Sept. 1937).

TWENTY

The Reorientation of Education to the Promotion of Mental Hygiene

THE CONCEPTION of mental hygiene has been gradually clarified and enlarged, first by the differentiation of mental hygiene from psychiatric diagnosis and therapy, and second by the realization that mental hygiene aims at something more than the prevention of mental disorders. This recognition of mental hygiene as an effort to foster saner, happier, and more co-operative personalities has focused attention upon education and its reorientation.

We may approach education as a cultural process and look for clues to the promotion of mental health in an examination of what cultural education involves for the individual. Here we face an initial difficulty because we are, for the most part, unaware of what culture does to and for the individual. Perhaps we can gain some perspective on this question by approaching the situation as follows:

While as organisms we *exist* in the common, *public* world of other organisms, objects, and events, and are subject to the natural processes of gravitation, heat, and cold, and other physical, chemical, and biological operations, it is evident, upon further reflection, that we *live* in a *cultural* world which gives to the common, public world the peculiar meanings, significances, and values, the highly formalized patterns of repression and expression, and the multitudinous tools, technics, and rituals with which our society attempts to meet the exigencies of life. This cultural world, which is more real and compelling than the public, physical world in which we exist, is transmitted from one generation to the next by a process of education which begins at birth and continues on into adult life. In other words, each child must be initiated into our culture world and made a participant in our society by a process of education which makes him see the world in terms of the meanings and significances and values, and the prohibitions and compulsions, that are cherished by our culture.

What we are now beginning to realize with increasing clarity is that the personality of the individual develops out of this process of culturizing—this education procedure that attempts to mold him into the kind of person favored by his culture, and to give him the training and socialization necessary for living in that culture.

Here we can only briefly outline the major features of this educational procedure, noting especially that the cultural training begins at birth, in the requirement that the infant should adapt himself to the prescribed schedule of infant feeding and frequently early weaning, shall accept toilet training, and shall learn to manage his emotional reactions. In so far as these practices drastically interfere with his physiological processes and involve severe deprivations of what the young organism needs for adequate infantile functioning, the child is forced to surrender his physiological autonomy and accept cultural control over his bodily processes, subordinating his organic needs to the prescribed patterns favored by his parents.

It is now becoming clear that these familiar, homely events, which we have all experienced as children and as parents, are fraught with lifelong significance for the child, because they involve deprivations and interferences which create acute tensions and organic distortions, and, above all, strong feelings of resentment, of anxiety, and of guilt toward the world, which may and usually do persist throughout his life.

In addition to these prescribed physiological adjustments, the young child is also required to learn other cultural patterns that carry further threats to his mental health. He must learn to respect the inviolabilities that culture imposes upon things and persons— what we call private property and the sanctity of the person. These lessons are exceedingly difficult because the child must learn to build up within himself the inhibitions that will prevent him from taking, approaching, or attacking freely accessible things and persons, despite strong impulses to do so. The child is also required to learn the many patterns of conduct that are prescribed for social

THE REORIENTATION OF EDUCATION

life, such as language, manners, and etiquette, masculine and feminine roles, and the extraordinary variety of rituals and symbolic practices (money, buying and selling, voting, and so on) that custom and tradition have ordained.

Mental hygiene is helping us to see that this early cultural training is necessary and inevitable, since the young child must be socialized, not only for the protection of society, but for his own guidance and self-management. But mental hygiene also makes clear that the mental health of the individual may be seriously jeopardized by the way in which these interferences and deprivations, these compulsions and prohibitions, are taught to him, and by the way authority in general is administered. That is to say, the personality of the child and his adjustment to society depend upon the way he *feels* about people and situations and especially about himself. If the educational process of weaning and learning to accept foodstuffs, of toilet training, of managing his emotional reactions, is administered harshly and cruelly or severely, that is, too early in life or too rapidly and without affectionate reassurance to allay the tension—then the child will *feel* deprived and regard the world as hostile. If the inviolabilities and the prescribed social practices are taught with stern discipline and punishment, without the love that alone can make these prohibitions and compulsions emotionally acceptable, then the child will *feel* that other persons are his enemies and will develop a resistance to authority. Moreover, if all this education serves to humiliate him, as if he were a bad, wicked, sinful, and wholly unworthy person, the child can only conceive of himself in those terms and either act out the role of bad child or express his feelings of guilt or resentment in various disguises that are antisocial or self-defeating. It is, therefore, not only what culture demands and imposes upon the individual, but the way in which this early education is conducted, that makes or mars the mental health of the individual.

As we see the young child emerging from this family training, bearing the impact of these cultural lessons, we can begin to evaluate formal schooling in terms of its contribution to mental health or its accentuation of the already established personality difficulties in the young child. Here we see the child entering school at five or six to face the demands for standardized academic achievement, for rigid conformity, and for adjustment to his contemporaries, bringing to these encounters all the perplexities and anxieties of his family background and training. It is evident that much of what is now done in the schools is inimical to mental health, since the child is confronted with more anxieties and exposed to frequent and devastating humiliations. Thus many of the attitudes and feelings he brings from his family training are crystallized and intensified by the school program and discipline.

If and when we are convinced that mental health must be conserved in education, we will call for teachers who are genuinely concerned with the personalities of children and not interested merely in their mental processes, who will continuously recognize the emotional needs and problems of the little boys and girls in their pupils of all ages. Faced with these cultural demands, children need warm, affectionate, human relationships and personal recognition all through school, from nursery school through college; indeed, we never outgrow these fundamental personality needs even though we change our modes of expressing them and of seeking fulfillment as we grow older. Today our greatest social need is not so much for intelligence and trained minds as for sanity and the courage to live, for we now realize how intelligence in a distorted, unhappy individual can be used, like science, for aggressive, destructive purposes, for defeatism and escapes. The highest academic competence does *not* guarantee a socially minded career or a humanly desirable design for living. In the interest of social welfare and human happiness, we could wisely sacrifice much of our present academic achievement for better personality integration and social adjustment, since only sane, co-operative personalities can deal with our present social disorder.

In education we see quite clearly that, just as parents inflict upon their children the distortions and anxieties from which they have suffered, so teachers feel it necessary to impose upon their pupils their anxieties and the intellectualisms they have used as defenses against anxieties to meet their personality problems. Thus they find it difficult, if not impossible, to shift the school program from an impersonal training of the mind to a concern for the pupil's feelings and his efforts to adjust to life. Those schools and colleges that have made an attempt to help individual personalities to reach a saner, more mature level of functioning are regarded with suspicion and disdain by the others who cling to the purely intellectual program in which alone they feel professionally secure.

THE REORIENTATION OF EDUCATION 243

The irony of this situation is that the emotionally distorted, unhappy individual often makes the best scholar or scientiest, because he finds a socially sanctioned way of living with his maladjustments in an academic career, wherein he sacrifices all else to his professional work as defense against mental ill health. Thus we are forced by the shining example of a few brilliant but neurotic professors to sacrifice all other students upon the altar of intellectual achievement.

We should begin, therefore, to scrutinize carefully the personality of all the cultural agents who, as teachers, physicians, psychiatrists, ministers and priests, youth workers, and in other capacities, are teaching and counseling children and youth. We will find that many of the ethical, moral, sex, and social ideas now being offered represent the projection of the individual's own lifelong anxieties and defenses, especially in regard to sex ethics.

Here it is necessary to point out, with all the emphasis possible, that these various cultural lessons—the physiological adjustments, the inviolabilities and patterned conduct and sex regulations—are necessary for any organized society. They must be taught to children in order to free the child from his own physiological compulsions and impulses and from coercion by emotional reactions, which otherwise would dominate his life and prevent him from doing much else but exist on a purely organic level of functioning and fighting. They are also necessary to protect him from the aggressions, the invasions of his property and person, the disregard of his rights and privileges by others. Private property and sanctity of the person, it must be remembered, are learned ways of conduct toward objects and persons which permit individuals to enjoy possession and personal integrity without constant watching and fighting. Our whole legal system is predicated upon these learned patterns of conduct and upon the observance of such rituals as ownership and possession, contract, barter and sale, orderly litigation, and courtship and marriage. The individual needs this education in socialization more than society does because he must have guidance and sanctions to order his life. When a child receives inadequate socialization or ambiguous and vacillating teaching, so that he never is sure of what he can and cannot do, he may become prey to constant anxiety and worry over the necessity of deciding every action, or be left to the mercy of every impulse.

The mental-hygiene orientation of education carries no support for the often preached doctrine of unrestrained freedom in the education of the child, because it is clear that neither the child nor the adult can tolerate such freedom; we need culture to pattern our behavior into socially acceptable conduct, to manage our impulses and emotions, to give values and purposes to our activities, and to rescue us from the intolerable isolation of our private worlds.

What mental hygiene asserts without reservation is the necessity of providing this socializing education with the minimum of damage to the personality, by guarding the child's feelings during the prolonged tuition he must undergo. The most effective protection of the child's personality is through warm, affectionate love, not love that exploits the child to assuage adult frustrations, nor love that dominates and crushes the child for adult satisfactions, nor love that cruelly and harshly disciplines the child "for his own good." The love and affection that the child needs is that which is non-possessive and non-demanding, but rather is a continual affirmation of his individual, personal worth and value and "belongingness"—which expresses itself in adequate breastfeeding; patient, almost casual toilet training; firm, but kindly management of emotional reactions; and sympathetic, understanding tolerance of his fumbling efforts to master the lessons in socialization it has taken mankind thousands of years to learn.

Mental hygiene in education should stress again and again that these cultural lessons, despite their familiarity, present the most exacting demands that the mammalian organism has ever had to meet throughout the whole of its evolutionary development, because they involve the continuous control of the most primitive, elemental processes and impulses by the cerebral cortex, itself only recently evolved. Socialization, even under the most favorable parental guidance, involves tension, anxiety, resentment, and guilt which the individual may carry throughout his life. If, therefore, we want to educate sane, socially well-adjusted men and women, we must strive to make social life, with its necessary and desirable frustrations, repressions, and compulsions, *emotionally* acceptable to the child. Only when he can and does accept culture and learns to tolerate its restraints, while enjoying its protections and privileges, can he "face reality," to use the contemporary phrase for adjustment to social life and acceptance of one's own limitations and capacities.

It must be recognized that adult conduct toward members of the

THE REORIENTATION OF EDUCATION

opposite sex is governed largely, if not wholly, by the early experiences and teachings of the family about sex, about masculine and feminine roles, about the significance of the love life and the place of sex functioning in adult living. Here, again, it is clear that it is not only *what* is taught, but *how* it is taught to the child that makes the important difference. Nor can it be too strongly emphasized that the child's own perplexities about sex are intensified by the secrecy, the shame, the ambiguity, and the often violent emotional upheavals of his parents and teachers whenever he seeks understanding or attempts to explore his or another's genital organization. Just because sex is so pervasive and so powerful and must be regulated and patterned for the sake both of society and of the individual, the education of the child in this all-important area of life demands the utmost of sanity, of sincerity, and of decency. But alas, sex education is usually distorted, insincere, and obscene. In consequence, the emotionally warped child, with distorted ideas of sex, grows up to be the unhappy, maladjusted husband or wife, or one of those adults whose lives are preoccupied with sex conflicts outside of marriage. It is safe to say that rarely, if ever, do we find a sex offender, a prostitute, a homosexual, or other sex deviant who has had an honest and truly humane sex education. The price we are paying for this prevalent mishandling of sex education of children is beyond calculation, and the tragic irony is that the pathetic eagerness of parents to protect their children from sex damage is so largely responsible for these tragedies.

It is indeed melancholy to reflect upon the immense amount of time, energy, and anxiety expended in homes and schools in the attempt to socialize children and then to see the large number of delinquents and criminals, of mentally sick, of sex offenders, of prostitutes, of celibates, of unhappy wives and husbands, of harassed, anxious, insecure businessmen, politicians, professional workers, and of those who are expressing their anxiety and repressed feelings through physiological disturbances. These are the babies of yesterday who were twisted and distorted, frustrated and anxious, made acutely unhappy and resentful by their early family training, who are spending the rest of their lives trying to "get even" by aggressions against others or by disguised outlets for their feelings of hostility, resentment, and guilt. These are the school children of yesterday who were taught formal academic lessons and coached to pass examinations, while inwardly they seethed with resentment or sulked and daydreamed, or reacted blindly against a world of adults who callously ignored their unhappiness and their loneliness, misunderstood the meaning of their failures and delinquencies, misinterpreted their scholastic ambitions and achievements. These are the adolescents of yesterday who pathetically groped for enlightenment and guidance in making adjustment to the other sex, who sought vainly for emancipation from parents who would not allow them to grow up and mature, who looked for some design for living in a confused, disorderly world and found no helpful answers to their perplexities and aspirations. These are the same little boys and little girls today, hiding behind an outer mask of adult size and social, business, and professional positions, pretending to be rational, mature adults, while underneath they are hoping, fearing, hating, and despairing, as year by year they grow older, finding no one who understands or cares for their lonely, unhappy personalities. These are also the parents of to-morrow's adults upon whom they will impose much of the same distortion and unhappiness of their own childhood, because, unless aided from the outside, they can but repeat the patterns and treatment of their own rearing and make their children suffer as they suffered.

Primarily the task of mental hygiene is to break the continuity of those cultural traditions and family patterns that now lead to unnecessary personality distortions. We have inherited a conception of human nature and conduct as fixed and unchangeable, born to be antisocial; so long as we hold to that belief we are unable to understand what the education of the child involves. Moreover, so long as we retain those older ideas about human nature we cannot free ourselves from the convictions that now compel us to punish the child, frighten and terrorize him, withhold our love and threaten him with the most awful consequences for his natural infantile and childish activities.

As we assimilate the idea of man as a product of mammalian evolution, with an incredibly long past during which he has developed new capacities and powers, notably intelligence, without having lost any of the most primitive functions and needs, we can begin to reshape our education in the home and in the schools toward mental health.

The home and family offer the greatest opportunity for such a program, since it is essential that we begin to change the present practices of child training—which, alas, carry the added sanction of prevailing medical teaching and approval. Parent education is designed to reassure parents that they can trust human nature, and so they need not coerce and punish, terrorize and humiliate their children to make them sociable and well-adjusted. But parent education is more than the teaching of formulas and techniques of child rearing, as some have supposed; its purpose is to communicate, so far as possible, understanding and insights, to provide reassurance to parents and to help to translate the newer ideas of human nature and conduct into the daily life of the family. If we can do that, and through family consultation and guidance help parents toward a happier personal and married life, parent education will justify all the time and money we can spend upon it, because it is directed to the time and place where the matrix of personality is formed. The mental health of the child is in the hands of the adults who are responsible for his rearing.

It is evident that the high schools and colleges can and should provide the basis for this parental education, especially since adolescents are desperately in need of help in human relations, particularly in their relations to their own families.

Just because boys and girls must face so many exigent questions, they are emotionally ready, if not eager, for the understandings and insights that will make for mental health. The high schools and colleges have a unique opportunity and a social responsibility because the adolescent is usually seeking emancipation from his parents, feeling the need of becoming independent as the first step toward becoming a mature adult, able and ready to start his own family life. In this situation the teachers and administrators can, if wise and tactful, intervene with benefit to the parents as well as to the adolescent. They can provide helpful educational experiences through novels, plays, poetry, moving pictures, and radio dramatizations, since these aesthetic experiences enable the adolescent to gain insights and some understanding of himself and his needs by sharing the emotional experiences of others.

Closely allied to the question of the relations of the adolescent to his family comes the question of sex maturation, which depends so largely upon achieving emotional independence from the family. It is clear from present-day evidence of family discord and marital unhappiness, of sex offenders, prostitutes, involuntary celibacy, and the futile, pitiable sex experimentation of so many youths and adults, that our traditional sex ethics and teaching are sadly in need of revision. Sex reform has usually meant a plea for "sex freedom," which, as every experienced person must now know, is a neurotic dream. As members of Western European culture, we cannot tolerate "sex freedom," but must have some ethical justification and personality fulfillment for our sex functioning. What we are in need of today is a sex ethics freed from the degraded, obscene ideas and beliefs of the barnyard which now make the sex relations of man and woman so often hideously subhuman. Adolescents are rejecting the older defeatist beliefs about sex; they are seeking a human, decent conception of sex that can be reconciled with their ethical ideals and their growing realization of woman's dignity. The present-day attempts at sex education are too biological and too much concerned with procreation; they are not sufficiently concerned with the cultural and emotional problems of youth who want to know how to make sex a part of human living and personality fulfillment. They are seeking a conception of sex that is not merely exploitative, that no longer treats woman as an impersonal sex object to be used by the exigent male, but sees in sex a way to achieve intimacy, a means of communication, "another language" through which one lonely person can communicate with another. To displace the older sex teachings, with their great authority and sanction, we must offer youth a saner, more human, and more fulfilling conception, which will be not only more rewarding than our traditional ethics but also more demanding, especially upon the male. No one need fear that libertinism, promiscuity, or any other sex looseness will come from giving youth more wholesome ideas of sex and a belief that sex relations demand the sincerity and integrity of personal intimacy and affection for personality fulfillment.

The mental-health reorientation in education awaits an ethical guidance for youth toward a society in which human personality will be conserved. The high schools and colleges, in presenting social studies and social problems, only emphasize the individual's feelings of helplessness in the face of large institutional complexities. What youth wants is some direction to his or her own personal life that will contribute to social values as well as bring individual fulfillment.

We may counsel youth to "face reality," but if we mean that

they should learn to accept the present social disorder and confusion, the frustration of human needs and aspirations, and the ghastly degradation or destruction of so many human values, then we are guilty of the worst defeatism and sabotage of human nature.

If we are persuaded that mental hygiene has the significance we have here assumed, and if we are to be guided by the implications of our growing knowledge of personality development, we must acknowledge that most of the contemporary careers we urge upon youth are in truth but defenses against anxiety and emotional defeat—competitive struggles for power, prestige, or property that reflect the childhood insecurities from which the individual is fleeing and that threaten him with new insecurities from the other aggressive individuals he must challenge. Such designs for living are neither mentally hygienic nor socially desirable, but at present they are the only socially approved uses to which youth is asked to dedicate his life. The youth of today, no less than the youth of other days, wants to be given tasks that arouse his enthusiasm and promise fulfillment of his aspirations. If we are to be sincere, we can but point out the futility of the competitive struggle that leads to no personal fulfillment because it arises from inner personal distortion and insecurity which no amount of achievement, property, or prestige can assuage. In contrast, we can try to give youth an understanding of how his own personal life may be made significant and enriched, not merely by achievement or acquisition, but by the quality of human relations he can sustain.

If any one doubts the adolescent's urgent need for new goals and purposes, he need only look abroad, where the anxieties created by the present uncertainties and confusions of our disintegrating culture have evoked the authoritarian states which do not scruple to exploit the desire of youth to be sacrificed to some authority and purpose greater than merely personal ends. In place of the programs of unrestrained aggression and sacrifice to power-seeking of the dictators, can we not offer a richer, happier life to be won by wiser, saner conduct and devotion of self to sane living for human values? These are exigent mental-hygiene needs of youth and adults today that cannot be ignored in our preoccupation with the immediate clinical problems of individual mental disorder. Only the mental-hygienist, with the authority of clinical evidence, can assert vigorously that the surest, most direct road to social betterment is through a saner, more integrated development of individual personalities who do not need to exploit others politically, economically, or sexually, nor to defeat our economic, political, and social purposes for defense against, or release from, their anxieties. Can we make that assertion meaningful and emotionally convincing to youth today, and help both boys and girls to find the supreme courage to be sane in a world of neurotics and psychotics who are bent on destroying themselves and society in their frantic efforts at defense or escape?

We should recognize, however, that even the sanest and most integrated personalities today are suffering from the cumulative disintegration of the basic ideas and conceptions that have for so long served to organize the world and order human experience. Every culture provides a conception of the universe, of man's place therein, of his relations to the group life, and of human nature and conduct with which individuals build up their own framework of ideas and beliefs, construct their private worlds, and establish their criteria of credibility. We have inherited from theology and philosophy the ideas and beliefs that have served Western European culture to order events, organize the world, and regulate conduct. But modern science, beginning with astronomy and physics and then continuing in geology and biology, anthropology, and then psychology, have made those ancient beliefs untenable for increasing numbers who can no longer believe in a geocentric universe wherein man was specially created a few thousand years ago. Man has found a new history in his mammalian ancestry, and through anthropology he is discovering how plastic human nature really is and what diverse cultures and social arrangements can arise to organize and regulate human conduct. Recent studies of personality development are undermining the older idea of man as a wholly rational, volitional super-animal being, since he is being revealed as a creature of impulse and feelings who has only lately developed intelligence, which, however, cannot obliterate or deny his more primitive and compelling functions and feelings without disaster to the individual and to society.

These new revelations about the world and man are profoundly disturbing because they have left so many of us uncertain about what to believe, fearful of the immensities outside and also inside ourselves. We also have lost the older cosmic sanctions for our ethics and the guidance they gave to our conduct. The newer

THE REORIENTATION OF EDUCATION

scientific findings and conceptions have not yet been formulated into a meaningful synthesis that is emotionally satisfying and inspiring to the new way of life. The newly discovered mammalian history has made possible a new future for mankind, but until man has really understood and emotionally accepted that history and its implications, he cannot begin to live or even to dream of his new future. It will be the task of education tomorrow to interpret these new ideas and beliefs, not as intellectual facts and scientific laws, but as meaningful conceptions and aspirations for guiding our lives.

Perhaps only a new generation of children who have escaped the older formulations and the prevalent distortions of today can assimilate these startling new ideas and beliefs coming from scientific research, can face the new world now being created and accept the new human nature, and thus begin not only to build the society that is to come, but to reconstruct our culture.

It must be clear, therefore, that mental hygiene is not merely an added embellishment or auxiliary service to be added to education. It is a far-reaching and all-embracing conception for the reorganization of our culture in terms of human needs and values and the creation of a social life dedicated to human conservation. Democracy is an aspiration that goes beyond universal suffrage, free speech, economic enterprise, and representative government; it is a continuous assay of our culture and our organized society in terms of human values that cannot be achieved so long as the personalities of men and women are warped and corroded by fear, anxiety, guilt, and hostility. We are just beginning to realize how limited are the traditional ideas of freedom and liberty that stress the opportunities for choice in overt conduct, but neglect entirely the inner emotional distortions of the personality which coerce and dominate the individual more despotically than any laws, government, or dictator. Democracy demands toleration of other individuals and protection of their integrity, however different from ours, but such toleration is possible only to those who are emotionally free and mature, who have first learned to tolerate and accept themselves and so do not need to exploit, dominate, or defeat others. Indeed, the lack of this emotional stability and inner security presents the gravest danger to democracy because distorted, immature, unhappy personalities will sacrifice freedom and follow demagogues and dictators with joyous abandon for the emotional release found in submission to a strong outside authority that sanctions aggression and retaliation.

Mental health and democracy are goals to be achieved anew by each generation who must give to their children a faith in human nature and a courage to live with love and understanding that can be transmitted only by warm, intimate human relationships. If each generation will strive to free its children from its emotional handicaps and personality distortions and bid them go forth to live fully and sanely, mental health and democracy will be secure. A program of mental-health education must enlist families and schools and all other agencies for human guidance in a united effort to protect and cherish the personalities of all children, if we are to realize our human potentialities.

(FROM: *Mental Hygiene*, 23 [1939]: 1–15.)

TWENTY-ONE

Mental Health in Schools

MENTAL HYGIENE has been concerned primarily with the diagnosis and treatment of individuals and their care in institutions. Even though mental hygiene organizations have fostered clinics for even young individuals in order to discover and, if possible, prevent more serious difficulties later, they have been oriented until recently principally toward these remedial efforts.

Medicine generally has been preoccupied with diagnosis and treatment of individual patients. Indeed the training of the medical student makes it difficult for him, usually, to think in terms of preventive medicine or health care. Even the work of public health agencies, organized to police the environment against hazards to health, is focused upon the more specific sources of disease and the application of vaccination, immunization, etc.

Health, physical and mental, has been left as a somewhat vague, ill defined condition which was thought of as governed by many diverse, but largely uncontrollable processes, or just good fortune. Therefore little in the way of concrete programs for health care, or even preventive care has appeared, beyond the hortatory efforts of health educators, appealing to people to do, or to refrain from doing, what they offer as protection against specific diseases; tuberculosis, cancer, poliomyelitis, rheumatic hearts, and so forth.

Only recently has it become clear that health, as a positive goal, might be projected ahead in terms of increasingly specific practices and improved ways of living. Thus it has been asserted that, if there is to be any preventive medicine or health care and any mental *hygiene* the primary responsibility rests, not upon the physicians and psychiatrists, but upon the family and the schools, beginning with nursery schools.

To maintain and protect the health of the growing child, the family must provide the needed nutrition through family meals, the required sanitary care and cleanliness through good housekeeping, laundering, dish-washing and similar daily chores, adequate sleep and warmth through provision of beds and quietness, and of clothing. All the daily activities of home-making and child care and rearing (including care of minor ills, like colds) offer the only way preventive medicine or health care can become meaningful and operational.

The housewife-mother is revealed as the primary agent for health care and upon her rests the basic responsibility of preventive medicine if that term is to have any real significance. The physicians can and must help her, guide her, and assist her when the infant or child is threatened by acute illness or failure to grow and develop appropriately. But the wife-mother-housekeeper is the primary agent for the health not only of children, but of all members of the family—her husband and any others in the household.

Likewise, to guard and foster the emerging personality of the developing individual, the parents, especially the mother, must provide the warm, comforting, unconditional love and patient care and rearing through which the infant gains confidence in the world and learns to accept the many and often severe frustrations, deprivations, interferences, and coercions which are involved in his socialization. We are only just beginning to realize what is involved in the familiar homely practices of baby feeding and weaning, of teaching regularization and control of elimination, of helping the child to manage his emotional reactions, especially to these many threats and compulsions. Likewise, we are becoming aware of how difficult it is for the child to learn the prescribed conduct for social living—to respect private property and the person of others, to perform all the required practices of manners, etiquette, cleanliness, and the masculine and feminine roles, to respond to and use language, all of which require him to take over and exhibit what it has taken the human race thousands of years to learn.

Moreover, we have scarcely realized the difficulties and hazards to the emerging personality of the child in learning to live in a symbolic world in which every object, animal, event, situation and person is given a symbolic designation or name, and is defined in symbolic terms, with explanations, sanctions and all the other complicated ideas of our traditional religion, philosophy, laws, folklore, and arts, plus increasingly our science.

It is the office of the parent, as cultural agent, to transmit these traditional ideas, beliefs, and patterns of conduct and of feelings to children, thereby inducting them into our cultural and social worlds. How it is done and how the child "takes it," especially when the parental training is too severe, too hasty or premature, too harsh and uncompensated with love and reassurance, are of major significance for mental health. Thus, if we are to have mental hygiene, in the sense of prevention of personality disorders, or if we want mental health, in the form of robust, courageous, emotionally balanced and socially adequate personalities, they can be developed only in the family setting through the informed and cherishing care of parents and all those who, as physicians, nurses, and others, are involved in infant and child care and rearing.

These considerations explain why health care, physical and mental, has lagged and why the task is so difficult because parents, especially mothers, must be given renewed confidence and helpful guidance for doing what only mothers can and must do in the family. Today so many women have lost confidence in themselves, largely because they feel that only the trained specialist, pediatrician, nurse, nutritionist, psychiatrist, psychologist, educator, can do anything of significance for children.

It becomes necessary therefore to make a specific effort to reassure mothers, to explain to them their immense responsibilities and their equally great opportunities to foster and maintain the health and personality of their children. What takes place in the home and family in these daily activities of housekeeping and the baby and child care and rearing is the focus of preventive medicine and mental hygiene. Through these homely, seemingly trivial practices, the mother stands guard over and actively promotes the health, physical and mental, of her family, especially her children, as no physician, nurse, or other specialist can or will. These are the basic processes of preventive medicine and mental hygiene, and of culturization, through which as a people we can even more effectively discard those traditional beliefs and practices that foster human defeat and distortion, replacing them with new conceptions and practices that will more effectively advance our cherished values and aspirations.

In the same way it is being discovered that for continuing health care and mental hygiene for children, the schools are the chief agency. Not the clinics and the many specialists who can diagnose and treat the various ills, defects, and handicaps, but the school personnel, especially the classroom teacher. What she does to and for children, as one personality acting, reacting, and inter-reacting with members of the class is the active, daily process of mental hygiene.

But teachers are in many cases much like mothers today. They have been impressed by the specialized knowledge and training of the physicians, the nurses, the social workers, the psychiatrists, the psychologists, and other professionals, and so many have lost confidence in themselves as teachers to do what only teachers can and must do for growing children.

The teacher in the classroom is the strategic person for mental health because he is the only one in the position to do what must be done to help children and youth grow up and achieve maturity with some degree of sanity and of adequacy for social living. But teachers themselves must realize and accept this by revising their image of themselves and by redefining their roles and their functions in the light of these larger opportunities before them to make their work more significant socially and more interesting and absorbing professionally.

Too many people are engaged in telling teachers what to do; in consequence they are often confused and bewildered by the variety of often contradictory advice and instruction. Likewise they are often resentful of the way they are told to do this or that or stop doing something else, and this feeling may sometimes distort and pervert even well-meant advice.

Those who are concerned with education and teaching, even those eager to develop mental health programs, are apt to forget that teachers are personalities. They have their own idiomatic ways of thinking, acting, feeling, their own personal convictions and their fears and hopes. Moreover, as personalities they have their own highly individualized patterns of human relations, toward others, including their pupils.

Instead of telling teachers what to do, it might be more helpful and illuminating to consider how teachers might become more aware of themselves as personalities, and of their characteristic ways of dealing with others, especially pupils. This is difficult and professionally unprecedented because teacher training programs have fostered the belief that a teacher, as a professional with the prescribed courses of instruction and practice teaching, was a sort of impersonal, wholly objective, rational, intellectual being, who left his personality at home when going to teach in school.

Like the little boy who insisted the king had no clothes on, to the consternation of his subjects, anyone who asserts that teachers are personalities, not just pedagogic robots, is apt to provoke various reactions of uneasiness and even resentment. But it seems clear that without such a recognition, not much can be done in the way of discussing mental health programs in schools.

To recognize that teachers are personalities, with their personal life history, their web of personal human relations to their own parents, to their husbands and wives and children, to others close to them, is essential then.

This does not imply any desire to make teachers self-conscious, analytical, and worried over themselves. It points rather to the professional question of how teachers, as professionals, can develop a larger capacity for seeing and meeting the personality needs of pupils, even though that may involve a high degree of self-disciplined and self-restrained conduct on their part.

For example, a physician learns, more or less effectively, that he must approach patients as individuals who are "frightened people," to use Elton Mayo's phrase. They are worried, often acutely anxious because they are sick; they need the reassurance of someone who offers the security of professional knowledge and skill, who offers needed treatment and restores their morale. The physician is trained to face the most disturbing bodily conditions and situations, which are often overwhelming or revolting to the layman, and to provide his best medical care to patients who are often repulsive and despicable to anyone else. Likewise, nurses learn to treat patients, often querulous and unreasonably demanding, loathsome in their personal bodily habits and conditions, and to give them what they can of care, patient treatment, and a feeling of being recognized as a person.

All the professions concerned with individuals, the ministers and priests, the social workers, the psychiatrists and so on, with greater or less effectiveness are taught to provide for those they help what each individually needs without letting their own personal feelings and reactions toward such persons interfere too much with their professional practices. This does not mean that they are impersonal and lack feelings, or that they are "all things to all people." It does mean that they have a professional ideal of serving and helping individuals apart from their moral or ethical or personal judgment of the individual before them. They have become aware of their personal bias and prejudices, of their likes and dislikes, and have learned to give professional help.

Those who, like the physician or psychiatrist or minister or priest, are in a peculiarly personal relationship to the individual, also recognize that to be effective in their professional services they must gain and hold the confidence of the individual. Here we are learning that there is a great difference between *teaching*, telling others and instructing them in certain content and methods — and *learning*, which is what the individual remembers, what he understands, accepts, and uses in his personal life.

For *learning* there must be some readiness to accept what at first may not be meaningful. There must be a taking over and translation into the individual's own idiomatic system of ideas and conduct. Then too, much learning takes place beyond what is taught, as the individual (pupil, for example) learns a variety of things from experiencing events, personal reactions, and expressions of feelings which the teacher and others exhibit often without realizing what they are doing.

It would seem both desirable and necessary to ask teachers to reflect upon their professional image, their conception of the teacher's role, and of the teacher's relationship to pupils, as a basic element in the classroom situation. This is especially important because teacher training programs give little or no consideration to this, contenting themselves with the more formal aspects of training teachers.

Then it would seem appropriate to consider what teachers, as personalities as well as socially sanctioned guardians and instructors of the young, can and should do for guarding the mental health of children and youth.

First, they can more clearly realize the significance of what they so often complain of — namely, that the child's family have either neglected his early education or have done things to and for him that show in various forms of undesirable, even disorderly behavior, of emotional instability, or withdrawn, sulky detachment from his group. It is customary for educators to denounce parents and scold the family for these conditions, but it may be questioned whether this is either professionally sound or socially desirable. If the physicians and nurses, the hospitals and clinics, the psychiatrists, and others who face children suffering plainly from parental neglect, maltreatment, and even abuse, shrugged their shoulders, soundly scolded parents, and threw the children out as too troublesome, too disorderly, too far gone to warrant their time and effort, we would question their professional fitness for their posts.

Now teachers today are being confronted with more and more children who are exhibiting conduct that is disorderly or negativistic. They are tried, often beyond endurance, by these unsocialized children who will not, and often cannot, conform to classroom requirements and accept the prescribed instruction because they are suffering from so many forms of parental neglect and mistreatment, from the disorderly and often sub-human conditions of bad housing and demoralized neighborhoods. Others coming from economically well-favored homes and good neighborhoods show various neurotic traits, from the marital conflicts at home, the preoccupied fathers and busy mothers, also often neurotic, and other family situations that block and warp the emerging personality of the child.

If the schools are to meet these conditions, which will probably get worse for another generation or so, then it will be necessary for them to reconsider both the school programs—what they now require of children in the way of knowledge and skill, and the role and functions of the teachers as agents for mental health who can and should provide the utmost possible to help these children escape from their past experiences and to go forward more courageously and adequately.

A generation or two ago when the family was relatively stable and secure in its undisturbed beliefs and familiar home practices, when the basic education of the child was conducted by the family and the church, children came to school with certain expectations and attitudes—they expected to learn what was taught, to work hard, to be obedient, to accept authority of teachers and principals, and thus generally to conform.

The school could set its program and authorize the teachers to conduct their classrooms in certain recognized patterns, understood and accepted by families and children. But today this prior family-church education and preparation of children is rapidly breaking down as shown by the problem children in schools and the growing demand for child guidance clinics which are already overwhelmed. The schools cannot go on putting out these problem children as if they were still operating in the 1890's.

The school, as indicated by various experiments and new programs, are trying to modify and adapt their programs to the needs and possibilities of the children of today. In general these are trending toward more group activities and expressive programs, to help these children to develop a greater capacity for group living, for interpersonal relationships, for self-discipline, and orderly activity, as contrasted with the older classroom ideal, each child sitting quiet and passive at his desk, not talking and not moving until the teachers gave permission or orders, not working with others since that was considered disorderly and cheating.

We are realizing that the older schoolroom program and situations, however appropriate and effective a generation ago, are now more than questionable. They put the individual child in a "psychological straitjacket" in which he is compelled to sit quietly for hours, often mute, while he mulls over and rehearses internally his phantasies, his frustrations and hostilities, and his escapes—physically present in a group, but psychologically cut off from the very social living he so urgently needs.

Likewise we are recognizing that the older practice of an authoritative teacher who maintains order by imposing her authority and discipline upon pupils is also questionable. It perpetuates the dominance-submission, passive relationship which handicaps the emerging personality in achieving a more mature personality who can accept the self-discipline essential to a free society. This has become almost the central problem of a democratic social order, because each individual citizen must assume the burdens of freedom and exhibit orderly, responsible conduct if we are to have such a social order and avoid dictatorship.

The classroom offers the most promising place for mental health programs in view of the difficulties of family life today. If the teachers will more clearly recognize in their pupils these idiomatic personality make-ups and needs that have emerged from family backgrounds and more effectively interpret what the child is telling us daily in his speech, his conduct, his displays of emotion, in everything he does, just as each profession has learned to look for and interpret the different symptoms and indicators, so teachers can become more sensitive to the appearance and meaning of children's behavior.

Day by day the child exposes his individual personality make-up and feelings—his "private world," which give the observant teacher clues to what is going on inside and what he needs. This does not mean that teachers should become amateur psychiatrists, attempting to diagnose and treat personality problems. It means that, as teachers, they can and should be alert to what the child is telling them in these various indirect or overt but disguised expressions so that they can deal with the child as a personality, not as a passive doll to be taught or disciplined for showing any resistance, inattention, or disorder.

Everything a child does is meaningful. His way of sitting and standing, of writing and speaking, his errors and mistakes in school work are symptomatic, not merely of inattention and lack of effort, but more often of a fundamental confusion in his whole orientation to life. Likewise, his free drawing or painting or modeling, his story-telling and other activities such as reactions to classmates, are also revealing to the observant eye of how he thinks, believes, and feels toward life.

Our previous philosophy of education stressed the importance of molding the child's mind and conduct to the socially sanctioned patterns and goals which family, church, and nation accepted. Resistance or failure to conform or to achieve the prescribed standards of work and conduct were interpreted as willful disobedience or moral weakness. Likewise, the young offender or delinquent was adjudged a deliberate enemy of society, tried and, if found guilty, punished by imprisonment.

This philosophy of education and of law was meaningful and more or less effective a generation or so ago, but within recent decades the social-cultural context of our lives has broken down; we have lost much of our personal security and become more and more confused. Moreover, we have gained new insights into these personality expressions and so are recognizing the delinquent as either an unsocialized individual coming from disorderly family and neighborhood life, or as an emotionally disturbed, often neurotic, personality whose illegal behavior is a symptom of his profound internal conflicts and unhappiness.

The permeation of these insights into education and the application of this new understanding and these recently developed practices for helping children and youth marks the ongoing transformation of the schools into agencies of child conservation, of preventive medicine and health care, of mental hygiene, increasingly prepared to provide what children so acutely need today, especially to reinforce and often replace the family care and socialization.

It should be emphasized again and again that this does not mean converting the schools into child guidance clinics, of subordinating education to other and alien purposes. It does not mean turning the schools over to the psychiatrist and psychologist to run, although it does mean closer working relationships and better mutual understanding with these specialists.

Primarily mental health in the schools is the responsibility and the opportunity of educators, particularly of classroom and other teachers (physical education, art, and shop), to do to and for pupils what they can uniquely do. Moreover, the most promising practices and methods for fostering mental health in the schools are coming from the experiments and new programs being developed by teachers themselves. The psychiatrists, the psychologists, and others have much to contribute to education and have indeed helped in many of these new programs. But the responsibility is that of the educators, and the methods and procedures which will effectively guard the mental health of school children are essentially group and individual classroom procedures and relationships.

What is needed immediately is a gathering up and critical review and integration of these experiments and procedures, a detailed and effective presentation of what has been developed and tried out by teachers for the training of new teachers and the guidance of teachers now in service.

The guiding principle for these endeavors is to start with children, their growth, development, and maturation and their emerging personality, their needs for help in meeting the requirements of social life and in building an orderly, more or less peaceful "private world" through the human relationships which can effectively supply what they so acutely need. This means flexibly adapting curricula, methods, course requirements, and the whole of the formal procedures to the children, thus recognizing that, as individual personalities with unique needs, ways of learning, and maturing, each child in the group should be encouraged and guided *in his own way and at his own rate* to meet the school requirements or such modifications thereof as are necessary in the interest of the child's development.

Thus what the individual child is curious about, what he wants to know and do in order to resolve his perplexities and often anxieties, gives the clue to what he is ready to learn and will accept as meaningful, as contrasted with the prescribed content to be taught under penalty of failure and of humiliation for failure.

It is astonishing how much teaching has relied upon threats and punishments to coerce children, deliberately humiliating the child before his group and family, as a way of "motivating" him to learn and to achieve. What the child learns from these experiences in the way of resistance to formal education, hatred of reading and other intellectual pursuits, resentment toward all authority, evasions and escapes into phantasy or overt truancy and delinquency, to avoid these intolerable situations or to "get even"—these are the lessons we are learning from the child guidance clinics which, as Dr. James Plant has put it, have tried to find out what school *means* to the child.

Until they have been effectively crushed and deprived of interests and curiosities, children are eager to learn. They ask questions, explore, adventure, and persistently seek to understand, but they are just as persistently *dis*couraged, intimidated, misled, or ignored and otherwise robbed of these desirable qualities by parents and schools conscientiously trying to discipline and teach children but ignoring the mainsprings of learning, development, and maturation.

The schools can foster and when necessary revive curiosities and eagerness as various school programs have shown, but it calls for a giving up of fixed, prescribed programs, set time schedules, and other rigidities that seek to compel children to fit the school instead of fitting the school program to the children.

Much of the resistance to such changes and the uneasiness of the teachers (if not their anxiety) arises from what is now an out-of-date, unfounded belief about human nature and personality development. Teachers are apt to become fearful that all social order and morality will break down if children are not kept under strong discipline and threatened by all manner of punishment. They are caught by their loyalty to the older, terrorizing practices of child rearing and the actual misbehavior and disorder of the children in their classrooms. They strive to maintain order by sheer force of dominating the children—scolding, threatening, humiliating, disgracing and punishing them (personally or by higher authority). They can and often do succeed in keeping a semblance of order and getting some school work done by such methods which usually exhaust the teacher and increase the internal tensions and external pressures for the children.

Thus the children may go through school finding nothing to help them achieve self-discipline and internal peace and go out into the world, often a menace to social order and to themselves, as we see in delinquents, alcoholics, drug addicts, sex offenders, and others who undermine social order or defeat themselves.

It takes a courageous belief in children and a patient, understanding realization of what is needed to help children, slowly, very slowly—like recovering from a serious illness—to release their accumulated feelings in ways that are not destructive to others or to themselves, and to build up a faith in the fairness and justice and friendly attitudes of adults (to replace their frequent belief that grown-ups are oppressive and antagonistic). If the child is given opportunity to find release, especially through symbolic and play activities (art, dramatizations, music, story-telling, and "planned success") under guidance of an adult he feels he can trust, he will, like a patient who passes a crisis in his illness, begin to improve.

But if supervisors and principals insist upon quiet and order and mark teachers as incompetent when they try to give children needed releases and helpful activities, even the most inventive and concerned teachers will be discouraged as we see so frequently happen among the young teachers who come eagerly to our schools and meet with antagonism and professional discouragement, sometimes from other teachers.

It is scarcely fair to ask teachers as individuals to expose themselves to these administrative hazards and resistances. The school systems as a whole or at least the school as a unit must have some guiding philosophy and make a commitment to mental health if teachers as individuals are to go forward along the lines already explored and developed by other teachers and by those who have been working with children in group therapy and similar adjustive situations.

If we are to keep our free society and carry on our efforts to achieve a democratic social order, the schools have a large, inescapable responsibility to guard the mental health of children. Moreover, if we are to take seriously our belief in the value and worth of the individual personality and the dignity of man, then we must begin to respect the emerging personality of the child and treat the child from infancy on with more regard for his dignity as a person.

How radical and far-reaching the foregoing statement is will be discovered by looking at what we now do to and for children in families and in schools. How far we fail to respect the personality and accord dignity to the child is written large, in the many forms of human defeat and maladjustment, indeed in our whole social-economic, political life and in all our human relations.

It is the quiet, devoted work of some parents and some teachers, patiently, day by day, helping children to meet the tasks of life with courage and with adequacy, giving them a sense of belonging and being loved and accepted, which offers the major hope for the future.

(FROM: *Education*, vol. 66, No. 9 [May, 1946].)

TWENTY-TWO

Art and Living

IF WE ARE to resolve the present confusion about art and life, we must seek a better understanding of the part that aesthetic experience plays in shaping conduct and satisfying human needs. For this purpose we should consider some of the recent views of human behavior put forth by psychologists and psychiatrists.

For our present discussion the most significant aspect of behavior is that the individual only sees, hears, or otherwise perceives what experience has prepared him to receive. That is to say, he selects out of each situation those aspects that he has learned to regard and ignores all else. To this selected scene he responds in definite patterns which transform his impulses to behavior into meaningful conduct. Put in another way, the individual faces a world of meaning, significance, and value because he has learned to see it in those terms, and he deals with that world through the patterned conduct he has developed under the influence of his cultural tradition. This means that there are no objective, unequivocal situations: not only man but all other organisms see the world in terms of their needs, life experience, and heredity. If man finds the world congenial to his desires or austerely valuable, it is because he has imputed those meanings and values to the world, projecting thereon his own imaginings and hopes. Out of the myriad aspects the universe wears, man everywhere has selected the few he will attend to and, assuming the relationships he deems important, has built up his culture.

The essential characteristic of human behavior, then, is this selective awareness and the patterned response, which give rise to what we call conduct, with its implication of past experience. This, then, brings us to the threshold of our inquiry, because the source of these selections and patterns is immediately the cultural tradition, and that, in turn, is the product of artistic creation. Whatever man has learned to observe and the manner of his dealing with the world of events and people have come from the insight and imagination of the artist, poet, religious or philosophical seer, or the creative scientist—all those who fashion ideas, conceptions, and forms that give meaning and value to life and furnish the patterns for conduct. It is they who have constructed the "world" we live in, and by their several arts persuaded us to accept it as the one among many worlds we should prefer. Human conduct, then, may be viewed as the way the individual accepts this artistic-cultural guidance, reconciles it with his own unique self, and utilizes the arts for such reenforcement and "escapes" as he needs to fulfill the demands of social life.

First we may note that every civilization or culture has developed around certain conceptions of the universe and man's place therein which have dominated the social life. It is enough to refer to the world conceptions and moral ideas of the Hebrews whose poet-prophets created the framework of Jewish culture and set the major problems of its people. Contemporaneously Egyptian civilization was flourishing upon different conceptions and values, while somewhat later the Greek culture arose with still other conceptions and ideals of life. In each the individual learned to regard those aspects of the world and of human activity to which the artists, poets, philosophers, and priests had sensitized him by their several imaginations. Thus we see how the very quality of a civilization is the product of artistic creation, the fruit of those valuations that the genius of the race or people has placed upon nature and man.

Since abstract conceptions and moral aims can operate only through concrete activity, in each culture we find definite patterns of behavior through which the ideals and values of the people are to be achieved and conserved. Here we find the artist supremely powerful since his imaginative embodiments of those issues really direct the conduct of life. More than we realize, significant education occurs through aesthetic experience of stories, drama, and poetry wherein a person realizes the valuations and the patterns that emotionally satisfy him. He identifies himself with the characters of the artist's creation whom he strives to emulate, or develops an aversion to others who affront his sensibilities and outrage his values.

In artistic creations he responds to stimuli for the evocation and channeling of emotional reactions; suddenly he finds himself moved by hitherto unsuspected aspects of life, now revealed in poignant form and action. Again he discovers patterns for behaving that give rise to unique conduct or an altered response to familiar situations. Often he finds interpretations of experiences that have long troubled him by their discrepant, if not incongruous, character, forcing him to harbor conflicting beliefs and fears; the artistic insight, piercing through these experiences, integrates them into a coherent and meaningful whole. Sometimes he receives an awaited answer to his anxieties, when the artist offers him a pattern that resolves his doubts and hesitations by crystallizing his suspended action into an expression he had never dared to hope for.

We need only remember the history of man's sex behavior and relationships to find examples of these artistic contributions to life. In every culture, the primitive, elemental desires of man have been fashioned and patterned by the artistic imagination that has compelled an acquiescence no force or coercion could evoke. How art serves to pattern sex life is vividly seen in early adolescence when the youth and maiden, suddenly impelled by a new flood of sex awareness, turn to fiction, drama, and poetry for patterns into which they may direct their conduct and express their feelings.

Beyond these values and instrumental patterns, art offers the purely aesthetic experiences, which, because of their sheer artistic perfection, are seized upon by man, hungry for organized and coherent experience, in a world where, for him at least, only art can minister to such a need. It is just this perfection of form, in the general sense of that term and not merely in spatial proportions, that gives art its compelling power over man—who must continually suffer from the distorted, warped and asymmetrical experiences of daily life. The capacity for aesthetic experience and the ability to respond may be enormously extended and refined by experience that further sensitizes the individual and sharpens his receptivity, as witness the career of the artist himself who must patiently attain a mastery of his chosen medium and the possession of a sensitive awareness.

When an individual undergoes an aesthetic experience, he passes through a critical and pervasive change in his whole self, wherein not the intellect or mind alone, but the whole organism responds. The visceral, emotional response is prominent, and the glands are called into play. Suddenly he awakes to a feeling of kinship or relatedness to some thing or person heretofore ignored or viewed indifferently, or he turns in revolt against long-cherished or tolerated situations.

As Thornton Wilder in *The Woman of Andros* has said, "We can only be said to be alive in those moments when our hearts are conscious of our treasure." That consciousness is essentially the fruit of our aesthetic training and experience wherein we have become aware of the treasures that the artist or poet has shown us, not alone in works of art, but in nature and human relations. If we possess treasures in the objects of the world or in the person and behavior of others, we owe them to the artists who have taught us to see and to value those aspects of life.

Art is socially significant because it provides the patterns and the aesthetic experiences that rule human conduct, above and beyond all factors in man or in life. Whatever we are or may become we derive from the artist, however he be named or labeled, and in his creations we find our ideals, our hopes, our values and meanings which set our goals and dictate our conduct. The artist gives the form or pattern for human activity and invests our otherwise dull and shabby lives with significance and purpose. We toil and suffer, strain and renounce, because we are under the sway of patterns he has laid upon us, and when we rejoice and are glad we do so because the artist has in a real sense created the occasions out of the drab round of our organic necessities. The very tonic of achievement that sustains and rewards us, far beyond the actual rewards or goals attained, comes from the artist's subtle attribution of value to those ends and to the process of striving.

Just because these patterns are so compelling that we can violate or ignore them only at our peril, art is socially necessary to provide the aids to morale, to courage, to the sustained activity necessitated by their coercion. If life demands effort and the renunciation of easily won goals, we need artistic reinforcements to be found in the aesthetic experiences of religion, music, art, both conceptual and plastic, and the group ritual wherein we reaffirm our patterns and our beliefs.

Every simple culture has these artistic aids, and the more it is faced with the raw impact of nature, the more importance it accords to them. In primitive cultures rituals dominate every activity as the group endeavors to sustain an unceasing relation to the world of its imaginative creation. Indeed it is the function of religion to provide man with a conception of the universe and his relations thereto that will give him a purpose and a sense of security without which life has no meaning. In the arts, religion has always found its most potent ally, as we see in the devotion of European art to the great Christian epic.

While art furnishes the patterns of human conduct and the aids to their performance, it also serves to provide the "escapes," through which man turns his back upon the world of duties and necessities, forgets the austere consolations and aids, and finds sheer delight in a wholly imaginary life portrayed for him by the artist. Therein he finds release from burdens, relaxation of his exigent tensions, and freedom, if only momentarily, from the continual anxieties he bears within him. He turns to these escapes because he wants experience that will lift him completely out of himself and his normal preoccupations and he finds therein an indulgent world that accepts him with all his follies and his weaknesses.

Whosoever can create these escapes through aesthetic experience may command society. He may have any rewards he chooses, far out-reaching the payments given to the sober worker in any other field, however exalted. Nor does he need to observe the ordinary restrictions and requirements put upon the normal citizen, since to him are accorded privileges and immunities that defy the law. Such rare individuals become the focus of interest and attention, public characters with whom the audience makes an identification, wistfully living a vicarious life of bright energy and full consummation of frustrated desires. In their creations or performances they are the most potent individuals in the group, since during their brief ascendancy they outrank and overlay all other claimants to the public attention. How pervasive and effective their influence may be we can never tell, since we are unable to discover how often their skillful performance has lured an individual away into the world of phantasy from which he has returned with new vigor or endurance. We can see today in the following of popular actors, especially in the movies, how vitally the patterns and escapes provided by art are regarded by the public, even those which may be as enervating as habit-forming drugs.

If we are so dependent upon art for values and patterns, for reinforcement and for escapes, what happens when our dependency fails of adequate response by the artist? The answer is found readily enough, for we today are witnessing on a large scale the conflict between the cultural patterns and the recently arisen demands of life in an industrial society. The old patterns are no longer congruous or applicable and we exhaust ourselves attempting to make the stubborn situation conform to the pattern when the situation is beyond such control. Along with this futile struggle to impose these old patterns upon alien situations of an industrial, urban society, we suffer grievously from the lack of any unequivocal direction, since there are so many competing voices bidding us to follow, but none speaking with the authority of aesthetic insight to which we can hearken. These conflicts and anxieties, these frustrations and perplexities, reveal themselves in overt form that may easily be recognized in irritability, worry, and other forms of mild confusion and in the more acute signs of distress or mental disorder and criminal action, where we see the individual who has been driven from the scene by his anxiety and confusion or has broken through the prescribed rules. A society must have a body of common values, ideas, conceptions, and beliefs to give it any integrity and cohesiveness and to provide the individual with socially sanctioned patterns.

When, in addition to the incongruity of the patterns offered us, we have insufficient art to bolster our sorely tried morale and to provide escapes that are not too enervating, then we have widespread despair, suicide, sterility, and general failure, while those who are not so seized throw themselves into activities where they dare not reflect or question lest they too be plunged into darkness. We have records of such periods to ponder upon and compare with our own. The increased urgency for escapes is a natural corollary of such low periods in human history and, as might be expected, the escapes are correspondingly more crude and enervating since, even in his phantasy, man cannot endure too robust creations when his morale is low and his direction is wavering.

If we ask people generally what art does for them, we will be met by the reply, nothing: art is too highbrow or complicated or meaningless. But, as we have just seen, every person is living on artistic creations; his very patterns of behavior, actual and ideal, are gifts of the artists and prophets of yesterday, and he turns to aesthetic experiences to console and sustain him against the strains and tasks of living. In his patronage of the movies, the comic strips, the fiction magazines and novels, in dancing and music, especially jazz, he finds escapes all of which are artistic creations, however poor in quality or aim some may believe. We all are living on art and only dimly aware of it, while we are completely ignorant of the treasures of art that we might tap if we had the wit or intelligence. It is as if we were living on chaff and muddy water while rich stores of good food and drink lay waiting, only occasionally being visited by a select few who, by the very character of their aesthetic snobbery, serve to repel the curiosity of the famished others. We do need an artist to reveal the resources of art for daily living.

What, if anything, can we do to foster art and develop artists who will create the new patterns for which an emerging industrial society so desperately awaits? Through what process can we rear the artists who will help to liberate us from the old loyalties and coercions which, by their very persistence, increase the difficulties of this emerging new culture? Especially do we need this emancipation in our personal lives, since we cannot advance under the weight of those dying ideas bequeathed to us by the culture of the past. As D. H. Lawrence has put it:

It is the way our sympathy flows and recoils that really determines our lives. And here lies the vast importance of the novel, properly handled. It can inform and lead into new places the flow of our sympathetic consciousness, and it can lead our sympathy away in recoil from things gone dead. Therefore, the novel, properly handled, can reveal the most secret places of life: for it is in the *passional* secret places of life, above all, that the tide of sensitive awareness needs to ebb and flow, cleansing and freshening.

But the novel, like gossip, can also excite spurious sympathies and recoils, mechanical and deadening to the psyche. The novel can glorify the most corrupt feelings, so long as they are *conventionally* 'pure.' Then the novel, like gossip, becomes at last vicious, and, like gossip, all the more vicious because it is always ostensibly on the side of the angels.

How can we stimulate the creation of the artistic reinforcements needed to sustain our courage and provoke our efforts toward the great achievements involved in developing a new culture? And how can we evoke the artists who will furnish us those escapes we so greatly need as the social life around us of necessity becomes more highly organized and controlled by plan and instrument? As the means of living continue to become more standardized and uniform (as they must become and properly so), human life can be liberated from those preoccupations with nutrition and shelter that have for so long dominated human society. When so liberated, the energy thus available will need new ideals and patterns not only to give life significance and meaning, but to provide opportunities for exercise of the courage, perseverance, and *élan* man has developed through aeons of struggling against hunger, danger, and enemies in an hostile environment.

Finally, let us note that with this realization of the human origin of our values and ideals there has come a leaden despair, a disillusionment so acute that many assert the game is up. It is true that man creates his own values, and most of those he has cherished are obsolescent if not dead, but it is also to be remembered that the human needs and functions that found expression in those values continue to exist, awaiting formulation in new patterns.

Is it not possible to hail this discovery of the nature and function of values, their inception in artistic insight and formulation in aesthetic patterns, as the most hopeful discovery of our time? It immediately delivers into our hand the very inmost secret of personality and of conduct, and if only we have the artists who can speak in the new language of our times, we can remake man and his society. The really crucial problem is to evoke the artist and infuse him with a passionate conviction of his own insights which he can then communicate to others while remaining aware of his social significance.

But what of the artist upon whose bounty we are so dependent? What is the source of his inspiration and his artistry, and what role does artistic activity play in his life? We are singularly uninformed about the artist since he is usually so incomprehensible to his fellows that he rarely attempts to reveal the secret of his own dreams and longings. From what we do know, it is clear that the artist is one who somehow is never completely caught up into the current of contemporary life, but rather is gifted, often tortured, by detachment, a sense of isolation that gives his vision a different perspective upon the ordinary affairs and objects of life. He sees situations and relations out of focus, judged by the common man's way of looking at things, and by that distortion from the obvious, transforms the everyday and ordinary into a thing of beauty or significance. Or, as today, he is so irritated and disturbed by the aspects of disorganized life he sees, which others complacently accept, that he gives himself to a destructive fury.

One who has this warped vision with the sensitive awareness that often accompanies it, and the deftness of tongue or finger to project his insights, can never be content with the routine affairs of life. They are devoid of meaning beside the shining reality presented to his sharpened gaze, and so he must, with almost frantic zeal, attempt to communicate what he has glimpsed of forms, situations, relations, values, and meanings, and the subtle nuances of life that are the heart of artistic performances. The artist is such an one because he must be such, although his way of life might be immensely more productive and wholesome if, as Leo Stein has pointed out, he were accepted by society as sane and normal.

For the thousands who are drawn to artistic activity, there may be but one who is sufficiently gifted to produce the patterns so essential to life. Only by the multiplication of artists, however, can we hope to find several such as we need today. It would be wise, therefore, to encourage artistic activity, especially among the young, where we may perhaps foster a talent or a genius that otherwise would be buried or diverted into less important work. We can today with good grace undertake such encouragement because, as we are discovering, even the most fumbling artistic efforts may yield a large satisfaction to the individual. Indeed, as our leisure time grows, it is probable that artistic activities, so long confined to the relatively few, will become a resource of all but the dullest, as we find in them new avenues to expression, new resources of reassurance, and new escapes from perplexity. With the growth of artistic activity, even though most of it be upon an elementary and pedestrian level, there will be a realization of the nature of the artistic purpose and a closer sympathy with the real artist and his strivings. Then and then only will our social life have attained a maturity of deliberate purposiveness and the artist will begin to feel at home in the world.

(FROM: *The American Magazine of Art,* 24 [1932]: 325-30.)

TWENTY-THREE

Science and Culture

THERE is a growing interest in the relation of science to society as evidenced by the increasing number of public discussions, papers, and books focussed on this question. For the most part these discussions are concerned with the changes coming from applied science and technology or are carried on in terms of large abstractions, such as Science and Society, with a capital "S." Little attention is being given to the influence of scientific advances upon the traditional Western European culture upon which our society and our personal lives are organized.

Discussion of this topic is difficult because at present we have so few clear ideas and little or no adequate terminology. Indeed it may be said that we are only beginning to gain an awareness of culture, a realization that we live in a culture and, as we shall point out later, that culture is in us. In offering this discussion, therefore, it is hoped that the reader will be patient if it seems somewhat circuitous and at times puzzling. If, however, we are seeking some understanding of the meaning and significance of science for culture, we must first seek a clearer picture of what culture means and does.

Man as an organism exists along with all other organisms in the geographical world of physical, chemical, and biological events and processes that we call nature. Throughout the long period of animal evolution every other species has come to terms with nature by differentiation and specialization of structures and functions for its life zone or environment. The persistence of some forms seemingly unchanged from the more remote horizons of geological time is convincing evidence of the effectiveness of these adaptations for survival. It is also eloquent testimony to the price that has been paid for survival on these terms because it has involved fixity and sacrifice of any further developmental changes.

Man, as we are beginning to realize, is unique because, unlike all other species, he has not made an adaptation to nature by organic specialization and bodily differentiation; but through ideas and the use of tools, he has created a human way of life; thereby he has retained his organic plasticity, remained biologically young, unspecialized and capable of continued development. Until we pause and reflect on this human way of life, we may not realize the full significance of what man has attempted. Instead of accepting one of the innumerable modes of biological existence on the level of organic functioning and impulsive behavior, man has attempted to live in a world of his own creation. To do so it has been necessary not only to forego life on a biological level, but also to create the assumptions and the concepts upon which he could build this human world.

At this late date in man's history it is impossible to speak with any surety about his early days, so that at best we can but hazard some surmise and suggest a few clues to an understanding of that past. Perhaps the most fruitful interpretation we can offer is to realize that from the beginning man has faced certain persistent tasks of life, namely:

1. To come to terms with nature in order to gain sustenance, to find security, and to achieve survival in a world both precarious and problematic.
2. To organize a group life so that individuals can live together and participate in the division of labor, which group living both necessitates and makes possible.
3. To transform organic functioning and impulsive behavior into the patterned conduct of group life and of human living as distinct from biological functioning.

This contrast between man and other species provides a clue to the understanding of what we call culture. It must be clear that if man was not to follow other species he must develop certain assumptions or beliefs about the world and himself that would not only justify but also compel him to act toward the world, toward other individuals, and himself in ways that offered some solution to these persistent life tasks.

Here we face one of the major difficulties in discussing such a topic because in the endeavor to formulate this unique relation of man to the world and his fellows, the most extraordinary variety of ideas and concepts has been developed. Whenever we attempt,

SCIENCE AND CULTURE   277

therefore, to discuss this question we are almost inevitably betrayed by the very language we employ for that purpose. Let us briefly pause, therefore, to see if we can make this situation clearer without importing into the discussion the usual mystical and subjective implications with which this topic has for so long been burdened.

Each species has worked out a way of life by learning to deal with certain selected aspects of the environment. Thus we find in the same life zone insects, reptiles, birds, and mammals finding sustenance and achieving survival, each, as it were, living in one of the many worlds which the environment provides for its selective awareness, specialized needs, and differentiated capacities. These diverse but coexisting worlds are created out of the totality of nature by what each species responds to and what it ignores or disregards — by the perspective which the environment presents to each organism.

In these terms we may conceive of man as attempting to work out his way of life by and through the specific meanings, significances, and relationships which he imputes to, or imposes upon, this same environment. He is still living in nature and he is still dealing with the actual world, but whatever he sees, thinks, feels, and does is governed by these concepts and assumptions that he makes about that world and himself.

Culture, then, is the process by which man creates and maintains this peculiarly human world and mode of living, built in terms of the ideas and conceptions that he himself has created and imposed upon nature and himself. All over the earth, therefore, we find different groups of people existing in this same geographical world of nature but living in distinct cultural worlds of their own historical creation.

Each of these different cultures may be looked upon as a different solution proposed by man to the persistent life tasks in terms of its four basic organizing conceptions, namely:
1. The nature of the universe; how it arose, or was created; how it operates; who or what makes things happen, and why.
2. Man's place in that universe; his origin, nature, and destiny, his relation to the world; whether in nature or outside nature.
3. Man's relation to his group; who must be sacrificed for whom; the individual's rights, titles, obligations, and interests.
4. Human nature and conduct; man's image of self and his

motives; what he wants and what he should have; how he should be educated and socialized.

From these four basic conceptions derive the systems of thought and logic, the conventional patterns of feelings and sensibilities and the criteria of credibility with which the great historical cultures have been built. All these are expressed in the religion, the philosophy, the law, and the art of each cultural group.

It begins to appear then that what we call culture is a way of giving meaning and significance to the environing world and to man himself, in terms of these basic organizing conceptions. Thus whatever exists and happens in the world will be seen and interpreted in the context of the ideas, beliefs, and conceptions provided by each culture as the only socially sanctioned way of believing, thinking, feeling, acting, and speaking.

Just as we find in different species sensitivities or irritabilities to a given range of stimuli or energy transformations, so that while existing in the environing world of nature they nevertheless live a restricted life in accordance with this selective awareness and the patterned responses, dictated by their organic structure and functional capacities, so in the same way we may look upon man as creating his special cultural world out of the totality of nature and living strictly within the limits of its formulations and prescriptions.

Again it may be emphasized that while almost every other species has, through the mode of organic adaptation and specialization, reached the end of the road, so to speak, man has, through culture, developed what is often as coercive and limiting as organic adaptation, but still susceptible to modification and change, whenever he can and will change his basic ideas.

Thus we may emphasize that culture is this historically developed way of ordering events, of organizing experience and of regulating conduct, which man himself has constructed and placed between himself and nature. Whatever man does to gain sustenance, protection, and security and to deal with his environment will be governed by his basic conceptions; whatever tools and technology he develops will arise as implications and consequences of these conceptions and will be used only in accordance with these conceptions. Moreover, whatever regulations of his own functions and whatever prohibitions and compulsions that he lays upon himself and his conduct will be dictated by his conception of the place of man in that universe, his ideas of the relation of the individual to the group, and his conception of human nature and conduct. Whatever he does and whatever he refrains from doing will be expressive of an idea or belief about the world and himself. Even when he repudiates and revolts against the dictates of his culture and the requirements of his society, he still acknowledges these ideas and these beliefs because only in the terms of his culture can he see, feel, think, or act.

As we see in the religion and philosophy of each cultural group, these four basic organizing conceptions are interdependent, each giving and receiving sanction and support from the other three. The specific formulations that derive from these basic conceptions are expressed in law, the arts, and the innumerable other formulations through which a culture declares and maintains itself. Moreover, these basic concepts, together with the selective awareness and sensibilities that they foster, and the patterns of thought, feeling, and conduct that they sanction, permeate the whole complex of language and symbols, rituals and ceremonies, institutional practices such as contract, barter, sale, marriage, political organization, and so forth, through and in which the social life is organized and carried on.

Since man everywhere has found the same nature and faced the same persistent tasks of life, there is a more or less universal pattern of life to be found in all cultures, each of which, however, has utilized different concepts, different meanings and purposes within this general framework. In most cultures, moreover, there is a theory of origins which tells how these basic organizing conceptions of life, this extraordinary complex of beliefs, patterns of conduct and feeling, have come, usually from some superhuman or supernatural source which may therefore neither be questioned nor tampered with.

Only recently, therefore, have we begun to realize that culture is a historically developed effort of each group to meet the persistent tasks of life—the human creation of man himself in an attempt to order events, organize group life, and regulate his conduct as an alternative to a purely biological mode of existence. It is only recently, also, that we have clearly understood that this immense cultural organization depends for its continuation and maintenance upon the acculturation of each generation of children, who must be taught these basic ideas and conceptions, this selective awareness, these sensibilities, these socially approved ways of thinking, believing, acting, and feeling for meeting the persistent life tasks that each generation must face.

Only in so far as children learn to see the world in these terms, to accept these cultural formulations, to observe these group-sanctioned patterns of conduct and speech, only thus does a culture persist. Moreover, only in so far as each child is socialized and taught the socially approved rituals, symbols, ceremonies, and patterns of conduct will the social life continue. It is evident that what the family teaches the child will be one version of the required cultural lessons and socialization, biased by the family's predilections and warped by the parental feelings about those lessons and toward the child. Moreover, the child will learn from those lessons only what they mean to him and always in accordance with the feelings aroused by the parents and their requirements. The great diversity of individual conduct, beliefs, and feelings therefore become explicable in the light of this process that creates the idiomatic individual and his unique personality.

We must continually remind ourselves that there is nothing in the natural, biological situation which requires or necessitates any particular culture or social organization. Nature, as it were, has been patient of the amazing variety of cultural formulations and social organizations which all over the world man has laid upon nature and himself.

The ancient belief that culture and society are super-organic, superhuman organizations, operating through large-scale, cosmic forces like gravitation, wholly above and beyond human direction and control, becomes increasingly incredible as we begin to recognize culture and society as the answers proposed by man himself to the same persistent life problems. If and when we do recognize the human origin of culture and of society and understand them as attempts to order events, to organize experience, and to regulate conduct, then we can understand more clearly what the activity we call science means to our culture.

As suggested earlier, each culture is built upon the four basic organizing conceptions through which each group has attempted to give meaning and significance and order to its life.

In these conceptual formulations are expressed whatever knowledge and understanding man has about the world and himself, organized and interpreted by reflective thinking, creative imagination, and the aspirations and sensibilities cherished by the group. We may, therefore, say advisedly that each culture is an expression of the knowledge and beliefs that were available during the period of its creation and formulation. Every culture is pre-scientific. In every other culture but ours, once these formulations had been achieved and translated into a living and continuing society, they have become final and unquestionable, and the major efforts of the leaders of each group are directed to preserving and strengthening the continuity of their traditions and the full force of their sanctions.

This almost universal preoccupation with the maintenance of the cultural traditions against any doubt, skepticism, or change becomes explicable when we realize that the whole structure of a culture and of the social life of the group rests upon the affirmation and acceptance of certain ideas, beliefs, and concepts. If man is to have any order in his group life and any meaning and design in his personal living, he must make such affirmations and perpetuate them through inculcation in his children. Thus in every group, so-called primitive or so-called civilized, there is this unformulated but intense conviction that the children must be instructed in the group-sanctioned ideas, beliefs, and patterns of conduct and forced, often by terror and brutality, to accept and conform.

Western European culture is unique in that it has developed, and today is now institutionalizing, what has been called the "technique of habit breaking," that is, a systematic, critical examination of every idea, conception, and belief about the universe and its operation, about man's origin and place in that universe, and every time-honored, traditional pattern of social life and individual conduct.

Seen in this context, therefore, what we call science may be interpreted as the most recent of man's cultural inventions. Not content with having built up a cultural world and thereby giving human life the orientation and direction that has made man a unique species, we now see that same human impulse directing man toward a continuous, critical examination of his culture in the attempt to escape that same crystallization and fixation in his culture as in his biological evolution. If we can see science in these terms, we will see it not as some special, outside force or agency, but as a part of western European culture, a further development and refinement of the creative activities which led man to create his culture in the attempt to order events and organize experience.

If, however, we are to understand the present situation in western European culture and the occasion for discussions such as these, we must look back and see how the four basic organizing conceptions of our culture were developed through a long, historical process of many converging streams, coming from the major cultural groups around the Mediterranean Basin, chiefly Egyptian, Chaldean, Assyrian, Hebraic, Greek, Roman, and Arabic, and later the northern European groups.

Slowly there was evolved out of these many cultural streams and influences a more or less unified body of ideas and beliefs and conceptual formulations expressive of the best knowledge and understanding then available. Within the past four or five hundred years this traditional western European culture has been under critical scrutiny; beginning with Galileo, Copernicus, Kepler, and Newton, the basic organizing conceptions of Western European culture have been rendered increasingly untenable and incredible.

First astronomy made obsolete the historical conception of a geocentric universe of limited spatial dimensions and temporal duration. The classic conception of the order of events and the relationships among natural processes became increasingly unacceptable as physics, and later chemistry, brought new understandings and concepts. More recently we have seen how geology and paleontology have necessitated a further revision of our basic conceptions of the world and of man, have enormously increased our time perspectives, and brought a new conception of man's place in the universe and his relation to nature. Within our own generation biology and anthropology and historical research have led to further revisions of our traditional beliefs about the nature of man, his relationships to group life and his social, economic and political theories and organizations. Today, biology, psychology and psychiatry are bringing a new conception and understanding of human nature and conduct, the implications of which are so far-reaching that we can scarcely grasp their significance.

The critical situation in which we find ourselves today may therefore be described in these terms. Western European culture, like all other cultures, is a historical creation in terms of certain basic organizing conceptions which expressed the best knowledge, understanding, sensibilities, and aspirations at the time of its formative period. Within the framework of these concepts and the culture to which they gave rise, western European peoples have faced the persistent tasks of life, of ordering events, organizing their experience and regulating their conduct, achieving what is writ large in their historically developed societies. This same culture has given rise to the dominant character structure and has fostered the personalities, the bearers of which are the active agents in social, economic, political, and international affairs and so are responsible for the persistent disorder, conflicts, and destruction recorded by that history.

For several centuries these basic concepts and beliefs of western European culture have been losing their validity and their credibility. Just as we have seen how other cultures have disintegrated with increasing social disorder and individual demoralization under the impact of European ideas, techniques, and teachings, so we are beginning to realize that our own culture has been cumulatively undermined by what we call scientific investigation, so that we no longer can accept or believe the older ideas and concepts. This process of disintegration has not been uniform, so that we find not only different groups of people, but also single individuals reflecting these changes in different areas and to different degrees. Thus some sections of the population have been relatively untouched by any new ideas, and so they continue to live in terms of the traditional formulations untroubled by any doubts or anxieties over the crucial aspects of life. Other sections of the population only partially accepting new ideas are attempting to live in terms of the old and the new, facing increasing difficulty and strain while trying to reconcile the growing incongruities and discrepancies in their lives.

If time permitted, it would be interesting to examine some of these ever-widening chasms in our individual and group lives, as, for example, our demand for modern medicine while we continue to reject man's mammalian ancestry which gives modern medicine its validity. Likewise we might reflect upon the difficulty of administering the law upon assumptions about the cosmos and human nature that are becoming progressively obsolete and absurd. But such an inquiry would lead into every aspect and phase of society and individual living, where we see increasing disorder, conflicts, and confusions as we face the persistent tasks of life for which our culture no longer provides guiding concepts and patterns and sanctions. From this cultural viewpoint, the bewildering array of social problems, of internal and of international chaos and conflict, as well as the mounting anxiety and insecurity in our personal lives, appear as symptoms of the breakdown of the older western European culture.

In the midst of these alarms and conflicts, the question of what men of scientific persuasion can do becomes one of the crucial issues of our time. The task of rebuilding our culture, of constructing a new framework of concepts and beliefs to give order, meaning, and significance to life becomes ever more insistent. But it must be clearly recognized, this is essentially an artistic task, of creating a consistent picture of the universe and of man that will not only satisfy our new criteria of credibility, but also express the new aspirations and sensibilities through which we seek to attain the enduring human values. It must be emphasized that we need more than abstract scientific laws, generalizations, quantitative findings, and formulas; we are waiting for a statement of the *meaning* of scientific knowledge in terms of its emotional significance for living, so that modern astronomy, geology, and biology will provide the equivalent of "Now I lay me down to sleep," in which the traditional cosmology, biology, and psychology were expressed. More concretely, we must courageously and imaginatively recreate the four basic organizing conceptions essential to culture—the nature of the universe, man's place therein, his relations to his fellows and his society, and human nature and conduct—utilizing our recent scientific knowledge and understanding for that purpose just as our predecessors utilized the best contemporary knowledge and understandings available to them for constructing the culture they bequeathed to us.

The more clearly we realize the stupendous achievements of the past in building up western European culture and sincerely recognize our indebtedness to those great leaders who created this amazing structure of ideas and beliefs and aspirations, the greater are our obligation and responsibility to do for our time what they did for their age. This is the very ideal of scientific endeavor, to carry forward the task of ordering events, of reorganizing our ideas and procedures, in our never-ending pursuit of understanding the world and all it contains, including man and his culture.

Until we formulate the *meaning* of modern science for these essential concepts and beliefs, we must continue to live anxiously and contingently, unable to achieve any order in our society or our personal lives, because we lack this unified set of concepts through which alone we can order events, organize experience, regulate conduct, and find dimensions for our values and aspirations. To find the courage and faith for such a gigantic task, amidst the chaos that now threatens, we shall have to remind ourselves and our children that, however dark and threatening the future, man can now imaginatively project ahead a culture dedicated to the conservation of those human values that for long he has vainly sought.

In the years to come it is probable that this discovery of the human origin and development of culture will be recognized as the greatest of all discoveries, since heretofore man has been helpless before these cultural and social formulations which generation after generation have perpetuated the same frustration and defeat of human values and aspirations. So long as he believed this was necessary and inevitable, he could but accept this lot with resignation. Now man is beginning to realize that his culture and social organization are not unchanging cosmic processes, but are human creations which may be altered. For those who cherish the democratic faith this discovery means that they can and must undertake a continuing assay of our culture and our society in terms of its consequences for human life and human values. This is the historic origin and purpose of human culture, to create a human way of life. To our age falls the responsibility of utilizing the amazing new resources of science to meet these cultural tasks, to continue the great human tradition of man taking charge of his own destiny.

(FROM: *Scientific Monthly*, 50 [1940]: 491-97.)

TWENTY-FOUR

What Is Social Order

INTEREST in the question of social order has been steadily mounting during the past few years. Today probably more individuals, both professional and lay, are aware of this question than ever before, since the issue raised by the proposal to establish the New Order in Europe has been made acute by the war and by the anxieties over a postwar world.

1

THERE IS a widely held belief in the existence of an over-all superorganic social system or organization which operates through large-scale social forces that govern our whole social life. This belief in a social mechanism not only is held by the general public and by those who speak and write on public affairs but is also accepted by various groups of social scientists who are studying social life. In both the textbook presentations of economics, political science, and sociology (although the latter has been changing very rapidly in the last two decades) and in the monographs and research publications by members of these disciplines one finds either an explicit statement or a more or less implicit assumption that whatever happens in a society is to be viewed as the outcome of the operation of large-scale social forces, which, acting at a distance, produce all our social events. Whenever anything goes wrong in our society and the customary institutional practices of economics, politics, and social life fail to operate as expected, the statement is made that someone or some group has been violating or interfering with the operation of social forces or economic laws. Therefore, the only remedy for our difficulties is to conform to the requirements of this assumed social system and to accept the operation of these social forces with full recognition that they alone can bring resolution of our difficulties. Consequently, it is believed that the only hope for attainment of order and intelligence in social affairs is through the slow and painful disclosure of the major features of this assumed social mechanism or system and through the quantitative determination of these assumed social forces.

This general conception and mode of thinking about social life is so familiar and so widely accepted that we must pause and reflect upon its implications before we can begin to realize just how extraordinary these ideas really are.

No one has ever been able to point out or to identify any kind of structure or organization that corresponds to this belief; indeed, the conception of a social system or organization carries with it the unspoken but well-accepted implication that it exists somewhere out in space, between the earth and the sky, and operates like gravitation. Moreover, no one has ever been able to measure or otherwise detect the operation of these assumed social forces which are always inferred from the variety of statistical data of economic, political, and social activities, such as prices, wages, production and consumption of goods and services, votes, etc.

The persistent belief in these social forces is supported by the well-established practice among social scientists of deifying data into entities: prices, wages, rents, votes, and other formal records of human activity in these symbolic patterns are treated as actual events or entities with an independent existence and energy apart from the actors who create them. The changing aggregates of these data-entities are then treated as forces which do things to individuals and group life and to other entities.

A clue to the understanding of this curious situation may be found in the historical development of modern social theories, more especially in the elaboration of the political, the economic, and, later, the sociological theories that have arisen since the seventeenth century. What apparently occurred was that first the political theorists, attempting to find some basis for order in political life and to provide a substitute for the older absolutist conceptions of sovereignty (divine right), took over the conceptual apparatus of Newtonian celestial mechanics and began to formulate theories of government and social organization in terms of natural laws and the cosmology which Newton and his successors had developed. Likewise, when the economists attempted to formulate a theory of economic activities in order to rationalize the coming industrialism and foreign-trade economy in England, they likewise used the Newtonian formulation and conceived of an *economic system* operating through large-scale economic forces, following closely the pattern of Newton's idea of the solar system and his conception of gravitation as a cosmic force acting at a distance. Thus it was that Adam Smith could develop his polemic against the older institutional and legislative framework that was obstructing the early development of what we now call modern industry; and thus he could formulate his theory of economics, which encouraged and guided those who were eager to exploit the new machinery and opportunities for trade. In his formulation he could, with entire confidence, rely upon the operation of the "unseen hand" because he was so thoroughly convinced that all economic activities were governed by this assumed economic system and regulated by the operation of these assumed economic forces.

A critical examination of the different schools of social theory will show that with a few exceptions, which have been either ridiculed or ignored, social scientists as a group have clung to this conceptual apparatus, one which offers a framework with which they can attempt to order and explain social events and group living. It is also interesting to note that, with the development of quantitative statistical methodologies that were welcomed as the instruments that would make social science "really scientific" — i.e., quantitative — the work of the quantitative students has been largely devoted to the attempt to demonstrate statistically the operation of these supposed social and economic forces and to establish beyond the possibility of doubt the existence of this assumed system of social and economic laws governing all human activities. Even the very recent studies of business cycles have been predicated upon the assumption — more often implied than explicitly stated — that the fluctuations in economics, industry, and business were the outward, visible signs of this assumed cosmic organization that governs all economic life. As indicated earlier, some of the sociologists have repudiated this search for a social mechanism or system and have begun to study human conduct and the institutional patterns of social living that give rise to various social data.

In accordance with the basic stock of ideas with which Western European culture has operated since Newton, the search for the order and meaning of social life and events has been directed by the hope of revealing an all-powerful, controlling system or mechanism that governs and directs all social life—a search directed also by the belief that helpless man could hope for security and peace only by learning to conform to this all-powerful system and its forces and powers.

This way of thinking has been supported by the theological, philosophical, and psychological beliefs with which western European culture has, from its early days, attempted to understand human affairs and explain social group life. One is struck by the persistence of what may be called a basically defeatist attitude in Western European culture in the sense that man has persistently viewed himself as at the mercy of something larger and more powerful than himself to whom or to which he must passively submit, be it an all-powerful deity or sovereign, an autocratic father, or some other authoritarian symbol or person or cosmic force.

With such a widespread belief in an underlying social and economic system operated by large-scale social forces and duly sanctioned by legal, philosophical, and even theological support, it is not difficult to understand how the discussion of social order, and especially the frequent discussion of so-called "social problems," usually falls into the familiar pattern. First, there is the presentation of the social difficulty arising from the inadequacy of the customary institutional practices for meeting social and individual requirements, such as poverty, housing, labor difficulties, etc., followed by a long recital of the various direct and contributing "causes," with the concluding demonstration that only in so far as we are prepared to stop interfering with the operation of economic or social laws can we hope for any mitigation of our difficulties or any resolution of our problems. The further discussions of social problems are carried on almost exclusively in terms of how to persuade individuals and groups to conform to the requirements of that system and its basic laws of operation.

2

IF SOCIAL order is not a part of the cosmos, arising from the operation of large-scale forces, how can we understand social life and its ongoing processes and events? Perhaps the most promising approach to that question is through more recent studies of culture and personality, which offer a dynamic conception of how group life is patterned and organized in and through the conduct and feelings of the individuals composing that group.

As we look over the world we see man existing as an organism in the geographical space of nature, from which he derives his nurture, his security, and his survival. Thanks to his mammalian ancestry, he can and does live in an extraordinary range of temperatures, altitudes, and geographical conditions to which he has adapted his very plastic organism.

Nowhere, however, do we find man living on an elemental level of physiological functioning and organic impulse as do his fellow-mammals. Everywhere he lives in groups which historically have each developed a cultural world and a social order as their way of meeting the persistent tasks of life—coming to terms with nature for sustenance and survival, organizing their group life, and regulating conduct. Thus we find man imposing upon nature and upon himself certain assumptions and beliefs, specific patterns of conduct and of human relations with which he has attempted to create a human way of life in place of an organic existence.

In order to come to terms with nature and obtain the sustenance, shelter, and security he requires, man has had to make certain assumptions about the universe: how it was created and how it operates and where the power and control over events are located. He also has had to conceive of himself in relation to nature— especially how he was created and to what end or purpose he is destined. Moreover, he has had to work out some scheme of the relation of the individual to his fellows and of their common group life in order to answer the exigent question of who shall be sacrificed for whom. Finally, he has had to develop a conception of human nature and an image of the self in order to regulate and direct his conduct.

From the reports on different cultures all over the world, as observed by anthropologists, we are learning that there is an extraordinary variety of these basic assumptions and beliefs in terms of which different groups have sought to make their lives orderly and meaningful, to give living some tension and purpose beyond eating, fighting, and procreating. In accordance with these convictions each generation rears its children to see the world and themselves in terms of its traditional beliefs and assumptions and to pattern their action, speech, beliefs, and feelings according to the group-sanctioned traditions.

Thus we find different groups attempting to achieve social order in and through diverse beliefs and ways of organizing human conduct and interpreting experience. Each culture, with its selective awareness and its more or less biased or warped aspirations, may be viewed as one of the many ways in which man has sought a design for living. As Ortega y Gasset has pointed out, culture is that which is sought in human conduct and each culture makes a virtue of its deficiencies—of what it ignores or neglects.

If, then, we think of culture as the regulation of human functioning and impulse, as the patterning of human behavior into orderly conduct in accordance with the basic assumptions and beliefs and the sensibilities of each group, we shall see that social order is not an inherent part of the cosmos but is that which is sought after or aspired to.

Culture exists or operates in human beings, who, by their patterned conduct and way of life, create whatever social order there is. Here we should recognize that what we call private property and the sanctity of the person are not properties of things or persons nor are they mysterious powers surrounding objects and people; they are the learned habits or patterns of respecting the inviolability of things and persons which children develop under the tuition of parents and teachers, who inculcate the necessary inhibitions in the young. Moreover, the various patterns of conduct exhibited by men and women—as masculine and feminine roles, as responses to the immense array of conventionalized situations and relations and of rituals and symbols—all these are learned conduct, painfully acquired by children, often under severe discipline and terrorizing threats of immediate or deferred punishment. Every situation and every object and person is defined by the parent or teacher in terms of what the child must not do—or may, can, or must do—according to his age, sex, status, class, and other categories of social participation.

Along with all these lessons in conduct the child is taught the basic beliefs and assumptions as formulated in what we call religion, law, ethics and morals, folklore and the arts, so that for every lesson in conduct he learns the group-accepted reasons and sanctions therefor.

Later, as the child grows older, he is instructed in the institutional practices of contract, barter, sale, employment, voting and litigation, courtship and marriage and divorce, and all the other rituals and symbolic patterns through which one individual approaches, negotiates, and comes to terms with another over property or his services or his person. Thus the multiplicity of individual activity in a group is limited and channeled into the group-sanctioned patterns and thereby gives rise in the aggregate to that observed order, regularity, and uniformity which have been heretofore viewed as the operation of an organization or social system.

Thus we can see how the appearance of large-scale social forces arises from the expression of human behavior in more or less stereotyped patterns of action, reaction, and interaction, even in the use of tools and technology, which is always governed by the customary practices of private property, contract, etc. Moreover, the co-called abnormal or antisocial behavior in crimes and delinquencies, alcoholism and drug addiction, sex offenses, mental disorders, and similar deviant activities is revealed as the conduct of those who do not conform to or abide by the prescribed norms of action, speech, belief, and feeling, because, as we are now realizing, their childhood experiences have failed to provide such patterns, or have so warped, twisted, and distorted them that such socially desirable conduct is impossible for them. Social adjustment is not therefore primarily to something outside, like weather or gravitation, but rather is the way an individual has tried to come to terms with his past experience and how he has accepted his forgotten childhood, with all the corroding feelings of anxiety, guilt, and resentment so often created by childhood experiences.

Out of the process of being culturized and taught to be a participating member of the group life each individual learns his peculiar idiomatic version of what his culture and society mean. In terms of these lessons and of the persistent feelings he has developed from such teachings, each individual develops his own idiosyncratic way of organizing and interpreting experience and reacting affectively — with feelings — toward other people. This dynamic process of organizing experience according to what it means for the individual is what we call the personality.

Social order, therefore, arises from the way different personalities have accepted and translated the teachings of their culture and have learned to use the group-sanctioned practices of institutional life as their personal design for living. Social order, therefore, is not some mysterious cosmic mechanism but human behavior patterned into the conduct approved by the group traditions.

3

IN THE light of the foregoing discussion the question that insistently rises is: How does this conception of social order offer any clues to the exigent social and international situation which we face today? If we cannot invoke any large-scale cosmic mechanisms or forces or laws with which to persuade or coerce groups to maintain social order and establish international peace, what, if anything, can we invoke, both as a process and as a goal, to meet the approaching threat of increasing social disorder and international anarchy?

Every great advance in human life has been initiated by a critical examination of traditions and by the formulation of new ideas and concepts and aspirations by means of which succeeding generations have grappled with the persistent tasks of life that face every group and have sought anew to realize the enduring human values. If we hope to develop a social order in which the amazing and rapidly increasing scientific knowledge and technology can be wisely and effectively used for human needs and values, in which some kind of decent social life can be established and maintained, and in which our basic democratic aspirations toward the recognition and conservation of human personality can be pursued, it seems obvious that we must seek a new framework of ideas and beliefs and a clarification of the persistent human values which have so long been frustrated and defeated.

No one who candidly examines the history of western European culture can believe that we have ever had what could validly be called "social order." The historical record shows exploitation, conflict, wars, and persecution—indeed, every form of social disorder, social degradation, and defeat; and be it noted that there has never been lacking a well-formulated body of justification and rationalization for all the disasters, disorders, and defeats man has suffered or inflicted upon others. Indeed, even today we are assured by some theologians, publicists, and social theorists that what is happening is a well-merited punishment or divine retribution for man's misdeeds and mistakes, with the implication or even the explicit declaration that man is essentially and completely helpless in the face of divine and cosmic processes.

The major obstacle we face today, therefore, is this essentially defeatist tradition expressed in the various conceptions of social order described earlier, as above and beyond all human control, if not understanding, and in the reiterated belief in man's innate depravity or fall from grace, from which only divine help can rescue or restore him.

In this situation, therefore, we can and must find the courage to view social order as that which must be achieved by man himself. Then the most promising approach to social order is through the reformulation of our major assumptions and beliefs and through the modification of the process of education by which our culture and our social patterns are inculcated in the growing child. No other promising alternative seems available unless we accept some form of imposed or authoritarian order.

More specifically, this leads to the question of what kinds of character and personality are being fostered by our traditional methods of child-rearing and education, under the influence of our historically developed conceptions of human nature and conduct and of the relation of the individual to his group. As long as we believe that human nature is fixed and unchangeable and continue to accept the theological conceptions of man as one who must be disciplined, coerced, and terrorized or supernaturally assisted into being a decent human being and a participating member of society, so long will we continue to create warped, twisted, distorted personalities who continually threaten, if they do not frustrate and break down, all our efforts toward social order.

It must not be forgotten that, while an occasional saint arises, the ideas and beliefs and processes of child-rearing produce the many unhappy, malevolent personalities who make life for themselves and for all others a tragic defeat. What is becoming increasingly clear from both clinical and experimental studies of human conduct is that if, during the process of early childhood education, the individual has been unnecessarily deprived and frustrated, coerced, harshly disciplined, or terrorized by parents and other adults, he may and usually does learn to conform outwardly, but he develops persistent affective reactions toward life, with strong feelings of anxiety, guilt, and especially of resentment

WHAT IS SOCIAL ORDER

and hostility. Carrying these often intolerable burdens of feelings within him but forbidden to release them in any overt activities, he seeks all manner of surreptitious and disguised outlets, finding in business and professional life, in politics, in educational endeavors, in marriage, in family life, and in parenthood—indeed, in every socially sanctioned occupation and activity—innumerable occasions in which to express these persistent affective trends, with consequent injury to others and to social order.

If such persons are anxious and insecure, their major endeavor in life will be to build up strong walls of defense through a thousand and one neurotic patterns that make life a burden to themselves and to others with whom they come in contact as they obstruct and oppose every endeavor that seems to offer a threat to their own precarious positions. In every organized activity of life we find such individuals engaged in quiet but effective sabotage and opposition to others, continually alert to frustrate others and especially to oppose every program in which they can interfere because it provides a release for their anxiety and an outlet for their malevolence. If they come to adult life suffering from strong feelings of guilt that have been imposed upon them by parents and adults who have scolded and punished them for childish misdeeds, then they will engage in a wide variety of activities through which they may vicariously atone or else project their guilt on others whom they can vigorously attack, as is seen so clearly in the lives of fanatic reformers and others who spend their lives in passionate attacks on other individuals or in persistent efforts to convert others to the particular form of doctrine which they have embraced as an aid to carrying such burdens of guilt.

Still others who have grown up feeling that they are worthless and useless, that they are unwanted and unloved, will go through life with corroding and resentful feelings toward life; they will spend all their days in a persistent endeavor to "get even," to retaliate, to block and destroy others in order to release the hate they feel. Often this resentment becomes a strong hostility toward the world which drives them to every manner of destructive, antisocial activities, including war and destruction. Even though they gain nothing by what they do, nevertheless, they are driven by this inner pressure of hostility to attack and destroy wherever possible.

If these strong affective threats appeared only in the well-recognized individuals suffering from mental disorders or engaged in what we call delinquency and crime, they would be serious but not fatal threats to social order. What we must face, however, is that the major activities in our social life, carried on through our group-sanctioned institutional practices of business, politics, and professional life, are, to an unbelievable extent, dominated by these destructive personality trends. The evidence is in the clinical records and the reports of what has been happening in our social activities—the breakdown of ethics and the rise of racketeering in almost every group and professional activity. It should scarcely be necessary to point out that a free society demands self-discipline and the highest standard of personal and institutional ethics; otherwise social order and freedom must be maintained by authoritarian commands, policing, and submissive obedience.

If we genuinely seek social order, we must therefore begin to think in terms of culture and personality and to conceive of social order as that which must be achieved. Moreover, we must attempt to reconstruct the underlying ideas, conceptions, and beliefs of western European culture—a Promethean task, but one that we cannot evade since those historical conceptions and beliefs are all obsolete, if not archaic, and no longer credible or even useful for ordering experience and giving meaning and significance to our lives. Our historically developed social patterns and institutions, based upon those obsolete ideas and looking to our legal and religious sanctions for support of such archaic beliefs, no longer will serve to organize group living or to guide individual conduct; we cannot any longer believe in them or abide by their guidance. Moreover, our sensibilities are changing so that increasingly we are unable to tolerate the degradation and wastage of human life and personalities which the traditional social arrangements impose upon so many, even upon the so-called "successful" and "powerful."

The crucial question involved in every attempt to achieve social order is "Who shall be sacrificed for whom?" Today, underneath the conflict and disorders of a war-torn world, there is a growing demand for human conservation and for a social order dedicated to human needs and values. As long as we are at the mercy of the warped, distorted personalities who seek power and prestige in our political, economic, and professional life, at whatever cost to others, we are helpless; but in recognizing that it is our obsolete, archaic culture and our traditional practices of child-rearing which create these malevolent personalities, we can escape the ancient defeatism of the past and face a problem that is basically within man's own power to meet.

It is evident that there are, as indicated earlier, certain persistent tasks of life that can be neither evaded nor ignored. They present social problems that cannot be solved, since each generation must face those tasks and formulate those problems anew in the light of its knowledge and understanding, its insights and aspirations, and its sensibilities. There can be no utopian solution that will permanently endure. Man himself must courageously and hopefully look forward to an unending endeavor to achieve social order and to create a human way of life.

In these terms, therefore, we can begin to examine the problems of social order and the immense task of developing a world order wherein we can hope to realize some of the hopes and aspirations now arising in the minds and hearts of man. The most effective answer to the New Order of the dictators is a conception of social and of world order that will enlist the energies and sympathies of men and women of good will everywhere. Out of the present struggle and turmoil, black as it now appears, may then come an opportunity to seek anew, in a saner, more wholesome social order, the persistent human values that for so long have been denied.

(FROM: *American Journal of Sociology*, 49 [1944], 470–477.)

TWENTY-FIVE

The Historian as Therapist

IT MAY seem curious, indeed somewhat astonishing, to suggest that the historian consider his role as that of therapist. In the light of the earnest endeavors of recent years to make history as objective and scientific as possible, to suggest that history become a therapy, essentially an art, may appear to be a regression to an earlier period in historical scholarship.

Before dismissing the idea, however, it may be worth considering what the historian has done and still does for the culture of which he is a participating member. For a clearer realization of his role and function it will be necessary to rehearse briefly what a culture does.

All over the world man, a mammalian organism, is found existing in the geographical space of nature, subject to gravitation, climate, and the ongoing physical, chemical, and biological events to which he is exposed. Nowhere, however, is man found living on the level of physiological functioning and organic impulse, reacting impulsively to the objective, geographical environment and other organisms. Everywhere he is found living in a cultural world which he has created by imposing upon nature the basic ideas, beliefs, assumptions, and aspirations which make the world meaningful, using the tools and techniques that make it yield what he seeks for his sustenance and survival. He also imposes upon himself, in accordance with these organizing conceptions and the values and aspirations to which they give rise, the patterns of living and functioning and of regulated conduct and feelings through which he established and maintains his social order.

Culture therefore is not an entity or some mysterious, unseen superhuman mechanism, located in space beyond man's reach or understanding, despite the awesome, supernatural sanctions everywhere invoked to give these cultural traditions an inviolable, unquestionable status. Culture is what man himself, with imagination and artistry, has created as a way of life or design for living, a preferred pattern of organizing and interpreting experience. Culture gives nature and his own living more meaning and tension, more form and significance than organic existence alone could provide. Culture, as traditional beliefs and assumptions and practices, is what man cherishes as his history.

Social order likewise is not a superhuman, cosmic organization or mechanism despite the long accepted formulations of social science which invoked the Newtonian conception of an equilibrating system, operated by large scale forces, acting at a distance to control all social events. Social order is not given as a part of nature but is that which is sought in human conduct by the patterning of man's impulses and functional needs into the group sanctioned expressions and repressions and by the channeling of his conduct into the institutional rituals and symbolic practices of person-to-person relations as specified in laws and customs. Thus, social order and culture are in each person who observes what is forbidden and what is required or permitted, who utilizes the socially sanctioned practices of contract, barter, sale, courtship and marriage, litigation, and voting, to carry on his life activities.

The cultural framework and the social order expressing these basic ideas, assumptions, and organizing conceptions, are historical creations, slowly developed by each group and carried along by each generation according to its interpretation of the past. Thus it may be said that each cultural group is endeavoring to live according to its history, that is, according to these historically developed ways in which man views his life—both his private personal career and the group life. Each culture therefore offers a series of time perspectives, which give to the past, the present, and the future, their basic dimensions and significance.

Culture persists by being transmitted to each generation of children who are taught the group sanctioned ideas, beliefs, assumptions, and patterns of conduct so that they will learn to see, think, and act according to tradition and to interpret the symbols and the records and the monuments of the past piously.

Every person, having been culturized and socialized in his childhood, carries in his organism and in his personality the persistent modifications and adjustments derived from the experiences to which he reacted when they were occurring by a variety of responses and feelings that have become part of his present, living self. The past of a person is in him today, as the modifications which previous experience has produced and made persistent. Every person is continually engaged in reorganizing his past, rearranging and resolving it according to the exigencies of the present and his changing understanding of that past. Every person likewise is projecting his interpretation of the past into the future as the hopes and fears and expectations which he sees in the present as forecasts for tomorrow. The cultural traditions as interpreted by his parents and teachers have directed all his experience and defined every object, animal, person, and relationship. Thus his past experiences as regulated by adults have given him the traditional patterns of action, speech, belief, and feelings, but each person has learned these with idiosyncratic bias and distortions as variations upon the larger traditional themes.

Every man therefore is a historian, of himself, of his family, and of his group, creating and recreating a picture of the past as he sees it in the light of his ongoing contemporary life and changing understanding and needs. Sometimes he gains new insight into his past that compels him to revise his interpretation of his past history, giving it a new meaning and, with that alteration, he may find emancipation from, or accept further submission to, his past. Whatever he does and whatever he projects ahead find sanction and support in his interpretation of his past history wherein he finds his image of himself, his sense of dignity, worth, and purpose or absence of such values.

Whatever a person feels about people and situations and about himself derives from his forgotten childhood, often the warped version of his childhood when he reacted to situations and people with strong emotional reactions that became persistent feelings toward other people and himself.

When personalities become warped and distorted, and emotionally disturbed so that they can no longer pursue the usual "normal" life activities, they may seek therapeutic help. Psychotherapy is an art, fundamentally historical, like clinical medicine, which undertakes an extensive exploration of the patient's life history to discover when and how he became "twisted" and emotionally disturbed. If successful the psychotherapist can by a variety of procedures persuade the patient to revise his past and redefine situations either by renouncing the often mythical and distorted version he has cherished as his "true past"—true because that is what it meant for him, or by helping him to reinterpret his actual past history in terms which permit him, with his more mature understanding, to develop a selective version of his life experience which will no longer be so conflicting and destructive. Psychotherapy is essentially the practice of historical therapy which explores the patient's past in order to help him reconstruct his past and provide him with an internally consistent image of himself. Thereby he can live more sanely and adequately in the present and face the future with less of the anxiety or guilt or resentful hostility that may be driving him to self-defeat or destructive and malicious conduct.

Every cultural group, like the individual patient, is governed by its interpretation of the past, which exercises a compelling direction upon all its present activities, its fear, expectations, and aspirations. Just as the individual patient's personality arises from his picture of self, his past experience and feelings, so nations live by and for their traditions. "Only through history does a nation become completely conscious of itself," according to Schopenhauer. And as Fustel de Coulange has emphasized, "Patriotism is not love of the soil but love of the past; it is respect for the generations that have preceded us," whose courageous endeavors must be emulated.

The coercion of the past is so compelling that despite frequent claims to modernity and pride in scientific knowledge and techniques, men today are, apart from the limited use of technology, living by the ideas and patterns of centuries ago. This persistent coercion by tradition, often obsolete or even archaic, presents one of the most baffling of human problems—how to use the past instead of being dominated by it. As Otto Rank said, "We cling to the past, not because we love the past, but because we are afraid of the present," and often are terrified by the future.

It seems reasonably clear, as Swain so cogently pointed out some years ago, that history is written, not because of interest in the past but because of concern for the future. By interpreting or reinterpreting the past, energies and aspirations can be redirected toward whatever goal may be selected as the historically determined destiny or chosen goal of a people. The various nationalist revivals have been preceded and accompanied by a historical reconstruction of their past that has spurred on the people to new and hitherto undreamed of achievements, all made to appear inevitable by the interpretation of the past as leading to just that particular future they now must seek.

Out of the past come the enduring values and aspirations and, above all, the image of the people that serve to direct their collective lives. As Hans Kohn has stated:

> Among the realities of national life the image which a nation forms of itself and in which it mirrors itself is one of the most important. Though the everyday reality, in many ways, does not correspond to the image and falls far short of its ideal perfection—sometimes even contradicts it in the countless and conflicting trends of the complex actuality—nevertheless, this image, woven of elements of reality, tradition, imagination, aspiration, is one of the most influential agents in forming the national character. It helps to mold national life; if it does not always act in a positive direction, it acts at least as a constant brake . . .

It has been the high office of historians to study and to interpret the past, guided by the conception of their function which they cherish as their professional and cultural roles, but directed largely by the problems and needs of their own time. But as Huizinga has recalled, history is

> . . . never the reconstruction or reproduction of a given past. No past is ever given. Tradition alone is given. If tradition were at any point to make the total reality of the past accessible to us, still no history would result; or rather then least of all. The idea of history only emerges with the search for certain convictions, the essence of which is determined by the value which we attach to them. It makes no difference whether we think of history, which is the result of researches strictly critical in method, or of sagas and epics belonging to former phases of civilization. History is always an imposition of form upon the past, and cannot claim to be more. It is always the comprehension and interpretation of a meaning which we look for in the past.

The form put upon the past derives from present perplexities and concern for the future, as clearly shown by the rewriting of history in each generation, not merely to present new findings but to meet this need for reinterpreting the past to illuminate the changing present as it is seen today.

Man appears to be consulting the past, learning the "lessons of history," but he is looking at that past in terms of his present anxieties and preoccupations, seeing and learning only what he is prepared to learn from the past. It is worth remembering that in the more slowly changing societies with intact traditions and a more or less static culture, this urge to rewrite history is not so strong. Indeed the pressure is to perpetuate the time-honored story of the past in the most pious manner. In a changing society the past is seen as selectively organized and interpreted by present needs and concerns. MacLeish has stated in *The Fall of the City*, "The future is a mirror where the past marches to meet itself," but it is always the past as man reconstructs it.

A nation, or a larger cultural group like the people of the Western European culture—to which Americans belong—is like a patient who is at the mercy of his past, actual or mythical, that drives him onward to the destiny he himself has created for his own coercion and destruction. With the repetitive persistence of the neurotic or the psychotic, peoples of European culture have for centuries compulsively repeated the same traditional patterns, generation after generation, teaching their children to follow the same beliefs and accept the same goals and purposes. The record of European wars and conflicts, the ambitious careerists in politics or military or economic activities ruthlessly sacrificing nations for glory or power; the international disorders and human exploitation and defeats differ from country to country and age to age in minor details and personages, but the pattern is monotonously and tragically the same.

Today thoughtful persons are timidly beginning to ask how one can minister to a sick society, how can one treat a humanly defeatist culture? It no longer seems impious to be critical and to scrutinize the cultural traditions and the sanctions that have heretofore been unquestioned and unquestionable. Indeed critical thinking and scrutiny of traditional beliefs are essential to scientific research. Nor is it wholly Promethean to propose the possibility of attempting to develop a social life and a world order that are conservative of human life and conducive to the persistent aspirations and values so long frustrated.

But before any forward steps toward such goals can be taken, the help of the historian as therapist is needed to release man from the coercions and distorted versions of his traditions, of his "past," especially the interpretations of that past which have been given by various groups—theologians, philosophers, humanists, and especially historians. Man is at the mercy of these versions of his past, these selectively organized presentations of traditions and events from which he derives his cultural heritage, his image of himself, and his ideas of his future.

If one will reflect on the notion of progress and study the implications of social change, it will be realized that a group can change and be progressive only by emancipating itself—that is, its members—from its past, by interrupting the continuity of the cultural traditions so that new patterns of action, speech, and belief may be created to supersede and replace the old. Therein lies the essential difference between a static, tradition-bound society wherein the traditions of the past largely control life and the progressive societies which permit and, to an increasing extent, encourage criticism of traditions. Even when it has undermined the most venerable beliefs, man has learned to foster the creation of new ideas and practices. Much of our social disorder and conflict are generated by the persistence of obsolescent beliefs and outworn rituals which are no longer compatible with the lives man is endeavoring to live or the aspirations he cherishes. Indeed, behind every human activity which threatens human life and values and jeopardizes social order will be found a belief or assumption or a pattern of conduct derived from the past which blocks human welfare and frustrates human intelligence.

As Teggart remarked in *The Processes of History* in 1918 and more recently has reiterated, so long as man clings to fixed, archaic ideas and anachronistic patterns of action, he continues to produce the conflicts which they must inevitably generate; if one scrutinizes the past one will see that every human advance has come through release from the beliefs and conceptions that held man in their fixed grasp, blocking him from seeing and doing what a later generation found so obvious. That is why wars and migrations have been the occasions for the major human advances because they served to free men from traditions.

Kemp Smith, in his inaugural address at Edinburgh years ago, likewise observed that "the history of human intelligence is a record, not so much of the progressive discovery of truth, as of our gradual emancipation from error." How to use the past for enlightenment, instead of being coerced or frustrated by it, is indeed the crucial question faced in group and personal lives today. That is the problem of cultural reconstruction.

Here let it be clearly realized that every culture has with greater or less clarity formulated its major aspirations or values by which it has endeavored to guide its conduct of life, as a group and individually. Just as in science a continuous effort is made to enlarge and improve knowledge and understanding through revision of the theories and methods which each generation has developed, so cultural reconstruction presents a similar task of reformulating the persistent aspirations and enduring human values of culture in new terms and new patterns expressive of growing knowledge, insights, and changing sensibilities. The debt to the past is paid by striving to do for today what the great figures of the past did for their times.

Much the same kind of therapy is needed for modern culture that the psychotherapist gives his patient, enabling him to revise his "past," actual or assumed, and escape from its coercion. Men cannot create an image of themselves as a people nor project ahead the constructive ideals and aspirations needed for peace and world order so long as they are fixated by the image and ideals derived from the history of yesterday and today.

Specifically, European peace and order will not be possible so long as each nation or group cherishes a history that perpetuates the patterns of action, speech, beliefs, and feelings which give rise to the continual social conflicts and accentuate every aspect of life which separates people and antagonizes them toward all others. Germany can be helped to a place and function in Europe if she can have a new history with a less destructive image of herself to guide her conduct and her relations to others. If and when Germany is defeated, who will provide the new history to be given her children and youth that will help them take up anew the tasks of social order upon a basis of human decency and freedom, ready to participate in world order?

In postwar planning the revision of education in Europe and the provision of new histories are urgent tasks on which the many refugee scholars here and in England could begin now to write for the reconstruction period. A general conceptual framework that would recognize national-cultural differences in each group but also would foster world order could be developed as a group enterprise in which American and other scholars could all participate. The recent flood of histories of Germany showing she has always been this way, since Tacitus, may be emotionally satisfying while fighting Germany, but they offer little help to the reconstruction of Germany after defeat. As others have suggested, one of the major difficulties with Germany is the lack of a coherent and emotionally acceptable history; the German people are dangerous because they have no consistent traditions, but rather they reach into the past for whatever role and sanction seem desirable or expedient at the moment. Obviously such a people will alternate between Beethoven and Bismarck, between the extreme of high ethical and artistic endeavors and the worst cruelty and ruthlessness, depending upon the circumstances and the exigencies or opportunities they face. This duality in German conduct reflects a similar childhood "past" in German adults.

Here the scientific historian, if he has read thus far, may protest vehemently. All the painful effort to achieve scientific detachment, pure objectivity, and impartiality are seemingly threatened if not destroyed by this proposal. The modern historian, he will assert, is no myth-maker but rather a cold, detached observer and sifter of evidence who tells the unvarnished tale of the past for others to interpret or misuse for partisan purposes if they must. History must be aloof and above the turmoil of contemporary conflicts, however urgent the need for interpretation and guidance. This ideal of detached objectivity, however, strongly held by the university scholars, is not binding upon those who write the histories used in schools and colleges as texts or the histories which are offered for public perusal.

It has largely escaped the attention of many students of human affairs, that to be completely objective means to abolish culture and destroy all values, since culture is a rejection of the purely objective, organic world for a world of meanings and values, of aspirations toward that which culture proposes and man strives to attain. Surely the historian need not be reminded that the cultural world of assumptions and beliefs by which each group has attempted to make nature and man over into their preferred images is not an objective, biological world. Moreover, what is now believed and cherished as tradition has been in large measure the work of previous historians who have provided both the image of a people and the courage to meet crises, as seen today in the many recent volumes on early American life. It should not be necessary to recall that ideas and beliefs are more potent than objective "facts"; otherwise the war would be over and the Nazis would be dominant.

Historian-therapists are urgently needed to free man from the coercion of his traditions, from those versions of the past as he now sees and feels and understands it. Only by emancipation from that past can the past be utilized with intelligence and the new resources of science and critical thinking be invoked to create a peaceful world order. The present war, attributed to so many different "causes" and trends, may be viewed as a crisis in man's efforts to escape from his "past," in order to achieve a more humanly, desirable future, a process he began when he first created culture and projected ahead his values and aspirations. For this is needed a larger grasp of cultural diversities, the many varieties of cultural framework and ways of life that have been developed all over the world. The historian who limits his vision to Western European culture helps to perpetuate the parochial, self-centered thinking of Europeans that has been so blinding and destructive.

Some groups must accept this responsibility for an historical therapy, and if the historians, as a professional group, reject this role and neglect that task, then some other therapists must be found who have the imagination and courage to re-create the "past" so that mankind can advance toward a future freed from the tragic defeat, the frustration, and destructive coercion of its older historical traditions. It is not fair nor wise to unload the whole burden upon the historian. Their help in escaping from the past is necessary, however, so that the artists can create the new symbols and sensibilities so anxiously awaited today.

(FROM: *Psychiatry: Journal of the Biology and Pathology of Interpersonal Relations*, VII [1944], No. 3 [August]: 231-36.)

TWENTY-SIX

Dilemma of Leadership

NOTHING is more familiar than the continual cry for leaders in the democratic countries, with their unending search for methods of selecting and training youth to be future leaders. It is not, officially at least, recognized that the professed rule of the majority depends upon someone to tell the majority what they should desire and how to get it. Today, when the issue of democracy versus dictatorship is so acute, it may seem to some unwise or inexpedient to discuss this situation critically, but serious students of personality and culture should examine the question of leadership in political life, in scientific and professional life, and in academic, educational programs.

Individuals, with the rarest exceptions, do not know what to do with their lives—how to act, what to desire and hope for—and so we need leaders to guide our aspirations, to project goals and to spur us on toward those purposes. That is the office of culture, to order events and experience, to regulate conduct, and so to organize group life; but culture becomes effective only when translated by one personality into the life of another.

This continuous need for guidance and for stimulation or coercion provides the occasion for the would-be leader who needs to use other people for his own personality fulfillment. Thus the leader finds what he requires in the plastic, waiting-to-be-led mass, who in turn find in the leader the one who will define their goals and purposes, urge or drive them on, and use them without scruple.

The causes to which the leader urges on the led may not have any relevance to the real needs of the mass. Indeed, the more the cause demands sacrifice of their personal interests and needs, the more compelling it may be, because the mass wants to be used. Just as a woman may find fulfillment and emotional completion in surrendering to her biological functions, allowing herself to be used by the growing child in her uterus, by the process of labor that brings delivery of the child, and then by the nursing child who sucks at her breast, so the mass, mostly men, seek a similar experience of being caught up in a forceful ongoing purpose that uses them as childbearing uses the woman.

But just because the majority of men need this leadership they forever risk being destroyed or betrayed by these leaders, who ruthlessly pursue their own private purposes and use their followers as instruments for their achievement. To be a leader of masses of men one must have this terrific drive, this insatiable need, this utterly unscrupulous capacity for exploiting others in the striving for goals of one's own choosing; otherwise the followers will not be led nor be willing to be used. Followers do not yield willing obedience to a leader from mere admiration or approval of the program or goals he announces. They look to him for leadership because he boldly tells them he wants them for his own purposes and demands that they sacrifice themselves for him, personally; his program and goals are merely the focus of their efforts and the feelings aroused by the leader's personality. Once that relation of led to leader is emotionally created, he finds them hungrily looking for guidance and self-sacrifice, and they find him ready to take their lives and use them as he will; then the leader can make any program he wishes, altering the plans and the purposes as he may wish or be compelled by changing events, and the loyalty of the followers never wavers. Even when, as sometimes happens, the leader completely reverses himself, his power over his followers is not diminished.

Leadership, then, is a dynamic emotional relationship in which the personality of the leader orients the personality of the followers so that they are directed toward him by reason of this reciprocal relationship between one who dominates and those who wish to be dominated and used by him. This capacity for leadership is a personality trend in which there is often great hostility which supplies the boldness, the ruthlessness, and the usual destructiveness of the great leaders of history. With such characteristic powers and drives and the vitality or energy to express them, the leader does not need any superior intelligence. Indeed, intelligence might hamper his leadership and inhibit the ability to arouse and play upon his followers.

The curious and highly significant aspect of a leader is his own personal submission to the compulsions that dominate his life which he can neither control nor understand. Just as the followers are willing instruments in the hands of the leader, so the leader is a plastic agent for the emotional feelings and obscure impulses that have assumed control over him. The leader is able to rationalize his life of compulsive striving and exploitation of others only in terms of large group programs and strivings that appear to him as destined goals for the people he leads. What he tells his followers, the way he arouses their enthusiastic response and claims their personal devotion is his effort to make his own life and personality reasonable and to express those feelings he cannot otherwise understand. Every leader has then the feeling himself of being led or guided by a daemon, as Socrates said, or by a spirit or other superhuman, private oracle and prophet and sustainer of his faith in his own unique destiny. Just as the leader yields to the guidance of his "familiar spirit," finding justification for what he does in the imperative commands he must obey, so the mass of men, lacking a personal guiding spirit, yield to the leader. Their willing surrender to him and their submission to his program seem wholly desirable and reasonable, just as are his surrender and submission. The sacrifices he makes to his guiding spirit call for equal and greater sacrifices of the followers to him. Whoever opposes or challenges the leader is manifestly wrong because the leader is uniquely guided and has access to a higher Truth and a more penetrating Vision. Whoever is fainthearted or skeptical is obviously weak and vacillating when the occasion demands full and complete devotion to the leader's needs.

Leadership fulfills urgent personality needs of the leader who is driven to his work by these needs that can be met only by obedient followers, eager to do as they are bid in pursuit of ever receding and ever enlarging goals. Leadership also fulfills the personality needs of the followers who crave the security of a firm and coercive program in which they can, by obedience and submission, find their place in life. Neither leaders nor followers, because they are both driven, can have any insight, any awareness of their personality make-up or needs.

The leader then uses his followers, and the more he uses them ruthlessly the more they blindly obey and revere him. Even when the leader is defeated, the loyalty of his followers continues and often is enhanced by the feeling of injustice done to their hero-leader. As he uses people and finds them more eager to be used, the leader becomes ever more bold and ruthless, his power over people and his use of it growing with exercise and success. The hostility that impelled the leader to assert himself, to oppose those in power, and to demand what he sought as goals, because strengthened by practice as more and more people yield obedience to his commands and successful achievement justifies his boldness. So soon as the leader feels that he may express his hostility, unrestrained by fear of successful opposition or retaliation against himself, then he has reached the apex of his career as leader, regardless of where he stands in relation to his announced goals. The dynamic emotional character of leadership thus conditions the career of the leader who can go on capturing new followers only in so far as his own aggressive impulses continue to seek expression in action; when he can no longer feel any restraint outwardly or inwardly upon his hostility his leadership may go on from the dynamics of the situations it has created, but it will not expand or grow.

Thus we see that the leader does not have definite ambitions or aspirations for specific goals, as in the ordinary gifted man who makes a design for living around that sought-for attainment. The leader has only a fund of initiative, boldness, enterprise, whatever we choose to call the way in which hostility is expressed, and so he continually projects ahead further goals and larger purposes that will provide release for more of his tremendous hostility. When the last inhibition or restraint has been removed, that is signalized by a cessation of the driving purpose because each new goal in his career has meant a further release of hostility.

But the followers likewise find in the leader's ruthless commands an opportunity for their own release of hostility. Now they can be ruthless and cruel and hostile in a cause, sanctioned by the leader's words and authoritative commands. Each step forward in the leader's program of increasing reach and power captures a further group of followers who require that cumulative attraction to the leader's cause in which their hitherto disguised or repressed hostility can be released more openly and with group sanction. As the leader's aggression reaches its climax, so the growth of his followers reaches its peak, since the latest to rally to his standard are those who were least repressed and so needed this cumulative influence to gather them in. Continued success of the leader will also bring in many who have no emotional loyalty to him, but who join the cause for reasons of prudence and fear of being on the wrong side.

Leadership and mass following are two expressions of hostility which cannot be released without some sanction and guidance, the leader finding his in the feeling of being guided from above, the followers finding theirs in feeling guided and commanded by the leader, but both leader and followers submitting to this superior guidance as essential sanction for expressing their hostility.

This hostility drive also operates to make the leader's program always destructive, a struggle against an enemy or an antagonism against another group who must be hated. As the hostility of the followers is thus focused and directed against a common enemy, the coherence and solidarity of the followers is increased, for all their aggressiveness is now being released toward an out-group whom they can freely hate. In the opinion of many, social solidarity is possible only when the hostility of each member of the group is focussed on a common enemy or despised class. Under such a regimen of shared hostility, the leader receives a loyalty and devotion that further justifies his course of action and frees him from any remaining restraint or timidity and thus encourages more destruction.

Nationalistic programs, imperialistic programs, militaristic programs, all the diverse drives toward the outer group have their characteristic phases of growth as the insatiable needs of the leader carry him on to ever more grandiose attempts at conquest and domination. Likewise arise the movements within a group that aim at overthrowing the existing control of the government or of those who wield power behind the government, against which the leader rallies all the discontented and unfortunate who have suffered from the regime he attacks. These revolts or insurrections or mass movements grow with the prestige and the influence of the leader who arouses his followers to a passionate devotion to him and obedience to the cause he preaches, which must always be destructive, an attack upon some group or class. A purely constructive program that aims to change similar abuses and maladjustments but proposes only the positive changes and reforms rarely arouses such whole-hearted devoted loyalty to such a moderate or constructive leader or such blind obedience to his cause.

Leadership, to be effective, must arouse an emotional response in the followers that will bind them to the leader in loyal, unquestioning devotion to him and belief in his program. Without this emotional tie the leader cannot build up his following, since he can enlist only the reasonable men, who act upon reflection and approve his program only for its intrinsic merits. This is one of the dilemmas of leadership in a democracy that requires leaders but can have them only by surrendering to them emotionally and accepting their destructive, aggressive programs. The followers must allow themselves to be used by the leader for his own purposes and needs that he may rationalize in terms of a social program ostensibly for their benefit but primarily addressed to the destructive ends that the leader's personality demands as release for his aggression. Like the bale of hay that forever lures the donkey along the road, these remote gains promised by the leader must always wait upon the removal by force or coercion of yet one more group or class institutional obstacle. The more self-seeking followers who press for reward may receive some tangible gains when the leader feels the need of allaying their clamor, but for the mass of followers the leader has only the call for more obedience, more self-sacrifice, more faith in the ultimate goals when all the difficulties and hardships will be over. The mass of followers find emotional release and exaltation above their petty lives and their drab occupations in this call to service, in which they may at once find a reason and a cause for their lives and a release for their hostility.

Democracy, as it is conceived in representative government, in majority rule, in defined power of government, in personal freedom and liberty of conscience, in the many other characteristics imputed to democracy, needs leaders, but is at their mercy since the self-constituted leader who arises spontaneously and raises a following has no obligations, no defined duties or responsibilities, no scruples or limitations upon his ruthless use of his followers for his own purposes.

Historically, the development of democracies has been the work of these self-constituted leaders who have started with existing discontents and grievances and fanned the flame of overt revolt or political upheavals. The very conception of political democracy in the Anglo-Saxon tradition reflects these waves of protest against the existing regime of political-economic control. The slogan of equality of opportunity came to represent those who wanted opportunity to compete and defeat others by the exercise of their initiative or aggression. This history and this dependence on a leader suggest that democracy is essentially dependent upon protest and discontent and the channelling of the hostility impulses of individuals into the socially sanctioned patterns of economic striving and political struggle. So long as the leaders restrict their programs to these regularized patterns, there may be social unrest and much economic-political struggle but no great destructive mass movements. The essential social organization and control is not threatened except by individuals who can reach positions of power in the hierarchy by personal efforts or maneuvers.

There has been for a long time a realization of these dangers of leadership in a democracy as indicated by the reiterated faith in education to make people more intelligent and reasonable in their social conduct. The traditional American faith in education as the bulwark of the institutions and government rests upon the assumption that education in skills and knowledge will protect men from being misled by undesirable leaders. But today this faith is less strongly held than before, even by educators who are coming to see that the formal teaching of subject matter and training in skills that has been going on for several generations gives little evidence of having influenced men's political and economic conduct or of protecting them against the rabble-rousing of aspiring leaders. Indeed the ability to read and write, the elementary knowledge gained in the schools, and the confidence born of being educated are being revealed as making people more susceptible to the appeal of leaders who can now play upon these standarized acquirements with more surety than when they had to combat the cautious folk-lore and canny wisdom of the unschooled but shrewd folk mind.

Education has not proved a reliable protection against unscrupulous leaders nor has it done much, if anything, to build up a desire for trustworthy leadership. This may be the result of the now acknowledged lag in formal education which has neglected political-economic questions for the more formal subject matter

DILEMMA OF LEADERSHIP

and non-controversial fields of knowledge. It is likely, however, that even the most modernized curriculum of subject matter will not make a change in the susceptibility to leaders of the character described, because that modernized curriculum will not touch the emotional lives of the students nor modify their repressed but ever-present hostility waiting for a leader to bring release in a cause or program of attack and destruction.

Education has not and apparently will not take seriously the question of emotional reactions through and in which the major aspects of personal and group life are expressed and controlled. Yet in the countries where democracy has been repudiated for authoritarian government, the skillful patterning of the emotional reactions, the evocation of hostility toward the hated classes or groups or enemies, and the summons to loyal, devoted submission to authority are carried on from earliest childhood through adult years. What the schools teach is not only carefully selected for its meaning but is presented in an emotionally toned setting that makes the educational program a satisfying, fulfilling experience, not merely discipline in knowledge.

It is as if the authoritarian governments had rationalized the leader-follower emotional relationship and established a social program of education, formally in schools and informally through radio, moving pictures, and mass demonstrations, that carried on the incitement to devoted, self-sacrificing adherence to the leader but saved him from the continual effort of keeping his followers emotionally attuned and blindly obedient.

Leadership has, as it were, been institutionalized and built into the very fabric of social life so that it functions pervasively and effectively, with little opportunity for any contrary ideas or feelings to be expressed or received. This, however, is not new but a revival of the older pattern of life that the individualistic movement of the past three hundred years had so largely destroyed under the impact of scientific curiosity, skepticism toward authority, and the waning of supernaturalism. Before these disturbances the pattern of life was woven from the same material and with the same design, and every activity was infused with the common body of belief, faith, and loyalty. The thirteenth century unity, as Henry Adams has described it, was a unity of authoritarian government and religion which not only the new governments abroad wish to reinstate, but many of our medievalists, such as Ralph Adams Cram, G. K. Chesterton, and Hilaire Belloc ardently hope to recover.

The perplexity of democratic governments arises in large measure from the persistent belief in man as a rational being in whom emotion is controlled by sheer reason and intelligence. Educational programs shrink from any frank acceptance of the underlying personality make-up and emotional reactions of students as entering into the educational situation, because to do so would bring a widespread collapse of the whole educational philosophy and undermining of approved pedagogy. Moreover, it would necessitate recognition of individual differences that involve not merely quantitative differences, as in intelligence ratings, but qualitative differences which cut across and negate the aim of education to create a common, socialized group as like-minded, with as similar conduct, as possible. This aim to bring about uniformity is what public education is established to do, and it gets its justification from the apparent need, in a democracy, or in any social group, for like-minded equally socialized (and therefore less individualized) people.

This educational program in socialization starts earlier than the schools, as the family insists upon conformity to the established patterns of conduct, of restraint and dutiful observance, so that the child will not deviate from the social norms. But, as we are learning, this very process of socialization, with the deprivations and repressions it imposes upon the child, is responsible for creating those strong emotional reactions, especially of hostility and resentment, which make possible that emotional relation of leader to the followers, as previously described.

What happens here is worth noting carefully because it points to the crucial issue; the child needs socialization of his functions and impulses, the protection of himself against his biological, reactive processes in order to be free to live and work and to get along in a communal life where some uniformity is essential to the co-operative, reciprocal activities of group life. The group life, therefore, depends upon this socialization being given to the child to fit him for the group life. But the way the parents treat the child during this necessary socialization creates the personality and emotional reactions of the child and provides the driving power for the leadership that threatens the established social order, because the severity or the over-indulgence of the parental training creates the resentful hostility of the leader, and also of the followers who dare not reveal or express theirs until a leader provides the sanction and the occasion.

Education, sharing the common pretense that man is a rational, volitional person, is fearful of recognizing these powerful emotional reactions and susceptibilities of children and adolescents, because of the tacit agreement to ignore them all through social life. The law asserts that man is rational and volitional and asks the jurymen to weigh evidence and calmly decide the issues but permits and approves of the most outrageous play upon emotions by attorneys to influence the jury's verdicts. Politics, likewise, assumes an air of specious reason and logical argument while actually relying upon the crudest and most elementary exploitation of fears, prejudices, and repressed hostility to rally its supporters. Industry and business likewise wear an air of strict impartial reason and non-sentimental businesslike exactions while operating with all manner of emotional appeals and expressions; the more critical and important the issues the more business men and bankers are swayed by feelings and emotions ("business confidence") and irrational desires, prone to mass hysteria as we have seen during the recent depression. The churches more or less openly acknowledge their appeal to emotions and play upon feelings on one hand, but on the other join with other social institutions in the general conspiracy of pretending that emotions must not have any place in human conduct.

With this general attitude and pretense and the neglect of emotional reactions in education, it is inevitable that adult men and women are usually infantile emotionally; no one receives any education or training in emotional maturation except suppression of feelings so that they do not appear directly or openly. Discipline consists in being taught that one must not feel but only think and be rational and if one does feel one must not show it or acknowledge it.

Thus men and women are generally in a state of overt conformity to social norms but inward emotional disturbances that they ignore, deny, and attempt to repress. Since the bulk of people have had unhappy childhood training they have more or less resentful hostility toward life that awaits occasion for release when a leader more capable of overt aggression and initiative provides the long awaited opportunity. Our educational procedures and social myths about rational man are constantly preparing for the self-constituted leaders who will exploit their emotional needs and infantile susceptibilities.

These susceptibilities are today dangerous to democracy because the well-established patterns of social norms are no longer coercive and people are therefore more ready to listen to programs of action proposed by leaders who seek further to arouse their perplexed discontent and exploit their resentments and hostility.

An educational program designed to foil the demogogic, dictator leaders would be a program of emotional education that would, by provoking repeated emotional reactions in controlled situations of adequate provocation, create a gradually rising threshold of susceptibility to these destructive leaders, just as training of soldiers, firemen, policemen, nurses, and others dealing with emotion-arousing situations are trained to act in definite patterns that inhibit or reduce the emotional response. Emotional susceptibility is greatest when the emotion is denied, repressed, or evoked by an experience for which there has been no preparation. Acknowledgment of the emotion, acceptance of the excitement, and the pressure of impulse to action, and training in handling the situation effectively, as the fireman or soldier, eliminates the emotion or reduces it so that it merely reinforces the learned pattern of action.

But rarely in education, except occasionally in a few nursery schools, is the need for this emotional education recognized or given any attention. If the democratic governments were concerned to protect themselves against authoritarian leaders, they could begin with such emotional education that would, however, expose the larger social situation, with its sedulously fostered myth of rationality, to such a reorganization that a social revolution would probably ensue.

Such an educational program could not be permitted because it would strike at the heart of these elaborate pretenses and of the systematic exploitation of the mass of people who are played upon and used so unscrupulously by active men in political, social, business, and religious life. The men who direct and control these affairs are not prepared to give up this most effective method of manipulating people to their own ends. Like the leaders who arouse their followers to an emotional response which they then direct to actions, so these political bosses, captains of business and finance, and others engaged in controlling human affairs for their own purposes need this emotional immaturity and these susceptibilities to run their affairs. So long as this kind of emotional exploitation is parcelled out among competing individuals the extent of their control is necessarily limited since they check and offset each other and restrict their activities to certain fields. Only when these local or lesser leaders come together and pool their followers, as in a national political party, does a national following get built, but here the local leaders can always threaten withdrawal of loyalty if they feel threatened or if they are denied their share of rewards. It requires a leader who can override these local leaders to gain full political control through arousing an emotional response so elemental as to be a common bond throughout the formerly localized groups. This is the risk that politicians run of having a leader snatch their following away by making a stronger emotional appeal and by creating a greater loyalty than they can maintain by lesser and more local appeals. They prefer this risk of being superseded, to the risk of being outmoded by an educational program in emotions because they feel able to maintain their places in the total political picture by various deals, intrigue, and chicane, according the rules of the great game of politics.

The collaboration of business and financial controllers is more of a threat to democracy, because their attempts at concerted action, to exploit the mass of people through arousing emotional responses such as fear and anxiety, are more likely to escape the disruptive pulling and hauling of local political leaders and so can be organized and executed more effectively. It is well recognized that the political maneuvers are largely a reflection of business and financial pressures utilizing the political organizations for their own advantages against other business and financial pressures. When the individual or group of business men forsake this indirect for more direct concerted action they can very quickly exert pressure on the mass of people, mostly wage-earners, and thus create the anxiety and fear reactions that permit them to gain control over governmental affairs.

Here the mass of men are exploited by a group which, unlike the leader who creates an emotional relationship to himself and releases a common hostility, operates on the basis of repression of action through arousing fear and anxiety that forbids group loyalty and any expression of aggression.

This kind of mass control has been the more frequent interference with democracy in the United States as is shown by the history of economic crises until recently, when first the financial repressive control was tried but soon abandoned for the political movement under Franklin Roosevelt, who is not a true-to-type leader of the aggressive variety and whose following has not the true-to-type emotional loyalty and submissive obedience to a destructive program of attack. We are too close to these events to gain much insight or have a perspective upon the situation.

The movement initiated and directed by a leader who uses his followers as instruments and exploits their emotional needs usually involves eventual disaster for the followers, who live gloriously while caught up in the movement, but come to the final phase, with collapse or loss of the beloved leader, often more miserable and deprived than before, but too tired and apathetic to care or struggle further. The concerted action by a small group to exploit the mass through playing upon their fears and anxieties brings no emotional release of aggression or self-sacrifice but merely deprivation and hardship and every more ruthless exploitation that brings misery and discontent. Then is the golden opportunity for the leader to arise and offer a destructive program of attack upon the exploiters which provides for expression of hatred, hostility, and aggression, with devotion to the leader.

Such historic situations produce leaders, often many at one time, each contending for supremacy, with one becoming the real leader to whom all others rally with a growing following that looks to early realization of their long deferred hopes of better days. Then comes the all too frequent betrayal when the exploiters of the mass, whom the leader has promised to destroy, quietly "make a deal" with the leader to turn the aroused hostility of his followers upon some other class in the group (religious) or upon an outside enemy. War to allay social discontent and drain off hostility that threatens economic political control is a traditional device for manipulating the emotions of the mass so that the dominating control may be continued.

It is idle to expect those who rely upon this emotional exploitation and manipulation to favor education in emotional maturity which would prevent such control. Thus again we see the dilemma of leadership in that the situations that are used for controlling and exploiting others create the need for leadership that threatens

DILEMMA OF LEADERSHIP

that control and if not bought off will destroy it, only to set up another form of control.

The struggle for power over others is unending, and is sought either through arousing an emotional response to an individual, who can then use that loyalty in bargaining or in conflict with others having a following, unless the individual becomes an undisputed leader, or through the creation of fear and anxiety which can be played upon to permit direct exploitation. The more the mass of people are oppressed by anxiety, the more they become ready for the leader who will command loyalty and self-sacrifice and who will permit overt aggression. Education for democracy has yet to face this situation or even realize it exists behind the objective data of social, economic, and political "problems" offered to students for discussion.

But even if education of emotions were to be accepted as necessary for a democracy, the danger of attenuating the feelings of discontent with the existing economic and social disorder would be so great that no one could be certain that such an educational program would not become a means to further exploitation by those who would not scruple to take advantage of any lessening of discontent.

Leadership is not limited to political and social affairs of a democracy. In every field of human activity there is expressed a similar need for able and intelligent leaders to guide the affairs and scientific, professional, or other human activities. Here is revealed another kind of dilemma of leadership, because however great may be the need for someone who can guide and direct activities or thought more fruitfully and effectively, the resistance is equally great.

The need for leadership in any field arises from the fixed, rigidly unchangeable patterns of thought and performance in that field on the part of those who, by position or seniority, control affairs. Where there is pliability, eager and hospitable reception to new ideas and methods, readiness to abandon the old and familiar for the new and experimental, there is rarely expressed any crying need for leaders, as is shown, for example, by physics today, rapidly changing and eager to push its ideas ahead, contrasted with the law, where every law school and bar association repeatedly assert the need for competent leaders.

This gives a clue to the dilemma of leadership in these fields which have a need for leaders only because they are caught in a situation from which they cannot escape; they want a leader to guide them out of that situation but the very fixity and rigidity of those in the field offers a resistance to any leadership that attempts to change the situation. This need for leadership is peculiar to scientific and professional groups that are, by the very training for practice, opposed to change, antagonistic to new and different ideas, hostile to improved methods and techniques that threaten their hard-won competence in the old.

There is in truth a need, not for leaders, but for some solvent of resistance to change. Paradoxically then they call for leaders who will force them to give up their accustomed ways and conceptions but they hate everyone who essays to perform that task. The historical record of antagonism and hostility to every one who brought a major contribution to the advancement of his profession, of the most bitter and violent opposition and attacks, personal and professional, upon the innovator, and of reluctant grudging acceptance of what in another generation will become the glory of the group, that record is available to each group but rarely considered or taught to the student.

It is not mere stupidity or blind, ignorant opposition. In scientific and professional work, the able men are those who, with native ability, can assimilate the prevailing ideas and conceptions and learn to use the theoretical and methodological instruments so thoroughly that they can do their scientific teaching and research or practice their profession with great skill. This devotion to the accepted body of knowledge and acquisition of skill in the use of prevailing methods are essential to competent performance and to that self-confidence so important in professional work. Skepticism and professional skill are antithetical and mutually exclusive for most men who must shut their eyes to all other possibilities and cling loyally to one, the learned, procedure.

The resistance to new ideas, the opposition to new discoveries, the neglect of new techniques and methods are all necessary, apparently, to professional competence, but equally obstructive to professional improvement. That apparently is the reason so many advances come from outside the professions, from amateurs, often dilettantes, who, with perhaps inferior ability and little or no training, nevertheless see possibilities, explore new leads and contrive new techniques. Just because these outsiders lack professional

DILEMMA OF LEADERSHIP

prestige and standing their contributions are under a double handicap, of novelty and of unprofessional origin.

This resistance to the new is especially characteristic of many professional and graduate schools in our universities in which able young men with ideas are disciplined into acceptance of the correct theory and the right conceptions and abandonment of their own original views and ideas. Being young and insecure and dependent upon approval of the professors who control the award of degrees and placement in jobs, the able young men, except in a few departments such as the natural sciences today, are rarely encouraged. It is just those fields and professions that exercise this regimented indoctrination of the official teachings and discourage original ideas that are most clamorous for leaders and are most opposed to new points of view and new problems.

One who has ability and originality and aspires to leadership in such fields faces a difficult situation. He must expect opposition, ridicule, and perhaps bitter antagonism from those in his field whose work and theories his contributions challenge. Only in so far as his own work does go beyond or contradicts the accepted views and findings will it be original and capable of advancing knowledge. But those very qualities may prevent even a fair hearing for his work.

What then impels a man to go ahead, despite professional opposition and in the face of this prospect of resistance and perhaps persecution? Every major discovery and innovation has had much the same fate, so that the individual so inclined knows he will be opposed. How then does leadership arise, and what personality need drives the individual forward against ridicule and scorn?

It is not merely intelligence or special ability in a particular line, although those may be present in more than average degree. It is rather the attitude toward authority, the emotional reaction toward those who exercise control in a field. Most individuals, despite their intellectual gifts, come to maturity with a feeling of acceptance or submission to what is required and what is forbidden. If intellectually superior, they will contrive to find opportunity in their fields for distinctive, high quality work, but not often original, since original work is just that pushing against the known, the accepted, the approved, for which the acquiescent or submissive person has no drive or impulse.

The individual who is to do original work, and be creative, cannot be tolerant of authority and submissive to the accepted; he must feel that the authoritative conceptions and approved methods of his field represent the stage that was reached by the push of the latest creative person before him. He regards these not as barriers that he must respect but as boundaries of previous exploration from which his own efforts should start, as a point of departure. Authority then for him is not that which controls but that which has ordered and cleared the way for further advance. This is essentially an emotional reaction that makes the individual see the field of work, not as restrictive, but as provocative. If he feels only resentment or hostility toward authority he may be destructively critical but rarely original and creative. Sometimes the hostile individual by the very vehemence of his attack upon accepted theories and authoritative teachers destroys much that stands in the way of new ideas and discoveries and so stumbles on important new leads.

Just because he is not submissive or hostile the creative individual need not feel either cowed or fearful of those in authority nor antagonistic to them; they exist in their areas as indicated, but his work lies beyond, where authority does not yet operate and consequently where he need not destroy or defeat others in order to achieve something, as do those who compete within the approved, accepted, authorized area of work. This is the mark of the creative mind that avoids controversy because it is emotionally irrelevant and unnecessary and because argument is concerned so often with alternatives upon a single accepted position, while the engaging problem is beyond the bounds of contemporary controversies.

The original mind, then, is artistic, and as Otto Rank has pointed out, is impelled to reconstruct the world that he finds uncongenial or inacceptable. But that very impulse to go beyond and reconstruct what others accept as correct and satisfactory arouses resentment in those who feel insecure or inadequate when the creative mind proposes something beyond their reach and competence. Thus the creator is opposed and ridiculed by his contemporaries who continue to assert the need for the very leadership they are rejecting. Such resistance, however, is not significant to the leader, who derives his confidence in the essential value of his work from his own inner necessity of creating something that is personally acceptable and rejecting what is professionally or socially imposed. Thus, as in the destructive social, political leader who is impelled by a conviction of personal destiny, the scientific-artistic leader is impelled by a similar conviction of unique creativity that he must express in discovery and achievement beyond the contemporary boundaries. But unlike the destructive leader, the creative leader does not seek or need a following with personal loyalty to himself, who will obediently carry out his program at whatever sacrifice. The creative leader does not need to use others for his own purposes and does not seek to exploit every situation for his own advantage or the advancement of his cause. He asks only to be allowed to work, to create, to explore for the new and more creative, which, however, he is rarely permitted to do by his contemporaries because his work undermines their own security and complacence.

Thus this dilemma of leadership appears as the continued need for creative leaders but the total inability to recognize them when they appear or to accept their contribution until years later, usually after the leader has died. The record of this unvarying pattern is voluminous and impressive but it has no influence upon the professional and scientific world which continues to cry for leaders and blindly reject them. This is the reverse of the situation with the destructive leader, who is immediately accepted with a full surrender of their lives by his eager followers craving to be used and guided in every thought and deed.

In the creative leader appears one who is rejected, while he asks nothing in the way of a following, makes no attempt to exploit others for his own purposes and offers his creative work for their advantage; in the aggressive leader appears one who is not only accepted but exalted while he demands loyalty and submission in his followers and exploits their self-sacrifice to no constructive ends. Well may we stress the dilemma of leadership and ask if there is any escape from such paradoxical results.

These recurrent situations are tempting for an *ad hoc* type of psychology or historical theory and for specific remedies, as we can see in the popular and educational journals. But these relationships are too deeply inward in the personality make-up of people and in the culture patterns to be resolved by any neat formula or prescription. The selection and training of needed leaders, of the processes to be brought out of the accidental into the area of purposeful social planning, must be predicated upon these fundamental human and cultural needs and limitations if they are to be effective.

If a commission of wise men were established to select and train the leaders of tomorrow they might, if clear sighted and honest, recommend that for the present nothing is possible because in our present state of knowledge whatever we attempt in any organized fashion may be directly opposed to our goal. But there is little likelihood of any organized attempt by a group of wise counsellors being made in the near future, while many unwise and shortsighted plans are being made and put into execution every year. It will do no harm and may prevent some damage, then, to examine into the question of how to select a future leader and then what to do to or for him that will be helpful to his leadership in the artistic-scientific-professional fields.

All over the country schools and colleges, universities and outside boards and foundations are seeking potential leaders to be assisted by scholarships and fellowships and the various programs of training established for different fields. Standards for judging candidates are measures of excellence in achievement. Academic standing, shown by grades, marks, examinations, and test results are the most frequent criteria of ability and it has been repeatedly shown that a good academic record is generally a reliable indicator of future competence; those who do good work in high school do good work in college usually, in graduate or professional schools, and in subsequent professional life. But it is not clear that such achievements are indicative of creative original minds who often cannot, or will not, expend themselves in the required tasks of academic work that arouse no real interest or enthusiasm.

It is an accepted doctrine of education that until an individual is disciplined by training in doing what is required of all, by learning what others have found out and believed, he cannot possibly do anything of significance or value. This doctrine is unassailable for the training of competent skillful workers in every field, but is wholly irrelevant to the development of the creative, original mind that can go beyond the accepted only by being psychologically resistant to the teachings of his contemporaries. Only by rejecting the authoritative teachings of his time can the leader escape from their limitations and bias, but that may involve a cavalier and ineffective response to the requirements of formal training. Moreover, the eminent men with prestige and authoritative positions in the field all feel that they are leaders even when they are spending their lives in defending a certain theory or technique against any criticism or change. The strong feelings they develop in this process of defending their position is one source of the professional resistance shown to the creative leader whose work renders their achievements obsolete.

Here we may note one aspect of the academic and professional situation that is of large importance to the selection of future leaders, namely, the inevitable feeling by those in the field that since they have had to undergo the training and discipline, accept what they were taught, and convince their teachers by their conformity to that teaching that they were competent, of necessity everyone else must be similarly treated. This attitude is wholly reasonable for a professional group that is concerned with maintaining and raising standards of training and performance in the men who will continue the professional work. In professional associations and boards the members are usually those who are the more aggressive individuals or more politically competent and so can win elections and appointments to office where their administrative abilities can be exhibited. These qualifications for offices in professional organizations do not often go with creative ability but frequently blind these individuals to the significance of a less conventional thinker and worker. But these are of no relevance to the original creative mind that alone can become the leader so much desired by the profession. Indeed every step in the direction of raising formal requirements for admission, demanding longer periods of schooling and of apprenticeship to eminent teachers, and presenting more difficult examinations and tests for competence may be creating greater obstacles for the prospective leaders in that field. Thus the educational logic is unassailable when taken in the restricted situation of training competent workers but irrelevant, if not inimical, to the discovery and development of leaders.

The initial selection of leaders for development today rests upon an inadequate understanding of the psychological characteristics and needs of the future leader, and any attempt to recognize these in selection of candidates would probably be violently opposed as undermining the profession and threatening collapse of hard-won standards. This is entirely justified since the approval of nonconformity to requirements and of deviations from established standards would immediately let in all manner of incompetents and low grade candidates because the customary procedure is to grade individuals, not as personalities, but as performers of prescribed tasks. To the candidate seeking entrance to a professional school the situation is largely an accounting transaction; if he can produce enough grades and credits of sufficiently high rank, he can, so to speak, buy his way in; thereafter his task is to demonstrate his ability to meet the successive tasks imposed.

The inadequacy of this situation even for the run-of-the-mine normal candidate has been recognized, and various aptitude tests and measurements have been devised, but these are essentially standardized versions of what the majority of professional workers should exhibit in interests, curiosities, and attitudes, and they are predominantly concerned with the intellectual (often motor) abilities and predilections. The personality make-up and trends that are of such large significance in the professions do not enter into the selection except in the casual interviewing that seeks to discover the outward social adjustments of the candidate, or the standardized inventories and rating scales of personality characteristics.

Within each individual, however, and usually wholly unrecognized by himself, are the personality trends and needs that will direct the individual's life and govern how he uses that intellectual capacity and whatever professional competence he may have or acquire. This is not the occasion for an extended discussion of personality needs in the professions, but it is essential to recognize that the creative original personality is one that may be entirely outside the range of what is regarded as "normal," desirable, or acceptable. If the individual had a personality that would allow him to conform, to accept, to be obedient to superiors, and to feel satisfied with achievements that bring prestige and high positions in the profession, then he would not have those other characteristics that are necessary for creative original work beyond the contemporary ideas and practices. The steady academic progress of the student who meets all requirements, does high grade work and pleases his teachers, who thereupon highly praise him for his ability, rules out just these unusual qualities that are necessary to leadership, but unsuited to the formalized academic pattern. What gives him the drive, to use a current term, and the direction to his energies is just these unusual personality trends and needs that cannot be satisfied with the ideas or the achievement that others find acceptable.

In the personality of the creative leader there is a need for something that others do not have or want. To use a current phrase, his level of aspiration is higher than that of others, so that what brings satisfaction and a feeling of adequacy to them, marks only his beginning of striving toward a further goal from which no obstacles or difficulties will deter him. This reaching out and beyond may arise from several life experiences, apparently being generated by the individual's attitude or feeling toward authority. If the early life has been an authoritative, repressive experience that has created resentment against all those who exercise authority and demand obedience, there may be a persistent drive to challenge authority, to assert a superiority over all requirements and even to remake life, or a portion of it, so that the existing authoritative rules and limitations are abolished. This resentment and dislike of authority are common, so common that they are the usual attitude, as shown in reluctant obedience or hostility toward others, often disguised to avoid retaliation or punishment. But in the creative original mind the attitude toward authority, instead of expressing itself in emotional reactions or ineffectual outbreaks or infractions of discipline or even surreptitious rebellion, becomes a steady driving power toward original work, a creative demonstration of ability to go beyond the authoritative and set up new ideas and procedures more congenial, because self-imposed.

Another attitude toward authority may be generated by a life experience of non-repressive tolerant direction that instead of creating resentment or hostility develops an attitude of outer compliance to requirements, when necessary, but a constant conviction of the purely contemporary character of all constituted authority. The aggressive personality develops leadership to express its resentment of authority; in this other personality who develops into a leader, the creative ability is released by the very absence of authoritative barriers to original achievement. In other words, the individual of this characteristic personality needs to show that he can work and conduct his life without constraint or coercion or rules because his own personal direction is sufficient to guide him. One is struggling for freedom from authority by escaping from the authoritative in his field, the other is ignoring the authoritative which his personality neither resents nor feels coercive and so he does not submit to the established beliefs and the prestige of position.

Too much discipline and repression or its absence in early life will create these personality trends that fight against what is prescribed or observe the rules only in order to go beyond them. Emphatically, personality alone will not make a creative-original leader, but without these personality trends and needs, creative original work is not done.

In the development of these leaders especially of the non-aggressive trend, the major process is the continual raising of the level of aspiration beyond what is required by the schools and professional work. This occurs when the individual is permitted and encouraged to set up goals and purposes for himself to which he personally aspires as contrasted with the achievement of tasks set by teachers and superiors. By this aspiration toward self-selected and self-imposed goals the individual releases his ability and generates a drive that others, not so impelled, can rarely show.

This quality of personality gives a clue to the seeming paradox of these leaders who may appear in youth as less vigorous and energetic than others whose work they can easily surpass, and who may show few signs of their real ability and originality in the standardized performances of school or college work examinations. These prescribed tasks may evoke little or no interest or effort in the individual whose life career is self-directing and focussed upon the work that lies beyond the regular channels. The selection of future leaders then waits upon the recognition of these personality trends that at present are ignored for the quantitative records and standardized tests and inventories.

The proposals for training leaders likewise rest upon a neglect or more often denial of the peculiar requirements of these original creative personalities. In general, it is assumed that prolonged and rigorous training is the essential process for future leaders involving persistent indoctrination in the accepted ideas, beliefs, and methods. But such training not only thwarts the emergence of original ideas by blocking and obscuring steps beyond what is accepted; it also discourages the sensitive awareness of the original creative mind who, because of that nature, must always feel that what is known and accepted is the chief enemy to advance of knowledge.

This points to the curious situation in scientific and professional work where the contemporary opinion and state of the arts is regarded as solid and final. Scientific discoveries are hailed as the revelation of eternal Truths, generalized statements of relationships are announced as final laws, and new techniques and instruments are produced with the claim to permanent worth. These practices and convictions are born of the authoritarian, absolute tradition that modern science inherited along with the philosophical preoccupation with "the quest for certainty." They express the need of investigators and professional workers for some personal security and the social, professional prestige of making profound discoveries. Each worker builds his life upon his activities and his bid for fame and so invests the known, the accepted, the professionally recognized with a strong emotional meaning that he attempts to give his students and subordinates. This is an understandable personality twist but one that presents serious obstacles to the advancement of science and professional arts because it hampers the full free flow of inquiry and experimentation and especially frustrates the creative original minds.

The universities and research institutes are everywhere caught in this personality difficulty as distinguished men of science and the professions stand astride the road to new knowledge and improved methods, blocking, diverting, and sometimes sabotaging the work that threatens to go beyond their own personal reach and convictions. Their training of younger men is of necessity the indoctrination and preparation of disciples who will carry on the teachers' own personal theory and practices unchanged except for minor improvements and elaborations. Often students are used as polemical agents to fight against a rival teacher or conflicting theory or as defenders of the only truth, as that laboratory or school passionately insists. Young men of ability and promise, and occasionally the creative original mind, are drawn into these feudal loyalties to a chief and sacrificed unscrupulously by him for offensive or defensive tactics against rival feudal lords. In scientific and professional life the same personality trends appear as in politics or business or military affairs, since the personality make-up and needs of the scientist and professional worker are no different from others. But these practices in science and the professions, despite the official credo of disinterested, objective search for knowledge, find justification in the time-honored beliefs in Truth, in absolutes, in authoritative laws and generalizations, and the other survivals from the older rationalistic, absolutistic, metaphysical traditions.

With such a background of belief and of strong convictions that derive from personality needs for security and prestige, if not for aggressive, hostile release, it is not difficult to understand how the training of neophytes so often is thus distorted and biased, nor is it hard to see how individual scientists and professional men can, quite sincerely and vehemently, insist upon the absolute, unchanging character of their discoveries, their theories and conceptions, while teaching the slow, cumulative development of their disciplines, with frequent overturn of accepted ideas. They can describe these past changes, glorify the historic rebels who forced their discipline into new channels and created new conceptions and theories, giving every detail of the official opposition and blindness, and yet insist that their work and their theory is the final truth, that must not be touched or doubted.

This seeming inconsistency and the delusion of finality are not to be considered reprehensible or personally shameful. It is the inevitable bias and distortion of viewpoint that the personality needs and emotional reactions of every individual, trained and untrained, impose upon him, but which he can rarely realize or acknowledge. The immense prestige of the rational tradition has obscured the pervasive role of feeling in all human activities, even in science, where emotional congruity dictates the structure of our ideas and conceptions about the universe. This basic, alogical, non-rational feeling or affective reaction cannot be eliminated and should not be. It is dangerous and destructive to scientific work only because it is denied so vigorously and repressed so sternly that its influence is always disguised and distorting.

The history of science may be viewed as a continual effort to recognize the emotional bias and personality needs that were dominating scientific thinking and observation. The prescientific or protoscientific views of animism were the naïve projection of man's feelings into nature, viewed as operating under the whimsical or malevolent control of spirits of humanlike motivation. The anthropocentric universe, the geocentric cosmology, all the marvellous ways in which man has conceived of nature, were born of his need for ideas and beliefs that were congenial to his feelings. The development of rigorous scientific methods has been marked by the growing realization of the innumerable ways in which feelings could invalidate or warp observation. The latest redirection to scientific outlook has been the recognition that the world is not fixed, immutable, governed by absolutes and unchanging truths, but is changeable, inconstant and relative, according to the design or scheme of order we prefer to impose upon our experience of events. Very tentatively, then, we hear a few scientists announce that personal human bias is unavoidable, is indeed inevitable, in any attempt to understand events, since our very science is a selective awareness of the all embracing manifold that might yield many other and conflicting perspectives.

These recent shifts in our climate of opinion indicate a trend toward explicit acknowledgment of the non-rational, affective influence, if not controlling bias, upon all scientific work; and they mark the passing of the absolutes, the unchanging generalizations of the past. This must eventually have a large and ever widening reflection in educational work and the training of scientists, with important consequences for the future leaders, since it points to the clear emergence and acceptance of the belief that the greatest contribution a man can make is to prepare the way for his successor who will supersede his work; because, as Kemp Smith remarked years ago, "the history of human intelligence is not so much the progressive discovery of truth as our gradual emancipation from error." Thus each person's work will be recognized and accepted, without blame for him or any feeling of guilt (that arouses professional controversy and enmity), as a human being with a personality and affective trends that enter into his work. Moreover each theory and conception will be viewed as a contemporary stage in the ongoing development of ideas, expressing the prevailing climate of opinion with its selective awareness and unawareness. A man who will then vehemently proclaim his unchallengeable rightness and assail all who do not accept his views, or who will insist upon making his students into proselyting disciples, will be recognized as a personality problem to be treated as such, not to be confused with scientific issues. In time it will become as dangerous to a man's reputation to exhibit the emotional outbreaks, now so frequent, or the obstructive self-centered preoccupation with his own ideas, as it is to be caught using sloppy methods or drawing illegitimate and unwarranted inferences from insufficient data.

Such a revolution in scientific mores impends and will bring a change in the education and training of scientists, as already foreshadowed in a few areas or fields. Such changes will make the training of future leaders a radically different process. So many of the men who dominate scientific work in their institutions are the mature product of the aggressive, destructive trends that early in their careers led them to attack the existing ideas and accepted theory, offering more or less original substitutes, depending upon their creative ability. The emotional drive to challenge authority in their youth has been gradually transformed, with increasing age and prestige, into the frequent pattern of polemical attack on any new work that threatens their achievements and frantic defense of their position, in which students, as indicated earlier, are used as helpless agents for attack and defense. Such a transformation of the rebel into the conservative is an almost inevitable change when the impelling drive has been hostility against authority that has successfully established the rebel as an authority who will tolerate no other in his field. Hostility in any activity runs the same course to the same reactionary stand because the activity is directed primarily toward the breakdown or overriding of authority, not the objective achievements in the field of activity, which are purely instrumental or subsidiary. Once that authority has been successfully challenged, the same hostile impulses are expressed in the building up of prestige and an unassailable position and its continued defense. Only the leader who does not need to destroy other persons or their ideas because his drive is to go beyond the accepted and familiar in creative endeavor can achieve and then tolerate and even encourage successors who will explore ahead and often render his own work obsolete. Such a pattern of disinterested and constructive endeavor has long been the ideal of scientific work, and the recognition of its defeat by these personality needs will serve to strengthen and reinstate it.

Scientific training then, in addition to the theoretical exposition and the methodological training, will of necessity expose these personality difficulties and needs as obstacles to scientific advance, of equal, if not greater, significance than the limitations now formally taught. This will be of far-reaching significance, because it is quite clear that today scientific advances are being retarded by these personality problems among scientific workers. Moreover, potential leaders of creative ability are being jeopardized, if not ruined, by apprenticeship to these dominating teachers and investigators. It is true that such persons do much valuable and important scientific work and that the controversies in which they are continually engaged help to clarify situations and reveal errors, but this process of making scientific progress is akin to the tale of burning down the house to get roast pig, a process to which many wish to cling for personal predilections. Much time and energy and space are being sacrificed to the practice of controversy, which is primarily an expression of personality clashes irrelevant to scientific advances.

In professional organizations and work the situation is similar except that the absence of the minimum scientific requirements permits aggressive individuals to assume dominance and to block any changes that threaten their position or prestige. Moreover, the very practice of a professional lends itself more readily to use for personal ends and satisfactions that can be rationalized in terms of professional needs and goals. Professional schools favor the more aggressive individuals who in professional practice soon reach elective or appointive positions in associations where they can exercise their hostility drives for power over others. Proposals for modification or improvement of professional work, other than restrictive limitations upon aspirants, are continually frustrated by these powerful individuals who can manipulate affairs and block changes which would interfere with their personal activities. The less aggressive members of the professions, more inclined to strictly professional than political activity, are unable or unwilling to devote the time and energy required to get past these entrenched and resistant personalities. When leadership is demanded in professional associations, the more able are reluctant to take any action or even speak, knowing that only aggressive destructive action will be able to affect any improvements. The more strongly dominated professions express the strongest call for leaders, which is answered only by those who want prestige and power more than professional improvement. These aggressive leaders therefore rise to power in their groups, only to dominate and use the group which gets this leadership at the cost of progress.

The situation in scientific and professional fields, like the situation in political and economic fields, is similar with respect to leadership. The cry for leaders continues unabated, because the majority of men, even the highly trained scientists and professional practitioners, do not know what to do with their lives or where to proceed with their work and so must, in the fact of often appalling conditions, wait for someone to arise and take control: they want an authoritative power to tell them what to do and how to do it, what to believe and why. They get leadership in response to this need that does tell them authoritatively, so much so that the pronouncements of many of the authoritative states are no more absolutist and dictatorial than what many scientific and professional "leaders" say or would like to say. The difference is in the permission still available here to reject these pronouncements if the rebel will take the risks involved of scientific or professional ruin. Of course, some scientific fields and some professions are far from dictatorial, but there are even in these few fields vociferous voices asking for control and regimentation, always in the name of professional standards.

Leadership presents this apparently inevitable dilemma because only aggressive leadership can and will emerge and find acceptance. The rare individual of original creative power who does not seek to dominate or use others for his own purposes does not evoke a large following of devoted and obedient followers; he would be greatly embarrassed if he did because, being non-aggressive but creative, he does not need to exploit others for his personality fulfillment. Moreover, the latent and partially or wholly repressed hostility of the majority of men, lay or professional, will not accept anyone who does not aggressively compel their obedience and win their devotion by directing them into conflicts where they may express hostility in sanctioned forms. But it is just this hostility that blocks their own activities and that of all others, save the very energetic and ruthless, since their hostility diverts their interest and thought from the scientific or professional problems or social situation to the personal conflicts they enjoy and continually seek, usually on behalf of the leaders they have accepted. Yet the need for leadership is just in this non-personal area where new ideas and conceptions, new awareness and insights can bring advances. The leadership we now have is a leadership in the direction and control of individuals and groups; the advances such leadership brings are a by-product of the destructive conflicts the rising leader has with those leaders he challenges. "Every movement towards emancipation brings but new chains." In that struggle for personal supremacy the older ideas and practices championed by the defeated former leader are weakened if not destroyed, to be replaced by the

DILEMMA OF LEADERSHIP 337

pronouncements of the new leader, whose rigid coercive control again generates the need for a new leader.

It is of the utmost importance to realize then that the apparent need for leadership is a need for emancipation of a group or a whole people from the loyalties to which they are fettered that prevent them from changing to their advantage. Only the aggressive, ruthless leader can bring such emancipation because he provides them with another loyalty that makes possible renunciation of the old.

This rhythmic process of fixation and consolidation followed by upheaval and disorder that yields another fixation and consolidation has been the very process of change as one leader has succeeded another, dragging his followers along to a new position that they adopt only because of the leader's demands. The pendulum-like oscillation between radical and reactionary positions in all fields, the often observed contrast between succeeding phases of a changing society or activity, are but reflections of this general need to follow someone, to be guided and directed. Thus is generated the contrary position taken by each rising new leader who out of his aggressive drive challenges the reigning leader and his views with opposition. The ironical part of this historic process is the utter irrelevance of the position taken up as a challenge, which the emerging leader espouses as if it were his most cherished possession, whereas it is but the vehicle of his progress to leadership. Once that position is attained the leader ceases to challenge and proclaims that which may not be challenged because it is his Truth. This process of alternating change then is not to be sought in the mysterious nature of the universe or of society or of scientific knowledge, but in the dynamics of leadership and the dilemmas thus produced by the leader and following relationship. Here apparently we see the psychological aspects of the dialectical process.

Must this alternating rise and fall of leaders and contrasting changes continue unchanged, or is there any possibility of interrupting the swing of the pendulum? The answer is equivocal because insight into the process of change and into the personality needs that are being expressed offers the possibility of modifying the situation, but that possibility is limited by the resistance offered to a recognition of the dynamics of personality. There is tremendous opposition to any view of human behavior that imputes man's conduct to emotional drives and unrecognized impulses even by those who are overtly playing upon those emotions. Every professional assumes an air of superhuman rationality and objectivity that obscures the acute emotional needs it channels and manipulates. The ordinary individual likewise is ashamed to confess that what he is doing is nonrational and alogical, the release of feelings, and even when most violent in his anger or rage or most partial in his sentiments he will rationalize his conduct as purely and entirely objective.

It is this desperate anxiety against acknowledging the role of affective reactions in human conduct that creates the seriousness of the situation. Such feelings and the reactive capacity of man can not be eliminated, and if they were, life would be impossible, as we see in the unfeeling, wholly anesthetic victim of dementia praecox who acts in a cold, calculatory manner to perform diabolical outrages. Emotion is an essential function in man, so necessary to his existence as man that the often preached doctrine of complete suppression of emotions is palpably a neurotic dream of those who are afraid of all feeling. It is not emotion and feeling that is man's treasonable enemy and source of disaster but the distorted and warped feelings such as resentment and hostility that urges man to destructive conflict because all other more benign forms of feeling have been denied or distorted.

This is not the place to discuss the source of the aggressive drives that so dominate leaders and their followers, but it is evident that the hostility and resentment are created in the child by the manner of his parental care and discipline. Whenever authority is imposed brutally and coldly it creates hostility that seeks outlets overtly or in disguised fashion while awaiting the sanction of leadership to be openly destructive. The exercise of authority benevolently or benignly to avoid creation of resentment, hostility, and destruction becomes the central problem of human life. When we can learn to tolerate our emotional natures and can avoid the distortion of childhood, then the creative original leaders will flourish and be accepted. Mankind, instead of opposing and ridiculing or destroying its benefactors, will turn to them with grateful and reverent affection because the love of mankind thus expressed can be accepted and returned when individuals no longer are driven by unrecognized but powerful impulses of hostility.

(FROM: *Psychiatry*, 2 [1939]: 343–61.)

TWENTY-SEVEN

Time Perspectives

1

THE "quest for certainty" in a precarious and ambiguous world has everywhere led man to believe that his ideas and values were permanent, unchanging truths. Time, of necessity, has been conceived as the enemy of man, forever threatening his most cherished possessions and, paradoxically, as his greatest sanction for these treasured beliefs. Only recently has time become the focus of sustained inquiry and reflection as we have begun to realize that time is not merely a variable in scientific study but is also a process, a multidimensional and highly variable continuum, with a relativity no less than space. Indeed, it is already evident that for years to come we will be confronted with the task of clarifying the many and far-reaching implications of the more recent conceptions of time.

The conception of a four-dimensional manifold in which occur the events that are now becoming the focus of scientific thinking has brought space-time as the successor to the preceding conception of three-dimensional space and single-dimensional time. This space-time is not merely three-dimensional space, with an added dimension of time, but an integral fusion of space and time, since three dimensions of space, to exist anywhere, must exist in a time continuum. It would indeed be equally appropriate to speak of time, with three-dimensional space as further characteristics of existents, but it is more desirable to consider space-time as the four dimensions of every existent. Moreover, this space-time is not absolute and unvarying but changeable, according to the frame of reference used, so that both space *and time* are relative. The gradual recognition of this altered conception will bring far-reaching changes in scientific theory and investigations, especially in biology where static structures have been for so long the preoccupation of morphology, with little or no apparent relation to functional activity. The space-time conception leads to a reformulation of our ideas of structure and function and to a realization that they cannot be separated but are the spatial and the temporal aspects of organisms. Time is being seen relatively, as having different rates according to the field (physical or organic) in which it is observed. The conceptions of physiological time and of biological time have been advanced recently to indicate a difference in the time dimensions within living organisms and the variation in time with aging of the organism, as contrasted with the apparently uniform time or duration measured by sidereal motions or displacements. Moreover, recent work in embryology and child growth is showing that growth, differentiation, and maturation have characteristic time rates that are peculiar to each organism, so that chronological age offers little or no basis for grouping or comparisons.

Perhaps no area is more in need of exploration for its temporal implications than the field of human conduct and none offers more promise of fruitful reward for imaginative speculation, since all human conduct (and probably all organic behavior) are conditioned by the time perspectives of the individual and of his culture.

Since this subject is so elusive and baffling we may wisely consider at the outset some rather homely and familiar aspects of human conduct, as seen in infant and child behavior. The immediate and pressing physiological needs of the newborn child demand and ordinarily receive early expression and fulfillment. The hunger contractions, with falling blood sugar, of the infant who, during intrauterine life, has been uninterruptedly nourished and must now accept the regimen of periodical feeding, are expressed in cries, restlessness, and then eager sucking at the breast or bottle. No less insistent is the pressure of urine and faeces that rises recurrently and stimulates the sphincters that permit their release. In this early infant behavior we have a physiological process, something approaching a purely stimulus-response situation, in which the infant may be observed behaving naïvely and directly as his organic processes require.

But this naïve naturalistic behavior is in most cultures not permitted for long. In various ways the infant is coerced into surrendering his physiological autonomy to the control of the duly sanctioned culture patterns that now are imposed upon him. With greater or less severity of tuition he learns to endure hunger; he learns also that the direct, immediate response to bladder or rectal pressure by release of sphincters for evacuation is not encouraged or permitted; he must learn to sustain these pressures until the duly sanctioned place and vessels are reached, when he may void. Such learning is not simple nor easily achieved and, as we are beginning to discover, it may bring profound emotional disturbances to the child.

What takes place in this familiar domestic process of toilet training may be described as a surrender of physiological autonomy to cultural control as imposed by the mother or nurse; the establishment of intraorganic events (pressures) as behavior cues or admonitions to prepare for the socially sanctioned release later to the appointed vessel; and finally, the first step in the process of creating or finding the socially approved stimulus-situations to which the individual may respond with approved conduct. Here then begins the characteristically human career of man who, not content to be ruled by hunger and other physiological functions, transforms them so that hunger becomes appetite, bladder and rectal pressures become occasions for modesty, cleanliness, etc., and later sex becomes love. This transformation of naïve behavior into conduct involves the acceptance of values, or, more specifically, necessitates value behavior and time perspectives wherein we see the individual responding to present, immediate situation-events (intraorganic or environmental) as point-events in a sequence the later or more remote components of which are the focus of that conduct.

A simple illustration of this statement may help to reveal its meaning for this discussion. If we let A represent one of the immediately impinging situation-events facing an individual, either within his organism or in the environment, it is clear that A is the first of a sequence A, B, C, D, . . . N. When the infant responds naïvely to A (physiological need) by a physiological process (evacuation) he behaves organically and directly. As training in toilet habits proceeds he learns to recognize A (the internal pressure) as a preparatory signal or behavior cue, not a stimulus to immediate releasing behavior; the bladder pressure A now becomes the first term in sequence A, B, C, D, . . . N, leading to the appropriate later term N which may be the household toilet. This response to A in terms of its consequences then becomes the prototype of value behavior with an almost infinite regression toward the future, for again we see that N (voiding at a specified place, in privacy, and keeping the clothes dry) is itself a first term or A in another sequence of holding or earning the much needed security of parental approval and love and a wider social approval and acceptance by teachers, schoolmates, and so on.

What looks like a simple, childish achievement of control of eliminations assumes, upon reflection, a large significance for understanding human conduct and the question of values within a time perspective. As will be realized the various time perspectives of a culture give the dimensions of the values that are operating in the lives of those living in that culture by specifying the conduct that must be observed in response to each situation, wherein that immediate situation is to be seen as instrumental to a more remote or deferred situation. Again we may illustrate this statement by a simple diagram in which we may indicate the importance, significance, or coerciveness of any stimulus-event by the size of the symbols used to denote those stimulus-events. Thus a large capital A might symbolize for the infant the immediate coerciveness of bladder or rectal pressure to which he will immediately respond by sphincter release. But as the infant grows, develops and learns to accept toilet training, these dimensions change. Where earlier there was

$$A\ b\ c\ d\ \ldots\ n \quad \text{we now find} \quad A\ B\ C\ D\ \ldots\ N \quad \text{or} \quad a\ b\ c\ d\ \ldots\ N$$

indicating that A has become attenuated by its position in the sequence leading to the toilet. A time perspective has been imposed upon events which thereby assume an altered meaning or value that is a function of that time perspective, similar to the spatial perspectives which the individual imposes upon the objective world, enlarging and contracting dimensions by reasons of their nearness or remoteness and learning to observe these distortions in his conduct. We might also say that cultural training creates a "field" in which events, both internal and environmental, are warped or distorted, contracted or expanded to dimensions that are relative to the specific individual who is so trained, since each person will receive that general training in a highly indiosyncratic manner because of the parental stresses and emphases and his own peculiar idiomatic organism. Thus we begin to see how in a common, public world of objects, persons, events, and situations, each individual creates a private, personal world by "structuralizing his life space," as Kurt Lewin has termed this process, in accordance with his life experiences. Probably the most important differentiating aspect of these private worlds is the value (or significance) we give to the various constituents of the surrounding world, according to our individual time perspectives.

As we reflect upon these relative dimensions of common events, we are struck by the very complicated scheme of time perspectives operating at any one period in a culture where we see each individual living with and in radically different time perspectives. The very young person will have time perspectives of limited range, while the successive age groups will show more extensive ranges, but again with wide individual variations as we may note in those who seem to live almost entirely in the immediate present and those who apparently live almost entirely in the future. To a certain extent we might say that the depth of the future time perspective, as we shall later see, varies with the depth of the retrospective time perspective. But this changes with the age of the individual: in childhood time passes slowly for the child living in the present, while in maturity time passes rapidly for the adult living in the future and the past but during senescence lives in the present and the past. Whole social classes may be described by the time perspectives that dominate their lives as revealed in the range of their planning, their prudential calculations, their forethought, their abstinence, and so on. These traditional virtues are indeed the consequences of the time perspectives in which the immediate events are viewed, wherein the large compelling A's of today are diminished in dimensions and potency because they are seen in the perspective that leads to the more remote rainy day, old age, life after death, and similar anticipations. But it must be emphasized that human conduct is always in an immediate present, and concerned with direct, impinging events and situations, so that we have apparently the retroactive influence of future events upon the dimensions of the present that must be recognized as controlling; and that means, if we are to avoid mystical conceptions of futurity, the operation of a time perspective in which the present gains these apparent, but highly relative, dimensions. These differences among individuals and social classes are, as we have indicated, due to the training individuals receive in regulating their behavior and the manner in which they have accepted that teaching. Thus a single individual may develop a variety of time perspectives, each applicable to a different aspect of living, so that he may view economic events in one dimension, political in another, social in another, sexual in another, and so on, with little or no apparent conflict; or he may develop a more or less homogeneous set of dimensions for all aspects of life, bringing his conduct into a well-integrated pattern. The more remote the focus of his time perspectives, the more he will exhibit preparatory or instrumental behavior that uses the present only as a means to the future; the more immediate the focus the more he will exhibit consummatory behavior and react naïvely and ignore consequences. This he may also do if the future focus is so remote that it loses all potency over the present.

With increasing maturity an individual may alter his time perspectives, seeing certain events in a more remote focus and others in a more immediate. The present then is reconstituted, with shifting values and conduct, from year to year, but always with a forward reference since the individual can rarely forget that each immediate present event is part of a forward sequence that succeeding hours or days will bring closer; what is done today will in large measure "determine" that future. Of course, that means only that, in so far as the individual deals with the present in terms of its consequences (sees the dimensions of A as set by B, C, D, . . . N), his behavior will be addressed to that set of sequent events, and so he will be ready for them. Perhaps the most interesting aspect of man's behavior is seen in contracts wherein he binds his future conduct by agreement with another to perform certain acts or to refrain therefrom, thus imposing upon himself a future time perspective specified by another because that other person also has accepted a time perspective which specifies what he will do. Our laws are primarily concerned with the rights, titles, powers, and obligations of individuals and their alteration, all of which are but different phases of future behavior. The often quoted statement of man's transition from status to contract refers to the power to contract away the future instead of having it fixed by status. The ironical tragedy of the human race has been the

TIME PERSPECTIVES 345

inability of man to find the appropriate time perspective for each of the multiplicity of events that crowd in upon him, so that he has continually been misled and frustrated by his own hopefully or fearfully devised dimensions imposed upon events that refused to accept such a setting or dimensions. Training for professional work involves discipline in the highly specialized time perspectives of each pursuit that change with each generation's reorientation and knowledge.

It has been the great office of culture, and specifically of religion, to provide the major time perspective of conduct by insisting upon the relative dimensions of the immediate present as seen in the focus of eternity. Culture, as transmitted by parents and other cultural agents, prevents man from acting impulsively and naïvely, as his needs, urges, and desires might dictate, and so compels him to regulate his conduct toward the opportunities around him, which he sees in the time perspective of life after death or other forward reference. The Hindu belief in reincarnation and endless striving toward perfection is probably the most attenuated and compelling time perspective that sets every event and human action in this ever-receding perspective from which there is no escape. Each culture and each religion presents its own time perspective and emphasizes the necessity of patterning human conduct in its focus, so that one culture will repress and another foster sexual functioning, one will favor and another repress acquisitiveness, and so on. Thus asceticism, continence, and all the other virtues may be viewed as responses to the dimensions imposed upon the present by religious, ethical time perspectives, many of which reduce the present to insignificance except as a preparation for the future in which this ascetism will be rewarded.

To insist then upon time perspectives in human conduct is to recognize the ages-old significance given to the future, but to bring that future into the manageable present and give it an operational meaning by showing that *the future is that name we give to the altered dimensions of the present.* Every scientific discovery that reveals the sequence of events and thereby shows that a specific point-event, A, is the antecedent of B, C, D, E, ... N, immediately alters the time perspective of those who are informed of this discovery; thereafter they can no longer ignore A, nor regard A, as an isolated event or as a part of the sequence taught by folklore and superstition (early scientific attempts); they see A as the initial step leading to N, to be responded to in terms of B, C, D, E, . . . N.

Scientific investigation therefore is constantly remaking our time perspectives and forcing us to revise the dimensions of our values and thereby automatically changing our conduct.

Frequently scientific knowledge brings release from supposed necessities by showing that the meaning we have long imputed to a particular event is baseless and that such an event does not belong to the sequence in which we have treated it. The progressive emancipation of human behavior from spurious meanings that have forced man to practice all manner of curious rites and have denied him the use of nature's bounty is probably the most amazing and engrossing aspect of human history. Scientific knowledge also reveals events as parts of unsuspected sequences wherein unwary man has been repeatedly betrayed and damaged because he reacted to the event naïvely in its immediate, apparent dimensions and was then caught inexplicably later by subsequent events that appeared to have no antecedents. Scientific discovery of these sequences places events in a time perspective that man may ignore at his peril.

As we reflect upon this cumulative exploration of the world and discovery of the sequences of events, it is obvious that the area for spontaneous, unreflective behavior is being progressively restricted. Every event is being revealed in its own natural time perspective and sequence. The world, ambiguous and immediate, in which early man lived precariously but spontaneously, is losing its ambiguity and becoming ever more precisely known and controllable, but no less hazardous, since scientific knowledge is giving every aspect of the present a significant dimension that man is forced to recognize in his individual and group living. The future is crowding in upon him in that every event is being reshaped and revalued by these newly revealed time perspectives that compel man to walk increasingly warily, weigh more and more consequences, and assume a larger load of anxiety lest he forget or mistake the appropriate conduct. At the same time scientific research is showing man how to avoid the undesired consequences of his behavior by interposing between the immediate A and the succeeding events various interferences that permit him to limit or abolish the usual consequences. In this direction scientific research is freeing man from the threat of innumerable disasters and

TIME PERSPECTIVES

unwanted outcomes, as in birth control, whereby his value behavior is altered.

2

THERE IS a strange paradox in this enhanced significance of the future because, for all the weight and influence of religion and the eternal future it has stressed, man has been obsessed by his past. Not only his own previous experience but the accumulated experiences of his culture have been his constant preoccupation and concern. The past has been the storehouse of wisdom for the conduct of life, and piety has demanded that he respect that wisdom and obey its teachings, since, in an uncertain world, that at least, was definite and fixed.

But if we look at the past intently, examining the individual's past and the group's history, we find another time perspective stretching away from the present to the beginning of things, not unlike that which is focussed toward the future. But in this retrospective view the relationships of immediate to remote are seemingly reversed: in the perspective of the future the dimensions of the present are shaped by the focus of the future; but the dimensions of the past are shaped by the present which imposes upon previous events a perspective that is governed by the necessities and the values of the present.

If we use the same diagram as before we see how the present, P, now looms large and the past is attenuated to the focus of its dimensions.

$$z - y - x \ldots\ldots c\, b\, a\, P.$$

Immediately we begin to realize, as we study this situation that the present, P, is coincident with the A of the future perspective that had its dimensions set by the focus of the future N, so that the diagram should show

$$z - y - x \ldots\ldots e\, d\, c\, b\, P\, b\, c\, d \ldots\ldots N$$

wherein human conduct is seen as an event occurring always between an immediate past and an immediate future. The important question then arises how the time perspective of the past enters into the time perspective of the future or, more significantly, *how does the future reconstitute the past?*

It is ancient wisdom that we can know the future only through the past; events are recurrent and what has been experienced once will be repeated in the future; history is prophecy; the values of the past, as set by the retrospective time perspective, can be the only values of the future. But, curiously enough, human behavior does change, despite the frequent assertions to the contrary and the professional demonstration of the unchanging *mores*, the "residues" and the "derivations." In the cultivation of fertility, the oldest of man's activities, the ancient rites and ceremonies of the wisdom of the past, that were piously re-enacted, generation after generation, to make the earth and animals fertile, are only survivals in out-of-the-way corners of the world. From innumerable laboratories and experimental stations, the techniques of agriculture and animal husbandry are being refined and elaborated and communicated, so that the conduct of these arts is being radically changed. In this evolution all manner of A's have been found to be irrelevant to the future events they were supposed to initiate and new and unsuspected A's were revealed as having critical importance. Only by repudiating the past as a guide to the future, by superseding a future time perspective governed by the dimensions of the past, could this transformation occur.

Again we see in written history how the past is used to construct the future time perspective, since, as J. W. Swain has suggested, we write history only because we are interested in the future and our desire to influence others' values by showing how the trend of the past makes such values alone desirable. It has been repeatedly shown how the national revivals of the past century or so have been accompanied, if not initiated, by the rewriting of the history of the country, always with the intention of creating a new time perspective for the past that makes the present an inevitable step toward the desired future of national greatness. In this use of history we see how myths are employed as Plato urged, to give people the meanings and values that are needed to direct their conduct toward future goals. It is as if the remote past were focussed upon the present, whereas it is the immediate present and its perplexities that are focussed upon the past, giving the past the dimensions of our present needs and values, which in turn

TIME PERSPECTIVES

are constituted by our future time perspective and aspirations.

Here we face a confusing, almost baffling relativity of time since it would appear that the past is constructed by projecting backward sequences of events that start with the present events we now experience. But this is not so absurd as it appears, since the past, like the future, appears as a multiplicity of sequential events, inextricably mixed up together (although each sequence of events is beautifully ordered and simple), and we impose upon that multiplicity and simultaneity of events, the specific sequences that we prefer. Thus, just as we project forward the sequence of events that fear, hope, tradition or science have taught us to believe flows forward from the particular situation we are confronting, so we project backward a sequence of events as we prefer to see the trends of history. In these projections forward and backward, the largest influence, unless somewhat checked but never eliminated by scientific methods, is the immediate present with its beliefs, necessities, perplexities, and emotional feeling tones.

We stand astride time, as it were, and, Janus-like, face the future and the past, looking at once forward and backward and seeing events in both directions in a time perspective that is never fixed. For if we are prone to view the future in the dimensions of the past, it may be because we are so fearful of the present, as Otto Rank has suggested, not because we love the past. But our fear of the present is born of the future time perspective that gives the present a threatening aspect, making our present situation the antecedents of events we dare not contemplate.

But that very past we see so clearly and in such definite dimensions is not divorced from the future. Indeed it is the future that creates and recreates that past, so that as we stumble forward we are continually reorganizing our past, individually and socially.

Let us see if we can find some order in this seeming confusion of past, present, and future. We view the present in a forward time perspective that gives the present its dimensions and values. We see the past in a retrospective time perspective that has the dimensions imposed by the present. Thus the actual present has no validity for our conduct, except as it is the threshold of the future toward which our conduct is oriented with varying degrees of focal length. Moreover, the present is valued only as it is seen in the retrospective time perspective that it imposes upon the past to give the immediate situations and events their meaning.

But then we are confronted with the realization that our future time perspective is itself generated by the experiences of the past that have created expectations and awareness and knowledge of the sequence in which events occur. Moreover we cannot forget that our interpretation of that past experience and our awareness of that past depend upon the present situations in which we find ourselves since those immediate situations and the emotions they arouse govern the dimensions of our retrospective time perspective; as our feeling about the present and the immediate future changes, so our past changes its dimensions, assuming a new meaning and value.

Seemingly then the future determines the present, the present controls the past, but the past creates that future and so imposes its values on the present. Is this but juggling of terms and obscurantism or does it reflect the actual processes of human conduct that our traditional teaching of philosophy, ethics, and much of psychology have heretofore obscured under the pretentious conception of man as rational, volitional and autonomous? We might inquire first into the meaning of these terms, past and present and future, where, in accordance with man's inveterate habit of deifying processes into abstractions we are prone to think of past, present and future as actual entities. But it is clear that the future is only a name, not a specific thing or an event; it is a term we apply to our way of dealing with immediate situations, to which we respond with certain expectations, since that present is one step in the sequence of events; thus when our behavior is oriented or directed to that whole sequence it appears purposeful and intelligent. These modifications of behavior to meet the present in this preparatory or instrumental fashion have to be learned (except for occasional sudden and unintentional discoveries that we stumble upon and remember) and so the past enters into our behavior toward the future. But the past also is but a name, a way of describing the altered organism that has registered experience in its modified structure-function-irritability, so that in responding to the immediate present these alterations and modifications condition that present behavior by a forward reference which, as we have just seen, is merely imposing these learned modifications upon the present conduct. When, as frequently happens, especially today in scientific procedure, man deliberately tests that learned behavior by observing carefully whether the future time perspective and expected sequence of events are valid, then he can often reorganize his conduct and change the retrospective time perspective of the past. He must, however, definitely repudiate the past and unlearn what proved experience has taught, in order that the new experience may be assimilated into a new expectation for the future.

Past and future then are but two aspects of behavior, the past being the persistent modifications in the behaving organism and the future the controlling direction or pattern imposed upon the unfolding behavior according to those persistent modifications. As the organism accumulates more and more modifications through experience, the pattern of behavior may be changed or become more fixed and persistent depending largely upon how experience has been received.

Here we come to another seeming paradox since this past, that so largely creates our future and therefore controls our present, is most controlling when it is lost or, as we say, forgotten. The experiences we have had but cannot recall are the masters of our destiny, for they operate in us, as selective awareness and patterned responses persisting from those prior experiences and directing our behavior to endless repetition, despite the incongruity and often destructive, self-defeating character of such responses. We behave in this frequently absurd, irrational manner because the forgotten experience has remained in our organism as selective awareness and patterned response that cannot be reorganized or changed until we can recall the original experience, that is, rehearse it and so integrate it into our present and future, by giving it new dimensions appropriate to the period of its occurrence. The most striking illustration of the powerful control exercised by forgotten experiences of the past is exhibited by those physiological adjustments, reflexes, and regulations that our organism learned in the dim past of evolutionary development, so long ago that we have little or no capacity to modify or even recognize their operation in our lives. The emotional reactions of fear, anger, rage, and grief are the expressions of these primitive response patterns over which we gain control only partially and slowly.

The most powerful experiences that exercise the greatest control over our conduct and are most often forgotten are the emotional experiences of childhood when we were intensely moved or disturbed but cannot later recall the occasion for that feeling. A screen, as it were, is interposed between us and the particular past experience that is most significantly at work in our present behavior and so we are moved, as by an unseen hand, to behave in a specific manner, often against our will, as we say, meaning despite the future time perspective in which we view events. Sometimes these compulsive responses are fears that seize us in situations in which no one else is apprehensive or anxious. Sometimes they are compulsions that force us, as if hypnotized, to perform certain acts that have no relevance to the situations or our needs. Sometimes they are anger or rage reactions to situations or persons who offer no provocation, or sudden and overwhelming grief for a particular thing or person long lost to us. These emotional revivals may even be disagreeable and crippling physiological disturbances or serious illness that appear and reappear in certain situations or with specific persons and frequently they are inexplicable blockades or interferences with actions we start but cannot complete, even when we eagerly desire to go further.

The amazing character of these forgotten but coercive experiences is seen when the individual, thus controlled by incongruous emotoins, recalls the original experience, piercing through the amnesia to the events, perhaps long past, and remembers how, in certain circumstances, he then acted and felt. As if released from a trance or hypnotic state, the individual, recalling the experience, may be suddenly transformed. He gains insight, as we say, into his previously incomprehensible behavior and sees it as a way of responding to that long forgotten experience, persisting into the present where it is no longer appropriate or relevant, but acts to distort the present dimensions that otherwise would conform to the future time perspectives of his more mature understanding.

In these aberrant forms of behavior we see how one experience in the past, because apparently it was so highly charged with emotion, is forgotten but nevertheless operates in the organism to control and direct his behavior in that one area, resisting the modifications that later experiences impose upon other phases of behavior. What does forgetting mean, then, since these forgotten experiences are more coercive than those we remember? Forgetting, in this naturalistic account, can be given no mysterious psychic interpretation but must be seen as an aspect of the organic modification in and through which alone the past has meaning. Thus approached we may view amnesia or forgetting as the isolation of an experience from the ongoing process of experiencing, responding and modifying behavior. The particular emotional situations we forget are those that have been so overwhelming, so disturbing, so painful or otherwise unacceptable that, despite the profound and lasting modifications they make in our organism, they cannot be fitted into the ordinary process of experience: we dare not, as with ordinary experiences, construct a future time perspective based on such events that promises a repetition of such shocks, since life would then be unendurable; nor can we use the present to order and reorganize the past so far as these shocking experiences are concerned, since nothing in our present will enable us to focus such a past experience into a perspective congruous with the present. Since so many highly significant emotional experiences occur in infancy and early childhood, before language to handle those experiences has been acquired, it will be seen that those early experiences, especially when traumatic, will exercise a persistently strong control over later life but we cannot describe them. We can only bury the shocking experience, try to ignore or forget it and even deny it happened and so live with it, like an encysted infection or bullet, that is walled off from the current stream of life but nevertheless continually interferes in our conduct whenever a situation arises that has the same meaning as the original experience. We forget the situation, event, or experience, but remember the meaning.

In similar fashion a highly disturbing experience may likewise control our present behavior not because we have forgotten it but because we cannot forget it, which means that we cannot fit it into the retrospective time perspective created by our more mature present. Such events then resist the usual attenuation that marks the ever remote past and persist in their original terrifying dimensions, so that they are more compelling than the present and thus they compromise or distort the future. In the classic conception of fate we see this belief in the mystical potency of the past over the individual's present and future life which he can never avoid nor escape. Likewise we see this same conception in the belief in the irrevocable character of sin (past misbehavior) from which we can be rescued only by a supernatural power to be invoked by prayer and atonement (conduct restricted to the inhibition of many otherwise permitted activities). In many respects the more categorical statements of infantile trauma in the theory of personality may be viewed as a modern version of the old conception of fate since these experiences are viewed as having a coercive power over all the rest of life from which the individual can never wholly escape, although psychoanalysis may help him to reduce their potency by attenuating the dimensions of that early past. Some critics of analyses assert that many of these recalls of early experience are fictitious but nevertheless are therapeutically helpful because they serve to bring the patient's past life into an ordered perspective that assuages the individual's anxiety and guilt and so releases him from their control.

Man thus lives with a forward and a retrospective orientation, hopeful and expectant or anxious and guilty. There should be a continual reorganization of experience as the individual grows older, the past being reordered and given new dimensions and the future being forever reshaped. If a person has this capacity for living with his past, assimilating it to his present and ordering its dimensions, repudiating it when necessary to accept a new prospective time perspective, he can meet life sanely and more or less effectively. But some become enamored of the past or so preoccupied with the perplexities of the past that they abandon the future, then the present and live wholly within their accumulated organic memory, inaccessible to their surroundings except for purely metabolic functioning. Others live only in the future, rejecting the present as valueless because they are focussed to a remote or impossible future for which they can never find a present approach; they live in dreams and delusions that bring a spurious realization. These we call the insane whose time perspectives have gone awry.

But what is reality in a world where time is so protean and elusive? In every age man has asserted reality to be that which he has learned to expect: the curiously complicated interplay of past experience upon present behavior that is addressed to the future. But as man learns more about the world in which he lives he expects different things and so modifies his conception of reality. The reality picture has been altered again and again, most recently by our scientific studies and theories that have compelled us to give up so many older conceptions and world views. Astronomy, geology, paleontology and biology have, during the past three hundred odd years, given us a wholly different time and space perspective, in which our earth no longer occupies the central position of a recently created universe. The earth has been displaced, relegated to an insignificant place in the cosmos, but with a past history so vast we can scarcely comprehend it, since temporal remoteness attenuates our understanding more drastically than spatial remoteness. Moreover, man himself has been given a radically changed history, in which he no longer appears suddenly upon earth by divine creation a few thousand years ago, but slowly emerges and evolves from an incredibly long ancestry of mammalian prototypes and these in turn from an ever receding horizon of living forms. We are today struggling to revise our time perspectives of the past and timidly beginning to explore for the inevitable revisions that they involve in our time perspectives of the future. Already the focus of personal immortality in an eternal heaven has begun to shift and therefore to change the dimensions of our present. The ascetic conduct that was addressed to the immediate present, seen as but a proving of our virtue for eternity, is beginning to lose its coercive appeal. When the present is no longer attenuated by the focus of eternity, reinforced by the expectation of everlasting punishment or bliss, human conduct is bound to change. A revision of our past, an alteration of the retrospective time perspective, brings about an amazing change in man's future time perspective and expectations, and hence in his conduct. Morals and ethics founded upon the older time perspectives lose their authority with every change in the dimensions of time that undermine the cosmic sanctions and necessitate new standards of conduct more consonant with these altered perspectives. How shall the new future be constructed from this new past, so that again we can deal effectively with the present, instead of the groping, conflicting and frustrating impasse we are increasingly feeling today?

There is indeed a need for new time perspectives to give dimensions to our values and order to our lives. We cannot assimilate our past experience until we do construct this new time perspective for the future, since only by projecting the past into the future can we bring it into relation to our present. If we focus ahead for only a brief span, life becomes insignificant, meaningless and dreary, since the present leads to nothing of enduring value. Such a short time perspective means only eat, drink, be merry, for tomorrow we die, but man cannot live for long on a purely organic level. On the other hand, if we focus toward the most remote future the present is rendered equally valueless and dreary because nothing humanly desirable or satisfying is permissible. We wait then for a time perspective that has a "vital sensibility" to use Ortéga y Gasset's term, wherein a sufficiently long future focus will give meaning and significance and tension to our lives, because our present endeavors point to a constantly receding but ever inviting future; but this focus must be humanly significant so that living is not forever sacrificed to something that denies life.

The Christian time perspective offered an eternal focus for the life pattern, promising the individual who treated the present as a prelude to eternity an early translation to that eternity at death. Such a personally realizable approach to remoter goals is needed because only a few can continuously live and strive toward an inaccessible future and then only by renouncing all that is human.

So long as man's past was fixed and sanctified he could but accept the future made inevitable by that past, just as the individual, whose frozen past coercively dominates his conduct, faces a future that offers no hope of escape or release for living. Now that man has found a new past for himself and the earth through astronomy, geology and paleontology, he has suddenly been endowed with the power to create a new future. It is no wonder that he is dazzled, if not blinded, by this dramatic appearance of a future of almost unlimited possibilities and undreamed of plasticity, as he timidly explores ahead in the light of an incredibly long past that shows his amazing evolution as a continuous and continuing development, because he has retained the supreme capacity for modifying his behavior. For the first time in his history, man has realized that human nature can be changed because it is constituted of the ever-changing past, and the ever-changing future time perspectives that he himself imposes upon what has happened and what will happen. This is the emancipation that psychology is giving man today, as he learns courageously to face his past, attenuate it to the dimensions that free his present and render pliable his future.

Perhaps in this new realization of man's prolonged past and the ongoing evolution of his humanness, we may find the future time perspective we seek, for we can, by learning from the past, project a future of further evolution, growth and development, stretching into the remote future so far as to be eternity; but this future becomes personally realizable in and through our children who become the living embodiment of our movement toward the future and the living achievement of our values. Instead of sacrificing the child, as we have from time immemorial, to the values of our other-worldly and superhuman time perspectives, we create a time perspective that expresses the potentiality of childhood as its supreme dimension, to be realized in and through conduct that recognizes the worth of human life, of mating, child bearing and child rearing and the fulfillment of man's physiological and psychological needs. This will bring the further realization that in the past of everyone there have been all manner of infantile actions, primitive emotional outbreaks, misdemeanors and other childish behavior, none of which we need be ashamed of since only by accepting that past can we relegate it to its appropriate dimensions.

In such a view of life we identify ourselves with the ongoing stream of life, recognize the immortality of the germ plasm and find significance for our lives in devotion to this biologically and socially valuable ideal, in which the past is recognized and accepted. So long as we deny man's past, refuse to acknowledge his biological make-up and functions, his need for mating and child bearing, we cannot project wholesome, sane goals of conduct. These denials not only frustrate his adult living but they distort and twist his personality, especially during childhood. The cumulative evidence indicates quite clearly that the treatment of children that is so destructive is predicated upon just this denial of man's essential biological make-up, needs, and functions, as taught by the older, nonevolutionary time perspective of man's past. Moreover, it is the guilt and anxiety fastened upon childish explorations and gropings that so often makes the past such a handicap, either as forgotten or as unforgettable experiences that interfere with the adult's mature time perspective on life.

When man has accepted his biological and social history and projected a new future consonant therewith, then the individual can build his personal time perspectives and face the future with hope and confidence, because he can live, untroubled by his past, in the present, where life alone is possible. We can see how living in its fullness and richness becomes possible in the timeless present of esthetic experience when we are swept away from our usual preoccupations and calculations and caught up in the compelling experience of the drama, novel, poetry and music, when we live in the *now* that makes ordinary life seem drab and feeble. Or again we find a timeless now, with no past and no future, in the fully developed and shared, mature sex orgasm that carries the man and woman together into ecstasy—but only when they are free from the distorting past and a threatening future. Happiness is just this sense of being alive in a present *now* that is completely adequate, with no worry about tomorrow or regrets for yesterday to cloud the full measure of the present (Omar). "We can only be said to be alive in those moments when our hearts are conscious of our treasure," said the Woman of Andros (Thornton Wilder), with a keen realization that only as we feel this immediate, close present in all its richness of fulfillment do we really live. Likewise Boethius, centuries ago, defined eternity—"to hold and possess the whole fullness of life in one moment, here and now, past and present, and to come." Freedom for the individual means that the present is neither dominated by the past nor sacrificed to the future, because he, the living man, is himself that past and that future, which he continuously reorganizes and reconstitutes in the living present.

(FROM: *Journal of Social Philosophy*, 4 [1939]: 293-312.)

TWENTY-EIGHT

Man's Multidimensional Environment

MAN FINDS himself in a series of environments to which he exhibits varying degrees of contingency. If we view human activity as occurring within a series of fields of which man's behavior may be regarded as a function, we may take one large step toward clarification of the present confusion and conflicts among students of human activity.

We may recognize initially therefore a number of environments, namely:
(a) The geographical environment of nature.
(b) The internal environment of the mammalian organism.
(c) The cultural environment of group life.
(d) The social environment of community living.

Each of these environments conditions the functional processes, the activities and the conduct of man, but with varying degrees of coerciveness.

THE GEOGRAPHICAL ENVIRONMENT

The basic geographical space, our natural environment in which all organisms exist, may be conceived as a series of ongoing processes and events—physical, chemical, biological—which occur in sequential patterns in accordance with the fundamental transformations of energy. More generally, we may speak of organisms existing in geographical space, subject to gravitation, radiation, barometric pressure, heat and cold, and all the many impacts to which they are exposed in their several life zones. Consideration of this geographical environment and of its meaning for human activity has been directed largely to the more dramatic events that have brought either disaster or good fortune to man, with a consequent neglect of the continuous dependence of man upon the operation of these ongoing processes and events for his continued existence.

To say that we are waiting upon broadly conceived formulations of man's relationship to the natural environment is merely to recognize how greatly we need a new conception of the relation of man to the universe and realization that man is a part of nature, not outside nature, as our theological traditions have for so long insisted. As Alfred N. Whitehead has so cogently remarked in *Adventures of Ideas:* "It is a false dichotomy to think of nature *and* man. Mankind is that factor in nature which exhibits in its most intense form the plasticity of nature."

The evidence is slowly accumulating in support of the conception of man as a cosmic resonator to a wide variety of energy transformations so that he is continuously absorbing, directly or indirectly, energy in different intensities as in sunshine, ultraviolet light, electrical energy, infrared rays, etc. Moreover, it is being shown that man is precariously dependent upon an adequate supply of the various minerals necessary for organic functioning and the various vitamins which he cannot manufacture for himself. How dependent man is for the constant supply of these substances is shown by the way in which his health and his sanity are threatened, if not lost, after any prolonged deprivation thereof.

To understand adequately man's relationship to the geographical environment of nature we must realize the many implications of man's mammalian ancestry, recalling the millions of years of evolutionary development, both in the mammalian and in the pre-mammalian forms, through which he developed the capacity for existing in this geographical space and maintaining his amazingly complicated physiological processes, including reproduction, that are necessary for man's continued existence and perpetuation. Only recently have we begun to gain any understanding of these mammalian processes which are being revealed as the slow achievement of successive evolutionary forms culminating apparently in mammals and especially in man, who has the widest range of existence of all mammals, from the arctic cold to tropical heat, from high altitudes to sea level and below. This then brings us to consideration of the next most important environment in which man exists.

THE INTERNAL ENVIRONMENT

Man's capacity for existing under such diverse and continually changing climatic conditions arises from his ability to maintain a relatively stable internal environment—an ability which, as indicated, was slowly evolved by his mammalian ancestors. As recent studies have shown, the various organ systems and glands of internal secretion interacting through the blood and lymph and the nervous systems are engaged in continual readjustments for the maintenance of what W. B. Cannon has so well termed "homeostasis." Through a series of amazingly delicate interacting adjustments, the mammalian organism is able to maintain its internal environment within fairly narrow limits of fluctuation, or to recover stability very quickly after it has been displaced through some external event or pronounced organic activity. Thus the mammalian organism is able to exist in a fluctuating, ever-changing environment, responding to the variations of heat, cold, barometric pressure, oxygen tension, as well as meeting the impact of traumatic events, of infections, and the like, and also carrying on in the mature organism the internal functional activities associated with reproduction and lactation.

Just because this capacity for maintaining a stable internal environment was "learned" through millions of years of evolutionary development, these processes take place ordinarily with little or no awareness on the part of man and with little or no conscious effort except that involved in seeking food and drink and in eliminations. It cannot be too strongly emphasized that these achievements of our mammalian ancestors have conferred upon us an amazing degree of freedom, not only to live all over the earth under the widest range of climatic conditions, but to carry on an extraordinary variety of sustained activities that are possible only because these basic organic processes are continually taking care of our organic requirements and needs.

Because we think of the environment as something outside or surrounding organisms, it is necessary to this discussion to re-emphasize the statement that man, as a mammalian organism, exists in the geographical environment *and* also in this internal environment. It may be said that man lives between the external and the internal environments so that their interaction is continually being mediated by him through internal readjustments or overt activities. At this point it may be appropriate to point out that man derives much from his mammalian ancestry, but unlike all his predecessors he enjoys a unique status, in that as an organism he is relatively young and plastic, having escaped that differentiation and specialization of structure and function which has marked the end of the road for all other species. Man is indeed unique, as Julian Huxley has recently emphasized in *Man Stands Alone* since he has survived without paying the price of fixity and sacrifice of further development possibilities, exacted from all other organisms. It may also be desirable to emphasize that man, as pointed out years ago, has a prolonged infancy, much longer than any other species, during which he is engaged in further growth, development, and maturation and therefore is capable of considerable learning. In addition, man also has a much longer adolescence than any other species, which also makes possible further learning and adaptation before he reaches the adult steady state and more or less fixed patterns of activity of the mature organism.

It is indeed astonishing to realize how little has been known about man, his evolutionary and hereditary background, his gestation, his growth, development, and maturation. As we will have occasion to point out later, all of our traditional ideas, conceptions, and beliefs about man are derived from the most extraordinary myths and fantasies which can no longer be accepted in the light of the growing knowledge of human development.

Many of those who are interested in studying man and trying to understand his activities have attempted to escape from these traditional mythologies by developing a rigorously biological conception of man. They have invoked the foregoing picture of man, the mammalian organism existing in the geographical world of nature, as acted upon by the ongoing processes and natural events and in turn reacting to these through his inherited mammalian capacities. These attempts to develop a more rigorous biological conception of man are highly commendable and are very much needed if we are to gain a better understanding of human activities. It must be obvious, however, that to stop with a formulation in terms of man as an organism reacting to the geographical environment is to give a picture that is fundamentally inadequate and incomplete, since nowhere do we find man, even among the so-called most primitive groups, living on a basis of organic functioning and biological impulse.

Man, as indicated earlier, is indeed unique because, unlike all other species, he has made his adaptations, not by organic specialization and bodily differentiation, but through ideas and the use of tools; indeed, what distinguishes man from his fellow mammals is the development of the cerebral cortex, which has not only made possible what we call human social life, but apparently has made it necessary for man to develop a mode of existence other than that of simple organic functioning and impulsive behavior.

While it has been customary to think of man as driven by fear to build up defenses against a threatening environment and natural enemies, it may be suggested that to a considerable extent man may have been compelled to develop what we call social life, and especially the arts, by sheer ennui and boredom. Having a large brain, he could not be content merely to exist on an organic level. It may also be suggested that since man, as man, appeared relatively late he found various life zones more or less pre-empted by older species that had established themselves through their specialized structural and functional capacities and could maintain themselves therein more efficiently than could man when he attempted to live on a purely biological level. Thus it seems probable that both through boredom and through the need for developing a mode of living that was compatible with his needs and capacities and the opportunities available to such a late arrival, man proceeded to develop in his early days what we call culture.

THE CULTURAL ENVIRONMENT

The conception of human culture as environment has not been very widely used or accepted except among anthropologists and the students of prehistory; therefore, it may be desirable to approach the discussion of the cultural environment by indicating what at this time may have been the probable origin of culture. Let us recall that from his earliest beginnings man has faced certain persistent tasks of life, namely:

    1. To come to terms with nature in order to gain sustenance, to find security, and to achieve survival in a world both precarious and problematic.

2. To organize a group life so that individuals can live together and participate in the division of labor, which group living both necessitates and makes possible.
3. To transform organic functioning and impulsive behavior into the patterned conduct of group life and of human living as distinct from biological functioning.

Each species has worked out a way of life by learning to deal with certain selected aspects of the life zone in which it lives. Thus in the same life zone we find insects, reptiles, birds, and mammals finding sustenance, achieving survival, but each living in one of the many worlds which that same life zone provides for the selective awareness, specialized needs, and the differentiated capacities of each species. These separate worlds may and frequently do conflict or interlock in the sense that we have predators, parasites, and symbiotic species; but it is not unwarranted to speak of these diverse but coexistent worlds as being created out of the totality of nature by what each species responds to and what it ignores and disregards in that life zone. We might say that nature presents a different perspective to each species which attempts to live within the dimensions of the life zone revealed by its own specific phylogenetic history.

In much the same way we may conceive of man working out his human way of life by developing the specific perspective which he imputes to or imposes upon the geographical environment of nature in which he finds himself. Here we have to face one of the major difficulties in attempting to clarify this larger problem of man and his environment, since we are prone to adopt a more or less unidimensional or absolute picture in accordance with our whole rational, intellectual tradition. We must make a special effort, therefore, in order to be able to think in multidimensional terms, which means that we must recognize that man, as a mammalian organism, *exists* in nature and reacts to the ongoing processes and events of what we call the "real or physical world," but at the same time he develops a highly specialized picture of that world in accordance with the basic conceptions and assumptions that he makes about the world and himself. Thus he exists in the geographical environment of nature and responds thereto with his inherited mammalian capacities, but nevertheless he builds up a highly selective version of that world and responds thereto in the rigorously patterned functions and conduct prescribed by his culture.

Culture, therefore, might be described as the process by which man creates and maintains this peculiarly human world and group way of life, this cultural environment which he imposes upon the geographical and the internal environments, upon nature and himself, in accordance with the basic ideas and conceptions which he himself has developed. All over the world, therefore, we find different groups of people all belonging to the same human species but with minor variations of color and size, existing as organisms in the same geographical world of nature; yet each group lives in a distinct cultural world of its own historical creation. Each of these different cultures may be interpreted as an answer proposed by man to the persistent life tasks which he has faced, and these answers may be said to arise from the four basic assumptions or organizing conceptions of each culture, namely:

1. The nature of the universe; how it arose, or was created; how it operates; who or what makes things happen, and why.
2. Man's place in that universe; his origin, nature, and destiny, his relation to the world; whether in nature or outside nature.
3. Man's relation to his group: who must be sacrificed for whom; the individual's rights, titles, obligations, and interests.
4. Human nature and conduct; man's image of self and his motives; what he wants and what he should have; how he should be educated and socialized.

With these conceptions or assumptions man has attempted to order events, to organize experience, and to give meaning and significance to the environing world and to his own life. Whatever exists and happens will be viewed and interpreted in terms of these basic ideas, beliefs, and conceptions which are expressed in what we call the religion, the philosophy, the law, and the art of each cultural group. They provide the only group-sanctioned ways of believing, thinking, acting, feeling, and speaking, giving rise to the *eidos* and the *ethos* of each culture.

The more we reflect upon the cultural environment, the more amazing it becomes, because we see that under the coercion of his own historically developed culture man has rigorously limited himself to what he may, may not, and must do, often depriving himself of the rich opportunities offered by his life zone for meeting his needs and requirements as seen in the extraordinary variety of taboos and inviolabilities which he has established for his own observance. Moreover, we see man engaged in a bewildering array of rituals and ceremonies, designed to deal with the environment as conceived by his culture, which in the light of our growing knowledge of natural processes and events are often erroneous. No better example of this can be cited than the amazing variety of fertility rites that man all over the world has practiced and still practices, hoping by sympathetic magic or other practices to enhance or modify the fertility of plants and animals upon which he depends for sustenance and also his own fecundity. What is perhaps the most remarkable aspect of the diverse cultural environments that have been developed all over the world is that man has been able to survive, *despite* the misconceptions and erroneous assumptions he has made about nature and himself.

What we need to emphasize here is that this cultural environment is a highly elaborated series of possibilities, of compulsions and of prohibitions, which very specifically define the geographical environment of nature, the internal environment, and man's interactions therein. In any attempt to understand human activities full recognition must be given to this cultural environment since it is usually more coercive and restrictive than the geographical environment of nature and the internal environment of man's own organism. Moreover, it must be evident that man cannot, except perhaps when psychotic or wholly lacking in intelligence, live on a biological basis of simple physiological functioning and organic impulse. Here we see why the well meant efforts of many scientists to foster a more objective and realistic view of human existence, however laudable their attacks on superstition and folklore, are inadequate and must be rejected, since man cannot accept and live upon a purely objective basis. To be wholly objective means to deal with the environment only in terms of the processes, events, and the biological functions of nature and to reject any patterns of conduct which involve aspirations, inhibitions, functional patterning, and the other aspects of human conduct as distinguished from organic behavior.

Moreover, culture, by the very demands it places upon man and the limitations it imposes upon his naïve organic demands and functioning, frees him from the coercive control of hunger, sex, and emotional outbreaks. If he did not learn to modify his internal environment by transforming hunger into appetite for the food favored by his group, eaten at the prescribed intervals, he would be driven incessantly to seek and appropriate available food and eat continuously like many organisms. If also he did not build up some respect for the inviolability of things and persons—what we call private property and the sanctity of the person—he would be continually subject to invasion of his body and goods by others or driven to attack others. Moreover, if he did not develop the awareness and the rather rigidly patterned emotional expressions and repressions, as favored by his group, he would miss most of the richness and significance of life and be at the mercy of every emotional impulse in himself and others. Indeed, we must recognize that whatever we cherish and value in life derives from the cultural formulations that have given meaning and richness to nature and living, all of which would be lost or destroyed by a purely objective mode of acting and thinking.

What culture does is to establish a selective version of the geographical environment and also a more or less rigidly controlled or restricted internal environment, so that both environments operate upon man to foster the kind of conduct and functional activity favored by the group traditions.

The necessity for recognizing the cultural environment and its coerciveness appears more clearly when we view the process by which this cultural environment is established. Unlike the geographical environment of nature and the organic patterns and functional activity of the internal environment, the cultural environment depends for its continuation and maintenance upon the process of culturation, that is, educating each generation of children in terms of the basic ideas and conceptions, the selective awareness, the sensibilities, the socially sanctioned ways of functioning, thinking, believing, speaking, acting, and feeling. Only insofar as children learn to see the world, including other people and themselves, in terms of their cultural traditions, learn to observe the group-sanctioned patterns of functioning, conduct, and feeling, will a culture persist. Each child in all the different cultural groups throughout the world arrives on the scene as a more or less plastic organism who is rapidly molded into the patterns approved by the group, so that the cultural environment in which he grows up becomes the only valid and acceptable way of seeing, thinking, acting, and feeling. Indeed, this parochialism of cultures by which the individual learns what the group traditions teach, and how he grows up to believe that that is the only valid way of looking at life, is one of the very curious aspects of human existence as expressed in intolerance and other forms of narrow-minded suspicion of all that is different.

We must continually remind ourselves that the cultural environment is a human creation which depends precariously upon the continuity of tradition, that is, upon inculcating these basic patterns in children. There is nothing in the natural biological environment which requires or necessitates any *specific* cultural pattern or social organization although, as indicated earlier, it seems clear that some form of culture is essential to man. Perhaps we might say that nature has been patient of the amazing variety of cultural formulations which we find all over the world.

The coerciveness of the cultural environment upon man derives from the very process by which it is established, namely, the education of the young child, who, as he grows up and reacts to his internal environment and to the external world, is continually supervised and admonished by his parents and other adults so that he is forced to accept what he is taught, at least to the extent of adopting the larger patterns of his culture, as we will see later. However, even the most coercive teaching does not produce a uniform result, since each individual will accept these teachings in his own idiomatic fashion.

Undoubtedly the persistence of cultures, despite the anomalies and the almost unbelievable practices, has been due in large measure to the sanctions that have been invoked for maintaining the culture. Every culture apparently has a theory of origins which usually teaches that its particular culture is a superorganic, superhuman, if not supernatural, creation which may not be criticized or questioned. Thus we find that each group believes that its culture is a part of the cosmos and operates wholly above and beyond human direction and control. To criticize or to challenge these basic conceptions and beliefs is considered impious because the culture is believed to be the product of some supernatural revelation that has been given to man for his guidance. Thus theology, philosophy, law, and art reiterate and reinforce the basic cultural formulations and support the social life which they provide.

THE SOCIAL ENVIRONMENT

As pointed out earlier, the persistent life tasks which have faced man from the very beginning arise from the necessity of coming to terms with nature, of organizing some kind of group life; and of imposing some patterns of conduct upon human activity. Here again we find that the social environment, like the cultural environment, may be regarded as a field of limited possibilities of human conduct, within the range of which the individual must carry on his life activities. We may gain a better understanding of this social environment if we will recall how the young child, beginning shortly after birth, is inducted into the use of these socially sanctioned patterns of conduct. The infant undergoes the process of socialization, as it has been called, wherein he is called upon to surrender much of his physiological autonomy and accept group sanctions, customs, and patterns. He learns to adapt his physiology to the food and eating practices of the group; he accepts certain patterns for the control of eliminations, and he submits to certain patterning and regulation of his emotional reactions to others. Here we see how the culture supports the social life which in turn imposes upon the individual certain basic patterns of functional activity that are considered desirable, if not necessary, to the group life so that the infant soon accepts which the social life demands and permits as the appropriate way of living.

The young child also is inducted into the use of language and rapidly learns not only to respond to the verbalizations of others but to utilize those verbalizations for communication to others. As the study of comparative linguistics has shown, while there is a limited number of larger categories of language, nevertheless there is an amazing variety of language systems, each of which is adapted to express the ideas and concepts of each culture, with a vocabulary that represents historically the development of the group life. The young individual is also taught to recognize the wide variety of symbols and their meanings, which involves the recognition of highly specialized meanings and significances that are imposed upon the common features of everyday life because they have received that conventionalized significance. As soon as the child has become more or less oriented to life and capable of asking questions and understanding, he is taught the basic ideas and beliefs of his culture so that from his earliest days he learns to see and interpret the world around him according to cultural prescriptions, and he is thereby progressively transformed into a participating member of his culture and of his society and learns to live in the cultural and the social environments provided by the group life.

As pointed out earlier, the major problem of group life is to transform the naïve, impulsive behavior of individuals into patterned conduct so that they can live together, participate in the group life, and, above all, can and will accept the requirements for social order. It is evident that if each individual is free to express his impulses and aggressive actions there can be little orderly social life and not much opportunity for any other activities than those observed among animals which spend most of their lives in hunting food and defending themselves from attack. Thus we find that each cultural group builds up an orderly social life by inculcating in the young the observance of the inviolability of objects, places, and persons which we call private property and the sanctity of the person. This comes about through the process of prohibiting the naïve, impulsive action of children toward objects and people, often by more or less severe punishment, until they can learn to tolerate exposure to biologically adequate stimuli without responding thereto. Thus we see how the prohibitions laid upon children by adults are transformed into self-administered inhibitions which prevent the child, even when beyond adult scrutiny, from approaching, taking, or attacking. It may be suggested that the concept of inviolability is probably one of the basic aspects of all cultures and all societies, since some observance of inviolability of objects and of persons, particularly those of the other sex, has been found in all groups thus far observed.

The young child must learn not only to observe the inviolabilities described by his society but he must also learn to perform all the different actions which are deemed necessary and appropriate, such as those that are defined by the masculine and feminine roles and kinship relations, by the group-sanctioned scheme of rank, caste, class, and similarly prescribed conduct. Thus the child grows up under the constant tuition of his parents and other adults to learn a repertory of conduct of what he must not do, and what he must and what he may do, and his status in the community is largely defined in terms of these prohibitions and compulsions. The whole scheme of owning property and of the control and the regulation of sexual activity and mating, therefore, is based upon these fundamental lessons in inviolabilities and compulsory activities.

Preparation for the social life starts with these fundamental lessons of inviolability and compulsion, but in order to provide for the orderly patterned relations between individuals the group life must provide more or less well-prescribed institutional practices and rituals such as contract, barter and sale, courtship and marriage, property owning, litigation, and the various political practices such as voting, negotiation, and the various activities associated with war and defense. It is these more or less stereotyped institutional practices which everyone must utilize in daily living that direct the conduct of each person to another who responds with the appropriate pattern. Thus the aggregate of patterned individual conduct gives rise to that appearance or order, regularity, and uniformity which has been interpreted as the evidence of a social mechanism or system.

What we should observe here is that through these lessons the young individual is taught the various patterns of conduct through which he can carry on his life activities, and through which he is given the aspirations and goals, the picture of a life career in terms of which he will direct his energies.

One of our most venerable beliefs is that our social life is a part of the cosmos, a sort of superhuman mechanism or organization, existing somewhere between earth and sky and operating through large-scale forces like gravitation which we call "social forces." The belief in this so-called social organization is widely accepted by social theories and social philosophers, deriving in large part from the historical fact that when the philosophers and political theorists and economists and later sociologists attempted to order events they took over the Newtonian conception and utilized it as a conceptual scheme for the discussion of social life and group activities. It must be evident, however, that what we call the social environment is essentially a historical development of man's own creation which he has imposed upon himself in the endeavor to achieve some form of social order, and that its persistence depends wholly upon the perpetuation of these patterns from generation to generation.

It must be obvious that group life and what we call social organization are essentially aspirations, an attempt to create some form of social order which is never given, but must be achieved by patterning the naïve and impulsive behavior of man into orderly and regular conduct. The observance of inviolabilities of things and of persons, and the performance of compulsory activities through the use of group-sanctioned stereotyped rituals and institutional practices, are essential for any large aggregate of individuals who live in close proximity with the increasingly differentiated division of labor which modern technology makes essential. It may be asserted with all emphasis that some cultural formulations and some kind of organized group patterns of conduct are essential; but the major question is "who shall be sacrificed for whom" or rather what sensibilities and values will govern the group life as thus established. With the current emphasis upon technology and scientific knowledge, it is necessary to assert vigorously that the quality of social life is governed primarily by sensibilities—of how we feel toward other persons, as we see when we examine what we call social progress wherein the development of new sensibilities has been the major factor in limiting or abolishing slavery and serfdom, child labor, and the other forms of human exploitation.

As soon as we recognize that social order is not given but must be achieved by building into individuals the patterns of conduct, the aspirations, and the sensibilities which govern the basic dimensions and quality of society, then we will realize that the social scientist and the technologist can tell us how to proceed, but they cannot tell us what to strive for. This is essentially a task for the artists who create and refine the sensibilities and the aspirations that will govern the group life. Above all the quality of the group life reflects and to a large extent expresses the personality-character structure of its members, since the individual, as an individual, while existing as an organism in the geographical world of nature and surviving through the operation of his internal environment, carrying on his life activities in the cultural and in the social environments of which he is a participating menber, really *lives* in his private world.

PRIVATE WORLD

To say that each individual really lives in a private world of his own may sound utterly absurd because we see others moving about in the common public world of our social life, using language, institutional practices, and the general patterns of social conduct and otherwise giving very compelling evidence that they are sharing the same world in which we live. We all do exist in the common world of geographical space as indicated earlier; we move about as organisms and interact with the geographical environment; indeed, one test body or instrument for recording this real world of geographical space is the human organism and its response to varying conditions of barometric pressure and temperature to say nothing of the response to gravity. Moreover, as we carry on our daily activities of buying, selling, negotiating, and otherwise participating in shared activities, we see clearly that we are participating in the public world of our traditional culture and our social life. Here is where it becomes necessary to invoke a multidimensional conception of the environment to enable us to grasp the conception of the individual human organism living in different environments for each of which there are highly appropriate data.

We may obtain a better understanding of this private world environment in which each individual lives if we will recall again the process by which the individual child is culturized and made a participating member of his society. Parents and teachers of the young all share a more or less common understanding of what the culture and the society prescribe and attempt to communicate these beliefs and patterns of conduct to the young, but each individual differs genetically and constitutionally and has had different life experiences, especially in the way he or she has developed an affective or emotional attitude toward life and toward this particular child who is being instructed. The lessons are supposed to be officially correct in accordance with tradition but are always warped and biased according to the parent's or teacher's own personality and emotional orientation. It happens, therefore, that the parent-teacher presents to the child what he believes to be the official socially sanctioned lesson, but it is a distorted and frequently bizarre version of the correct lessons. Therefore, not only is the child presented with a variation of the official cultural and social lessons, but what is more important, he receives this teaching always with a bias and an emotional significance that is uniquely his own. Here we must pause to point out that the individual organism, especially man, faces each new situation with a definite set or organic state which he carries over from his previous experience. Thus learning is a cumulative process, and what we call the past continues to operate in the present insofar as past experience has modified the organism in ways that persist into the present. Thus each new lesson presented to the child gains an emotional significance and is biased by what the child has experienced earlier. Moreover, insofar as the child faces an adult who is exercising authority over him which is kindly or more frequently severe if not brutal, he is reacting emotionally to his teacher.

We may, therefore, say that the individual child, undergoing the process of being culturized and made a participating member of our society, learns a highly idiomatic and idiosyncratic version of what he is supposed to learn. This is the basic process of human learning, as our whole experience of life confirms, namely, that each individual sees the world about him, including other people, always in terms of the highly specific meaning and emotional import which they have for him alone. Thus, the notion advanced earlier that the individual really lives in a private world of his own is but a confirmation of our own experience and the beginning of real insight into human conduct.

Another way of approach to this same situation is to recognize that each individual lives in his specific life space, which becomes organized or structuralized in accordance with his own peculiar life experience and feeling and emotional attitudes. In a very real sense we may say that the individual, moving about in the common public world in which all organisms exist, creates this very idiomatic private world or life space in which every object, situation, and person is given the highly specific and peculiar meaning with which he invests all his experience.

What we call personality may be viewed as this dynamic process of organizing and interpreting experience and reacting affectively to the situations and relationships which we ourselves impose upon events and people according to our life experiences. The personality might be likened to a rubber stamp with which we go about stamping situations and people with the particular set patterns of our personality. Whatever life has meant to us, especially in the earlier years when we have been building up this personality process, becomes coercive upon us so that we continue to see and feel toward life always in terms of these early established set patterns.

If we will reflect briefly on this situation our own life experience will confirm what we have said, because we realize how impossible it is for any one person to see life in the terms and with the meaning that each situation presents to another. Moreover, we know that even when a group of people are all in a small room listening to a person speak, each individual in that room will be seeing a different speaker and hearing a different speech, not what the speaker says but rather what each individual hears.

The individual personality has a highly developed selective awareness which picks out of the total situation that to which it will attend, and that which it will completely ignore. To a certain extent this personality process might be compared to a chemical valence, as we have learned to speak of the capacity of different substances to react chemically with others. Thus we know that if we apply a specific acid to all the different substances in a room it will react upon some and be unable to act upon others, and in each chemical reaction that takes place there will be produced a specific kind of salt, depending upon the kind of acid we employ. In much the same way the individual personality process will interact to certain situations and avoid all others, and when it does react it will always contrive to produce the kind of situation which that personality process requires.

The beginning of an understanding insight into human conduct comes with the realization of these private worlds in which we live and from which we can never escape. Only thus can we begin to understand the fears and compulsions, the anxieties, the hostilities, the prejudices and resentments, the enthusiasms and dislikes which each individual brings to life, and only thus can we begin to gain a sympathetic awareness of how certain individuals spend their whole lives in prolonged conflict or anxious concern over questions which, to an outside observer, appear to be utterly absurd and without substance. What we call the neurotic is essentially an individual whose private world is built upon some bizarre, if not fantastic, assumptions which he insists upon maintaining even though they may require all his energies and force him to renounce all other life activities. Indeed, the most astonishing aspect of human conduct is the way in which individuals dedicate their lives to utterly unreal but completely compelling beliefs and purposes that can be understood only insofar as we can sympathetically understand the private world that gives those beliefs and purposes their coercive meaning. Nor can we understand the amazing irrationality of human conduct unless and until we can realize how much of our thinking and acting is dictated by the persistent, affective reactions that were built up in us in childhood which continue to dominate all the rest of our lives and make us constantly feel anxiety and guilt, or resentment and hostility, and force us to be dependently submissive or arrogantly dominating to others.

As we come to understand and accept the environment of this private world in which we really live, we begin to see a little more clearly what human history means as we realize how individuals and groups have always been moved by the assumptions and beliefs of their culture and the coercive dominations of their private worlds regardless of how they differed from the so-called objective real world of nature. We may also begin to understand why the wholly rational arguments and programs that are offered man so seldom receive his recognition or acceptance. As we see in the more serious cases of mental disorders, the individual must at all costs to himself and to society strive to maintain the private world in which he lives. Only that which is emotionally congenial and can be incorporated into the dimensions of this private world will be accepted by individuals and by groups.

As we look back historically on our own culture and on the records of other cultures we see recurrent phases of extreme pressure to force the individual into developing a private world that is rigidly organized by outside authority or alternating periods when individual deviations have been not only tolerated, but encouraged. If the contemporary discussions of democracy with the emphasis upon the recognition of the integrity of the individual are to have any meaning, we must begin to translate that aspiration over into a program and a process that will attempt to foster the development of the individual private worlds that will be more sane and wholesome, that is, less conflicting and distorted by neurotic and emotional disturbances, oriented to the larger common purposes and goals through which alone a society can gain unity. Until an individual personality can live at peace with himself in his private world he cannot live at peace with his group life. For an orderly society we need individuals capable of orderly co-operative living who can bear the burdens of freedom and sustain social order in and through their own personal conduct and feelings.

We have inherited a series of ideas and beliefs about man and nature, many of which have become incredible in the light of new scientific knowledge and understandings and many of which have become intolerable to our more recently won insights and aspirations. If we accept this multidimensional conception of man's environment, we may clarify some of the present confusions and conflicts, not only in public affairs but also in scientific discussions.

It is evident from even a hasty perusal of scientific literature that each scientific discipline has developed its instruments and techniques for research and is inclined to formulate or to reformulate every question it investigates in terms of the assumptions and concepts of that discipline. Thus the biologists are eager to translate all questions concerning man and his behavior into biological questions and insist that only such questions are scientific. It can be asserted that purely objective methods and data are essential to biological investigation but not that man merely *exists* as an organism in geographical space. All his observable conduct and group relationships which are not objective are cultural and social. They are aspirations and ideals, like local distortions and aberrations of the geographical space that is bent or curved in the immediate neighborhood of the sun.

In similar fashion the physiologists and others who are concerned with man's functional processes, with the maintenance of his internal environment, are often emphatic in their assertions that only objective methods and data as found by their techniques are possible for the study of human behavior and conduct. Whatever can not be brought within the reach of these physiological methods they would ignore or rule out as irrelevant and worthless. Curiously enough this position has been recently undermined and rendered almost untenable by the cumulative evidence of how man's internal environment can be seriously and persistently disturbed not only by emotional reactions but by persistent affective disorders. Thus a man's heart rate or blood pressure may be enhanced by anxiety or hostility, which differ from fear and rage in that they are chronic tensions localized in one organic function while fear and rage are over-all, total organic reactions to some exigent or threatening situation. Even more significant is the demonstration that these persistent functional disturbances can often be reduced or even eliminated by treatment of the personality of the individual, especially by helping him to recall the often forgotten events which have been disturbing him.

What is of especial significance is that in the absence of an adequate biological stimulus-situation the individual reacts with an organic process wholly irrelevant to or incongruous with the actual situation in which he finds himself: his heart beats are accelerated as if frightened or under heavy load of exertion while seated in a room alone; his vascular system contracts, his respiration is accelerated or constricted, his skin blanches or is suffused with blood or exhibits local disturbances, and so on.

Thus the realization of how persistent affective reactions, derived from prior experience, chiefly from childhood, can disturb physiological functions, has made the criterion of purely objective physiological data rather complicated if not impossible, since individuals and experimental animals are reacting affectively all the time.

Psychologists have also proposed their formulations and applied their methodologies to man and his conduct primarily in terms of their specific assumptions and dimensions. There are of course many different schools of psychological investigation from the pure study of reflexes, similar in intent and scope to that of the physiologists, to the larger range of the social psychologists, the educational psychologists, and others who are more concerned with man's conduct and feelings. What should be noted is that each of these schools emphasizes one or more aspects of human behavior or of man's reactions to these different environments in its methods of study, and upon those limited data often erects a large edifice of theory concerning all of human conduct.

Social scientists are inclined to focus their attention upon the institutionally patterned conduct of social life as exhibited in the buying and selling of economic affairs, in the voting and other acts of political life, or in the varieties of deviation shown by delinquents, criminals, vagrants, and so on. It has been customary to assume, as indicated earlier, that there is a superhuman mechanism or organization which regulates economic, political, and social life through the operation of large-scale forces acting at a distance. The study of human conduct and of group life in terms of human conduct and of group life in terms of this assumed mechanism or organization ignores the biological and cultural environments and the individual personal private world. What is especially to be noted is that the activities of individuals in an institutionally structured social environment are registered in a wide variety of records—prices, votes, wages, consumption, production, and so on. If these different data are deified into entities, forgetting that they record human activities, then we may create problems that can never be solved because artificial.

Likewise, among students of the human personality there is a disposition to focus upon the individual's internal environment and private world and neglect the social-cultural world in which that individual personality arose and now is living. Thus, some formulate the problem of human conduct largely in terms of biological instincts to which they attribute most, if not all, of human activities, minimizing or ignoring how culture operates to modify the so-called instinctive processes which in men are less coercive than in any other species. Others use various "mental mechanisms" to explain human conduct and personality expression.

It should be evident that we need a multidimensional conception and methodology for the study of human conduct, wherein all the disciplines may collaborate by helping to observe and, wherever possible, measure the many dimensions of man's environment and of his patterned conduct and feelings.

(FROM: *The Scientific Monthly*, LVI [April, 1943]: 344-358.)

TWENTY-NINE

The Arts in Reconstruction

PLANNING for the postwar period, especially for the occupied and the conquered countries, has been focused upon military occupation and policing, relief, medical care and rehabilitation, political reorganization, agricultural and industrial restorations and operations, control of money and banking and distribution of commodities and similar activities. It is hoped that by careful and foresighted planning of all these practical arrangements and technical operations, and the establishment of new boundaries with new governments and a new international government to police the world, reconstruction of social order and restoration of customary modes of living will be achieved.

As we read reports of the actual situation since fighting ceased, these many and varied plans and programs, however necessary, desirable, and promising, however complete in their meticulous attention to the complex social, economic, and political needs, seem negligent of the most crucial task of all—namely, human and cultural reconstruction.

It must be evident that the bombing and all other wartime events have brought not only the destruction of homes, factories, railroads, utilities, schools and universities, and other forms of devastation but, in addition, for many people, have destroyed much of their traditional ideals, the cherished beliefs, and customary assumptions by which they have attempted to make their lives orderly and meaningful.

This war, following so closely upon the First World War, has accelerated the breakdown of the historically developed European culture (spelled with a small c and used in the anthropological sense), which long before the war had been disintegrating. The underlying conceptions and assumptions, the customary patterns of thinking, acting, and feeling by which, and for which, western people have lived, worked, and reared their children, maintaining social order and pursuing the goals and aspirations of their traditions, all these have suffered either collapse or profound alteration during this war.

All the varied plans for social, economic, political, juridical, and international reconstruction are predicated upon the existence and operation of these cultural traditions, since all these proposals assume that the different peoples will continue to exhibit some regular pattern of thinking, of orderly conduct and of feelings; will continue to practice the self-discipline and the highly ritualized, symbolic conduct which makes these social, economic, political, juridical, and international arrangements operate.

The people themselves, the men, women, and children, the youths and maidens, who are the carriers of culture, the bearers of traditions, the actors and the operators of these organizations and social practices, have greatly suffered from the war. Not only have they been starved or badly undernourished, exposed to hardships, cruelties and atrocities; but they have lost much, and for some, all of that naïve, often passionate, faith in their traditional beliefs and practices as the only right and necessary way of living. Many have also developed a cumulative emotional reaction to life from these traumatic experiences of wartime. They are filled with hostility or overwhelmed by despair, either burning with an intense, corrosive hate against those who have mistreated or misled them or sunk in an apathy of hopeless resignation. Everywhere people are ridden by anxiety because they can look forward with no dependable expectations for their future.

Probably never before have there been so many people emotionally disturbed, and these strong feelings, as we know fron cumulative studies, must find some release or expression, direct and overt, or disguised and surreptitious. If allowed to pour out their hate and resentment, people will exhibit every form of violence and destruction, as reports of "incidents" already have shown. If restrained by military or police force, these feelings of hate and hostility will poison and sabotage the efforts at social reconstruction and restoration, with a series of political crises and outbreaks.

However strongly we may emphasize the economic basis of

social order and the imperative need of food, shelter, and protection for existence, we must recognize that man lives primarily by memories and expectations. He must believe in something, must aspire and hope and strive, as daily he links his past, represented by traditions, with a future he pictures in terms of his customary expectations and aspirations.

When a people no longer hope nor expect anything, but merely "endure the slow misery of existence," they undergo progressive demoralization. They can find no energy for rebuilding their individual and group lives. They have no feeling of urgency for maintaining standards of conduct or attempting any achievement beyond mere survival. They are overwhelmed by apathy or paralyzed by despair. So long as relief is provided, people thus apathetic can exist on a minimum level of subsistence, but they have ceased to live as a people.

The people of Germany present an especially perplexing problem. Conquered by military force and subjected to all the drastic punishment, retaliatory measures, and demands for reparation now being imposed upon them, many are sullen, resentful, and suspicious. Most of them will have lost all faith, unable to believe in anything or anyone after the collapse of national socialism. If we face squarely the question of how the German people, who cannot be wiped out as a people, are to be treated, especially after the punitive measures have been applied, we must wonder what can we do or say to them that will have any meaning or effect. How can we persuade them to change their traditional culture, their dominant character structure, their way of life, so that they can learn to participate peacefully in European affairs and join in maintaining world order? We can punish and destroy and by force compel them to change everything we can reach and to "accept" democratic practices. But how can we replace their traditional patterns of thinking, of acting, of feeling, their customary patterns of human relationships, the innermost core of their personalities? Can we coerce them by force and prolonged military occupation into changing their image of themselves as a "master race," the supreme nation? The historical record plainly shows that "a cultural heritage in the long run never submits to force, but itself vanquishes force in the end."

Likewise with the Japanese, whose cultural traditions give them an orientation to life we find difficult, if not impossible, to under-

THE ARTS IN RECONSTRUCTION 383

stand. We can occupy their home lands, disarm them, punish the war criminals, and order them to reorganize their political and economic life. But none of these measures will touch the traditional beliefs and assumptions of their religion, their philosophy, their law, their family life, out of which come the way of life and dominant character-structure of the Japanese people. So long as they continue to maintain their traditional culture unchanged, we cannot expect them to become supporters of world order, because those traditions foster a belief in their divine origin and their mission to rule the world. Moreover, their traditions make self-government by the people themselves exceedingly difficult, if not impossible under an Emperor-God to whom the first duty is reverent obedience.

In the face of this situation, this overwhelming emotional disturbance and this widespread cultural breakdown and, above all, this baffling task of reconstructing German and Japanese culture, we must look to the arts as the only mode of communication which can reach people and begin to transform their hostility and resentful hate into more constructive channels, giving them courage and hope for the future. It has been the historic role of the arts, especially the drama, to do what must be done if there is to be any human and cultural reconstruction.

Never was a time more ready for the dramatist. The whole world today is ready, emotionally aroused as never before, waiting for the resolution of the drama to free them from the conflicts and frustrations of their destructive feelings and paralyzing anxieties, so they can take up again the persistent tasks of life. Only the dramatist, speaking with the power of aesthetic expression, can effectively focus the attention of a group and organize and redirect their emotions through the catharsis he provides. The dramatist compels each one of his audience, whose members are ordinarily shut within their private worlds, to see and hear and feel together, because each shares the same aesthetic experience, accepting the common images and symbols on the stage for his own private personal problems and hopes. Thus the drama offers the most promising instrument for the group therapy that a disorderly and despairing world so desperately needs today.

Moreover, only the drama can fully and effectively express the new assumptions and expectations, and persuade people to accept this reconstruction which is essential today because their traditional beliefs and patterns have become empty and meaningless, no longer capable of providing the guidance and courage people need for living.

If these assertions seem too bold or even fantastic, we must remind ourselves that the arts, especially the drama, have been performing these functions throughout the ages. In almost every culture we find the drama, aided by music and the dance, as the instrument through which the basic perplexities and the emotional needs of people are met, their daily anxieties and their sense of guilt and hostility are released, so they are able to live and meet their daily tasks. We need only remember our own commercial movies to recognize this function of the drama and its provision of phantasies.

This emphasis upon the drama and its presentation in moving pictures and radio is justified because the immediate situation calls for the dramatic approach and the use of the most effective techniques now available to communicate with people. If the German and the Japanese people are to have a new image of themselves as a people, a new set of values, especially human values and purposes, and are to develop the character structure appropriate to the attainment of those values, then only the drama can provide the aesthetic experiences for such transformations. No other means are available to bring about a reformulation of their masculine and feminine roles, of the relation of husband to wife, the reconstruction of parent-child relations, the redirection of adolescent aspirations and adult strivings. No other instruments or program can create the new sensibilities, the concern for the dignity and worth of the individual personality which are essential to the democratic way of life.

But all the arts are needed for this Promethean task, since the new hopes and patterns must be portrayed in every medium, reiterated by and orchestrated among all the arts, each in its chosen way and medium, helping to create the new awareness and sensibilities, the new patterns of conduct that recognize the common man and create the feeling about events and people needed for this human and cultural reconstruction.

Primarily this creative work must be done by the artists of each country who belong to the people and have grown up in the culture, and so can speak the language and use the ideas and symbols they will recognize. Probably the artists who can and will speak

THE ARTS IN RECONSTRUCTION 385

most clearly and effectively will be those who have suffered like their compatriots during the war, but can transform their suffering into the creative endeavor of art.

Among the youths and younger men and women in each country are the potential artists of tomorrow. To find these few individuals and give them the encouragement and assistance they may need to do this creative work offers an opportunity for imaginative philanthropy to contribute to the future of Europe in a most promising way. It is depressing to think of how much money and effort will probably be spent in attempts to restore dying institutions and obsolete patterns, and how little will be available for this essential creative work in the arts through which European culture must renew itself. It is to be hoped that some individual or foundation will have imagination and courage to undertake this most promisimg and significant contribution to the future.

In the light of what happened to the artist, especially in certain countries where the authorities tried to dictate what he should think and do and how he should create, no one must tell the artist what he must do in this situation. But we can in many ways aid the artists to recognize this opportunity and become aware of this urgent need for the help which they alone can give. Moreover, we can assure the artist, especially the dramatist, that today in talking moving pictures and radio as well as the stage of living actors, there are immense new resources for his use, with unprecedented new technical devices of tremendous potency for arousing peoples' feelings, such as the sound controls developed in the Experimental Theatre at Stevens Institute in Hoboken. Moreover, there is music with all its potentialities, not only to move people, to arouse and to calm them, but also to interpret feelings and characters, thereby enhancing the power of the drama for these tasks.

This, however, is not a short-term program of immediate postwar reconstruction, gigantic and complex as that will be. We in the Western nations face, from now on, the stupendous undertaking of renewing Western European culture, the historically developed body of ideas, beliefs, and assumptions, of patterns of conduct, of rituals and symbols, of institutions and formal practices, served by all our modern tools and technology.

It is becoming increasingly clear that the basic assumptions and organizing concepts of Western European culture have become progressively incredible, inadequate, and intolerable. They are no longer congruous with the new climate of opinion which is emerging with relativity, space-time, field theory, and their many implications, and which, with ever increasing acceleration, is rendering many of our traditions obsolete, even archaic.

Our ancient beliefs about the nature of the universe and how it operates, including the venerable traditions of man's place in that universe, of man's relations to his society and of human nature, these fundamental assumptions of our culture, expressed in religion, philosophy, law, education, and especially in the arts, plus many of the customary ways of believing and feeling, predicated upon those traditions, all these have been losing their once unquestioned and unquestionable validity for more and more people. If we are to have any order and meaning in our personal lives and in our society, if we are to conserve our enduring human values and our persistent aspirations toward human dignity, we must renew our traditional culture, providing equivalent formulations for all these obsolete, archaic assumptions and developing new patterns and roles through which we can live more sanely and fully and can more nearly approach our enduring goals and values.

It seems clear that, however these basic dimensions of a culture were originally created and formulated, they became operational in the lives of the individuals only as they were communicated through the arts. We have had a Western European culture which generations have believed in, guided their lives by, because the basic assumptions and beliefs of that culture were transmitted by parents to their children and reiterated by the artists who told people what to believe and feel and teach their children.

Our Christian tradition was established because it was painted, sculptured, dramatized, and sung for a thousand years. Thereby the intellectualized statements and subtle abstractions of theologians, of philosophers, of jurists, were transformed by aesthetic experiences into meaningful and directive patterns in our lives.

Here we see, then, that we must wait upon the artists to become fully aware of the emerging new climate of opinion, the new conceptions and new criteria of credibility now appearing—and to accept the task of translating these highly abstract and relatively meaningless ideas (at least to most people) through the aesthetic experiences they can create for us. We especially need new symbols for this cultural renewal, to replace those which now perpetuate the archaic concepts that defeat our efforts to live in the present. The essence of a culture is that it provides man with a symbolic world of meanings and values in place of the geographical world of nature. Man with a large brain and imagination cannot merely exist on a level of physiological functioning and organic impulse; it is too boring. He must have a culture to provide ideas and aspirations to live by and for, and art and symbols to guide his conduct; but his culture and his art must be credible and congruous with his advancing ideas and techniques.

Above all, we must wait upon the artists to create the new sensibilities — the awareness and the feelings of sympathy and concern which can transform the bare, abstract idea of human dignity and the worth of the personality into the daily conduct and feelings of individuals. If we really want a democratic social life with world order, the artists must create and maintain the sensibilities which are essential to democracy as a way of life.

Moreover, for understanding other peoples and their culture, their character structure, their design for living and their traditional ways of feeling, we have no more valid sources than their arts, wherein what they live by and for, the sanctions they obey and the purposes they serve, are presented in their essential, their quintessential, expression. Both for understanding a culture and for access to the sensibilities and feelings of a people, the arts provide the major approach. The arts, therefore, offer our chief resource for developing the awareness and understanding, the acceptance of the cultural diversities all over the world which must be accepted and orchestrated into world order.

The museums, with their collections of art and archeology and of anthropological materials, have an unrivalled opportunity to help create this awareness of other cultures and more sympathetic approach to and acceptance of these various designs for living.

This is the prospect we must face, now that the war has ended. This is the tremendous task we must undertake, and for such an undertaking we must give the artists the fullest opportunity and all necessary assistance and encouragement to play their historic roles in one of the crucial periods of human history. In view of the shabby treatment we usually give the artist, even those who profess to value the arts and concern themselves with Culture (capital "C"), we must vigorously reassert the primacy of the artist and his essential role in the reconstruction we must undertake.

Individually and as a group, all those who recognize this must demonstrate to a skeptical and indifferent public that aesthetic experiences are indeed the keys to the future, because, as D. H. Lawrence told us, "it is the way our sympathies flow and recoil that really determines our lives."

(FROM: *Journal of Aesthetics and Art Criticism*, IV, No. 3 [March, 1946].)

THIRTY

World Order and Cultural Diversity

THE IDEA of a world order has haunted the dreams of man for untold centuries. Again and again individuals have arisen to proclaim such a goal as the supreme endeavor to which man should sacrifice all else. Some have had a vision of a world united through acceptance of a transcendent religion or of human brotherhood, seeking in a common faith the resolution of conflicts and differences. Others have sought to create unity through the sword of conquest. Still others have relied upon the slow process of education or upon political and parliamentary devices for mediating opposing interests.

There have been innumerable roads to world order offered to mankind, but each proposal has demanded acceptance of the particular religion, philosophy, political organization, or military power of the proponent and the abandonment, if not utter destruction, of all other religions, philosophies, political organizations, and of independence. However lofty the aspirations, proposals for world order have been conceived primarily in terms of a single dominating power, authority, creed or belief, or an exclusive scheme of political and economic institutions to be imposed on all peoples. Even the Christian churches that have for so long asserted the ideal of human brotherhood and peace on earth have thought primarily, if not exclusively, of a Christian world in which the religions of other peoples would be eliminated or displaced by a militant Christian church.

1

IF WE are genuinely concerned with the establishment and maintenance of a world order, then we must begin to examine more critically the assumptions and the purposes implied by the various proposals for achieving such a goal. The crucial question then is how far does any scheme or program for world order recognize and accept the cultural diversity of mankind as the fundamental, inescapable basis of order. It is relatively easy for us to protest vehemently against Hitler's ideal of world order, with a master race of Germans running the world, while all others submissively accept their control and guidance. We are quick to resent the assumption of German superiority, of an exclusive possession of all wisdom and the right to govern others, and we hasten to organize all our resources to oppose the threat of an authoritarian government because we feel that our way of life and our aspirations are endangered by the German dream of world conquest. The issue here is clear and unambiguous, and to that cause we have dedicated our lives and our national resources.

But Western European culture, which we share with the other nations that stem from the Egyptian, Greek, Judaic, and Roman backgrounds, tends to ignore or deny the value and significance of other cultures. Toward the peoples of ancient lands, India, China, Japan, Africa, many of whom have cultural traditions, religions, philosophies, and ways of life far more ancient than ours, we have had a curious attitude of smug complacency and often outright disdain, if not contempt. Toward other peoples, especially those of a different color, we have usually acted as the "master race" which had all the wisdom and enlightenment and therefore was entitled to impose its ideas and religions, its institutions and social practices, and its political and economic control upon their lands and their peoples. The tradition of colonization and of empire, of missionary zeal and trade promotion and economic exploitation are predicated upon this assumption. Like the classical Greeks we still regard those who speak with a different tongue and attempt to order their lives to a different design as barbarians, to be pitied for their benighted condition and to be exploited or degraded whenever they find themselves in the path of the one wise, truly civilized, and really superior people, who bear the "white man's burden." What Hitler, with his assertion of a German master race has done, is to reveal, in all its stark ruthlessness and self-centered, almost paranoid, distortion, what Western European culture has accepted as the major premise of its international relations. The sordid and often brutal history of our devastating contacts with other peoples bears eloquent testimony to the operation of this premise in diplomacy, economics, even religion, and almost all other phases of our international activities.

Thus we face the searching question of what kind of world order do we seek: the dominance of Western European peoples and culture, of our religions and our peculiar scheme of political and economic activities, our relatively parochial way of life, or a world in which different peoples can live according to their own values and traditions, their own assumptions and beliefs and their peculiar sensibilities. If the four freedoms are to be established and maintained, can we continue our self-centered insistence upon our western European values and beliefs and refuse to accept those of others? Never have we had a greater need for a more sympathetic awareness and understanding of other cultures and peoples. Just because we are so myopic and culturally illiterate we need some longer, deeper perspective in which to view the world and its various people, including ourselves.

2

ALL OVER the earth we find man, a mammalian organism, existing in the geographical space of nature, subject to the impact of physical, chemical, and biological events, responding to gravity and weather and the threats from other organisms. Despite the obvious differences in size, shape, color, and in some physiological functions, man, as a species, is essentially alike everywhere. Moreover, despite variations in climate and local differences in flora and fauna, nature, the environing world, is essentially alike, operating through the same basic processes everywhere. Thus we have initially the more or less homogeneous human species existing in and upon this even more orderly, almost uniform earth.

But nowhere do we find man living as a child of nature or existing merely as a mammalian organism engaged primarily in functional activity and impulsive behavior; everywhere he is found living in a cultural and social world, which he interposes between nature and himself and imposes upon his own functional activities and behavior. Each group of men has established its culture, a human way of living, based upon its basic assumptions and beliefs, its aspirations and its feelings.

If we try to find some way of grasping the amazing variety of cultures that have appeared, or still do exist, all over the world, we can gain some understanding by recalling that man has, from his earliest days as man, faced the same persistent tasks of life: to come to terms with the environing world to gain sustenance, shelter, and security and to perpetuate his kind to organize some form of group life or social order wherein individuals can participate in the common affairs of life; to regulate human conduct by transforming naïve impulsive behavior into the patterned conduct and strivings cherished by the group. These are the persistent, inescapable tasks of life that have confronted man everywhere and continue to face every generation anew, since social order is not given but must be sought. To meet such tasks man had to make certain assumptions about the world and himself, and thus we find that he has created for his guidance a body of ideas, conceptions, and beliefs in terms of which he has built his culture and established his social life.

What is beginning to appear is that each group, faced with the same life tasks and compelled to make the same kind of assumptions about the world has, of necessity, employed the same *process* of meeting those demands and formulating those beliefs. The products, that is, the specific content or formulation of their beliefs and assertions, what they have developed as their religion, their philosophy, their art, and their patterns of social life, are so different as to appear completely divergent and contradictory. Yet those differences are only the variations in what are essentially similar or equivalent patterns.

If we can stretch our minds to grasp this idea of similar patterns underlying different expressions and formulations and can begin to realize how the same fundamental process gives rise to different organizations, functions, and activities, then we may find it less difficult to see the divergent cultures all over the world as different, but equivalent products or expressions of the same human process.

3

So soon as we begin to regard diverse cultures as so many different answers proposed by man to the same tasks or questions, so many different solutions offered to the same vital problems, then we may find it less difficult to think of world order, not in terms of a dominant, coercive imposition of one cultural formulation upon all others, but in terms of orchestrating cultural diversities to the larger theme of achieving meaning and significance, values, and order in human living. We can begin to see how these same vital tasks have been approached by different groups of people according to the various assumptions and beliefs they have developed for ordering events and organizing experience, guided by their peculiar sensibilities and feelings. Our Western European culture then appears as only one of the many historically developed cultures, with its peculiar religion, its philosophy, its art, and more lately, its science, which probably is its only valid claim to distinction. All else is essentially a parochial version of what other cultures have offered their people as a design for living.

Since the very purpose or operation of a culture is to affirm certain assumptions and beliefs and to attain certain standards of conduct, this necessarily creates anxiety and fear of anything different. When peoples of different cultures meet, this basic anxiety and hostility are aroused; each approaches the other with contempt or overt enmity, with destructive criticism and depreciation of the other's beliefs and practices. Yet the assumptions each rejects and the patterns each despises in others are essentially the product of the same process of striving to make a human way of life that produced its own cherished beliefs and patterns, and they fulfill the same function in the cultural context of its life.

Now that the world is shrinking through rapid transportation and even more rapid communication and is being forced by commerce and by world-wide war to seek some larger concepts and broader understandings, the older traditions of narrow, parochial intolerance appear in all their primitive destructiveness. Moreover, it is becoming evident that loyalty to these self-centered beliefs in an exclusive superiority makes possible the cynical manipulators, political and religious, who play upon these prejudices for their own purpose to perpetuate and intensify the antagonisms toward other peoples.

To believe that the English-speaking or Western European peoples can impose upon all others the parliamentarism, the peculiar economic, business practices, the esoteric creeds and religious rituals, and all the other idiomatic features of their Western European patterns, is the initial misconception and blindness in so much of present-day thinking and planning. As Ortega y Gasset has reminded us, a culture is that which is sought; but every culture is asymmetrical, biased, and incomplete, making a virtue of its deficiencies and its anesthesias. Each culture in grappling with the same problems has created patterns of action, speech, and belief, of human relationships and values that have accentuated certain potentialities of human life and have ignored or repressed others. Each culture seeks to represent itself by its aspirations, emphasizing its lofty ethical or moral goals as its essential character, usually ignoring or denying its shortcomings and its often destructive features.

4

WORLD order is not to be gained by a regimentation of all peoples to the same pattern of thinking, acting, and believing through a neutral blend of all in an undifferentiated internationalism or a rigid uniformity. No single culture can be accepted as the final and best for all peoples; we must recognize the unhappiness, the degradation, the misery, the incredible brutality, cruelty, and human wastage in all cultures which each tends to ignore while stressing lofty ethical aims and moral aspirations. At the same time we can and must recognize how each culture has selectively developed certain human potentialities and denied or repressed others. Each has formulated its beliefs and patterns which are outstanding achievements, giving human life and social order some meaning and beauty and fulfillment and security. Thus we may view cultures as we view the arts of different peoples as esthetically significant and artistically meaningful, each in its own context or setting.

Indeed, world order may be approached as in art, where the artist achieves universality, not by a composite blend of all scenes, peoples, and situations, but by the very individualized, idiomatic personalities and concrete situations he presents in all their multidimensional but highly specific patterns. So in the effort to establish a world order we must start with an acceptance of the diverse cultures all over the world, with a sympathetic understanding of their basic similarity of purpose and process, recognizing their diversity and their different emphases, as productive of the richness and color and variation that man has achieved in living and human relations. The brotherhood of man will come, therefore, through the realization that all men, everywhere, face the same life tasks, share the same anxieties and perplexities, the bereavements and tragedies, seek the same goals in their cultures: to make life meaningful and significant, to find some security, to achieve some social order and to regulate their conduct toward values that make life more than mere organic existence.

When we realize this basic persistent endeavor of all cultures, we may begin to assess them by what they do to and for the human personality, submitting our own culture to the same evaluation as all others. The humility and the pride we gain from a candid assay of what our Western European culture does to and for the personality, may then prepare us for the understanding and sympathetic evaluation of other cultures, some of which offer more humanly conservative ideas and patterns than our own.

Thus we can accept and respect all other cultures and their idiomatic way of life, which will recognize the basic value of the individual, will maintain freedom, will seek human welfare, and will co-operate in the endeavor to establish and preserve world order to those ends. Those who can and will accept these basic criteria and values, can also accept regulations for human conservation, such as labor regulations, safety provisions, codes for uniform procedures in economic and technological affairs, public health measures and medical care, and the many specific agreements among nations that now point the way forward to this sharing of knowledge and techniques and mutually agreed-upon practices for human conservation and welfare. These specific standards can be accepted and put into practice within the framework of the diverse cultures just as we translate agreements into different languages and symbols.

If we can think of world order in these terms, can envisage this immense, almost Promethean, task as the inescapable responsibility of all those who profess the democratic ideal of respect for the individual human personality, then we may be able, in the midst of the darkness and despair that now assail Western man, to muster the courage and find the faith that will enable us to take up anew the endless task of achieving human values and order, in company with all other peoples of the earth.

(FROM: *Free World*, III [June, 1942].)